ON THE EDGE
OF FREEDOM

THE NORTH'S CIVIL WAR
Paul A. Cimbala, series editor

On the Edge
of Freedom

The Fugitive Slave Issue in
South Central Pennsylvania,
1820–1870

David G. Smith

FORDHAM UNIVERSITY PRESS
NEW YORK   2013

Fordham University Press has no responsibility for the persistence or accuracy of URLs for external or third-party Internet websites referred to in this publication and does not guarantee that any content on such websites is, or will remain, accurate or appropriate.

Fordham University Press also publishes its books in a variety of electronic formats. Some content that appears in print may not be available in electronic books.

Library of Congress Cataloging-in-Publication Data

Smith, David G. (David Grant), 1964–
    On the edge of freedom : the fugitive slave issue in south central Pennsylvania, 1820–1870 / David G. Smith. — 1st ed.
        p.   cm. — (The North's Civil War)
    Includes bibliographical references and index.
    ISBN 978-0-8232-4032-6 (cloth : alk. paper)
    1. Fugitive slaves—Pennsylvania—History—19th century.   2. Fugitive slaves—Legal status, laws, etc.—Pennsylvania—History—19th century.   3. African Americans—Pennsylvania—History—19th century.   4. Antislavery movements—Pennsylvania—History—19th century.   5. Abolitionists—Pennsylvania—History—19th century.
6. Underground Railroad—Pennsylvania.   7. Borderlands—Pennsylvania—History—19th century.   8. Pennsylvania—Race relations—History—19th century.   I. Title.
    E450.S64 2013
    326′.809748—dc23

                                                                                    2011037748

Printed in the United States of America

15 14 13   5 4 3 2 1

First paperback printing 2014

To Valerie and Caroline, for all their love

Contents

Tables

Acknowledgments

I have incurred numerous debts completing this project, which I can only imperfectly acknowledge. Thanks to the community of scholars who encouraged this work or commented on parts of it, including Richard J. M. Blackett, Stephen Browne, Peter Carmichael, Margaret Creighton, William "Jack" Davis, Susan De-Wees, Robert Engs, Barb Gannon, Lori Ginzberg, Thavolia Glymph, Ervin Jordan, Christian Keller, Sally McMurry, Angela Murphy, Mark Neely, William Pencak, Robert Sandow, Constance Schultz, Manisha Sinha, Andrew Slap, Beverly Tomek, Nan Woodruff, and Karen Younger. Particular thanks go to William A. Blair, who generously suggested sources, approaches, and improvements. He also suggested the work's title, which became the organizing theme for the book. Special thanks also to Anne Rose, Allan Steinhardt, Beverly Tomek, and Heather Wilson for their encouragement. Christopher Densmore carefully commented on the entire manuscript, as did an anonymous reader to whom I am equally indebted. Several scholars created opportunities for me to present portions of this work, including Ted Alexander, Bill Blair (again), Carol Reardon, and James "Bud" Robertson. Peter Wallenstein and Bertram Wyatt-Brown graciously published my essay "Race and Retaliation: The Capture of African Americans During the Gettysburg Campaign," in their collection *Virginia's Civil War* (University Press of Virginia, 2005). It formed the basis for the central part of Chapter 8. Thanks also to my patient editors at Fordham University Press, Eric Newman and Wil Cerbone; to my able copy editor, Nancy Rapoport; and to Paul Cimbala, who gave this manuscript critical early encouragement.

I also owe a debt to archivists and local specialists. I visited historical societies in Adams, Franklin, Cumberland, Lancaster, and Chester counties in Pennsylvania, and Baltimore, Carroll, and Frederick counties in Maryland. I was greatly helped by Timothy Smith (Adams County Historical Society) and Christa Bassett and Richard L. Tritt (Cumberland County Historical Society). I also visited numerous libraries and archives; particular thanks to Christine Ameduri (Gettysburg College), Christopher Densmore (again; Friends Historical Library), and Stephen Miller and Max Grivno (Freedmen's Bureau Papers).

Independent researchers helped generously. G. Craig Caba graciously allowed me to visit the substantial resources of the J. Howard Wert Gettysburg collection several times. Peter Vermilyea, a pioneer in examining Adams County's African American community, was a great encouragement. Earl "Cookie" Johnson and his brother, the late Reverend Philip Lowther, talked with me at length about race and history in Franklin County. Late in the project, I met Debra S. McCauslin, who graciously shared her extensive knowledge of the Underground Railroad and Adams County's Quakers. Special thanks as well to W. Cullen Bengtson, who created an outstanding map of south central Pennsylvania.

I have been generously supported by the George and Ann Richards Civil War Era Center, the Department of History, and the Graduate Research Support Office at Penn State. This included fellowships endowed by the Lewis, Gold, and Stitzer families, and the Warren Hassler award. I also received a Breckenridge Travel Grant from the American Historical Society and a Scholar-In-Residence Grant from the Pennsylvania Historical and Museum Commission, and was selected to participate in the Pew Summer Scholars Graduate Program. Those weeks in Harrisburg with Linda Shopes, Karen James, Jonathan Stayer, and the staff of the Pennsylvania State Archives were a highlight of my graduate years. So were those at Notre Dame under Vernon Burton's able tutelage.

While it has been many years since I studied at the University of Virginia, I must thank my mentors there, H. C. E. Midelfort and especially the late Martin Havran. Finally, Carl and Lawson Sperapani and their family generously allowed me to stay at their house so I could work in Virginia and study in Pennsylvania. Lawson also read the entire manuscript. My family was also a great encouragement, particularly my father as well as my twin brother, Eric, who read several chapters, suggested some valuable changes, and was supportive throughout. My father is also to be thanked for instilling a love of history in me. He passed away just as this project was being completed.

The most important thanks go to my wife, Valerie, and my lovely daughter, Caroline. Both were wonderful gifts that helped me complete this project, and it is to them that this book is dedicated.

On the Edge
of Freedom

Introduction

*The Fugitive Slave Issue
on the Edge of Freedom*

In between the Black Belt South and the Yankee Upper North lies a lush middle ground, less explored by historians, particularly on the northern side of the Mason-Dixon Line. There, residents had views that often diverged from the views of inhabitants of both of those better-studied regions. A great historian once aptly captured this in twentieth-century terms: C. Vann Woodward, writing to Robert Penn Warren after reviewing the manuscript of his brilliant, cantankerous *Life* magazine article on the centennial of the Civil War, wondered if Penn Warren's "a-pox-on-both-your-houses" critique of North and South had not been influenced by his border state, Kentucky heritage. Woodward described Kentucky as an "Alsace-Lorraine of pragmatism" between the die-hard crusaders of the antebellum crises.[1] Similarly, the focus of this study, south central Pennsylvania—here defined as the counties of Adams, Cumberland, and Franklin—was part of the North's metaphorical Alsace-Lorraine. It was fought over, disputed, and changed hands in a both a physical and philosophical sense. This region was part of a vital borderland where pre-war conflicts over issues such as slavery and fugitive slaves were contested in the legislatures, in the courts, in town hall meetings, and in the backwoods, back roads, and back rooms.[2] Pennsylvania's antislavery activists were often radical in their goals but practical in their approach. The results of that contest—before, during, and after the war—continue to shape our nation's legacy of race and slavery.

Studying the impact of fugitive slaves and the fugitive slave issue in a particular border region of the antebellum North illuminates the processes at work in rural antislavery and antebellum grassroots mentalité and politics. The transition that saw this area move from permitting slaveholding to prohibiting it, and then having many of its residents oppose slavery elsewhere (the South or West), was fraught with difficulties and danger in this border region. This study examines key parts of this process in southern Pennsylvania through the lens of the fugitive slave issue, which also illustrates the development of pragmatic tactics for radical antislavery along the Mason-Dixon Line.

It is clear that the Lower North and the Upper North varied in their response to the fugitive slave issue. In 1850, Daniel Webster was denied the use of Boston's Faneuil Hall for a speech because of his support for the new Fugitive Slave Law, but he was applauded in southern Pennsylvania. In 1851, large biracial gatherings—nearly 3,000 in one case—tried to prevent the rendition of fugitives from Boston and Syracuse. In 1854, the Anthony Burns fugitive slave case convulsed both Boston and Worcester, Massachusetts, resulting in the death of a deputy and the removal of a Harvard lecturer and judge. Later in the decade, noted episodes of resistance to the Fugitive Slave Law occurred in Oberlin, Ohio; Troy, New York; and Wisconsin. No such mass interracial resistance emerged in south central Pennsylvania, and when rescues did occur—at Carlisle and at Christiana—they were led almost exclusively by African Americans.

In the Upper North, some antislavery activists were open about assisting fugitive slaves. Henry David Thoreau wrote freely about helping an escaping slave in *Walden*. Frederick Douglass, in upstate New York, complained that western abolitionists who published names of Underground Railroad "conductors" were much too cavalier with information that could mean freedom or reenslavement with possible torture or death for escaping slaves. This openness rarely characterized south central Pennsylvania, where some Underground Railroad routes were so secretive that they still remain unknown.[3]

In reality, the fugitive slave issue was more critical, in a practical sense, in southern Pennsylvania than it was farther north. Southerners knew that *every single fugitive slave* escaping by land east of the Appalachian Mountains had to pass through Pennsylvania, which is why the state, its laws, and the attitudes of its citizens were so important. South central Pennsylvania, Maryland's Cumberland Valley, and Virginia's famed Shenandoah formed one grand continuum, so the Pennsylvania region was a vital entry point for fugitives seeking freedom from the central agricultural regions of Maryland and Virginia as well as Baltimore and Washington, D.C.

One insight from this study is that near the border the fugitive slave issue, along with other forms of the slavery controversy, very rapidly became politicized. Volatile Jacksonian politics led groups who were determined to actively help fugitives and oppose slavery to realize early on that they needed whatever practical, political assistance they could receive. When efforts to engage in mass organizing along the border failed—after having been so successful in New England—these groups turned to the traditional tools of the political minority, including the petition and an appeal to the legal system. Such tactics, rather than confrontational activism, also aligned with the religious sensibilities of many involved.

These activists were responding to the initiative of the fugitive slaves themselves. As they fled from slavery, many became walking advertisements for its cruelties; also, the forcible seizure and repatriation of fugitives or free blacks, often carried out in the sight of border Pennsylvanians, illustrated the oppressiveness of the system. After one egregious example, white and black activists successfully pushed for a new personal liberty law that complicated fugitive slave renditions significantly. When fugitives and free blacks themselves fought back against the 1850 Fugitive Slave Law, most notably at Christiana, their actions profoundly influenced the politics of Pennsylvania, Maryland, and the nation.

To say that the fugitive slave issue became politicized is not to minimize its importance, but rather to emphasize it. Many abolitionists and antislavery activists saw the issue as profoundly humanitarian, but many also saw its political potential. By working within a legal and political framework, antislavery activists created space for border politicians, lawyers, and judges to define the meaning of Pennsylvania as a "free" state, and in 1860 to regard support for the state's personal liberty laws restricting fugitive slave rendition to be upholding law and order.

The fugitive slave issue does not unlock all the politics of this period; interest in the issue ebbed and flowed, and antislavery activists were often stymied by border Pennsylvanians' lack of commitment to the cause. The fugitive slave issue also truly divided the populace. At least as many people seemed willing to embrace cordial relations with Southern neighbors and uphold the law and the Constitution as were drawn by the sufferings of the slave to oppose slavery or at least its further extension westward. This split was sufficiently pronounced that the fugitive slave issue remained a significant point of contention after Lincoln's election in 1860. In a post-election campaign of petitions, meetings, and publications, Democrats hoped that by exploiting the issue they could forestall secession, impede the incoming Lincoln administration, and preserve the Union.

Secession and war did not end the fugitive slave controversy; it redirected it, and in some ways even intensified it. During the war the issue lived on in disputes over "contrabands," escaping slaves who congregated near the border. This controversy was part of a larger debate over citizenship and equal rights for African Americans, including their right to fight for their own freedom. When the war ended, Pennsylvania's African Americans hoped to experience the rights they had earned. To some extent, the antebellum border focus on the fugitive slave issue worked against this aim, for emphasizing individual fugitives enabled acts of humanitarian charity without necessarily challenging the existing social system. An antislavery campaign based on fugitive slaves was an uncertain foundation on which to support postwar aspirations for equality. During and after the Civil War, south central Pennsylvania actually became more Democratic and conservative, and the edge of freedom became a place of limited opportunity. Fugitives seeking the Promised Land found unfulfilled promises instead.

As befitting a border region of a border state, south central Pennsylvania contained contradictions. Two local families who were stalwarts in helping fugitives escape, the Wrights and the Wiermans, also put them at risk for recapture by employing them for months. In 1836, a new antislavery organization seemed as interested in politics as moral reform. Thaddeus Stevens, an antislavery giant, helped a slave owner retain his slave after he is generally regarded to have converted to antislavery eight years earlier. An itinerant salesman who allegedly helped slave catchers later rose to the board of the world-renowned Pennsylvania Railroad. Another slave catcher supported local Republican candidates. A minister and college president, Samuel S. Schmucker, boldly condemned any legislation that would force the return of fugitive slaves four years before passage of the 1850 law, and even hid some within his own walls. He also served, however, on the board of the state colonization society for nine years in the 1860s. James Cooper, a politician who stated publicly that he regretted that the fugitive slave clause was ever placed in the Constitution, became a key Senator who more consistently supported the 1850 Compromise, including the new Fugitive Slave Law, than any other Northern Whig. An area so pivotal to the fugitive slave issue before the Civil War became home, after it, to discrimination, attempted lynchings, massive Ku Klux Klan rallies, and lost opportunities. These paradoxes underscore the challenges of fully appraising antislavery activity along the border, with all its contradictions and ambiguities.

The Fugitive Slave Issue and Historiography

The challenges of understanding the fugitive slave issue and border antislavery result in part from the fact that the field has largely lain fallow for much of the twentieth century. Fortunately, there has been a welcome shift with recent scholarship regarding fugitive slaves and the Underground Railroad. Many of these studies examine the Underground Railroad in an area, or look at individual cases. This study seeks to contribute to this body of recent scholarship by examining the fugitive slave issue as a theme through nearly fifty years of sectional conflict, war, and reconstruction.

The earliest commentators believed that the fugitive slave issue was vital. Even before the Civil War, John C. Calhoun, who sought Southern unity, labeled escaping slaves, particularly those aided by northerners, "the gravest and most vital of all questions to us and the whole Union." Missouri's Senator Thomas Hart Benton, no friend to Calhoun, wrote in the 1850s that the fugitive slave issue was critical to the sectional crisis, and Pennsylvania's obstructive legislation especially so. After the war, Massachusetts antislavery Congressman Henry Wilson made the fugitive slave issue a key ingredient of over one-fourth of the chapters in his massive two-volume study, *History of the Rise and Fall of the Slave Power in America*. In Philadelphia, abolitionist William Still gathered over 500 pages of notes and recollections on the operation of southern Pennsylvania's Underground Railroad. Numerous Quakers recorded their reminiscences or wrote histories about their participation as well, including several who concentrated on southern Pennsylvania.[4]

Academic study of the fugitive slave issue reached a zenith around the turn of the twentieth century, when Harvard scholar Albert Bushnell Hart and his students emphasized its importance in a number of works. Their conclusion, synthesized by Hart in his introduction to Wilbur Siebert's *Underground Railroad*, was that the slaves' ability to escape introduced critical uncertainty into Southern slaveholding, forcing Southerners to remain politically aggressive to defend it. In short, for these Harvard and Radcliffe historians, the fugitive slave was a key ingredient to the coming of the Civil War.[5]

After Hart and his students reached these conclusions, however, a shift occurred. In the larger study of the antislavery movement, it was the highly literate Garrisonians who intrigued historians. Not only had the Garrisonians and their descendants written many of the first histories of the movement, they had left letters and publications, and expounded philosophies of vital interest to twentieth century intellectuals. Interest in Garrison and his followers expanded as historians grew more concerned with ideologies and radical philosophies and action, and less interested in rural folk helping fugitive slaves. William Lloyd Garrison himself worried that the fugitive slave issue, by turning abolitionists toward helping the individual fugitive, could divert their attention from destroying the institution of slavery. Until recently, many historians seem to have adopted his viewpoint and overlooked the importance of the fugitive slave issue to the antebellum conflict.

Other changes in the historical profession also marginalized the fugitive slave issue for much of the twentieth century. In the 1930s, Charles and Mary Beard emphasized large-scale economic and social factors in antebellum America; for them, the Civil War era was a massive clash of diverging civilizations, a drama in which the individual fugitive had little role. Other historians, influenced by the horrific bloodshed of World War I, argued that the Civil War was a blunder brought on by sensationalist journalists and incompetent statesmen. To them, the fugitive slave issue was important almost solely as an issue these villains agitated. The few who continued to study the Underground Railroad and fugitive slaves were outside the academy, such as Henrietta Buckmaster, a thorough researcher who wrote in a more popular style.[6]

As the historical discipline professionalized, historians embraced new forms of evidence. The adoption of "scientific" methods for the study of history also helped push fugitive slaves into the background. The personal reminiscences of individuals, even those of former Underground Railroad participants who conscientiously tried to write for the historical record, seemed far less important than more scientific forms of evidence. As scholars began to make increased use of the invaluable but flawed resources of the nineteenth century U.S. census, historians from James Ford Rhodes to Robin Winks relied on that data to suggest that few fugitives escaped north per year—only 1,814 fugitives were enumerated in the 1850 and 1860 censuses combined.[7] These figures, however, cannot be accepted uncritically. There seems to have been little incentive for slave owners to admit to the census taker, who could have been a neighbor, that they could not control their laborers.[8] Certainly many Southern politicians, especially from the border states, readily claimed that their state's loss of slaves was unacceptably high.

In another application of the scientific method to the fugitive slave issue, Stanley Campbell analyzed court records and concluded that slave owners prevailed in the vast majority of fugitive slave proceedings in the North, and that Southern complaints regarding enforcement of the law were unjustified. He failed to consider, however, that in large areas of the North, Southerners did not even bother to try to recover fugitives. The fact that this study remained the last word on the Fugitive Slave Law for over thirty years shows the academic neglect of the issue.[9]

Campbell's work helps illustrate an important academic strain of thought, which argues that the fugitive slave issue and the Underground Railroad have been overemphasized and, at times, mythologized in the literature. Even before Campbell, Larry Gara had sharply critiqued prevailing views of the Underground Railroad as unduly influenced by the romantic myth of valiant Quakers, cloaked lanterns, and helpless fugitives. Gara pointed out that many African Americans escaped north with no assistance from Northern whites, relying on their own resources or on African American helpers. He argued that the Underground Railroad was not an organized, systematic institution but an *ad hoc* one for which far too much influence was claimed. He also believed researchers relied too uncritically on local lore and rose-colored reminiscences, often written decades after the events by Quakers and others who consciously or unconsciously wanted to exaggerate their roles. Gara's corrective was needed, but was sufficiently harsh as to inhibit Underground Railroad research for several decades.[10]

Even some of the finest historical work has unintentionally slighted the fugitive slave issue. Eric Foner, in his magisterial study of the free labor ideology, considered the fugitive slave issue in the 1850s primarily as a tool wielded by radical Republicans to wrest control of the party from conservatives, not as an important issue in its own right. This was despite the fact that his study focused considerable attention on the influence of Ohio lawyer and politician Salmon P. Chase, whose early career included representing fugitive slaves. John Hope Franklin and Loren Schweninger, in their comprehensive study of runaway slaves, suggested that few fled north. They were most interested in the "rebels on the plantation"—those who "laid out" close to home.[11]

Recently, this neglect of the fugitive slave issue appears to be changing. A renewed interest in the Underground Railroad, with early assistance from the works of Charles Blockson and the initiatives of National Park Service, has led to new studies and perspectives. Individuals and communities have been rescued from scholarly neglect.[12] Harriet Tubman and Frederick Douglass, the most famous fugitives of all and leaders in the fight to help fugitive slaves, have received increasing scholarly attention.[13] Fergus Bordewich's wonderful sweeping treatment re-emphasizes the importance of Quakers and the Underground Railroad and glides past Gara's critique. Recently, specific fugitive slave cases in Boston, Pennsylvania, and Wisconsin have enjoyed renewed attention. J. Blaine Hudson and Keith Griffler have produced excellent studies of the Underground Railroad and fugitive slaves in border Kentucky and Ohio. The field of Underground Railroad and fugitive slave research seems to be undergoing a renaissance.[14]

New synthetic works have started to arise, which like Bordewich's *Bound for Canaan*, analyze trends over broad geographies and time scales. Perhaps the most significant new work of antislavery history that this work intersects with is Stanley Harrold's *Border Wars*, published as this work was in final revision. *Border Wars* is a valuable extension to Harrold's earlier work, *Subversives*, which focused on slave escape networks on the Eastern Seaboards.[15] That earlier study made a significant contribution in uncovering an entire web of border Underground Railroad routes and locations, with the whole operation extending to Philadelphia and New York and likely financed by Lewis and Arthur Tappan. *Border Wars* is an even more profound contribution. Its scope spans the entire border, although much of the early part of the book, covering the 1830s and 1840s, focuses on Ohio. Harrold contends that sharp conflict and near open warfare existed from the 1830s on between slaveholders and abolitionists around fugitive slave escapes. In some respects, he sees the Civil War as the culmination of this border violence. Harrold based his work largely on newspaper accounts and political statements, including from highly politicized pro- and anti-slavery newspapers. This may result in some exaggeration of the potential for violence, but it is hard to argue with certain reported facts, such as when fugitives were killed or slaveholders or abolitionists were badly beaten.

Harrold also shows the critical role that the Border South and the issue of slave escapes, kidnappings, and potential insurrections played in the critical debates of the secession crisis. Many in the Lower South were convinced that the threat to border slavery would make border slave states secede, but those states accurately perceived that after decades of complaining about Northerners enticing their slaves to escape, they were still safer in the Union rather than facing an implacable, well-armed Northern foe with little motivation to return fleeing slaves. The slaveholding Border and Middle South states hesitated; after Fort Sumter, half of them seceded, but half did not.

My work examines a border region of Pennsylvania with strong Quaker influence. I have not found as much of the violence characterized in Harrold's work, at least not until the 1850s, when the new Fugitive Slave Law brought about a violent turn. Why there seems to be a difference between the Midwest and the East, at least in the early decades of activism, is unclear. The Western regions had less established political institutions and history. Perhaps residents of these areas had more of a frontier mentality, with people more inclined to take matters into their own hands. Even John Brown, progenitor of the ultimate act of fugitive slave–related violence, was radicalized in part by his experiences in Kansas. Twenty years ago, Phillip Paludan provocatively argued that the Civil War could be seen as an attempt by nineteenth century citizens to restore law and order. In an era with tiny police forces, individual citizens felt that they, too, were responsible for maintaining law and order and policing society.[16] This concept may have had even greater resonance in the less established, more sparsely populated Midwest than in the more settled communities in the East. As Harrold points out, western slave states such as Kentucky and later Missouri felt surrounded on three sides by free territory where slaves could find refuge or were enticed to flee.

Another difference between this work and Harrold's is that like many historians, Harrold seems to portray an ascending arc of tension and conflict until secession. My work shows that, at least in the public press, the fugitive slave issue lost momentum along the south central Pennsylvania border in the mid-1850s. This area, which had no substantial natural barrier between Pennsylvania and Maryland and Virginia—as Robert E. Lee proved—carefully tried to back away from the precipice. John Brown made this impossible, but even then, many of south central Pennsylvania's activists were silent during the war-of-words petition battle in the midst of the secession crisis.

This work argues that neglecting the fugitive slave issue leaves out an important aspect of the sectional crisis and limits our understanding of the border North. South central Pennsylvania's antislavery activity, centered largely around helping fugitives, differed from abolitionism farther north because it was less confrontational and gave greater emphasis to legal and political remedies. Antislavery activity built around the fugitive slave issue led to legal and political engagement, which, along with Garrisonianism, was a vital component of antebellum antislavery. It resulted in protections for fugitive slaves and prosecutions for kidnappers, and made a substantial contribution to Pennsylvania's 1847 personal liberty law. This legislation deeply angered Southerners and helped lead to the 1850 federal law. In combination with similar developments occurring in Ohio and elsewhere, this approach could support political antislavery, which would largely become embodied in the Republican Party. Its limitations, however, can be seen in the failure to win meaningful postwar equality for African Americans along the "edge of freedom." In the postwar years, however, without the animating spirit of the antislavery activists, the law became a conservative force. By the 1920s, local writers condemned African Americans for breaking the laws of nature by passing as whites, and used law and order to disparage the Underground Railroad as a sentimental, illegal activity. And the Ku Klux Klan held large rallies just off of the Gettysburg battlefield.

As we consider the importance of the fugitive slave issue in border Pennsylvania, the central insights of Ed Ayers's work comes to mind. Ayers cogently argues that the "edges" of our antebellum and Civil War story—he cites Virginia, the Upper South, the Mississippi Valley, and Franklin County, Pennsylvania— significantly complicate our grand narrative. They cannot be omitted without obscuring the story. His work inspired the title to this study.[17] For years, many historians considered the North an undifferentiated monolith lying above the Mason-Dixon Line. Using the fugitive slave issue to examine the edge of this region reveals meaningful subtleties, shades, and variations.

Finally, this study may help illuminate the rural antebellum North. It supports David Donald's beleaguered contention that the rural background of many abolitionists in an industrializing America should be explored. Valid criticisms of his assumptions and demographics have been made, but this author, after nearly a decade of studying this locale, believes that Donald may have seen something profound.[18] The Underground Railroad, perhaps the largest form of civil disobedience until the 1960s, had a very significant rural component. In some ways, it is an example of a rural protest movement on a grand scale, part of a continuum that stretches from Bacon's Rebellion through the post–Revolutionary War upheavals of the Whiskey Rebellion, Shay's Rebellion, and Fries' Rebellion (Pennsylvania). This unrest lasted into the 1830s with Antimasonry (strongest in rural areas) and the 1840s with Dorr's rebellion and the struggle against the vast landholdings on the Hudson. Then rural protest seems to vanish until the post–Civil War movements of the Populists and the Grangers. Yet any time farmers or rural citizens helped a fugitive slave travel on, or offered one directions, food, or water, they may have been protesting unjust laws that they felt were corrupting the country and subverting America's purpose. Seeing the Underground Railroad and border antislavery as part of a historical continuum of protest in national and rural life gives this story abiding significance, even for today.

Notes Regarding Terminology and Methodology

In 1774, Pennsylvania reformers formed the Society for the Relief of Free Negroes Unlawfully Held in Bondage; in 1787, the group reorganized as the Pennsylvania Society for Promoting the Abolition of Slavery (PAS). Individuals who belonged to it were called, in the press, members of the "ABOLITION SOCIETY"; decades later, local historians would call PAS members "original abolitionists."

As a historian who wants to give voice to the people of the past, it is difficult not to call "abolitionists" individuals who self-identified themselves as such. Nevertheless, because part of the historical profession generally restricts the use of the term "abolitionist" to those who favored immediate abolition (itself a term with multiple meanings), I have, somewhat reluctantly, tried to conform to that usage. Some of the individuals in this study definitely did favor immediate abolition, and many more may have, but they either chose not to make it the central point of their message or I did not uncover their public advocacy of immediatism in my study of fugitive slave and antislavery materials. I also use the term "African Americans" to refer to Americans of African descent, although occasionally I used the term "black," primarily for stylistic reasons. I do apologize for having to use several egregious and offensive racial epithets to accurately convey the character of newspaper coverage of the time. To avoid gratuitous use of this terminology, I have limited this language to what is necessary to illustrate the racialized nature of social and political conflict in the late antebellum, wartime, and postwar periods.

Rural areas do not always offer the same rich concentration of sources as an urban study. This is particularly true in south central Pennsylvania, where the Franklin County courthouse and its records were burned by Confederate raiders. Despite these challenges, the history of the fugitive slave issue in this key border area deserves to be told. For this study, I have been instructed and inspired by Winthrop Jordan's *Tumult and Silence at Second Creek*, a stellar example of what can be accomplished studying events in a rural setting. Like Jordan, I have tried to piece together evidence from a wide variety of sources: newspapers, first person recollections, antislavery society records, census data, letters and diaries, legal and legislative records, local histories, and the holdings of private collections, local historical societies, and archives along the East Coast. The result is a fascinating collage from fragmentary sources. The chapters that follow are organized around particular sets of sources as well as the flow of events. In more cases than I would have liked, I have had to make reasonable suppositions about the linkages between events. There were very few "smoking gun" documents that explained the thoughts and motivations of the participants. I welcome future scholars—and there are a number working on Adams County alone—testing, improving, and extending these findings.[19]

1 South Central Pennsylvania, Fugitive Slaves, and the Underground Railroad

At dusk, a shadow crept parallel to a road from central Maryland to Pennsylvania, following the road while still avoiding exposure. A fugitive slave! Unaware of the precise moment when he crossed the Mason-Dixon Line, he silently entered south central Pennsylvania, a region with its own history of slavery, antislavery activism, and unequal freedom. Home to a significant free black community and an effective Underground Railroad, this area was also replete with slave catchers, informers, and those who resented fugitives. It was a place of both significant opportunity and substantial danger. In short, he was on the edge of freedom.[1]

South central Pennsylvania—defined in this study as Adams, Cumberland, and Franklin counties, with a particular emphasis on Adams—was home to multiple such "edges."[2] There was the well-known demarcation represented by the Mason-Dixon Line. After 1820, there was divergence between state and federal fugitive slave law. There were also "edges" in the community, divisions between those who helped fugitives and those who supported efforts to apprehend them or to intimidate their supporters.

Geographical, economic, cultural, and historical factors made this region a place of "edges" (see Figure 1). Initially, south central Pennsylvania was frontier. Its inhabitants feared attack by Native Americans, and trade with Philadelphia was inhibited by abysmal roads and the broad Susquehanna River. In 1814, nearly a quarter of a million dollars was spent to bridge the river. Even into the 1820s, south central Pennsylvania's social and economic ties to Virginia, Baltimore, and central Maryland were stronger than to eastern Pennsylvania. Improved roads helped, but it was the railroad that finally tied this region to Philadelphia. Even then, development was sporadic and Gettysburg, the seat of Adams County, was not connected to the railroad—as a spur—until 1858.[3]

The geography that encouraged social and economic links to the south also aided fugitive slaves escaping north. While there was no broad river of commerce along the border, like the Ohio in the Midwest, other features strengthened the

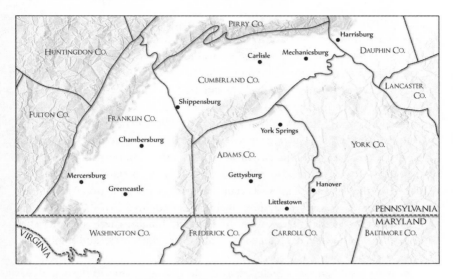

Figure 1. South Central Pennsylvania and vicinity. (W. Cullen Bengston)

ties between sections. The North and South Mountain ranges, which turn east toward Harrisburg as they pass through south central Pennsylvania, funneled in that direction the traffic, commerce, and fugitive slaves of Virginia's Shenandoah Valley and Maryland's Cumberland Valley. Correspondingly, much of the region's goods were directed southward. The mountain ranges were paralleled by a series of gentle ridges also running roughly southwest to northeast. In 1863, the two great armies at Gettysburg occupied two of these parallel ridges. Streams in the area generally ran north-south, also potentially guiding fugitives to freedom. As these waters eroded the limestone ridges over millennia, they contributed to the stunning fertility of the entire Great Valley region.[4] This in turn supported orchard crops and grain-based agriculture, which employed temporary labor, including free blacks and, sometimes, fugitive slaves.

This region was part of the great colonial era migration route, with settlers disembarking in Philadelphia and then crossing south central Pennsylvania before turning south to the vast back country stretching from Virginia to Georgia.[5] As the National Road was completed across Pennsylvania, Gettysburg and Chambersburg became important stage coach stops between Philadelphia and Pittsburgh. The region developed a booming carriage trade, and many customers came from the South for the distinctive "Gettysburg" carriage.[6]

Many different groups traveled along these paths. Quakers, while socially and economically influential in eastern Pennsylvania, competed with Germans and Scots-Irish Presbyterians in the south central part of the state, but they created space for their own institutions and mores. In this region, Quakers were important to fugitive slave assistance. The Quakers' practice of staged westward migration, often advancing county by county, meant that the area's Underground Railroad workers could connect to kin or trusted friends all the way back to Philadelphia.

The Quakers began as a radical sect in England, but gradually they traded much of their radicalism for sober thrift, accumulation, and organization. They often could be found running local banks, organizing financial networks, or participating in the legal system. As a result of their own persecution in England, they had a deep concern for the suffering, including fugitive slaves. Quakers were pacifists and most preferred to work non-confrontationally. These characteristics would contribute to the character of the antislavery movement and fugitive aid in this region.[7]

Pennsylvania, its Quakers included, had a long relationship to slavery. Slaves lived along the Delaware, serving Dutch and Swedish masters, before William Penn owned the colony. Although some Quakers protested slavery, beginning in 1688, many of the colony's Quaker leadership owned slaves, including Penn. As a result, although the Quaker-dominated assembly tried to regulate slave importations from 1703 on, meaningful action against slave owners in the Philadelphia Yearly (Quaker) Meeting was delayed until the French and Indian War (1754–63). Then Quaker abolition efforts accelerated under the leadership of reformers such as John Woolman and Anthony Benezet.[8]

The Revolutionary War resulted in a loss of Quaker influence because of the Quakers' pacifism and suspected Toryism. Still, slavery did not fit many patriots' revolutionary ideals. The antislavery movement started to pick up influential non-Quaker supporters, including Thomas Paine and Benjamin Rush. In 1780, the Pennsylvania assembly passed a gradual abolition bill, which freed no slave who was alive when it was passed, but would liberate their children—that is, those born after November 1780—at the age of twenty-eight. The law also established a registry for slaves, which in retrospect was a highly significant step, creating the presumption of freedom for every African American in Pennsylvania who was not registered. Slaveholders immediately tried to evade the law; a stronger version was passed in 1788, which regularized the registry and imposed kidnapping penalties for those who would take slaves out of state to evade the law's requirements.[9]

Pennsylvania's 1780 legislation contained an insidious feature. While the children of slaves born after 1780 would gain freedom at age twenty-eight, itself a significant compromise from the originally proposed age of twenty-one, their children would not be born free, but also would be enslaved until age twenty-eight. So would their children, their children's children, and so on. This provision was supposed to compensate the slaveholder for the resources spent raising slave children, but it provided the potential for perpetual slavery in the state. This was confusing, and in 1826, Pennsylvania's Supreme Court ruled that the children of slaves due freedom at twenty-eight would be free.[10] East of the Susquehanna, this decision was largely moot. Slavery there had vanished relatively quickly because of substantial Quaker pressure and because of access to an apprenticeship and indentured servitude system for African Americans that was nearly as oppressive as slavery. Elsewhere, however, slavery lingered, particularly in south central Pennsylvania.[11]

South central Pennsylvania's social geography was also shaped by the Pennsylvania Germans. German settlers, perhaps more than any other group outside of England, had heeded William Penn's call to religious minorities. Most migrated to the state's southern region, where they could practice a familiar grain-based agriculture. Pennsylvania Germans were so numerous there that it can seem misleading to call them a "minority." One scholar has estimated that in 1850, Pennsylvania Germans composed forty-nine percent of the population of Adams County, thirty-nine percent of Franklin County, and thirty-seven percent of Cumberland County. York County, adjacent to both Adams and Cumberland, was fifty-two percent German.[12]

Pennsylvania Germans had mixed attitudes toward slavery. Some of the first German settlers, fleeing European oppression, disapproved of slavery. In 1688, at Germantown, four German Mennonites and Quakers signed a memorial to their local Monthly Meeting urging equal treatment for all men, condemning slavery and the slave trade, and even positing a right of resistance for slaves.[13] This Germantown Petition ultimately reached the Yearly Meetings in both Philadelphia and London, but no action was taken. Other Germans, however, willingly adopted slave labor. Adams County historian Larry Bolin estimates that at least twenty percent of that county's slaveholders were of Germanic origin.[14]

The Pennsylvania Germans competed with the area's Scots Irish and English populations for prime lands and cultural leadership. Politically, in the nineteenth century, although some Germans were Whigs or antislavery, generally they formed the core of the region's Democratic Party strength. For example, a Pennsylvania German, Henry J. Stahle, edited Gettysburg's Democratic newspaper, the *Compiler*, for decades.

A third important demographic group was south central Pennsylvania's black population. They were vital to the local economy, to antislavery activity, and to aid to fugitive slaves. During the colonial period, skilled African American slaves had been invaluable. It was a classic case of labor control—with so much of Pennsylvania's labor force migrating westward down the Great Valley Road, there was substantial advantage to keeping skilled, experienced workers through force of law, backed by custom. Even after the adoption of Pennsylvania's gradual abolition statute in 1780, prejudice and discrimination closed off many employment opportunities for African Americans. Most worked long hours doing low-paid manual labor, often performing the dirtiest, least desirable jobs, such as working in tanneries and iron furnaces. African Americans also composed much of the region's service class of barbers, waiters, launderers, and livery stable attendants, although they faced competition with Irish and German women in domestic service.[15]

In the antebellum period, a significant percentage of the state's rural African Americans lived in south central Pennsylvania. Quaker influence in Philadelphia led to rapid emancipation there after the 1780 act, so a significant part of Pennsylvania's slavery became concentrated here. Once emancipated, many African Americans chose to remain in the area, where they had family, friends, or established business or labor relationships.[16] In addition, African Americans migrated into the area from Maryland and Virginia. Some were fugitive slaves, but most were freed slaves or free blacks. For much of the antebellum period, those two states required slave owners to transport manumitted slaves out of state, so some slave owners carried them just across the Pennsylvania line to free them. As Keith Griffler has noted concerning the border region of Ohio before the 1820s, southern Pennsylvania "gained a reputation as a refuge for enslaved African Americans freed by their repentant owners." Franklin County, with several villages located close to the Mason-Dixon Line, was a popular destination. Such immigration was often unwelcome. In York County, when a group of fifty-two slaves from Virginia arrived in 1819, a newspaper reported that "all is consternation and conjecture here," as locals feared that an influx of freed slaves would compete for jobs.[17] A similarly sized group of manumitted slaves arrived in Chambersburg in Franklin County as late as the 1850s. As Pennsylvania's abolition and indentured servitude laws became better known, instead of emancipating their slaves, some Southern slave owners took them to southern Pennsylvania and sold them as indentured servants until age twenty-one. The slave eventually became free, but the owner was compensated. This was illegal—slaves coming into the state to stay were to be freed immediately—but in some areas this practice may have continued until 1845.[18]

Other former slaves relocated in south central Pennsylvania voluntarily after escaping or purchasing their freedom. Although hazardous because the area was honeycombed with slave catchers and kidnappers, living in southern Pennsylvania enabled them to stay in contact with kin to the south, and to possibly purchase their freedom or help them escape. For farm laborers, southern Pennsylvania's grain growing economy, similar to that of central Maryland and Virginia, would have been familiar.[19]

Pennsylvania's slavery lingered from 1780 to 1840, although most slaves had been freed by 1830. Until 1850, the proportion of free blacks in Adams and Cumberland counties generally matched or exceeded the state average, as Table 1 shows. Franklin County nearly doubled the statewide average during those years. In 1820, nearly ten percent of the state's African Americans lived in the south central section. If the data for the counties of Philadelphia and Allegheny are excluded, as a rough proxy for Pennsylvania's urban population (Philadelphia and Pittsburgh), then in both 1820 and 1830, the three counties of south central Pennsylvania (out of the forty-nine remaining "rural" counties) held nearly sixteen percent of Pennsylvania's "rural" African American population.

The information on the free black population shown in Table 1 illustrates the weaknesses of early census data. First, the sizes of counties were shifting—

Table 1.1 Free Black Population in South Central Pennsylvania in Proportion to Total Population of Each County

| | Number of Free Blacks/ Percentage of Total Population in County | | | | | | South-Central Pennsylvania % of State's Population of Free Blacks /Rural |
Year	State	Adams		Cumberland		Franklin		Free Blacks
1800*	2.4%	189	1.4%	329	1.3%	664	3.4%	8.1 / 15.7%
1810*	2.8%	338	2.2%	265	0.9%	924	4.0%	6.8 / 13.2%
1820	1.9%	606	3.1%	728	3.1%	1547	4.9%	9.5 / 16.3%
1830	2.8%	592	2.8%	928	3.2%	1804	5.1%	8.8 / 15.7%
1840	2.8%	690	3.0%	996	3.2%	2033	5.4%	7.7 / 14.4%
1850	2.3%	555	2.1%	957	2.8%	1948	4.9%	6.5 / 11.4%

* = Data for free nonwhite persons excluding Indians not taxed

Cumberland County, in particular, underwent a dramatic reduction in size, as parts of it were carved off to form other counties. There is also reason to suspect, as Karen James of the Pennsylvania Historical and Museum Commission has suggested, that most Pennsylvania censuses undercounted the African American population. African Americans were often mobile or lived in marginal areas where census takers might be less diligent.[20] The reason for the absolute decline in free blacks in all three counties between 1840 and 1850 is unclear. The fear of kidnapping probably does not account for the entire decline. 1850 was the first year in which Pennsylvania census takers did not enumerate slaves. It is possible that many census takers, no longer required to distinguish between slaves and free blacks, took less care in enumerating the African American population in general.

This concentration of African Americans in southern Pennsylvania had important ramifications for fugitive slaves. Scholars of the Underground Railroad have long recognized that a strong free black population was an important component to successful aid to fugitive slaves. In Maryland, just to the south, nearly forty percent of the African American population was free by 1840, a higher percentage by far than any other Southern state. The presence of these two emerging free black communities—Pennsylvania's and Maryland's—created opportunities for networks based on race and kinship. In south central Pennsylvania, free blacks could shelter escaping African Americans, guide them through the region, direct them to additional help, or even entice slaves to flee. They could also ignore fugitive slaves, urge them to "move on," or act as informants or slave catchers. Whatever they chose, they are important actors in the story.[21]

Some of these African Americans formed the backbone of south central Pennsylvania's Underground Railroad. Others became prominent elsewhere. John Peck, a local barber, supported the Underground Railroad, helped lead Carlisle's antislavery society, and served as vice president of the Colored Men's Convention in Harrisburg. After relocating to the Pittsburgh area, he helped found a training institute for African Americans. His son, David J. Peck, became the first African American graduate of a U.S. medical school. South Carolina's Daniel Alexander Payne studied in Gettysburg, then became a bishop of the African Methodist Episcopal Church, and later the president of Wilberforce University. Some of the fugitives also became famous: J. W. C. Pennington fled through the area before becoming a prominent minister in New York.[22]

Certain white families also aided fugitives. One prominent family headed by William and Phoebe Wright began helping fugitives around 1819.[23] Other residents, white and African American, undoubtedly started sooner. The years

1816–19 are the earliest dates for which complete membership records exist for the Pennsylvania Society for the Abolition of Slavery (short title: Pennsylvania Abolition Society), an organization that helped lead the fight against slavery nationally until the rise of Garrisonian abolition in the 1830s.[24] The vast majority of the group's membership came from Philadelphia. From outlying southern Pennsylvania, however, the most members—four—came from Adams County. In Jesse Russell, George Wilson, Nicholas Wireman, and Samuel Wright, Adams County had more representatives than the more populous Lancaster, York, or even Chester counties, which lay next to Philadelphia and had a strong nineteenth century antislavery movement.[25]

While white Adams County residents participated in the statewide antislavery organization, there is also limited evidence of a local organization before the 1830s. In 1820, there was a newspaper notice calling for a meeting in Menallen township of an Adams County Protection Society "to protect the sable descendants of Africa from being unlawfully held and dragged into bondage." The notice proclaimed that slavery was inconsistent with Christianity and was an "absolute violation of our bill of rights." The society denied any intention to interfere in relations between masters and slaves, but vowed to protect free blacks from kidnapping (African Americans illegally "held" in bondage referred to those who were due freedom under the gradual emancipation law, but whose owners retained them by keeping their slaves in ignorance, or because of differences of interpretation about the law, which ultimately had to be litigated). Jesse Russell was the president, and Isaac Pearson, secretary. Despite this bold beginning, little more was heard of this organization.[26]

The scant record of an early antislavery society is matched by the limited documentation on fugitive slave cases. Records of the capture of fugitive slaves from this region appear non-existent before 1826, apparently because most Southerners exercised a "right of recaption" to recover fugitive slaves. Under this property right, if a horse wandered away, and the owner found it, he could recover it without legal process, unless someone objected. The same principle was used to recapture slaves until Pennsylvania passed new legislation in 1826.[27]

According to the 1793 fugitive slave law, slave owners or their agents were supposed to take fugitives before a U.S. judge or the magistrate of the county, city, or town in which the fugitive had been seized. In southern Pennsylvania, however, many slaveholders, agents, or fortune hunting slave catchers apparently did little more than travel across the border, grab individuals whom they claimed were escaped slaves, and carry them south. In some cases, the owner might go before a magistrate and make a perfunctory declaration of identification. Such a system was rife with potential for abuse, and, in many cases, the individuals seized claimed that they were not slaves. This led to an outcry against "kidnappings." Kidnapping had long concerned Pennsylvania's antislavery community. In fact, the Pennsylvania Abolition Society (PAS) had begun as the Society for the Relief of Free Negroes Unlawfully Held in Bondage (1775), essentially an anti-kidnapping organization—its goal was to ensure that African Americans who were supposed to be free were not held as slaves. It was a direct predecessor to the PAS, and even after the PAS was formed, the old society's name was still part of the group's lengthy official title, the Pennsylvania Society for Promoting the Abolition of Slavery and for the Relief of Free Negroes Unlawfully Held in Bondage.[28]

South central Pennsylvania, located near the Mason-Dixon Line and with its mixed black population of free, slave, and fugitive, was fertile ground for kidnappers. Reports of kidnappings were common across southern Pennsylvania, and in their memorials to the biannual American Convention on Antislavery, the PAS routinely decried kidnapping and made it a significant focus of its message.[29] Compassion was not the sole reason for these protests—kidnappings also symbolized liberty's general fragility. In the kind of "slippery slope" thinking common in colonial and antebellum America, there were fears that compromising any rights of any "freeman" could ultimately result in the loss of all rights for everyone.[30] So allowing African Americans to be wrongfully carried off could be the first step of a larger repression of all Pennsylvanians. This may not have been difficult for Quakers to believe, from their bitter history of their repression by the British Government, and they routinely faced persecution from Pennsylvania for refusing to pay militia fees or take oaths.

The 1826 law regularized the fugitive slave rendition process and mandated stiff penalties for kidnapping free blacks or selling them to be carried out of state. For either offense, an individual could be fined up to $2,000—a large sum—and jailed for five to twelve years, including hard labor and solitary confinement. One half of the fine would be payable to the people who brought the case. In order to recover a fugitive, the law mandated that the owner or his agent must swear to a judge, justice of the peace, or alderman that the individual claimed was his slave, and produce a legal affidavit from the jurisdiction from which the slave escaped, which included the slave's name, age, and description. Then the judge or magistrate issued a warrant empowering the sheriff or constable to bring the fugitive before the bench. If the judge was satisfied that the individual was indeed the fugitive slave sought, he was to issue a certificate, called a warrant of removal, "which shall be sufficient . . . for removing the said fugitive to the state or territory from which he or she fled." This warrant was to include the name and residence of the person alleging the escape of the slave, and the name, age, and description of the fugitive. The judge was to file a certified copy with the clerk of the court of Quarter Sessions.[31]

This law apparently changed some slaveholders' practices; they either tried to abide by it or realized their possible legal jeopardy if they did not. In early 1827, writs begin to appear in Adams County. There are only twelve in all, covering from 1827 to 1834. Like most fragmentary records, they raise more issues than they answer, but together with fugitive slave advertisements and slave narratives, they help provide a valuable portrait of those willing to risk the flight north to freedom.

Generally, the warrants of removal were granted by William McLean, a judge of the Court of Common Pleas in Adams County. An example of a warrant of removal is shown in Figure 2. It reads: "Adams County Ss[Sessions] Whereas John Ish of Loudon County Virginia, the regularly authorize[d] agent of Sarah Ellsy, of the County and state aforesaid, hath this day procured from the subscriber, one of the Judges of the Court of Common Pleas of said county, a Warrant for the Removal of Negro George, who acknowledges himself to be the slave of said Sarah Ellsy—He is black, about 5 ft 8 in high, slim make, between the age of 20 + 26 years—Given under my hand and seal the 12th day of June 1828 W McLean." In two cases, in 1827 and 1834, a local justice of the peace supplied the warrant instead.[32]

According to these writs, most of the slaveholders claiming fugitives were from Maryland counties abutting the Pennsylvania line. Eight of the twelve records

Figure 2. 1828 Warrant of Removal, Adams County Quarter Sessions. (Adams County Prothonotary's Office)

show warrants issued to slave owners from Washington County or Frederick County, Maryland. The close proximity of Gettysburg to these counties allowed slaves to escape more easily, but also permitted masters to respond quickly.

Some fugitives came from greater distances; records exist for escaped slaves (one case each) from Baltimore and Prince George's County, Maryland, and Loudoun and Culpepper counties in Virginia. These locales ranged from roughly 60 to 140 miles away from Gettysburg. In the vast majority of cases, the slave owner appeared personally to reclaim his property, rather than use an agent. In some cases, the trip may have been an adventure, a diversion, or an opportunity to buy Northern goods. Forgoing an agent also decreased the cost and may have increased security, as the owner could avoid dishonest agents who might sell a fugitive to slave traders rather than return him.

There was no doubt that slaves were valuable. Male slaves had the highest worth; according to the research of Ulrich B. Phillips, prime young male field hands were valued at $400 in Virginia in 1828–29. If they could be transported to Georgia or New Orleans, they could bring $700 to $800. Skilled laborers would be worth even more.[33]

Many of the slaves fleeing to south central Pennsylvania were skilled and in their prime as laborers and thus highly valuable. Of the thirteen slaves named in these cases, twelve were male, between the ages of eighteen and fifty (Ephraim Valentin, listed only as a "boy," may have been younger). Two men were approximately forty and fifty, but the overwhelming majority was between eighteen and thirty. Most were described as "stout," indicating that they were well muscled and would have been valuable laborers. Only one woman was mentioned, Mary, but she was young and had attributes such as a "lively gait" that indicated she could have been particularly useful as a laborer, household assistant, or potential source of slave children.

The frequency of the warrants decreased rapidly after 1828, when six were recorded. From 1829 to 1831, only one certificate was recorded a year, and then in 1834, there is one more case. This last example has a twist: Rather than just a record describing the issuing of the warrant of removal, there is an actual case in the Adams County court records, *The State v. Negro Jim and Ephraim Valentine*. The result of the case is also unusual: The judge did not issue a warrant for removal, but rather ordered the constable to arrest the two alleged fugitives, and to bring them in for questioning. While this may have happened in similar cases without any records surviving, this seeming change of practice may have indicated a growing reluctance to help slave owners. After Thaddeus Stevens died, area residents claimed that rendition of fugitive slaves had been very difficult, if not impossible, after his conversion to antislavery views. If true, it is possible that this change in practice in 1834 reflected a lessening of sympathy for the slave-holder in the Adams County legal system. This new process may not have denied slave owners their legal rights, but may have tried to discourage them by slowing the process. If there were individuals willing to help fugitives, magistrate Sampson King's actions in this case may have given them time to get organized.[34]

The lack of any records after 1834 may reflect a diminished willingness by south central Pennsylvania judges to participate in fugitive slave renditions. It could also indicate a reluctance by slave owners to rely on the southern Pennsylvania legal system.[35]

Additional evidence concerning fugitive slaves, their escape strategies, and their master's fears can be found in runaway slave advertisements placed in local papers.[36] Not all runaways, of course, struck out for Pennsylvania, or reached the south central counties. Some stayed near home, hiding out in the woods and staying in touch with family. Others headed for a city.[37] In this border area, however, with free states nearby, many runaways tried to reach the uneasy safety of Pennsylvania, as shown by ads placed in one of the Gettysburg papers, the Adams County *Sentinel* (or *Centinel*).

Twenty-eight advertisements, describing thirty-three fugitive slaves, appeared in the *Sentinel* from 1820 to 1828 (see Appendix A for capsule summaries). By 1828, the number of advertisements had begun to wane dramatically. With the progress of Pennsylvania's gradual emancipation law, there were fewer Pennsylvania slaveholders and local sentiment may have led to a diminution in the advertisements.

The advertisements generally followed a similar style: an account of when and from where the slave escaped, the slave's name, a description of the slave and his or her clothing, and the reward offered. Usually, the expectation was that the slave would be captured and lodged locally; the reward would typically be greatest if the jail were out of state and less as it approached the slave owner's locality. In one case, "reasonable charges would be paid if the slave was delivered back to the owner's house," in addition to the reward.[38]

The reward system was vital to recovering fugitives. In Pennsylvania, fugitives were often recovered through the cooperation of several individuals, and a large reward would mean ample payments to everyone. As commonly practiced, however, the arrangements seem backwards from the slaveholder's perspective, as he would pay the largest reward if the slave were farther away and would necessitate a potentially costly trip for his recovery. Two Maryland slaveholders recognized this, and offered a larger reward ($125 or $150) if their fugitive were lodged in

Frederick jail rather than the Gettysburg jail ($100). They were the exception, however.[39]

Slaveholders from nearby Frederick County, Maryland placed half the ads, especially those who lived only a few miles from Adams County. Other ads came from Hagerstown in nearby Washington County. Ads were also received, however, from Maryland's Montgomery, Baltimore, and Allegheny counties; Loudoun County, Virginia; and Georgetown in the District of Columbia. Only three advertisements were from Pennsylvania—two from Adams County and one from York. In two of those cases, the runaway was described as an African American indentured servant, not a slave, but in most cases the distinction meant little. Although there were African American indentured servants, many slaveholders simply called their slaves—who, under Pennsylvania law, would be free at age twenty-one or twenty-eight—indentured servants to avoid a term that might bring censure from their non-slaveholding neighbors.[40]

The warrants for removal were heavily skewed toward male slaves, and so were the advertisements. Only one advertisement is for a woman, Sophia, who had run away on September 2, 1820. She was about nineteen years of age, and so could have been valuable either as a bearer of children or for household or field labor. The owner was convinced that Sophia would be in Adams County, "as she has been there before."[41]

Most slaveholders advertised for their slaves immediately, but some waited several months, probably to see if the slave returned voluntarily. Near south central Pennsylvania, many slaves escaped around Christmas time. Most slave owners gave their slaves up to a week off then, and as the owners often stayed indoors or were visiting during that season, fugitives could have a substantial head start before their absence was noticed. Christmas was at the winter solstice, so the nights were long, which helped slaves who wanted to flee under the cover of darkness.[42]

Recent commentators on fugitive slaves, Loren Schweninger and John Hope Franklin, note that those who ran away to the North almost always needed money to be successful. What is striking about the Adams County advertisements is the number of the fugitives who are described as having money or, in one case, being an adept counterfeiter. One owner wrote that his slave's mother, who was free, had probably supplied him with money for his escape. Clothing was also a critical need. As abolitionist Graceanna Lewis remembered near the end of her life in 1912, slave clothing could be a gigantic badge of fugitive status in the north. Such clothes were often manufactured from cheap, coarse textiles, and sometimes carried striped patterns more commonly associated with nineteenth and twentieth century prison clothing. They looked very different from clothing worn in the North. These clothes would need to be quickly exchanged, and Lewis, free blacks, and others on the Underground Railroad helped.[43] Many slave owners, after writing a detailed description of the clothes that the escaped slave was wearing, resignedly closed by stating "but undoubtedly he will exchange his clothing." In the ads, many fugitives seem well-dressed with new, less obvious clothing, particularly if they escaped around Christmas. They had either waited for the master to distribute new clothes, or they had helped themselves to some when they fled. They often appropriated other assistance too—several had stolen horses or dogs.

Several advertisements support Schweninger and Franklin's claim that it is often the "most ingenious, persistent, and intelligent" fugitives who successfully headed north.[44] One accomplished slave spoke several languages.[45] The fugitive Frank Hill illustrates the resourcefulness and achievements of some fugitives, the options they had in border areas, and the resulting confusion that this could cause the slave owner:

$100 Reward. Ranaway [sic] on the 26th of December, from the Subscriber, living in Frederick County, Maryland, negro Frank, who calls himself Frank Hill; . . . He has a number of good clothes. He is a smart fellow, reads very well, and writes a tolerably good hand.

Frank has been accustomed to working in the house, and can also do any work which is to be done on a Farm, but is rather too much of a house servant to work on a Farm. He is an excellent knitter and has always been very anxious to live in Town. He is very neat in his dress; and persons not knowing him would suppose him to be a waiter. It is supposed he left Frederick-Town on the 27th of December, and I have no doubt he has made for Philadelphia and will endeavor to get employment as a waiter in a tavern, drive a hack or open a Blacking Shop . . . I have no doubt he will change his name. He has been seen in company with a negro from Ohio . . . and perhaps he may take the Ohio routes.

I will give the above Reward, if he be taken out of the state, and secured in any jail, and 40 Dollars, if taken in the state and secured in jail so that I get him again.

Lloyd Luckett

Living near New-Town or Trap, Frederick County, Maryland

Jan. 8, 1822 3t [3 times]

It is supposed said Negro is in the neighbourhood of Gettysburg.[46]

Such slaves, while perhaps more identifiable because of these skills, could support themselves while fleeing or in new communities. Their skills gave them options, making them difficult to locate. This ad also reveals that as early as 1822, area slave owners expected fugitives to flee to Philadelphia with its large African American population, and that Gettysburg lay on the route that they would take.

One famous fugitive who did just that was James Pembroke, later known as J. W. C. Pennington. In 1828, he appeared as a cold and wet runaway slave on the doorstep of William and Phoebe Wright in northeastern Adams County. Pennington was a blacksmith by training and had escaped from slavery near Reisterstown, in Baltimore County, Maryland. He took the "good road" between Baltimore and Gettysburg, after doubling back several times to avoid recapture. When he reached a tollgate near Gettysburg, he asked the woman there where he could find work; she directed him to the Wrights' house. He stayed there for several months, working in their stables and orchards while they improved his writing and taught him arithmetic. One day Pennington was frightened by the voice of Joel Wierman, Phoebe Wright's brother—it sounded like his master's voice. He determined to push on. It was a wise decision, as it was later learned that slave hunters were on his trail. Pennington traveled to New York, and eventually attended Yale Theological Seminary, receiving a license in 1838. In that same year he presided over the marriage of the just-escaped fugitive Frederick Douglass and his wife, Anna, in New York. The "fugitive blacksmith" became a leading nineteenth century African American divine. In 1849, he received an honorary doctorate from Heidelberg University, the first man of African descent to be awarded that honor. In his autobiography, he expressed great gratitude to the Wrights. His case shows that south central Pennsylvania was a place of both refuge and danger for fugitive slaves.[47]

In addition to Pennington's, only a few other antebellum fugitive slave narratives from this region have been identified. One involved another fugitive blacksmith, Charles Bentley. In 1841, Bentley and two other slaves fled north from Leesburg, Virginia. He and his companions traveled for ten nights, hiding by day. They suffered from hunger and exposure. Desperate for food, they accosted a lime-kiln worker, who immediately suspected that they were fugitives. He advised them, "If you travel on, by daylight you will cross Mason and Dixon's line, and get among the Dutch. Keep away from the big road, travel near it, but not in it,— walk during the daytime, but keep in the woods."[48]

Following the man's directions, by ten o'clock in the morning, they found themselves at a "Dutchman's" [German] house. There, as Bentley described it:

The man was out,—but the woman and girls set the table. We ate all they had in the house,—I ate until I was ashamed. The good woman told us to avoid Shippensburg, as six had been carried back from there just before. She told us, if anyone questioned us, to say that we were going to Horse Shoe Bottom camp meeting on the Susquehanna. We did accordingly, and soon struck the track of the underground railroad, which we followed into the northern free States.[49]

Bentley's narrative is one of the few existing first-person accounts of fugitive slaves moving through south central Pennsylvania. It shows that there, the escape of fugitive slaves was the result of the initiative of the escapees themselves, aided by informal helpers along the way, and, when contacted, a more formal "Underground Railroad."[50]

The Underground Railroad in South Central Pennsylvania

Helping fugitives could be a dangerous occupation, and some of south central Pennsylvania's abolitionists would pay in legal difficulties. The region's Underground Railroad appears to have involved more women, more secrecy, and more black and white cooperation than some historians have believed.[51] It utilized already existing networks of kinship, religion, and rural, social, and economic obligations.

According to local accounts, those actively helping fugitives escape were organized around family and kin groups. Religious and benevolent organizations could also play important roles in helping fugitive slaves. By far the most important aid to runaways came from free blacks in south central Pennsylvania. The leading African American communities in the area were located in or just outside of Mercersburg, Chambersburg, Gettysburg, and Carlisle. There, African Americans worked as day laborers, iron workers, laundresses, and seamstresses, and, according to unsympathetic census takers, as prostitutes, thieves, and card sharps. While some fugitives made their way through the area with little outside assistance, many others relied on the African American community to feed, shelter, and guide them, or to help rescue them if they were taken by slave catchers. However, not all border African Americans could be trusted. Carl Oblinger, a scholar of African American communities in southern Pennsylvania, believes that there was widespread resentment of fugitive slaves by free blacks there, because the poverty and crime some whites associated with runaways threatened to bring down repression on the entire African American community. No clear evidence of such sentiment exists in south central Pennsylvania, but certainly some individuals actively worked against fugitives. They helped capture runaways, either as spies or in some cases as active slave catchers.[52]

In southern Pennsylvania, an African American family in the border town of Greencastle was reportedly in league with the slave catchers. In Gettysburg, a Maryland-born hostler named Eden Devan rose to some wealth while allegedly helping return fugitives. In Chester County, near present-day Lincoln University, a prominent African American family was remembered in two divergent ways by the local population. Some lauded them as Underground Railroad workers; others remembered those activities as a ruse, allowing them to deceive fugitives before turning them over to slave catchers.[53]

While danger lurked even in the African American community, there were also resources for help. In December 1840, Gettysburg Slave's Refuge Society was established. Five African American men formed the founding committee (James Camron, Henry Butler, James Jones, Henry D. Chiler, and John Jones). The group's purposes embraced helping "our brethren groaning under the tyrannical yoke of oppression," including aiding fugitive slaves. The committee passed resolutions against Maryland's laws restricting the movement of free blacks into and out of the state. The society's founders complained that this prevented southern Pennsylvania's African Americans from attending "public worship" across the border in Maryland.[54]

This complaint likely had multiple motivations. Undoubtedly, church and camp meetings facilitated the escape of many slaves—Frederick Douglass used a camp meeting near Baltimore to help plan his escape—but the demand also points to a basic human need to see friends and kin. Nothing prevented a white resident of Gettysburg from visiting Hagerstown or going to church there with friends or relations. Gettysburg's free African Americans protested that they should be able to do so as well.

They could not do so because of restrictions stemming from Maryland's attempts to control its free black population. By 1850, over forty percent of Maryland's African Americans were free (by comparison, only thirteen percent of Virginia's African Americans were free). Maryland's African Americans were becoming increasingly important to their local economies, while Maryland's slave owners saw them as a threat to the security of their slaves. They hoped to drive them from the state or restrict their activities.[55]

While Gettysburg's free black leaders could do nothing about the Maryland legislature's determination to exercise increasing control over free blacks, the opportunities for worship in south central Pennsylvania were improving. Gettysburg's African Methodist Episcopal church (A.M.E.), which would become a fixture in the local African American community, was also established in 1840. The meeting to establish the Slave's Refuge Society was held at the A.M.E. church. The church reportedly played a leading role in helping area fugitives, as the denomination did throughout the North.[56]

These organizations strengthened the African American community for decades and provided space for organized political and social action. In 1847, for instance, when Gettysburg's African American community petitioned the state legislature to pass a strengthened personal liberty law, the petition may well have been drafted and "signed"—most of Gettysburg's African Americans were illiterate—at the A.M.E. church.[57]

A well-organized black community in Gettysburg and Carlisle, and a significant African American presence in Chambersburg and Mercersburg, while of great help, was sometimes insufficient for helping fugitive slaves. Other townships in south central Pennsylvania had no African Americans at all. Any concerted effort to bring African Americans to freedom—however loosely organized—had to adjust to this reality and develop contingency plans for an emergency. These plans might include relying on sympathetic white families. Few historians have commented on this regarding the border north, but social geography alone almost forced some degree of cooperation between white and black abolitionists trying to help fugitive slaves.

An example of this occurred in 1846, when an African American wagon driver with a cargo of fugitives, headed for a south central Pennsylvania iron furnace, was still on the road as day broke. He turned aside to a white farmer's house. When the farmer was sued for the value of the slaves, it became a celebrated Cumberland County court case. The potential legal liability that this case revealed underscored the necessity for abolitionists to have contingency plans and a system to rapidly pass fugitives through various locations, to minimize the legal exposure of any one set of Underground Railroad workers. Underground Railroad historian Larry Gara, looking at the movement as a whole, emphasized its *ad hoc* nature, but the situation along the border, where the potential legal exposure was significant, forced greater organization.[58]

Charles Bentley's narrative makes it clear that Gara was correct in stating that many fugitives escaped largely through their own resources, with occasional help from white or black residents. This was particularly true in Pennsylvania's dangerous border areas. Others, however, did contact the rough network of safe houses and escape routes in south central Pennsylvania, which constituted that region's "Underground Railroad." Unfortunately, the risks of the border meant that much of the work was unpublicized and undocumented, leaving little historical record. What we know today of escape routes for fugitives has to be teased out of legend, lore, and rumor.

Escape Routes

Discussing "routes" of the Underground Railroad immediately makes the escape of fugitive slaves sound too regularized. The main factor causing the Underground Railroad to be decentralized was the fugitives themselves. Almost none of them carried maps; some might have directions or know the name of possibly friendly families or communities. Many made it through risky areas on their own, unaware that there were willing helpers.[59] Because those areas also contained people, both white and black, who were eager to turn them in, many fugitives wisely relied solely on their own resources.

Sometimes Underground Railroad workers themselves deliberately contributed to this confusion over routes and tactics. Graceanna Lewis, a Quaker naturalist involved in helping runaway slaves, indicated that there were several directions in which her family forwarded fugitives from their Chester County home, depending on which heading seemed safest. A modern scholar of the Underground Railroad, Tracey Weis, has pointed out that multiple routes often increased safety because it lowered the traffic on any one route. If all fugitives went along the same roads and paths, it would be easy for the escape routes to become known and for fugitives to be recaptured.[60]

Many routes were determined by simple geography. The Appalachian mountain ranges extended into Pennsylvania, and many slaves in the Shenandoah Valley escaped northward, keeping the mountains to their left as a guide. Others chose to flee along the mountains themselves, a more difficult but possibly safer route. Once in Pennsylvania, the North and South Mountain ranges gradually turned east, acting as a natural funnel to direct fugitives toward Harrisburg on the Susquehanna. Historian William Switala suggests that Indian trails were often followed through the hills and woods. Pennsylvania's verdant forests also offered protection to the fugitive and temporary employment. Fugitives could work for a time in the state's timber industry, or could make charcoal for the region's iron furnaces.[61]

The road network also reveals why many fugitives escaped into south central Pennsylvania. While Gettysburg's status as a nineteenth century road junction led to the 1863 battle being fought there, it also led fugitives there. Good roads from Baltimore led to Gettysburg, Hanover, and York; roads from Washington converged on Gettysburg also. Fugitives faced several obstacles to traveling by the most direct route from Baltimore to Philadelphia, where the African American community's Vigilance Committee could protect them and they could seek urban employment. First, the road remained in Maryland much longer, increasing the risk of exposure within a slave state. Second, the fugitives would likely have to cross the Susquehanna River at Havre de Grace, Maryland. Some did, but it was generally safer to make that crossing in a free state, where ferrymen might be less likely to ask for papers. Traveling from the Baltimore area to York or Gettysburg, and then taking the road to Harrisburg, allowed the Susquehanna crossing to be made in Pennsylvania, at Wrightsville or Harrisburg.[62]

So all manner of physical geography—topography, the forests, and the road network—influenced the escape path of a slave. Many times, the natural routes through physical landscape were also modified by information the fugitive might have received. Fugitives might take a more difficult route if it was faster, if they were less likely to be seen, or if they knew of a friendly house along the way. A historian of the Kentucky borderland summarized this well, saying, "fugitive slaves . . . followed routes determined by the human, political, and physical geography of the region."[63]

Many fugitives from Virginia and central Maryland fled on foot. Some stole horses or, occasionally, carriages to transport their wives and family. Escaping by stagecoach was risky as some drivers reported their black charges, and departing by train or boat was very dangerous without an extensive set of corroborating papers.[64]

Some areas had reputations for being hazardous. Bentley's "Dutch" woman warned his party to stay away from Shippensburg. Gettysburg also could be troublesome. So could the Funkstown, Maryland—Mount Alto, Pennsylvania area. In south central Pennsylvania, slave catchers knew to hunt around the African American settlements at Mercersburg or among the Quaker farmers of eastern Adams County. William Still, chairman of Philadelphia's Vigilance Committee, remarked that Baltimore was "one of the most difficult places in the South for even free colored people" to leave, "much more for slaves."[65] Some who escaped fled in market wagons of sympathetic Quakers.

Washington, D.C., was significantly farther south than Baltimore, increasing the dangers for escapees from there, but almost all the major roads north led directly to Pennsylvania. Stanley Harrold has found that south central Pennsylvania was a key locale on an escape network leading from Washington, D.C., to New York City.[66]

Once they reached some degree of uneasy safety in Pennsylvania, relatively few fugitive slaves continued traveling until they reached Canada. Pennsylvania was a large state with opportunities for employment and community. Geography and climate also helped increase the attractiveness of southern Pennsylvania for slaves who wanted to stay. Fugitives who did not bring sufficient funds—or who did not make contact with activists willing to arrange train fares or wagon transportation—would not have walked from Virginia to Canada, especially if they had young children. Many accounts of ordinary fugitives, such as Benjamin Drew's *North-Side View*, depict even most refugees in Canada as having worked in the North for several years before pushing on.[67]

While historians have emphasized the ingenuity, persistence, money, skills, and resourcefulness required for a successful escape, some of these requirements can become blurred by proximity to the border.[68] If a fugitive lacked sufficient money to push on to Philadelphia or New York, he or she could stop in south central Pennsylvania and earn money, either at traditional rural occupations or by using any special expertise as a seamstress, blacksmith, barber, tanner, and so on. As Virginia's Shenandoah Valley had largely converted from tobacco to grain production around 1800, fugitives would not need to learn a new set of agricultural skills to work in Pennsylvania's rich grain belt. Many others undoubtedly chose to remain near their kin on the other side of the line—either to aid their escape later or to sneak back to see them. All of these factors made south central Pennsylvania a gateway for many fugitives and a stopping point for some.[69]

The routes in south central Pennsylvania are particularly obscure because of the dangers to fugitives and abolitionists in the area. The pioneering Underground Railroad researcher Charles Blockson stated that Franklin County was "a hazardous area of one hundred miles [that] contained the most secretive, tangled lines of the Underground Railroad." One central point was the African American settlement of "Little Africa," near Mercersburg. Here, the free black community could shelter fugitives and slave catchers faced considerable danger; in 1837, one fugitive killed a constable and wounded two others attempting to arrest him there. African Americans also ran Underground Railroad "stops" in Chambersburg, with fugitives sometimes directed to Carlisle or Harrisburg through Shippensburg. Other routes ran through the eastern part of the county: White abolitionist Hiram Wertz identified a route that ran from Rouzerville along the South Mountain to Thaddeus Steven's Caledonia furnace, on the border of Franklin and Adams counties. From there, fugitives usually went east toward Carlisle and Harrisburg.[70]

Although these are the supposedly "documented" routes of the Underground Railroad in Franklin County, in reality, of course, many fugitives reaching this area from Maryland or Virginia's Shenandoah Valley traveled through it on their own, following the mountains or feeling their way through the woods. Some-times they were helped by individuals giving them directions or food. Their ex-periences were more like those told by the fugitive Sam Davis from the safety of Canada:

> When I was passing through Orangetown, in Pennsylvania, I went into a shop to get some cake. Two men followed me with muskets. They had followed me from a village I had passed through a little before. They took me, and were go-ing to carry me before a magistrate—they said to Chambersburg. I walked just before. By and by, watching my chance, I jumped [a] fence and ran. They were on horseback. I got into a piece of woods—thence into a wheat field, where I lay all day; from 9 A.M. until dark. I could not sleep for fear. At night I traveled on, walking until day, when I came to colored man's house in the mountains. He gave me a good breakfast, for which I thanked him, and then directed me on the route. I succeeded, after a while, in finding the Underground Railroad. I stopped awhile at one place sick, and was taken good care of. I did not stop to work in the States, but came on to Canada.[71]

By the time Davis reached the organized "Underground Railroad," he had es-caped capture once, and received invaluable aid from an African American in the mountains.

Several major routes crisscrossed through Adams County. One followed the eastern slopes of the South Mountain to Bendersville, and then to Carlisle or Harrisburg. Fugitive slaves moving up the Marsh Creek could also wind up in the Bendersville area. William Switala believes that the Bendersville route be-came less significant later in the antebellum period when some Adams County Quakers (including the Wrights) moved to be closer to the Menallen Meeting (Friends) outside of York Springs. Still, in 1845 an African American family was kidnapped from near Bendersville, and a 1942 historical novel, *The Drums of the Morning*, described an important escape route from Chambersburg over the North Mountain to Bendersville.[72]

Around Gettysburg, the routes become confused. The town was dangerous because of the presence of slave catchers and informants, and many fugitives seem to have bypassed it. In the late antebellum period, one purported route led from African American farmhand and veterinarian Basil Biggs's residence on the McPherson farm to Edward Matthews's residence across the "Quaker Val-ley," and then to Carlisle.[73] Some fugitives who reached southern Adams County were directed up White's Run and avoided Gettysburg entirely. Another route led up the Rock Creek from Maryland to James McAllister's mill, where fugitives were hidden. From there they could be escorted to or around Gettysburg by Mag Palm, known in legend as "Maggie Bluecoat" because she wore an 1812 officer's uniform to be identifiable to fugitives. In defying the risks involved with helping fugitive slaves, Palm survived at least one attempt to kidnap her.[74]

Gettysburg's African American community was centered on the southern and western outskirts of town, and it was there that fugitives most likely were hidden. The Gettysburg A.M.E. church was the center for the Slave's Refuge Society and may have been a hiding place. Henry Butler, who signed the 1840 Slave's Refuge Society charter, reportedly was a leading conductor. Mag Palm resided for several years in the 1850s in a cabin by the Emmitsburg road on Abraham Brien's farm on Cemetery Ridge, south of town. Brien was an African American farmer who had to make do with the thin soils of the ridge. July 1863 put his property near the apex of Pickett's charge.[75]

If for some reason fugitives had to be taken through the county seat, sometimes a diversion was planned. According to J. Howard Wert, a Gettysburg College student in the 1850s, a group of young men and students from the college known as the "Black Ducks" would occasionally stage pranks or disturbances to disguise the fact that runaway slaves were passing through the town. These same individuals reportedly hid fugitives on Culp's Hill, a heavily wooded rocky prominence south of town. Some scholars doubt these claims, noting that Gettysburg College's president in the 1850s, Henry Baugher, was a notorious disciplinarian who would not have tolerated such activities.[76] Baugher was at least moderately antislavery, however, and several of the Black Ducks were not college students, and they apparently met off campus, where it may have been difficult for Baugher to control them. The group may have been aided by Jack Hopkins, the college janitor and a prominent member of the African American community who was rumored to be an Underground Railroad guide.[77]

A 1910 account by Underground Railroad participant Hiram Wertz stated that Steven's Caledonia Furnace was a waypoint for fugitives. There, Robert Black, the manager, would forward the fugitives east, through Gettysburg, Pine Grove, or Carlisle.

Although the Gettysburg area drew fugitives, a second major route through Adams County ran to the east, through York Springs. Some fugitives were taken there from McAllister's Rock Creek mill, bypassing Gettysburg. York Springs lay in a different economic network than Gettysburg, being closer to Cumberland and York counties than it was to the Adams County seat. It was also nineteen miles from the Mason-Dixon Line, rather than Gettysburg's seven. Helpers there may have been less exposed to economic coercion or social unpleasantness from pro-southern merchants and elites. William and Phoebe Wright, who were leading friends of the fugitive, lived in Latimore Township, north of York Springs. As local historian G. Craig Caba points out, they were surrounded by "passive helpers" in kin and friends. Sometimes they would warn the Wrights of approaching slave catchers; while they might not be involved in the Underground Railroad themselves, allowing fellow Quakers to get in legal trouble for practicing their religion was anathema to the Friends. The Quaker custom of "marrying in the faith" strengthened these networks of interrelated families. Some believe that the Wrights' house, "Plainfield," was specifically designed for service on the Underground Railroad. It was off the main road and up a lengthy lane that would give inhabitants ample warning of the approach of strangers. It also appears to have had several hiding places for fugitives.[78]

William and Phoebe Wright, and their children, were some of the most important figures in the Underground Railroad in south central Pennsylvania. Several nineteenth century historians credit them with helping hundreds of fugitives. Graceanna Lewis, in a brief manuscript account of her Underground Railroad activities written shortly before her death, discusses the Wrights first among all the Underground Railroad participants in south central and southeastern Pennsylvania. William Still, the head of the Vigilance Committee in Pennsylvania, listed them among forty-five families who were important friends of the fugitive, and included a profile of William Wright in his Underground Railroad memoir. William and Phoebe Wright married in 1817 and started helping fugitives around 1819, when William Wright and Joel Wierman rescued Hamilton Moore from recapture by his Baltimore County master. When the Wrights lived near Bendersville, the curve of the mountains helped guide fugitives to their home.[79] In 1828, another Baltimore County slave, James W. C. Pennington appeared on the Wrights' doorstep—but this time to their new farmhouse in eastern Adams County.

Ties of kinship helped forge links in the Underground Railroad in the dangerous border region. Both William and Phoebe Wright had the support of family members in their work. Phoebe Wright was the sister of Joel Wierman, another prominent Adams county antislavery activist, and Hannah Wierman Gibbons, a key opponent of slavery in Lancaster County. William Wright had a legacy of antislavery work from his extended family. One of his cousins and an uncle belonged to the Pennsylvania Abolition Society and brought "freedom suits" in southern Pennsylvania to compel slaveholders to free their slaves in accordance with the gradual abolition law.[80]

Several letters published in Still's work reveal William Wright's connections with abolitionists in Washington, D.C., including Dr. William Chaplin. Chaplin and others directed or transported escaping slaves to Wright, sometimes via McAllister's mill. The Wrights appear to be a key part of network of abolitionists, identified by Stanley Harrold, that forwarded fugitives through southern Pennsylvania using Lewis Tappan's vast organizational and financial network, coordinated by Still's Vigilance Committee.[81]

Although many fugitives from York Springs proceeded through York County to the home of another William Wright in Columbia, and then to Hannah and Daniel Gibbons in Lancaster County, there were also ties between the Adams County Underground Railroad and the Cumberland County routes to the north. Stephen Weakly helped link the Underground Railroad in the two counties. He lived in Cumberland County and was an active member of the Underground Railroad there, but he also signed the 1840 Annual Report of the York Springs (Adams County) Anti-Slavery Society.[82]

In Cumberland County the escape routes are obscure, but Carlisle served as a major destination for fugitives. Here we may see a divergence between this area's "white" and "black" Undergrounds. Some of the African Americans in Adams County's "black Underground," including Basil Biggs and Edward Matthews, are reported as having escorted their charges to Carlisle. In contrast, the white abolitionists living near York Springs appear to have sent fugitives to Boiling Springs or through to Mechanicsburg, Wrightsville, Goldsborough, and Harrisburg. Boiling Springs had several families willing to hide fugitives. Daniel Kaufman, who founded Boiling Springs in 1845, was an important figure. He was aided by his brother-in-law Stephen Weakly, and Philip Brechbill, owner of a tavern along the Yellow Breeches Creek. When Kaufman's property came into jeopardy during an 1840s fugitive slave case, Weakly assumed his legal liability and Kaufman dropped out of Underground Railroad activities. After that, Weakly and Brechbill hid fugitives on islands in the swamps of the creek instead of in barns and homes. John Harder of Carlisle was reportedly another key individual; a market man, his wagon was frequently used to convey fugitives because locals were accustomed to seeing it on the local roads. It was also hoped that as a prominent Democrat, Harder would be above suspicion. From Carlisle, fugitives were generally conveyed to Harrisburg, with Mechanicsburg occasionally mentioned as a stop.[83]

Harrisburg had a large free black community and prominent white Underground Railroad supporters. Fugitives sent on a more southerly route east from Adams County sometimes went to Harrisburg, but often crossed the Susquehanna at Wrightsville and passed through Lancaster and Chester counties toward Philadelphia. There, many would be helped by the Vigilance Committee. Some would be forwarded to New Jersey or New York; others went into Bucks County to work.[84]

As these descriptions indicate, understanding the importance of networks is vital to understanding the Underground Railroad in south central Pennsylvania. Free blacks had extensive networks of kinship, fellowship, and friendship in south central Pennsylvania and across the border in Maryland and Virginia.[85] Individuals with business ties to Pennsylvania and Maryland might be critically important; Basil Biggs worked as a veterinarian in both Carroll County, Maryland, and Adams County before the Civil War, an occupation that would bring him in contact with Southern agricultural slaves. He was reputedly an important member of Adams County's Underground Railroad, but Biggs was illiterate and left no proof.[86]

The networks of white abolitionists also extended into the Southern states. Joel Wierman's wife, Lydia, received permission to travel to Maryland and the Shenandoah Valley and speak at the various Quaker meetings. In letters she sent to an antislavery newspaper, she mentions discussing slavery with Southerners at these meetings, but her letters are understandably discreet.

Central Maryland also had significant antislavery sentiment. The Pipe Creek Antislavery Society and the Pipe Creek Protection Society had been formed in the 1820s in Carroll County, Maryland. Their charter was published by Benjamin Lundy in Baltimore (Lydia Wierman's half-brother). Carroll County was due south of Adams County, Pennsylvania, and members of the Pipe Creek Meeting met with their Adams County counterparts during Quarterly meeting.[87] Adjacent to Carroll and southwest of Adams County was Frederick County. For a locale south of the Mason-Dixon Line, Frederick County appears to have had an unusual amount of antislavery sentiment; hundreds of residents signed antislavery petition to Congress in 1829, an extreme rarity for a Southern slave state. There are reports of a secretive Underground Railroad in Frederick County, of necessity even more obscure than southern Pennsylvania's.[88]

In addition to networks of kin and religion, scholars recognize that into the twentieth century rural Americans lived in interlocking networks of mutual help and obligation. One farmer might help another raise a barn, then be repaid in crops or by help at the harvest. Sometimes these arrangements were sufficiently codified that farmers kept ledgers of help rendered and assistance returned.[89] This mutual dependency in rural life created networks of individuals who, if not motivated to help fugitives, at least would not be likely to help a stranger (slave catcher) with apparent ill intent looking for a friend's house. Local economic centers could act as focal points of these relationships; for example, the Wright family was surrounded by Wiermans and Griests, to whom they were related by marriage, as well as the Deardorffs, a family who owned the local mill. The Deardorffs and the Wrights reputedly occasionally helped each other in Underground Railroad activities. Another of the millers in the county, James McAllister, was very involved in the antislavery society and the Underground Railroad, as was Jesse Cook, who owned a mill in eastern Adams County. Another family, which owned Shriver's mill, may also have been involved. If you informed a slave catcher that a fugitive was at the Wrights, it is possible you might have to find a new place to grind grain if your involvement was suspected.[90] Similarly, area abolitionists occasionally had a sympathetic relative, such as Isaac Wierman, as the local justice of the peace. They also maintained a strong presence on the Gettysburg bank. This tactic, mirrored by western abolitionists in Cincinnati and elsewhere, held real promise for economic coercion. Cooperation with slave catchers might not only be met with difficulty grinding grain, but also getting a loan.[91]

The extant fugitive slave narratives, the Adams County fugitive slave cases, and advertisements paint a picture of determined fugitives traversing this divided border area. They often found their own routes through. They occasionally encountered networks of sympathetic white and black individuals and families, who helped them settle down or keep moving, including Henry Butler, Mag Palm, Basil Biggs, William and Phoebe Wright, and Joel and Lydia Wierman.

With Pennsylvania's own slavery dwindling and escaping fugitives bearing witness to the oppression of the Southern system, the 1830s might seem to slavery's opponents an ideal time to begin agitation. When they began in south central Pennsylvania, however, they collided with a society where some leading members opposed antislavery. Some had recently been slaveholders themselves; others belonged to an economy and culture that was tied to the South in many ways. Many south central Pennsylvania citizens valued mollifying white Southerners over protecting escaped black ones, and resisted open action for abolition. In the next few years, these tensions would erupt.

2

Thaddeus Stevens' Dilemma, Colonization, and the Turbulent Years of Early Antislavery in Adams County, 1835–39

South central Pennsylvania was liminal ground, lying on the dividing line between the border North and the Upper South. This physical circumstance, combined with a legacy of slavery lasting into the 1830s, gave the area a distinctive, almost Southern character. At the same time, many Quakers, Mennonites, and other non-resistant groups who had settled in the area opposed slavery, but preferred pacific forms of opposition. This environment would influence the tactics and development of the white antislavery movement in the area, which preferred legal and political engagement over public confrontation. As a result, antislavery sentiment in south central Pennsylvania evolved differently from abolitionism in the Upper North, particularly in New England. Along Pennsylvania's border, the antislavery movement had strong political as well as moral overtones from the beginning of the renewal of antislavery activity in the 1830s. Adams County's abolitionists, in particular, would be politically involved from the inception of their organization. The fugitive slave issue would be an important part of this border antislavery activism—but, for most of the 1830s, the principal contest was between two different proposed solutions to America's race problem: abolitionism and colonization. When Garrisonian antislavery lecturers traveled through the area, it would be a response in part to the political needs of the region's leading political figure, who had seemed to favor colonization just a few years before. The approaches that these lecturers had developed in Massachusetts, New York, and Ohio, however, would prove largely unsuccessful here, forcing the development of alternative tactics and strategy.

Viewing this early antislavery movement from a dual social and political perspective is valuable, because most scholars encounter the rise of antislavery through monographs about antislavery or reform movements. In these books, the overall narrative proceeds this way: Leaders such as Theodore Weld and William Lloyd Garrison inspired highly dedicated, religiously or idealistically motivated activists to organize antislavery sentiment throughout the North. Although these activists and their leaders did not abjure politics, they shared grave concerns about the morality of partisan activity. Initially, the work of organizing societies and spreading the antislavery gospel precluded political involvement. Once formed, according to these modern accounts, the societies engaged in an activity almost naïve from our perspective, moral suasion through petitioning of Congress. Eventually, these societies decide to question political candidates on their stands toward slavery ("interrogation"); when that proves unsuccessful, only then do some antislavery activists consider forming a third political party, in 1839. This splits the movement.[1]

In contrast to this dominant narrative, there have been hints of an alternative interpretation in which politics played a more central role. This interpretation emphasizes the emergence of antislavery activism in the midst of a mid-1830s political struggle over Jacksonian democracy. Particularly in areas where Anti-masonry was once strong, the antislavery movement's emergence looks suspiciously like a political tool being developed as the basis to rally Northerners against a new, politically dominant conspiracy. This time, it was not the secretive Freemasons, but the Southern slaveholders of the Slave Power Conspiracy who were to be the mortal enemy.[2]

Both interpretations could be true, with inspiring outside organizers being employed by politicians to build new constituencies against conspiratorial threats, and that seems to be closest to the case of Adams County, Pennsylvania. Antislavery there was born out of political turmoil occurring with the decline of Antimasonry. Indeed, it appears that the growth of antislavery organizations may have been encouraged in hopes that the movement would grow to be the basis of a Northern political party capable of defeating the Southern-leaning Democratic Party. The initial antislavery agents sent out by the American Anti-Slavery Society, at least the one who visited south central Pennsylvania, do not appear apolitical at all. And for a variety of reasons, Thaddeus Stevens, a leading regional and national politician, supported the new antislavery initiative with his newspaper, his funds, and, more cautiously, his own presence.

A transplant from New England, Stevens would be an important part of these developments, and he serves as a visible illustration of the tensions concerning antislavery in a border area. While Stevens would later become known for his strong, almost unique stand on African American equality, in border Pennsylvania, Stevens adopted an antislavery position slowly, and later than many of his biographers believe. When he finally did move to an openly antislavery stance, it would be in large measure a response to his political situation, in addition to any moral repugnance he may have felt toward slavery. In particular, Stevens confronted the choice between abolitionism and colonization, and sometimes embraced both. While not all antislavery activists shared Stevens' stark political concerns, his dilemma in choosing a new cause around which to build a political movement illustrated the pressures on antislavery reformers and politicians along the Northern border. In this regard, Thaddeus Stevens is not that different from other border lawyers and politicians negotiating the same issues, such as Salmon P. Chase or Abraham Lincoln. Because it can be documented, Thaddeus Stevens, his path to antislavery, and the emergence of strong antislavery sentiment among his constituency offer a valuable window into the explosion of border antislavery and anti-abolition sentiment in the mid to late 1830s.

Thaddeus Stevens was a significant, even dominant figure in south central Pennsylvania politics. Even after he relocated to Lancaster in 1842, he owned substantial property in the area, frequently spoke there, and served on the board of Pennsylvania College. His influence was profound, but it has also been misunderstood.

Stevens was a dynamic, divisive figure; in the 140 years since his death, historians and biographers have remained divided about this controversial politician.[3] Soon after his death, Stevens was either lauded by biographers as the consummate politician or reviled as a political antichrist who had destroyed America's Constitutional government. Much depended on the writer's attitude toward Radical Reconstruction, which Stevens helped lead. In the twentieth century, historians were more distant from the post-war animosities, but they still struggled with Thaddeus Stevens. Some denounced him as spiteful and hate-filled; Richard Current produced a scholarly biography of Stevens, which unsympathetically characterized him as a grasping, scheming politician. Popular chroniclers of the Underground Railroad, however, found Stevens to be a noble, even saintly figure.[4]

A shift in the academic view of Stevens commenced after World War II. Biographers treated Stevens more sympathetically, humanizing him. Fawn Brodie lauded Stevens as a defender of human rights, and as the Civil Rights movement progressed, Stevens was virtually canonized in certain circles, and portrayed as a man a century ahead of his time. His most recent scholarly biographer has largely followed the emphasis of the last forty years in his treatment of Stevens. So does a recent, exhaustively researched account of Stevens' early years in Gettysburg.[5]

There was, however, significant truth in the perspective of earlier biographers. Stevens was, as Current portrayed, first and foremost a politician, and his commitment to antislavery early in his career appears weaker than recent biographers have portrayed. To say this is not to diminish the principled, egalitarian stands Stevens took later in life, after he moved to Lancaster; it is simply to recognize that with Stevens, as with many other politicians, his positions were evolving early in his career. In fact, it was not until Stevens faced a significant political dilemma that his connection to antislavery rose to the fore. Understanding that dilemma requires understanding Stevens' early career.

The Early Career of Thaddeus Stevens

Thaddeus Stevens was born in Vermont in 1792, and grew up in hardscrabble poverty. After graduating from Dartmouth in 1816, he studied law in York, Pennsylvania. Learning that he could be indefinitely blackballed by local lawyers, he passed the bar exam in Maryland, then moved to Gettysburg to set up practice in September 1816.[6] This experience may have cautioned the bold Stevens against sticking his neck out too far in parochial south central Pennsylvania.

From the start of his career, Stevens encountered Pennsylvania's complex legalism of slavery and abolition. At first, this Vermont transplant seemed to have no problem with Pennsylvania's dwindling institution of slavery. In 1821, he represented a Maryland slaveholder whose slave was suing for her freedom under the 1780 abolition statute. This act mandated that all slaves brought from out of state be freed if they resided in the state for six months or more.

In this case, Charity Butler had been born a slave in Maryland and subleased to a Mr. Gilleland. In exchange for feeding and clothing Charity, he had her services until she turned sixteen. Soon after this agreement was reached, Gilleland separated from his wife, who went to live with her mother near the Pennsylvania line. She took Charity to look after her infant. Nearly destitute, Mrs. Gilleland traveled to find work as a seamstress, often going into southern Pennsylvania for weeks. When she finished a job, she and Charity returned to her mother's house. When Charity reached age eleven, she was returned to the original owner.[7]

Butler's lawyers argued that since her total residence in Pennsylvania was greater than six months, Charity and her two children, born afterwards, should be freed. Stevens, defending the slaveholder, contended that leasing slave property did not convey the right to destroy it by taking it to Pennsylvania. He also argued that the drafters of the 1780 law had intended six months' continuous residence, even though this was not made explicit. This "common sense" position matched the desires of the state's business elite. Many Southerners visited Pennsylvania annually to relax or shop, and merchants did not want them worried that by so doing, they would eventually liberate the servants who accompanied them. The court agreed with Stevens, citing in particular the need to be hospitable to Southern visitors at Pennsylvania resorts, including Adams County's York Springs. Charity Butler and her children were returned to slavery.[8]

Most of Stevens' recent biographers see the Butler case as a seminal moment in his career. They maintain that he was ashamed of his participation in the case and soon converted to antislavery opinions. As evidence, they cite an 1823 toast, at a large Fourth of July celebration, where Stevens proposed, "To the next President of the United States—may he have never fastened fetters on a slave!" Of course, such a toast had a political subtext. Stevens was migrating toward the Federalists, and their presidential candidate would likely be from New England, not from slaveholding Virginia.[9]

Stevens' biographer Fawn Brodie believed that this toast proved that Stevens was moving toward opposing slavery, and that he followed it with other antislavery actions in the 1820s. Other modern scholars follow Brodie; Hans Trefousse contends that Stevens' response to the Butler case led him to "[t]hereafter . . . invariably ma[k]e his services available to defend fugitive slaves, of whom there were many in the border region in which Gettysburg was located, and his neighbors remembered that he rarely lost one of these."[10] Records of Adams County fugitive slave cases involving Stevens, however, have been impossible to find, and most of the recollections Trefousse cites were written over forty years later, which is why Richard Current believed that they were unreliable. While his record regarding fugitive slaves is undocumented, Stevens did, according to other anecdotal evidence, perform stirring gestures of compassion for some African Americans. He reportedly spent $300 he had set aside to buy a law library, to purchase a boy out of slavery in Maryland.[11]

Whether Stevens' attitude toward slavery substantially changed after the Butler case appears less likely than most modern biographers claim. They fail to acknowledge that in 1829, Stevens was back in court on behalf of a slaveholder (*Cobean v. Thompson*). There he argued—using a dictionary—that a common sense understanding of the term "yeoman" was a sufficient indication of profession for registration of a slaveholder's occupation. This argument prevailed, allowing his client to retain his slave.[12] If there was a transformational moment for Stevens after his involvement in a legal case involving slaveholding, it may have been after this 1829 case.[13] If Stevens did alter his views after involvement in a slave case, possibly area residents looking back at Stevens' early career from forty years' distance, confused the Butler and Thompson cases. The fact that warrants of removal issued in Adams County fell off sharply after 1828 may support this, if Stevens began then to represent fugitive slaves.

By then, Stevens had become a sought-after lawyer in Adams, Cumberland, Franklin, and York counties. Some considered him the finest member of the

Pennsylvania bar, and he won nine out of the first ten cases he argued before the state supreme court. He aligned himself with Anti-Jacksonian and Federalist Party activities, serving as a member of the Anti-Jacksonian Committees of Correspondence in 1823, 1824, and 1828. By 1826, Stevens was one of the largest property holders in Gettysburg; by 1829 he was one of the wealthiest men in Adams County. Although prospering, he did not yet have corresponding political influence. That was about to change.[14]

Stevens' first major political cause would not be antislavery, for which he later became famous, but rather opposition to Masonry. In 1826, publisher William Morgan disappeared in New York state, after having written an exposé revealing the secret rites of Freemasonry. It was presumed that the Masons had murdered him. A popular antimasonic reaction soon became a political movement. Stevens participated in the first Antimasonic meeting in Gettysburg in 1829, and he and a co-investor acquired a newspaper, the *Star and Republican Banner*. Stevens asked two of his principal political rivals, Robert Harper and Jacob Lefever, to edit it. This was likely a crafty way for Stevens to get them both on the record as not espousing Antimasonry if they refused. Harper actually belonged to the Masonic order. Both chose to remain with the papers they were already editing, and the position fell to Robert Middleton. It was widely believed that Stevens was the paper's controlling influence, however.[15]

Through Antimasonry, Stevens expanded his political activities regionally. In 1830, he was a delegate to both the state and national Antimasonic conventions. He began to speak in Maryland and elsewhere. In 1833, Stevens was elected to the Pennsylvania legislature, the beginning of a long legislative career, which was dominated by Antimasonry at first, but in which antislavery and egalitarianism would play an increasingly prominent part.[16]

As Antimasonry was rising, Pennsylvania's own slavery was dying out, almost vanishing by the mid-1830s. Southern fugitives were still captured and carried back, but local papers no longer printed runaway advertisements, except occasionally in Franklin County. The reasons for this change of sentiment likely stem from the loss of a slaveholding constituency in Pennsylvania. The few slaveholders who remained lacked the political clout that the slaveholding class had once possessed, even a decade earlier.

Allowing slavery to die out in Pennsylvania was one thing; so was standing against its extension, as the Pennsylvania legislature did during the Missouri crisis. Actively pushing for its elimination in the nation was quite another, which usually required a worldview of slavery as sinful, aberrant human behavior. The origins of this area's antislavery sentiment were built on Pennsylvania's own legacy of gradual emancipation and its Revolutionary heritage. The American and French Revolutions had sparked a global interest in human rights and liberty, and the Pennsylvania Abolition Society (PAS), the first antislavery organization with national reach, fought to free slaves through legislative action and the courts. Through the PAS, area residents, including Samuel Wright, William Wright's cousin, provided legal aid to slaves and free blacks.[17] In the early nineteenth century, antislavery Quaker preachers had traveled through Pennsylvania, and since the mid-1820s, at least, the writings of the Quaker abolitionist Benjamin Lundy had reached the south central counties.[18] In fact, several of his children lived in Adams County before moving west in the late 1830s. Both his half-sister, Lydia, and his daughter married into the Wierman clan, a prominent local antislavery family. There are indications of a protection society in the area, even if it met irregularly.[19]

Pennsylvania's abolition acts, even if gradual, allowed white Pennsylvanians to avoid identifying with an institution increasingly perceived as brutal and oppressive. Consequently, an opportunity was created for greater animosity toward slavery and the South. In the 1830s, the abolitionists tried to capitalize on this and achieved hard-fought gains. The fact that they were even able to publicly criticize slavery at all in this border area was an accomplishment, but the degree of resistance they faced forced them to alter tactics and lessen their visibility. By the mid-1840s, the result was a new legal strategy, more confrontational than simply representing slaves in "freedom suits," but markedly different from Garrisonian-style mass organization.

It should not be surprising that tensions over slavery and the fugitive slave erupted in south central Pennsylvania in the 1830s—it was a turbulent decade throughout the United States, as Jacksonian populism merged with racism and ethnic and class resentments. Pennsylvania was particularly affected as a border state and a crucial swing state in national electoral politics. The state's electoral college delegation had gone narrowly for Jefferson in 1800, 8–7. After Jefferson's election, Pennsylvanian Timothy Pickering (who had been born in Massachusetts) became a thorn in his side, characterizing Jefferson's actions, including the Louisiana Purchase, as extending the power of the slave states. This partisanship only continued into the Jacksonian era, and south central Pennsylvania experienced tumult on various levels, from unrest concerning Irish laborers working on the railroad to a bitter theological dispute in Carlisle which resulted in Dickinson College collapsing as a Presbyterian institution and being reorganized as a Methodist one. Turbulent environments are made for politicians who can capitalize on them—such as Thaddeus Stevens.[20]

Thaddeus Stevens' Dilemma and Antislavery Organizations in South Central Pennsylvania

In the mid-1830s, Thaddeus Stevens faced a dilemma: what to do next. A political dynamo, he had ascended to prominence on the strength of his energetic leadership of Pennsylvania's Antimasonic Party. Nationally, Antimasonry had collapsed after its presidential candidate in 1832, William Wirt, carried only one state, Vermont. Largely because of Stevens' influence, however, it persisted as the primary political movement opposed to the Democratic Party in Pennsylvania from 1829 to 1834. After 1834, it had to share the opposition stage with the emerging Whig Party.

Thaddeus Stevens was both the driving force behind Pennsylvania's Antimasonry, and the movement's chief lightning rod. For example, in 1831, he gave an incendiary speech in Hagerstown, Maryland—one of several instances when he accused Masons of drinking blood from human skulls. No sooner had Stevens arrived in the Pennsylvania's legislature in 1834 than he began a controversial investigation of Freemasonry.

Stevens held other controversial positions as well. He championed public schooling when many taxpayers did not want to pay for other children's education. In his own county, Pennsylvania Germans feared efforts to Americanize their children through the public schools. They applauded, however, the state aid Stevens brought to Gettysburg's Lutheran college and seminary. Stevens, who owned large amounts of real estate and the controlling interest in two iron furnaces, also backed measures to increase internal improvements, and he promoted the Wrightsville, York & Gettysburg Railroad. His interest in Pennsylvania's industrial development would ease his later, reluctant move to the Whig Party. Stevens also would be one of the few antebellum politicians to oppose capital punishment. Despite this variety of political interests, in the mid-1830s, Stevens was still better known for his contentious Antimasonry than anything else.[21]

Even after a bruising fight over the school bill, Stevens' star continued to rise. In 1835, Pennsylvania's Democratic Party split over the national bank, the desirability of a state constitutional convention, and Democratic Governor George Wolf's support of the school law. This created a rare opportunity for the Anti-Jacksonians. Pennsylvania was traditionally Democratic—in fact, the leading political history of its early national period called it the "Keystone of the Democratic Arch"—but the possibility of victory led to a coalition between the Antimasons and the new Whig Party. Jacob Ritner, a Pennsylvania German who had been Speaker of the Pennsylvania House of Representatives, was the fusion candidate. Stevens campaigned strenuously for the Whig, and, in October, he was rewarded with his own reelection and the election of Ritner and sufficient Whigs and Antimasons to hold the majority in the assembly.[22]

These victories enabled Stevens to launch a more extensive investigation into Freemasonry. Chairing a special committee, which armed him with subpoena powers, he summoned numerous Democratic luminaries, including former Governor Wolf (1829–35), and George Dallas, a future U.S. vice president (1845–49). All declined to testify. Stevens' heavy-handed tactics backfired when the House refused to compel their testimony. The investigation also disrupted the fusion of the Whigs and Antimasons, and it hurt relations between Stevens and those Whigs who were Freemasons.[23]

Despite this setback, Stevens' successful efforts to have the Bank of the United States in Philadelphia rechartered confirmed that he was a leading politician in Pennsylvania, a state with a lot of political talent during this period. Whenever he tried to move to a larger stage, however, he was rebuffed. Suggestions that Thaddeus Stevens should be the Antimasonic candidate for president, or, in 1836, a possible Whig vice presidential candidate, never came to fruition. That same year, he tried to persuade William Henry Harrison that the Antimasons, not the Whigs, should be his key electoral ally in Pennsylvania. When his advice was ignored, an angry Stevens led a splinter group of Antimasons away from cooperation with the Whigs.[24]

As the 1835 fusion efforts had shown, and the divisions that occurred afterward reinforced, Antimasonry in Pennsylvania, despite Stevens' drive and political abilities, was unable to sustain a viable party. Stevens was safe for the time being because he had a strong political base. Adams County, named for the second president, had been one of the few to vote Federalist in 1800, and often opposed Democratic candidates. Stevens also came from a region where many religious sects opposed oath taking, a significant part of Masonic ceremonies. Nationally, however, the movement had waned rapidly. In Pennsylvania, Stevens' investigations drove away moderate and Whig support and contributed significantly to Antimasonry's eventual collapse.[25]

With Antimasonry dwindling, what were Stevens' political options? He could not join the Democratic Party. Even if he had not tried to investigate their leaders, to him they represented the aristocracy and the old guard. The Democratic Party had ruled Pennsylvania since the election of Jefferson in 1800, and the popular presidency of Andrew Jackson had cemented their hold.[26] While the Democrats broadened the suffrage and cast itself as the party of the people, in Pennsylvania, because of their long tenure in power, they also represented the elite that Stevens hated—the lawyers who kept him from taking the bar in York, for example.[27]

Stevens' distaste for Democrats was reinforced by his running battle with Jacob Lefever, the editor of the *Republican Compiler*, Gettysburg's Democratic newspaper. In the 1820s, Lefever printed several anonymous letters suggesting that Stevens had murdered a young, visibly pregnant black woman to cover up his affair with her. Stevens' responses to Lefever were heated, and he sued Lefever for libel. Nonetheless Stevens was willing to set aside a long-standing rivalry for political gain, and his animosity toward the Democrats underwent a brief thaw. In 1836, angered at the collapse of the Whig-Antimason alliance and the Whigs' refusal to back Daniel Webster, his favored presidential candidate, Stevens argued that while honest Democrats could become good Antimasons, Whigs could never do so. In reality, however, both temperamentally and practically, Stevens could not become a Democrat.[28]

The other major party in Pennsylvania politics was the Whig Party, which in the mid-1830s coalesced opposition to Andrew Jackson and the Democrats. In many ways, the Whigs were the successor to the old Federalist Party. Because they supported Henry Clay's "American System" of internal improvements, which attracted wealthy merchants and budding industrialists, it could be argued that they represented elitism and privilege even more than the Democratic Party. Stevens, however, believed deeply in the necessity of internal development, especially for south central Pennsylvania, isolated from the eastern Pennsylvania economy. Pragmatically, Whig support could also help Stevens as he sought appropriations for railroads to his iron works or money for the college in Gettysburg. Stevens firmly supported the national bank, which Whigs also favored. Stevens ultimately, if reluctantly, chose to become a Whig in the 1840s.

In the 1830s, however, Stevens did not want to become either a Democrat or a Whig. Instead, he hoped for another mass movement, another popular cause like Antimasonry. Where would such a crusade come from? In February 1830, he had been elected a manager of the Temperance Society in Gettysburg, and for some time played an energetic role in the temperance movement in Adams County. Stevens took his commitment to temperance seriously. He told others that he had "taken the pledge" not to drink alcoholic beverages, and it does appear that he drank very little the last half of his life. Even in 1836 and 1837, when he began his move to a political antislavery stance, temperance often occupied a more prominent part of the *Star and Republican Banner* than antislavery. Politically, however, temperance was not sufficient to inspire a successful electoral move-

ment in Pennsylvania, especially not in a county with a heavily German population. In addition, some of Stevens' political rivals—such as Robert G. Harper, the
editor of the local Whig newspaper, the *Adams Sentinel*—were also prominently
involved in the temperance movement. This was not a cause to which Stevens
could claim clear-cut leadership, even in his own county.[29]

Another promising cause for generating political momentum was the colonization movement. Colonizationists proposed solving Pennsylvania's "problem"
of poor free blacks by shipping as many of them as they could to West Africa
or other destinations. The colonization movement appealed to lofty aspirations
in pursuing its goal of an all-white America, through dreams of exiled Pennsylvania free blacks christianizing Africa. The American Colonization Society
had been founded in 1816, and counted some of the country's leading statesmen
as adherents, including James Monroe, James Madison, John Randolph, Francis
Scott Key, Henry Clay, and Daniel Webster.[30] Colonizationism was particularly
popular in the southern Pennsylvania counties, where both fugitive slaves and
recently freed Southern slaves swelled the native African American population
already present due to Pennsylvania's own legacy of slavery. In fact, as the decades of the 1820s and 1830s progressed, local and state legislation became more
restrictive against Pennsylvania's African American population. For example,
regulations were issued prohibiting African Americans from drinking in taverns
or staying at inns; in the past, such policies had not been codified, allowing for
exceptions. Now, some cities, such as Lancaster, required African Americans to
register in the "Negro Entry Book" when they reached the city. Harrisburg did
the same. According to historian Peter Vermilyea, Gettysburg never adopted
such restrictions in its legal code, but whether that border town had a markedly
different stance toward African Americans is unclear.[31]

These laws reflected a long-standing belief in the superiority of white Americans and a need to control the African American population. In the 1830s and beyond, these views were gaining academic backing. Scientific racialism, the conviction that science itself proved a "natural inequality" of the races, contributed
significantly. James Kirke Paulding, an ardent Northern supporter of Jackson
and Van Buren, was one early proponent who relied on "scientific principles" to
write a defense of Southern slavery. Samuel Morton, the founder of the American
School of Ethnography, measured the skulls of Caucasians, African Americans,
and Native Americans in an effort to prove the superiority of the white race.
Morton was based in Philadelphia, which because of its size, wealth, and location
in a border state was a major cultural influence in both North and South. In the
1830s and 1840s, Morton's purportedly leading edge scientific research was dis-

seminated into the mostly rural areas of southern Pennsylvania through newspapers and traveling "moral lecturers." These lecturers often sought to prove the
inequality of African Americans; crude racial stereotypes were also presented
through minstrel shows that traveled to Pennsylvania's cities and towns.[32]

The colonization's society's outreach was multi-faceted; the society also tried
to appropriate Independence Day to clothe its efforts in patriotism. Ministers
were asked to preach pro-colonization sermons around that day, and churches
took up collections; one Franklin County congregation took up a collection for
the American Colonization Society as late as 1849. Some area newspapers also
printed articles supporting colonization every Fourth of July. For example, on
July 4, 1837, the Harrisburg *Keystone*, a Democratic newspaper, ran an account of
the British capturing two horribly overcrowded slaving ships off of the coast of
Africa. Rather than use such scenes to condemn slavery, as antislavery publications often did, this paper asked who "can hereafter refuse to lend his aid . . . to
the colonization society, which . . . will in a few years put an entire stop to this
hellish slave trade, and spread the lights of colonization and religion over Africa."
The paper argued that this would do more to help African Americans than "the
emancipation of all of the slaves on our continent."[33]

For many, colonization seemed to be the progressive solution to the problem
of a supposedly inassimilable minority population. A number of leading educa-
tors in south central Pennsylvania favored the movement. Samuel S. Schmucker
was the first president of the Lutheran Theological Seminary in Gettysburg, a
founding faculty member of Gettysburg College, and a leading force in the drive
to create a Lutheranism tailored to America. His works would circulate widely,
especially among German Lutherans in Pennsylvania, Maryland, and Virginia.
Schmucker himself would change from a proponent of colonization to an important border voice opposing slavery.[34]

Schmucker attended the same colonization meeting as Stevens in 1835 and
offered a prayer on behalf of the movement. Just two years later, however, he was
telling Daniel Alexander Payne, an African American student, that the members
of the College's Society for Inquiry on Missions were "not colonizationists, but
abolitionists."[35] Other faculty, such as Henry Baugher, supported colonization. In
fact, both Schmucker and Baugher attended a meeting of the Young Men's Colonization Society in Gettysburg in 1835, and Schmucker subscribed himself and
the college to the *African Repository*, the American Colonization Society's journal. He was nominated to be a vice president of the Pennsylvania Colonization
Society (PCS) in 1838, although not elected. He did serve as a PCS vice president
from 1860 until his death in 1873.[36]

This academic interest in colonization was regional. In Marshall College in Mercersburg, a student, Theodore Appel, wrote an essay in 1841 for professor John Williamson Nevin, a leader in the irenic Mercersburg theology. Appel, who would later become president of Franklin and Marshall College, wrote a speculative essay titled "Our Country in Years to Come." As he tried to predict the country's future, he reflected the values of much of the area when he wrote:

> The traveler inquires into the history of the colored man, about whom so [much] debate has been raised by the Abolitionist, the Colonization-man and the Planter of the present day. . . . Their chains at last fell. The sea covered with sail with every wind bound up that which bore them to Ethiopia, to favor so noble an undertaking carried them on its billows to the land of their ancestors, where they have been formed into a kingdom, and are beginning to act the part on the stage of human existence, which destiny pointed out to them.

So Appel wrote in his first draft; then, upon reflection, he made an insertion to change it to "the sea . . . carried *a part of them* on its billows [emphasis added]," and added a concluding sentence, "The other part of the colored race remain with us, independent and free." The emphasis, however, was on successful colonization.[37]

Even some of the area's leading Underground Railroad workers did not oppose colonization. Despite historian Larry Gara's cynical and mostly accurate comment that the Underground Railroad removed more African Americans from America than the colonization movement ever did, there is little evidence that contemporary Underground Railroad workers thought of their work that way. In 1835, however, after rioting had rocked their community of Columbia in nearby Lancaster County, Deborah Wright wrote to her nephew describing how she had recently discouraged antislavery lecturers from visiting the area. Deborah and her husband, also named William Wright, were highly significant figures in the southern Pennsylvania Underground Railroad. They reputedly helped hundreds of fugitive slaves escape during the antebellum decades, putting their lives and property at risk. In her letter, Wright explained that as a Quaker, she preferred to work for change silently and unobtrusively. She believed that both the abolition and colonization societies were working toward the same ends, and praised the colonization society's recent return of an African prince to West Africa as a noble act that could not be criticized by even the staunchest abolitionist.[38]

Colonization could appeal to many through its seeming combination of American ideals of progress and humanitarianism; to other border residents, colonization simply offered a crude way to export African Americans from the

border regions, or at least force them to move on. Keith Griffler has described
how, in border Ohio and Indiana, African Americans seeking help were often
met with references to restrictive, anti-black legislation, and comments such as
"I cannot help you. You will have to go to Liberia."[39] While such poignant anec-
dotes have not surfaced regularly about the Pennsylvania border, undoubtedly
many welcomed colonization as a socially acceptable way to get rid of African
Americans.

With this broad base of appeal, supporting colonization could bring political
dividends. As he did with temperance, Stevens carried on an extensive flirtation
with the movement. Several historians have noted the prominent role he played
in a colonization meeting in Gettysburg in 1835, but if the pages of the *Star and
Republican Banner* are any indication, his interest in colonization began well before that and continued a number of years after.[40]

Stevens' relationship to the paper was complicated, but he was widely regarded
as "the power behind the journal." During a local political dispute, Stevens had
denied owning or controlling the *Star and Banner*, but in truth, he was one of the
principal early investors and likely exercised a controlling interest.[41]

As early as 1832, Middleton—and most likely Stevens—seemed quite interested in colonization, publishing material that supported the Pennsylvania Colonization Society and lauded progress in the colony being established in Liberia. On December 4, 1832, the editor took the unusual step of highlighting an
item he was reprinting from the *Baltimore Gazette*, recounting the efforts of the
American Colonization Society to raise funds and collect Bibles. After a special
printer's mark, Middleton wrote: "We call the attention of the public to the following article. Cannot the citizens of Gettysburg and vicinity aid in colonizing
the sons and daughters of Africa?"[42] That same year, Middleton noted a petition
to the state legislature from residents of Adams and Franklin counties, urging
restrictions on the migration of African Americans to Pennsylvania.[43]

On the first day of the next year, Middleton ran a prominent article about the
departure of African Americans for Liberia, extracted from the pages of the *African Repository*. Middleton blessed the philanthropists who were financing the
voyage, "God speed them in this Godlike enterprise. God speed them to make
a freeman of the slave and a citizen of the freeman, and to send him back to the
shores of his own radiant and verdurous soil."[44]

Stevens' support of colonization does not necessarily mean that he was racist or favored the elimination of African Americans from America, although
a number of the movement's supporters were and did. A few colonizationists
were sincerely seeking to end slavery as quickly as possible, but their efforts often

played into the hands of those interested in supporting Southern and anti-black positions. Leading Democrats often supported the colonization movement, as did Southern planters. Often, the motives of these colonizationists were more overtly racist and less humanitarian. One of the first pro-colonization petitions sent to the Pennsylvania legislature in 1827 makes this clear. This document listed a long litany of alleged African American misdeeds, including their purported disproportionate representation in jails and mental institutions. Believing that climate and their constitution made African Americans unsuited for the North America continent, the petition urged support of the American Colonization Society (ACS), which was founded in 1816, but came to prominence during the Missouri controversy.[45]

Throughout the 1820s, the colonization movement was largely unchallenged as it portrayed itself as possessing the solution to America's race problem. During the early 1830s, however, a new movement, begun in the offices of Benjamin Lundy's newspaper in Baltimore, was coming to the fore. William Lloyd Garrison, Lundy's assistant editor, had been persuaded by African Americans in Baltimore that colonization was simply a tool to eliminate free blacks, who wanted equality in the United States instead.[46]

Not only did Garrison advocate immediate abolition and equality, but he leveled a vituperative attack on the American Colonization Society, making that movement very controversial. His caustic *Thoughts on African Colonization* (1832), based largely on the writings and critiques of black abolitionists, circulated widely. Donations to the ACS declined precipitously, the society felt compelled to indicate that it was not an antislavery organization, and many Northerners began to distance themselves from the beleaguered movement.[47]

In response, colonizationists struck back, with mobs destroying abolitionist presses, intimidating editors, and shouting down abolitionist lecturers. Leonard Richards's study of the anti-abolition mobs of the 1830s showed that they were generally made up of laborers, including immigrants, led by prominent political and business figures, often Democrats—"gentlemen of property and standing." In border areas, these local elites would lose much if abolitionism caused a rupture with Southern customers and kin, or if Pennsylvania ceased to be aligned with the Democrats.[48]

A series of race riots with the characteristics described by Richards ravaged Columbia, Pennsylvania in 1835. This Susquehanna River town was a haven for African Americans because of the availability of work and the presence of a prospering free black community, including several successful African American entrepreneurs. The growing African American population was flexing political

muscle by beginning to vote. Under the sponsorship of wealthy black businessman Stephen Smith, they also began moving into areas where white workers
lived. Both actions were seen as a threat. The riots devastated the African American section of town and specifically targeted prominent African Americans such
as William Whipper. It was these riots that cowed area opponents of slavery and
caused Deborah Wright to affirm that colonization was a reasonable solution to
the area's racial issues. Anti-abolition and anti–African American rioting also
struck Philadelphia several times in the 1830s and 1840s.[49]

Riots were not the only response. The controversy that Garrison provoked
over the American Colonization Society, and the society's corresponding financial problems, caused many state colonization organizations to be founded or revived. These often were controlled by Northern state leaders free from any stigma
of cooperation with Southern slaveholders. Pennsylvania was no exception. The
Pennsylvania Colonization Society (PCS) was founded in 1826, incorporated
in 1830, and soon gained support along the border. Thaddeus Stevens played a
prominent part in an 1835 Gettysburg meeting of one of the PCS's auxiliaries,
the Young Men's Colonization Society, and agreed to serve on a committee to
canvass for donations. Some of Stevens' associates, such as Samuel Schmucker
and Henry Baugher of Gettysburg College, were also involved.[50] The mid-1830s
represented a high water mark for colonization in Pennsylvania; the PCS was
enjoying favorable publicity as a result of having established a colony in Bassa
Cove, Liberia, and there were hopes that the volume of African Americans leaving Pennsylvania would increase.[51]

The Garrisonian assault of the early 1830s drew a sharp distinction between
colonizationism and immediate abolition. Not all antislavery supporters were
Garrisonian, however, and for much of the 1830s, south central Pennsylvanians
did not always see a conflict between antislavery and colonization. Many individuals, Stevens likely included, would not have seen the two approaches as necessarily contradictory, despite Garrisonian abolitionism's sharp combat with the
colonizationists.

Stevens' public support for colonizationism in July 1835 was not an isolated
aberration; in this period, Stevens often supported colonization or opposed abolitionism. In September, he spoke at a public meeting on slavery, attended by
Whigs, Antimasons, and Democrats. The meeting, based on a similar Union
event in New York designed to reassure Southerners, passed resolutions condemning abolitionist agitation, asserting that slavery was not necessarily "un-
moral," and denying that there was a political or "moral right" to interfere with it.

The resolutions even proclaimed that the North was ready to help suppress slave rebellions if needed.[52]

During 1836–37, when antislavery lecturers supported by Stevens visited Gettysburg and the pages of the *Star* contained many antislavery items, pieces favorable to colonization still appeared. In early 1836, the *Star* published an account of the anniversary celebration of a Pennsylvania College literary and debating society. James Keiser, of Waynesboro, Virginia, spoke in favor of colonization. The *Star's* correspondent—who could have been Stevens himself, owing to his relationship to the College—wrote that Keiser spoke effectively on one of the "exciting topics" of the day. "With arguments as irresistible as the rays of truth," the paper proclaimed, he "made the cold and quivering *Abolitionist* turn pale!"[53] If Stevens wrote those words, then his feelings evolved, for on January 2, 1837, the paper reprinted an account in which a correspondent described how he had decided not to support the Young Men's Colonization Society but rather "immediate emancipation." Still, the *Star* continued to run pieces favorable to colonization for years, even after Middleton left for Lancaster in December 1838 and was succeeded as the *Star's* editor by Robert Parker.

Stevens' public ardor for antislavery varied in the early days as well, likely based on the changing political climate. In January 1838, during the contentious constitutional convention that debated African American voting and trial by jury for fugitives, Stevens responded to a request by the American Anti-Slavery Society to meet in the Pennsylvania statehouse. He proposed that representatives of both abolitionism and colonizationism be given a hearing. He characterized both movements as "honest and respectable," "benevolent undertakings," and suggested that by listening to both, members of the legislature might learn much "respecting two great enterprises."[54]

In the end, however, colonizationism was not the solution to Stevens' political dilemma either: It did not provide him an opportunity for distinctive leadership. Regardless of where such schemes may have fit into Stevens' evolving racial views, in Gettysburg, the colonization movement was already supported by Stevens' political rivals, including Robert Harper and Jacob Lefever. Promoting colonization would not allow Stevens to differentiate himself, and it appears that he decided that colonization was not the answer to Pennsylvania's "race problem" either.

The net effect was to leave Stevens where he had started. Although he was still a powerful figure, Antimasonry had collapsed nationally and was rapidly losing momentum in Pennsylvania. Temperance was not powerful enough to sustain a political mass movement, particularly in a heavily German area, and some of Stevens' political rivals were also heavily involved in the movement. Colonizationism seemed to hold promise, because it appeared to address a concern of both border Pennsylvanians and the nation, but the colonization high ground had already been seized by hated rivals such as Jacob Lefever and the Democratic Party. In addition, colonizationism was under sharp attack by William Lloyd Garrison and other abolitionists, and the movement may not have fit in with Stevens' reputed work on behalf of fugitive slaves, and his relationships with several African American citizens of Gettysburg.

Although Stevens was unable to capitalize on temperance or colonization to rally a new mass movement, by mid-decade, a solution to his dilemma began to appear. He may have been behind its emergence from the beginning, although it appears that reform-minded constituents gave him the opportunity by starting an antislavery society. In 1835, Stevens had supported colonizationism, and condemned abolitionists, although he also had spoken a few sentences against slavery in September.[55] The next year, 1836, his public position began to change.

That year represented a key transitional year for Stevens and his political support of antislavery. His sentiment may have altered, which was in itself an accomplishment in this border area whose geography and economy encouraged cooperation with Southerners and discouraged antislavery agitation. Alternatively, he may have recognized a potential shift in public opinion in the state or the North due to the rise of immediate abolitionism and the Gag Rule controversy. Both may have been true. Any aggressive position against slavery, however, was muted by the border environment in Pennsylvania and the controversy attached to antislavery positions. At first, Stevens was able to portray antislavery not as the controversial issue it was within Pennsylvania, but as part of an interstate dispute, involving the principles of freedom of discussion then seen as under concerted attack from Southern neighbors.[56] At this point, the importance of his personal convictions on the subject appear at least matched by the political considerations involved. Stevens appears to be staking out a position where his support for antislavery might enable him to build a committed political base statewide.

In February 1836, Stevens had reported a bill to the legislature to prevent kidnappings of free blacks. He took a stand against slavery as well. In late 1835, the legislatures of Virginia, Kentucky, and Mississippi had reprimanded the Pennsylvania legislature because of its toleration of "abolition societies and incendiary publications." Stevens drafted a committee report emphatically upholding freedom of opinion and denying the right of Southern legislatures to dictate to Pennsylvania on these issues. The report, issued on May 30, 1836, granted that the slave-holding states alone had the right to regulate slavery within their boundaries, but asserted not only that Congress had the constitutional power, but also that "it is expedient" to abolish both slavery and the slave trade in the District of Columbia.[57]

Thaddeus Stevens was not the only Adams County resident to begin staking out an antislavery position in 1836. On July 4th, a number of county residents picnicked near James McAllister's mill, southeast of Gettysburg. The flatland next to the Rock Creek was the traditional recreation spot for Gettysburg residents. This group gathered on the sixtieth anniversary of the nation's independence to discuss antislavery reform. This was not the first antislavery society in the area—in addition to the sparsely documented meetings in Gettysburg in the 1820s, there was an antislavery society in Carlisle, made up entirely of African Americans until seminary student J. Miller McKim joined it in 1832.[58]

Those organizations, however, had made little public impact; this one, perhaps due to the hidden hand of Stevens, generated sizable early controversy and publicity. At McAllister's mill, these antislavery activists proclaimed their key principles. They were troubled by slavery's continued presence in the nation. They believed that slavery was supposed to have gradually faded as the light of liberty progressed; failure to reach that end betrayed the Founders. They called for emancipation in the District of Columbia, affirmed the right of free discussion, pledged vigilant prosecution of kidnappers of free blacks, and boldly declared that all races were "of *one blood.*" Perhaps most radically, they maintained that the Constitution's fugitive slave clause directly conflicted with Scripture. This was based on the law of Moses, which states, "Thou shalt not deliver unto his master the servant which is escaped from his master unto thee: He shall dwell with thee, even among you, in that place which he shall choose . . . Thou shalt not oppress him" (Deut. 23:15–16).[59] This is the first reference to this idea in the region, but it became an important trope, with the same passage later appearing in newspapers and even a sermon of prominent Lutheran minister and college administrator Samuel S. Schmucker in 1846.

That the gathering occurred on the Fourth of July underscores the political and civic undertones. More partisanship was shown by the picnickers' motion to only publish an account of the meeting in the *Star* (Antimason) and Robert Harper's *Sentinel* (Whig), because these, and not the Democratic *Compiler*, were the papers that they considered the "free papers of this county." Already the group seemed to be deliberately antagonizing the Democrats. At the *Star*, Middleton supported the communicated article about the event by highlighting the emphasis on the rights of free discussion, as well the right of Congress to abolish slavery where it could. He also decried the emerging use of mobs to stifle abolitionism. Then, perhaps hinting at one of Stevens' motivations, Middleton predicted that "a few brief months will see the ANTI-SLAVERY PARTY control every free State in the Union."[60]

Such a prediction was soon to be tested. The Adams County antislavery society met two months later at Two Taverns, a stop on the Gettysburg road from Littlestown. It was September 17, "Constitution Day," the anniversary of that document's ratification. The society passed more resolutions, with the first two related to "free discussion."[61] That may also show the hidden influence of Stevens: Free discussion was a clarion call of the Antimasons against Masons who bound their adherents with oaths and who had silenced William Morgan by death. It was also a potent rallying cry for evangelical Christians; a restriction on that right might ultimately limit their ability to evangelize. The antislavery society also decided to correspond with other antislavery supporters in Adams County and to send letters to each of the candidates standing for Congress from Adams County, to determine their position on slavery and the slave trade in the District of Columbia. This practice, called "interrogation," became a common antislavery tactic during 1837–38. The interrogation tactic was not new—British abolitionists had used it, and Boston labor organizers employed it in 1833 to identify political candidates friendly to education for labor.[62] What was new was its application by U.S. antislavery groups. In south central Pennsylvania, Adams County abolitionists were using this tactic in 1836, before the American Anti-Slavery Society endorsed it the next year. While it is unclear and perhaps unlikely that the Adams County society pioneered the use of the tactic by antislavery groups, they were influential, as correspondence describing their effort was published by a leading regional antislavery newspaper. The practice soon became standard for antislavery societies.[63]

The unfolding of the "interrogation" and the response of the committee of correspondence appears to reveal a hidden political agenda. When the antislavery society's committee of correspondence received replies from the two candidates, James McSherry (Whig), and Daniel Sheffer (Democrat), both sought the abolitionist vote, offered evidence of antislavery commitment, and pledged to work toward future antislavery goals. Each candidate had been asked whether he believed that Congress had the power to abolish slavery in the District of Columbia, and whether he would work to achieve that end "regardless of all threats to dissolve the Union." As evidence of his commitment, McSherry cited his support of Stevens' report in response to the resolutions of the Virginia legislature. Sheffer, however, pointed to having signed an antislavery petition the preceding winter, and he promised to vote for abolition of slavery and the slave trade at every opportunity.[64]

If the society had been politically nonpartisan, a logical course might have been to endorse both candidates or to have refrained from making a choice. Instead, while commenting that neither candidate's response was wholly satisfactory, they decided that McSherry's remarks were sufficient and endorsed him. In this case, politics may have been thicker than blood. James McSherry was a Whig and a protégé of Thaddeus Stevens. This apparently had more weight than the fact that Sheffer was related to the Wiermans, a prominent area abolitionist family.[65]

By employing tactics such as interrogation, the Adams County antislavery society adopted political tactics from its inception. Other antislavery societies in the region were encouraged to follow its lead. This correspondence with the candidates was later reprinted by the Benjamin Lundy's *National Enquirer*, a Philadelphia journal with significant regional and even national scope. As the republication was in December, after the election, it could not have been intended to sway the votes of the paper's readership. Instead, it was probably intended to be an example for other antislavery societies to use in future campaigns. In fact, the interrogation tactic was widely used by abolitionists for the next several years, although it is not clear that the Adams County example was the cause.[66]

The public appearance of a new antislavery society largely coincided with the *Star* adopting a new perspective on antislavery. By November 1836, the paper was publishing a notice for the convention to form the Pennsylvania Anti-Slavery Society, and commenting that Gerrit Smith, *"once the active patron of Colonization,"* had been elected president of the influential New York Anti-Slavery Society. Four years earlier, it had called for a colonization society to be started in Adams County; now it asked, *"Can there not be an Anti-Slavery Society formed in Adams County?"*[67] Several years previously, the paper had linked Masonry and slavery. Now it returned to the issue again, for the first time linking antislavery and Antimasonry, through the principle of "Free Discussion," currently being highlighted by the Gag Rule controversy. "Take this right away," the paper warned, "and the press is powerless—the people are slaves."[68] Later that month, Middleton continued the offensive by urging attendance at the upcoming antislavery meeting. He echoed abolitionist concerns that Northerners could be summoned to quell a slave insurrection, and criticized the Three-Fifths compromise, reminding readers that for "all our boasted republicanism," "we live under laws which are made in part, by slaves" through an unduly powerful slaveholding aristocracy.[69]

This type of language raised emotions to a new level of intensity when the Two Taverns abolitionists met in Gettysburg in December. The town was not like the rural, eastern areas of Adams County, where Quaker influence was strong. The county seat was filled with merchants, businessmen, and lawyers who depended on custom from the southern states, especially Maryland and the Shenandoah Valley. Because Gettysburg was a stop at the junction of several major turnpikes, there was a ready market for carriages and the associated industries of carriage repairs, saddle making, harness repair, and livery stables. Controversy over slavery might drive away Southern customers. An organized antislavery society in town, which might be seen as representing town sentiment, would be particularly threatening. The Two Taverns group's attempt to establish itself in Gettysburg represented a bold move, certain to face resistance.[70]

It would be a largely unsuccessful move as well; with the call published in the local papers, the December 3, 1836 meeting was packed with opponents of antislavery. James McAllister, a wealthy citizen whose mill sheltered fugitive slaves, chaired the meeting. Professor William Reynolds of Pennsylvania (Gettysburg) College made a speech, which one unsympathetic spectator writing a letter to a local paper deemed to hold that "slavery was an evil and slave holders evil men." When Reynolds moved for an antislavery society to be organized, the opposition struck. Methodist minister Richard Bond, who had recently moved to the area from Maryland, took the floor and outlined alternate resolutions. These criticized abolitionism and deemed it "inexpedient and improper" to interfere with slavery in the Southern states. Significantly, however, even these watered-down resolutions called for the abolition of slavery in the District of Columbia and a ban on the admission of new slave states. The new resolutions were supported by Daniel Smyser and James Cooper, both protégés of Stevens. They were apparently opposed only by Reynolds, Charles X. Martin, and "a negro named Payne."[71]

"Payne" was Daniel Alexander Payne, a student at the Lutheran Seminary who would become a leading figure in the Washington, D.C. antislavery community in the 1840s. Eventually, he rose to be a prominent bishop in the African Methodist Episcopal church. At the time, however, he was nearly anonymous to this Gettysburg resident reporting on events. Probably he was the only African American in the room; as a native of South Carolina, he certainly had more firsthand knowledge of slavery than anyone else there.[72]

The dueling sets of resolutions reflected the deep split over antislavery in this border Pennsylvania town located less than ten miles from the Mason-Dixon Line. According to one abolitionist observer, "a very animated, almost violent discussion took place" over the proposals. After much debate, Bond's resolutions passed "by an overwhelming majority." When the hijacked meeting attempted to appoint delegates to an important upcoming antislavery conference in Harrisburg, the chairman, James McAllister, tried unsuccessfully to stop the proceedings and derided the opposition as "pro-slavery men." The antislavery advocates decamped and reconvened a rump meeting, where they passed their own resolutions, proclaiming that all races were of one blood, all men were created equal, and "immediate emancipation was the right of every Slave, and the duty of every slaveholder." The *Star*'s editor, Robert Middleton, acted as the organization's secretary. Meanwhile, at the original meeting site, James Cooper, a Gettysburg lawyer and eventual U.S. Senator, was elected chair. Despite receiving training from Thaddeus Stevens, Cooper's true inspiration was Henry Clay. Cooper had been born in Maryland and spent his political career, like Clay, trying to find the center on the slavery issue. Under his direction, delegates to the Harrisburg convention were selected, and they planned to demand admission to the convention or, in a dig at Stevens, they would decry the abridgement of their rights of free discussion. An anti-abolition "spectator" later charged in Gettysburg's Democratic press that Reynolds's intended purpose was to promote "amalgamation . . . but the people of this county are too intelligent to be caught in such a snare, more especially after they have witnessed the practical effects of his system as exhibited in the speech of his negro coadjutor [Payne]."[73]

Leonard Richards has shown how whispers of amalgamation and miscegenation were vital fodder for the opponents of abolitionism in the 1830s, voiced in hopes of stirring up a strong and visceral reaction in the white populace. As for the abolitionist observer, he hinted at his dissatisfaction with the man many believed would be Gettysburg's emerging antislavery champion: "It was expected that Mr. Stevens would have been present to advocate the cause of the Abolitionists; but business *unfortunately* compelled him to be absent."[74] That members of an ostensibly grassroots reform group would be irritated at the nonattendance of one of the area's leading political figures speaks volumes about the political subtext behind the organization, and Stevens' likely hand in it.

The attempt to establish an antislavery society in Gettysburg had been daring, but had largely failed. Still, the fact that even abolition opponents would pass resolutions urging restrictions on slavery in the District of Columbia and in the territories indicates a strong underlying opposition to slavery's expansion. Adams County's abolitionists were not completely daunted. In January, they gathered in York Springs, the second largest town in Adams County. York Springs was closer to the borders of York and Cumberland counties than it was to Gettysburg (three, five, and fifteen miles respectively). This distance allowed it to serve as an alternative cultural and economic center for rural residents of the eastern part of the county. It was close to the Menallen meeting of the county's Quakers, and while York Springs was a resort patronized by Southern visitors in the summer, it did not have as extensive a carriage trade as Gettysburg.

In this rural town, the antislavery society heard an address from C. C. Burleigh, a lecturer from the American Anti-Slavery Society. Burleigh was a striking, controversial figure, with a long, flowing white beard in an age when most men kept their hair short. According to Ira Brown, who has researched Burleigh's lecturing, the lawyer's typical stump speeches included references to fugitive slaves; in one of them, Burleigh made the point that every fugitive contradicted the Southern claim that slaves were happy. In a portent of what was to come, opponents of abolition attended this meeting also, apparently determined to best Burleigh in debate. A female observer, probably an abolitionist, stated that Burleigh's arguments were overwhelming, and, for the most part, were not opposed openly. Still, the fact that the opposition showed up in York Springs, just a couple of miles from Adams County's Quaker meeting house, shows their strength. The society determined to meet again in Gettysburg in March.[75]

The controversy did not deter Thaddeus Stevens. In December 1836, Governor Ritner, who owed much to Stevens, had given the annual gubernatorial state of the commonwealth address. Within this speech, he decried the loss of state's rights, and the "subserviency of Pennsylvania to the general Government." Of the collapse of the traditional Pennsylvania policy of independence, Ritner maintained that "worst of all, [was] the base bowing of the knee to the dark spirit of Slavery." The governor stated that Pennsylvania's own abolition of slavery, its 1819 pledge to oppose admission of new slave states into the Union, and its opposition to slavery in the District of Columbia were "cherished doctrines of our State." He concluded by defending free discussion, and he argued that if one section were to impose limitations on free speech on another, "union becomes subjection." The speech was well-received in northern abolitionist circles and John Greenleaf Whittier even wrote a poem in Ritner's honor. It was widely believed that Stevens, Ritner's close political advisor, had written this part of the governor's speech. In Gettysburg, the *Star* celebrated the message and emphasized the antislavery portions.[76]

It was in this atmosphere, with antislavery ferment peaking in both Harrisburg and Gettysburg, that a young Vermont minister named Jonathan Blanchard visited Stevens at the capital and appealed to both his opposition to slavery and his political ambition. Blanchard explained that his mission was to travel on behalf of the American Anti-Slavery Society (AASS), rallying support for the cause throughout southern Pennsylvania. He challenged Stevens to build a political organization based on antislavery, not Antimasonry, because the slaveholders would defend the institution and not deny their involvement, as so many suspected Freemasons had. Writing thirty years later, he claimed to have appealed to Stevens' political ambitions: "If you can turn your Anti-masons into abolitionists, you will have a party whose politics will not bleach out. The Slaveholders will not 'possum like the Freemasons, but will die game."[77]

Blanchard was just one of a number of agents whom the American Anti-Slavery Society was dispatching to rural Pennsylvania. This followed a strategic decision on the part of the AASS and its sister organization, the Pennsylvania Anti-Slavery Society, to avoid cities and concentrate their organizing efforts in rural areas of Pennsylvania. This approach had been advocated by the national abolitionist leader Theodore D. Weld, who urged that the antislavery message set afire the North's rural areas, and then "back fires" would ignite the cities.[78] The wisdom of this strategy may have been borne out by the fierce opposition antislavery speakers attracted in Philadelphia, including the burning of the abolitionists' Pennsylvania Hall in May 1838. The original motivation, however, was the great success that the AASS had had with similar programs in New York in 1836 and particularly in Massachusetts in 1835–36, where a rural lecture campaign had resulted in the formation of hundreds of antislavery societies.[79]

Border Pennsylvania, however, was not Puritan New England. The lecturers met with decided opposition everywhere. Blanchard had already been mobbed several times in Pennsylvania, but with Stevens' backing he hoped to gain a better reception in the south central part of the state.

Stevens agreed to give Blanchard his full support, and gave him a total of $90 on two separate occasions. As Blanchard left their meeting, Stevens warned him, possibly in jest: "Go to Gettysburg, and if they Morganize you, we will make a party out of it." This reference to the martyred William Morgan is another clue that Stevens was considering a political movement based on antislavery.[80]

Blanchard did travel to Gettysburg, where he spent several weeks holding meetings. Along with the December 1836 gathering, these events are the best documented examples of the conflict between Gettysburg's abolitionists and their opponents in the entire antebellum period. According to the *Star*, Blanchard's first speech occurred on Monday, March 13, when Gettysburg's opponents of abolition had organized a meeting to nominate delegates to a Harrisburg anti-abolitionist convention, "Friends of the Integrity of the Union." Antislavery activists packed it, just as anti-abolitionists had filled the December 3rd antislavery meeting. Blanchard addressed the meeting for an hour, with James Cooper and Daniel Smyser responding with anti-abolitionist resolutions.[81]

On Wednesday, March 15, Blanchard spoke in the Gettysburg Court House on the topic of "Will Abolition Dissolve the Union?" He argued that the Union was not threatened by abolitionists simply exercising their legal and constitutional rights, but by Southerners who threatened secession, suppressed the mails, and restricted speech. He reassured his audience that the South "would never secede." One reason was the fugitive slave issue: "If the Union were dissolved the separating line would be another Canada line and the slaves could not be kept on the South side of it." In addition, he predicted that Southerners would nullify the actions of their state governments if they did secede. In case his audience was unconvinced, he urged his listeners to trust God to preserve the Union.[82]

In a likely appeal to local sentiment, Blanchard closed by referencing the "Genius of Emancipation," also the title of Benjamin Lundy's first antislavery newspaper. Lundy's writings were widely read in the county; his current newspaper, the *National Enquirer*, regularly published accounts of Blanchard's wanderings.[83]

James Cooper, sometimes a political ally of Stevens, sometimes a foe, responded with a position befitting a border politician born in Maryland but now living in a free state. Cooper assured his listeners that he opposed slavery and believed that Congress could abolish slavery in the District of Columbia and ban it from the territories. He favored free, open discussion, but he believed that slavery was a domestic institution, which only the legislature of each slave state could ban. Cooper believed that expressing opinions on slavery was fine, but that "organized opposition is mischievous and wrong." He argued that there was a difference between expressing a constitutionally protected opinion on the laws of slavery and an "organized warfare" on them.[84]

Cooper also believed that the abolitionist scheme was impracticable: It hardened Southern resistance to emancipation, made the slave's lot more difficult, and endangered the Union. He hammered at the reformers' utopian perfectionism: Government was inherently flawed, he believed, and not perfectible. Since he regarded the Founders as the most virtuous of all Americans, they were more to be trusted than a "newer generation who would tear down their edifice." Cooper felt that abolition violated the spirit and the intent of the Constitution. He, too, alluded to Lundy: In Cooper's view, the "Genius of Emancipation" had been driven off by abolitionism and replaced by evil genii. In a typical anti-abolition argument, Cooper stated his belief that the legislatures of Virginia, Maryland,

Kentucky, and Tennessee had all been poised to abolish slavery before abolitionist agitation hardened attitudes and increased fears.[85]

Cooper recalled Pennsylvania's abolition of slavery as an example of prudent emancipation. It was gradual, and it was done by Pennsylvanians. There were no antislavery meetings in other states passing resolutions pressuring the Keystone state, nor were there out-of-state lecturers, like Blanchard, circulating through it, decrying its slavery. He challenged his listeners to judge the abolition tree by its bitter fruit, and he argued that Blanchard minimized the risks of disunion stemming from abolitionist agitation.[86] At the conclusion of Cooper's talk, Andrew G. Miller, a Gettysburg lawyer, attempted to offer resolutions hostile to abolitionists, but the crowd was too unruly.[87]

The excitement continued through the week. That evening, at a courthouse "again crowded to excess," a second meeting featured a debate between Blanchard and Daniel Smyser.[88] On Friday, Blanchard spoke at Clarkson's schoolhouse, arguing that Southern slavery was not justified by the Bible. In the evening, Blanchard lectured at the courthouse on West Indian emancipation; Cooper again took issue with the speech.

Here at last Stevens made his entrance, having traveled from the state legislature in Harrisburg. He defended his young friend and offered a resolution decrying the attempts to stifle the abolitionists and upholding the right of free discussion. He taunted Blanchard's religious opponents, saying that they would easily tolerate the speech of a Muslim, Jew, or profligate, but couldn't stand a few words spoken on behalf of antislavery. Stevens gave an eloquent address for free discussion, but, as one editor noted, "without taking sides either for or against Abolition."[89]

Still, Stevens' support of Blanchard was significant enough that during his time in southern Pennsylvania, Blanchard prevailed upon the American Anti-Slavery Society to offer Stevens his own position as an antislavery lecturer, a fact that remained hidden for nearly one hundred years. Stevens declined.[90]

After Blanchard left Gettysburg, the battle continued to be fought in the town's newspapers, as antislavery supporters and opponents tried to impose their version of events on local memory. Middleton, the editor of the *Star*, argued that no "serious disturbances" had taken place during Blanchard's speeches, although he did admit that during Monday's talk some attempted to abuse Blanchard, both inside and outside of the meeting place.[91] Gettysburg's Democratic newspaper, the *Compiler*, claimed—with pride—that Blanchard had been unable to finish his speech on the courthouse steps because he had been shouted down by an angry mob led by some of the borough's leading citizens. Moses McLean, Jacob Lefever's lawyer who would serve as the Congressman and state legislator from the area in the 1840s and 1850s, had reportedly shouted, "We do not have any slaves here, why do you come and trouble us?" William McLean, Moses's father and the judge who signed the lion's share of the warrants of removal in the 1820s and early 1830s, also led the efforts to shout down Blanchard.[92]

Like all of the AASS lecturers, Blanchard moved on. He spoke at Middletown in eastern Adams County and then Chambersburg in Franklin County. In Middletown, he was greeted with corncobs and flint stones that pelted the church building where he was speaking. In Chambersburg, he was mobbed.[93] The controversy over his visit rocked Gettysburg for several months. The *Star* printed many articles about the incident and about Blanchard's reception in Chambersburg and other parts of the state. They also printed the complete text of Blanchard's possibly truncated speech, particularly since the *Sentinel* had printed the rebuttal by James Cooper. Then, Stevens' *Star* went one better, and printed the complete text of Cooper's speech—twice—challenging the *Sentinel* to show the same reciprocity and print Blanchard's. The purpose was to goad its rival, but the *Star* may have also been subtly reassuring its readers it could support antislavery positions that were more moderate than Blanchard's. From there, the controversy degenerated into bitter name calling. The insinuation by the *Sentinel*'s editor, that there were no (antislavery) "heathen" (that is, individuals who believed in slavery) in Adams County needing conversion by Blanchard was twisted by Middleton into a suggestion that he had labeled those who supported antislavery as the "HEATHEN OF ADAMS COUNTY." For his part, Blanchard in Chambersburg unwisely suggested that the McLeans and his other Gettysburg opponents might be destined for hell. Because the McLeans were a prominent area family, this only polarized matters further.[94]

The end result of the controversy was that the antislavery cause gained significant publicity in Adams County, Thaddeus Stevens had defended an antislavery lecturer, but the antislavery society, at least in Gettysburg, had been cowed. One distressed area abolitionist, in fact, wrote a letter wondering if the organization had disbanded, because there was no activity on the next Fourth of July, in 1837. In response, Joel Wierman reassured Adam Wert that the society was still vital, but that there had been no requirement for it to actually meet then or at any other time! When we next hear of the Adams County antislavery society, it is meeting again in York Springs, in the northern part of the county.[95]

Thaddeus Stevens, meanwhile, had gone on to a leading role in the convention for a new Pennsylvania constitution. In 1837, Stevens, at the height of his power and leadership within Pennsylvania, was *de facto* ruler of the Pennsylvania Constitutional Convention. The combined Whig/Antimason delegation he led held a narrow edge in the convention. Stevens made what appeared to be a bold defense of the enfranchisement of African American men. Under closer observation, however, it appears to have been a conservative move to forestall changes to the state's constitution, and his proposal would have kept in place property restrictions that disenfranchised some whites. Stevens was really arguing for *status quo ante*, which would have kept recently arrived immigrants from voting. Under the old constitution, very few male African Americans actually voted, although they had a titular right to do so. Even noted members of the Philadelphia elite such as James Forten did not vote. Carl Oblinger believes that African American men voted in Columbia, Pennsylvania, and Robert Purvis and some other wealthy African American men voted in Bucks County, but their participation was highly controversial and launched a court case that took the right to vote away from African Americans even as the Constitutional Convention was doing the same.[96]

Stevens left the convention early, in part because he was under attack in the state's legislature, but also partly because he knew he was on the losing side. In his absence, the new constitution restricted the franchise to white voters. Stevens refused to sign it. He did not, however, take special steps to ensure he had his vote recorded against the disfranchisement of African Americans, as John Sergeant from Philadelphia did, and he was criticized in the abolition press for it. For 170 years, Stevens has been largely remembered as a valiant champion of African American rights in the convention. The truth is more complicated; like much else Stevens was doing in the 1830s, his actions there indicate substantial calculations of political advantage as well as suggestions of stirring principle. Stevens' convention record reflected the difficult position he was in, trying to organize a new political movement while dealing with a significant split in sentiment among his border constituency.[97]

While they did not succeed in establishing a regular organization in the county seat, the Adams County abolitionists were persistent. In 1839, they brought another traveling antislavery agent to Gettysburg, J. Miller McKim. McKim had local ties—he was born in Carlisle, and went to Dickinson College there. Reading Garrison's *Thoughts on African Colonization* had converted him to immediate emancipation. He ultimately decided, like many young, theologically inclined converts to antislavery, that the cause of antislavery was more important than his call to ministry, and he began to work with the American Anti-Slavery Society, headquartered in Philadelphia. McKim became a key figure in Pennsylvania abolitionism, eventually serving as secretary of the Pennsylvania Anti-Slavery Society. Accounts of his 1839 visit to Gettysburg are sparse, but he apparently received a reception much like Blanchard's at the courthouse. Again Stevens intervened to aid the speaker; this time, he cut right to the point. Whatever he might have said previously about the glories of free discussion, here he promptly threatened the boisterous crowd with jail time for refusing to let McKim speak.[98]

The turbulence from 1836 to 1839 had brought the issue of slavery into greater regional prominence, but the abolitionists' hopes of results similar to the previous campaign in Massachusetts—large scale conversions, the founding of many local societies, and the formation of a mass antislavery movement—had been thwarted. While the lecturers had stirred up controversy and made inroads in public opinion, their efforts had not been an unqualified success. Local antislavery activists in Adams County had been cowed. In the future, they would reappraise their approach.

This border antislavery movement had shown itself to be unusually politically involved from its onset. They had met on significant political holidays, they had criticized the Democratic press, and they had interrogated political candidates on their antislavery stands. They apparently chose to support the Whig candidate solely for political reasons. When their local political champion did not show at a meeting as expected, they grumbled. As they moved forward, they continued to use political and legal strategies, rather than relying extensively on a moral crusade or mass conversions to the cause. This political component implies that in this border area, partisan political conflict contributed heavily to the 1830s development of the antislavery crusade.

Other border areas evolved similarly. Political antislavery had much greater appeal in the border states of the Midwest, and Salmon P. Chase had a similar antislavery odyssey to Stevens. Like Stevens, Chase attended Dartmouth College, and he studied law under William Wirt in 1829. Wirt would later be the Antimasonic candidate for President in 1832. Chase gravitated toward defending fugitive slaves in 1835, but he, too, did not immediately advocate Garrisonian immediatism, but rather a form of political antislavery. Later, like Stevens, his views became more radical, and in the late 1840s and 1850s he advanced the concepts of "free soil, free labor and free men" and "slavery sectional, freedom national." During his early days, however, Chase, like many border politicians, clergymen, and leading citizens, placed much of his antislavery sentiment inside the framework of helping fugitive slaves.[99] Likewise, in south central Pennsylvania, many of the controversies of the next decade, and some of the decade following, would focus on fugitive slaves.

Notwithstanding the controversy and conflict stirred up along the border, in antislavery, Stevens had finally found a significant cause for a new political movement. Even when he eventually joined the hated Whig Party in the 1840s, he could do so as a "Conscience Whig," firm in his opposition to slavery. In fact, his fierce rival at the *Compiler* suggested that was what Stevens had been up to all along: using antislavery to stir up a new controversy just as Antimasonry was dying. He suggested "[abolition] is intended . . . to be a political party, and in Pennsylvania to take the place of antimasonry." Other critical observers thought the same; one commented in December 1836, "Anti-Masonry is defunct in Pennsylvania. What hobby can . . . be so appropriately mounted [by Stevens] as the abolition question?" One hundred years later, the noted political historian Richard N. Current came to the same conclusion. In the antislavery cause, and its particular resonance in rural, border Pennsylvania, Thaddeus Stevens had solved his dilemma.[100]

3

Antislavery Petitioning in South Central Pennsylvania

The failure of the antislavery lecturers to ignite a mass movement in south central Pennsylvania roughly coincided with disturbing events elsewhere, such as the martyrdom of Elijah Lovejoy and the burning of Pennsylvania Hall. Likely as a result, the Adams County Antislavery Society returned to two tools that had previously been employed by antislavery activists in Pennsylvania: the petition and legal action. These tools were supplemented by other methods of advocacy being adopted by contemporary abolitionists, such as distributing pamphlets and establishing antislavery lending libraries. All of these approaches helped the antislavery society move forward less confrontationally than with contentious public meetings and inflammatory lectures, although the petitions, the legal strategy, and the literature still had a radical edge. While the wide distribution of antislavery materials worked behind the scenes to change public opinion, it was the petitions and the prosecution of kidnappers that had the most visible results on the statewide level. They helped discourage fugitive slave renditions and inspire and pass a new, strengthened personal liberty law, which would place Pennsylvania's legislation on a collision course with federal law.

By revisiting these tactics, the society placed itself on a continuum that started in the 1780s and would stretch into the Civil War. Antislavery activists in Pennsylvania had brought court cases and "freedom suits" and circulated petitions since at least the 1780s. In fact, southern Pennsylvania activists played a leading role in the underappreciated petition campaign across the North organized by Benjamin Lundy in 1827–29, an important forerunner to the massive campaigns of the 1830s. While Garrisonian antislavery lecturers criticized the response they received in Gettysburg, that did not mean that all of the region's residents were "pro-slavery," as was sometimes angrily charged. It meant that the antislavery society had adopted tactics suited for their situation, in a border region of a border state.

At the national level, the society would be no more or less successful in its petitions than the hundreds of antislavery societies whose members signed petitions to Congress from 1835 to 1844. They did not achieve abolition, not even in the District of Columbia, but they did raise the level of attention to the issue and win broad support from Northerners concerned about Southern aggression or the right to free speech.

At the state level, however, the society was unusually successful. It successfully prosecuted individuals for kidnapping—seizing free African Americans and carrying them south. A later petition campaign in the 1840s inspired Pennsylvania's strengthened anti-kidnapping legislation, and would help define the state's relationship to the fugitive slave issue. Both the petitions and the legal cases would allow south central Pennsylvania's abolitionists to influence the legal environment in favor of the fugitive along the "edge of freedom."

The petitions allow us a glimpse into the antislavery community in terms of demographic makeup and geography. An analysis of an 1846 petition reveals that most antislavery activists, at least in eastern Adams County, worked in rural occupations. This petition, signed by white Quakers, and a significant petition the next year, signed by Gettysburg's African American residents, suggests a failure to integrate the white and black antislavery communities that would hinder the two groups' usefulness. The two sets of petitioners did, however, successfully apply pressure to create a stronger Pennsylvania personal liberty law. Similar analysis of petitions supporting colonization in 1860 hint that these rural champions of the fugitive may also have been older than colonization supporters, although it is difficult to be certain with the nearly fifteen year difference in campaigns.

Despite this unusual success in influencing the legislature, for the most part, the Adams County Antislavery Society developed in similar ways to many of the new antislavery societies forming across the North. After the tumultuous meetings with Jonathan Blanchard in 1837, the antislavery society began meeting in the York Springs area, in eastern Adams County, where many Quakers lived. When anti-abolition strife manifested even there, the gatherings moved to a darkened schoolhouse in the middle of the woods. In 1840, soon after the hostile reception given to lecturer J. Miller McKim in Gettysburg, a published summary of the society's activities inveighed against the Gag Rule in Congress, reported that petitions regarding slavery in the District of Columbia had been circulated, and celebrated the success of their pamphlet distribution and lending library. The library was under the leadership of William and Phoebe Wright's daughter, Hannah Wright. Six hundred publications had been ordered for the library and for distribution. Low cost lending libraries and pamphleting were major emphases of abolitionists at this time, and this tactic also corresponded with the less confrontational approach favored by many Quakers.[1]

Despite the mistreatment of Blanchard and McKim, antislavery lecturers still traveled to Gettysburg, but their accounts of their reception hint at resistance and resentment. In 1840, Charles C. Burleigh spoke in Adams County at twelve different places, including five lectures in Gettysburg. He was unsure whether he would visit Gettysburg again.[2] In 1842, Benjamin S. Jones and James Fulton traveled through the districts close to Maryland in Adams, York, and Lancaster counties, lecturing and distributing material in English and German. An antislavery convention was held in Gettysburg in 1843, as a result of a Garrisonian program to hold one hundred conventions in Pennsylvania, Ohio, Indiana, and the Northwest.[3] Quaker lecturer, feminist, and antislavery activist Abby Kelley spoke in Gettysburg in 1845, but she complained of the chilly response she received, and her traveling partner Benjamin S. Jones said that lecturing there was like the "building of a fire on an iceberg." Jones believed that because of the seminary and the strength of Lutheranism there, the town's residents were "afraid" of a woman lecturer and would "suffer not a woman to teach."[4] In 1846, Cyrus M. Burleigh, Charles's brother, complained of a similar reception in Gettysburg—no one invited him to stay, not even Professor Reynolds of Pennsylvania College, and only a few helped pay his meeting expenses. He did rejoice that toleration of kidnappers seemed to be waning, based on a recent conviction in Adams County court.[5]

All of these visits seemed inspired by the agenda of the national and state antislavery societies; Adams County activists seemed more interested in shifting away from controversial public meetings to alternative tactics such as the petition and using the law to win freedom for African Americans. Both of these techniques have been described by historian Richard Newman as part of an older, more deferential antislavery tradition, but they were also consistent with south central Pennsylvania's abolitionists' engagement with the political system. Their efforts resulted in significant changes to both the letter of the law and the legal environment.[6]

For south central Pennsylvanians, petitioning, even during the mass campaigns of the 1830s, was an established tactic, not a new one. In fact, Pennsylvania had helped lead the first sectional petition campaign, from 1827 to 1829, and petitioning was the first strategy returned to by Adams County antislavery activists when it became clear that antislavery lecturers had not won sizable converts in south central Pennsylvania.

Because of its widespread use by Garrisonians, the petition is sometimes considered solely as an instrument of moral suasion, aimed primarily at changing public opinion. Reformer and abolitionist Angelina Grimke defined it as such, as do modern historians such as James Brewer Stewart.[7] What historians sometimes miss, in the light of the later reluctance of some Garrisonians to vote or join antislavery political parties, is that this instrument was fundamentally political in intent. Petitioning a legislative body is a political act, which is why many female abolitionists, denied the suffrage, eagerly embraced it.

Quakers and other political and religious minorities in Pennsylvania especially treasured the right to petition. These groups were often far too small to elect a candidate or amass a legislative majority, but they could appeal to law and morality through petitions. For groups whose members chose not to vote— including some Quakers, some members of other peace sects, and some abolitionists—petitioning was particularly vital.

In Adams County, opponents of slavery began petitioning even before their society was formed. Daniel Sheffer's response to the new society's interrogatories indicates that petitions from Adams County were being sent to Congress during the "Gag Rule" controversy of 1835–36. When antislavery societies across the country flooded the Congress with petitions, Southern Congressmen passed a rule forbidding their reception.[8] This was actually before the Adams County Anti-Slavery Society's first meeting.

The Gag Rule restricting debate on slavery and the reception of antislavery petitions had to be renewed every year. Abolitionists, including the antislavery activists from Adams County, continued to petition Congress for its repeal. If slavery could not be abolished, the controversy over the rule would at least illustrate the Southern repression of the rights of petition and free expression. The minutes of the Adams County Antislavery Society show that a committee to "circulate petitions" was established in December 1837.[9] Members of the society had already been petitioning; on January 30, 1837, Congressman George Chambers (Pa.) informed Adam Wert that his petition to abolish slavery and the slave trade in the District of Columbia had been presented to Congress. Chambers agreed with Wert that "trafficking in human beings" was abominable, but told him that nothing would be done during that session. This did not discourage the society; later that year, Joel Wierman wrote Wert that he had a stack of petitions to send to Congress. In 1838, the new Adams County Congressman Daniel Sheffer, a Democrat, told Wert that his petition had not yet been presented, because it would not be received with favor by "the Southrons."[10]

These activities were part of a long tradition. Pennsylvania's Quakers had a history of petitioning Congress. Beginning in 1783, a petition from the Philadelphia Yearly Meeting asked the national government to abolish the slave trade.[11] This action was at the leading edge of a national and global reaction against slavery in the era of the American and French Revolutions. Similar anti-slave trade petitions were sent in the 1790s, along with petitions protesting kidnapping after the passage of the 1793 fugitive slave law. These early petitioning efforts by Quakers and the Pennsylvania Abolition Society (PAS) have been criticized as elitist or ineffective, yet they kept the slavery issue before the government in the early years of the Republic.[12] Generally, the memorials were referred to Congressional committees, which typically developed replies about how it was "inexpedient" to pursue them at the time. In the case of the slave trade, however, some petitions gained attention and in 1808, Congress did reconsider the trade, as had been pledged during the Constitutional Convention, and outlawed it.[13]

That action, however, did not lead to the extinction of slavery, as many had hoped. During the 1820s, Baltimore Quaker Benjamin Lundy (1789–1839) organized a significant antislavery petition campaign, likely the first such sectional campaign. Lundy was born in a part of New Jersey where slaveholding was not uncommon, and only gradually ebbed after gradual emancipation was passed in 1804. He observed the slave trade firsthand in Wheeling, [West] Virginia, in Missouri, and later in Baltimore. Determined to stop such injustice, he helped to organize antislavery societies in Ohio starting in 1816. This important early abolitionist wanted to start a national antislavery movement. He lived briefly in Tennessee, to support the Manumission Society of Tennessee. He also encouraged antislavery societies elsewhere in the South, including in Missouri, North Carolina, Virginia, and Baltimore, Maryland. Before Nat Turner's rebellion in 1831, some antislavery societies existed in the South, and generally advocated gradual emancipation. Beginning in 1821, Lundy wrote and published the first newspaper dedicated to antislavery, *The Genius of Universal Emancipation*. Lundy's campaign was probably the first mass petition campaign; the PAS often preferred to submit petitions with the names of a few politically prominent individuals. Lundy's three-year campaign ultimately attracted thousands of signatures, and was an important precursor to the massive flow of petitions in the mid-1830s, which initiated and sustained the Gag Rule debate.[14] South central Pennsylvania was on the leading edge of this campaign.

Because Congress had declared that states had jurisdiction over slavery within their borders, this drive focused on the District of Columbia, which Congress did control. In 1826, Lundy's newspaper, *The Genius of Universal Emancipation*, urged Charles Miner, a Federalist Congressman from West Chester, Pennsylvania, to advocate in Congress the abolition of slavery in D.C. Miner did as Lundy requested, but his resolution for gradual abolition was shelved. In 1827, Lundy turned to a petition campaign.[15]

The petitions were based on a memorial drafted by Lundy and his lawyer, Daniel Raymond. Lundy published it as a model in his *Genius of Universal Emancipation* and the Baltimore *American*. In 1827, the American Convention of Antislavery Organizations meeting in Philadelphia asked Lundy to chair a committee to distribute the petition to every antislavery society in the country.[16]

Two petitions from this 1827 campaign are in the National Archives. In addition to a petition Lundy sent in from Baltimore, Pennsylvania antislavery activists also submitted a petition. These documents, based on Lundy's form, did not narrowly criticize slavery in the District, as a cautious, conservative petition might. It also did not use restrained rhetoric—as historians suggest marks white antislavery protest before the rise of Garrison. Instead, the document sharply critiqued the institution. The Pennsylvania petitioners deplored the growth of slavery and identified it as a threat to the Republic. As the slave trade had been declared a heinous piratical crime, why not slavery itself? If it was immoral to enslave someone on the coasts of Africa and illegal to ship them to the Western Hemisphere, the petitioners contended that enslaving people born in the land of liberty was even worse. They argued that every African American born in America, slave or free, was a "natural born" U.S. citizen, basing this concept of citizenship on the Constitution's "no attainder" clause (Article 3, Section 2). Constitutionally, tainted parents could not work "corruption of blood"—the stigma and results of their serious crimes could not be passed down to their children. Under English law, individuals convicted of treason or other high crimes and under a bill of attainder could not pass property to their children and forfeited it to the Crown. In constitutional law, this clause protects a child from being punished for a parent's crime. Lundy's petitioners argued that even if parents were enslaved, their children should be free United States citizens.[17]

While opposing slavery in the United States generally, the petition specifically called for abolition in D.C. because it was the "exclusive jurisdiction of Congress" and because the Capitol was the "Temple of Liberty." Slavery there mocked the country's claim to be dedicated to freedom. Using their "no attainder" logic, the petitioners asked that Congress decree that children of slaves born in the District would be free. Because such law applied only to persons not yet born, they believed that no slaveholder could feel defrauded as a result.[18]

In 1828, Representative Miner joined Lundy in appealing for increased petitioning; eighteen petitions followed. These petitions were identical to the 1827 petitions, sharply condemning slavery and asking for its abolition in the District of Columbia through freeing the children of slaves. Over 1,200 Pennsylvania abolitionists signed the petitions. One of the first 1828 petitions was from Adams

County antislavery activist Joel Wierman, his father William, and a number of other south central Pennsylvanians (see Appendix B).[19] Samuel Taylor, who reportedly later stopped at least one kidnapping attempt in Cumberland County, signed another.[20] These petitions were all apparently circulated with at least the consent of the Pennsylvania Abolition Society.

Lundy was still not content, however. The next year he supported an expanded campaign with travel throughout the Northeast—what one historian has called "one of the epic journeys of the time." From May through December, he spoke at forty-three meetings in nearly as many cities, visiting every northeastern state north of Pennsylvania except Vermont. In December 1828, his half sister, Lydia, reported seeing him circulate a petition in western New Jersey. In all, Lundy would claim to have traveled 25,000 miles in the 1820s, visiting nineteen states and holding over 200 meetings.[21]

The trips paid off. In Massachusetts, he recruited a young William Lloyd Garrison to the cause. In 1829, antislavery societies from across the North joined the crusade, along with several from the South, making this the first sectional or even national antislavery petition campaign. Vermont activists submitted the most petitions—Garrison had moved to Bennington and had mailed or enlisted the postmaster to mail petitions to at least thirty-six Vermont towns. A notation on the Bennington petition reads, "The Postmaster is respectfully and earnestly desired to to obtain as many signatures as possible to the following petition." Southerners would greatly fear the influence of postmasters during the Gag Rule controversy and during the secession crisis after Lincoln's election, when there were concerns that Republican-appointed postmasters would subvert the South. Those fears, while greatly exaggerated and based primarily on the discovery of abolitionist literature in the hands of slaves, free blacks, or poor whites, may not have been entirely unfounded.[22]

Pennsylvania's activists submitted the second-largest number of petitions in the 1829 campaign, including one sent to the postmaster of Columbia. A number of Pennsylvania petitions came in from "inhabitants of western Pennsylvania." Dr. Francis Julius Lemoyne had formed a Western Abolition Society in Washington County in southwest Pennsylvania in 1824, and would help form the Washington County Anti-Slavery Society in 1835. South central Pennsylvania abolitionists, residing just west of the Susquehanna, could be influenced by his western Pennsylvania groups as well as by Lundy in Baltimore and the PAS in Philadelphia. Several south central Pennsylvanians signed these "western Pennsylvania" petitions, including Samuel Taylor and a Samuel Wright, possibly William Wright's cousin.[23]

Other petitions came from Indiana, Ohio, New York, New Jersey, Maine, Connecticut, and Massachusetts. Petitions were also received from Maryland, including a large one from Frederick County; Delaware; and the Manumission Society of Tennessee, and one apparently from the grand jury of Washington, D.C.

Charles Miner retired from Congress in 1829, and the petition campaign crested in that year. Pennsylvania abolitionists continued to submit petitions, however. In 1831, when former President John Quincy Adams returned to Washington as a Congressman from Massachusetts, his first speech was on slavery and the slave trade in the District of Columbia. He presented fifteen petitions on the subject from Pennsylvania Quakers. Adams indicated that he did not personally favor abolition in the District, but he thought that slave sales there might fall under Congressional jurisdiction. This protest was Adams's first step toward becoming antislavery's reluctant political champion in the 1830s and 1840s. The petitions that he used to introduce the topic were not an anomalous set of memorials from Pennsylvania, but a continuation of the earlier 1820s campaign.[24]

This overlooked petition campaign came years before the mid-1830s petition initiatives that sparked the Congressional "Gag Rule." Richard Newman has characterized the Pennsylvania Abolition Society's petitioning during the 1820s as a "conservative petitioning strategy," as he argues that the contentious debates over the Missouri Compromise persuaded PAS leaders to test the political waters before submitting petitions to Congress. Merton Dillon, Lundy's early biographer, admits that some Philadelphia Quakers hesitated to endorse the petition campaign at first, but outside of the Pennsylvania metropolis, other Quakers willingly followed the lead of Lundy. Still, through the American Convention, an umbrella group of antislavery organizations, the PAS implicitly endorsed Lundy's broadly scoped, vigorously worded petition campaign against slavery in D.C., even if some of the leadership did so reluctantly.[25] Whatever scruples some PAS leaders may have had against mass petitioning did not prevent hundreds of Pennsylvania abolitionists from sending strongly worded petitions and memorials to Congress. Newman aims to contrast PAS "elite," "conservative" petitioning with the mass petitioning tactics of later Massachusetts activists. The signers in the 1828–29 campaign were not elite, however, and the language they used harshly denounced slavery and declared it incompatible with Christianity.[26]

This suggests that there was not a sharp break between the petition tactics of Pennsylvanians and those used later in Massachusetts, but rather an evolution. In fact, the 1820s Maryland/Pennsylvania campaign, which became sectional, likely influenced later petitioning in Massachusetts. This could have occurred through the national efforts of Lundy and Theodore Dwight Weld, whose Western Pennsylvania Antislavery Society built on the work of Lemoyne's 1824 organization, which appears deeply involved in the 1829 petitioning. Weld became a leading figure in antislavery organizing and petition campaigns in Massachusetts in the mid-1830s. The transformation in petition strategy Newman identifies appears to have had its genesis in Pennsylvania in the late 1820s, not Massachusetts nearly a decade later, with south central Pennsylvania activists involved from the beginning.

Lundy's campaign did not achieve its object, but had focused attention on slavery in the District of Columbia. A special Congressional committee was formed. While they reported that it was "inexpedient" to consider abolition in the District, the debate in the committee rooms was contentious at times. The stage had been set for the petition debates of the 1830s and the accompanying Gag Rule controversy years before Garrison proclaimed that slavery in the District was the "first citadel to be taken," and John C. Calhoun declared that securing the right to refuse antislavery petitions would be the South's "Thermopylae."[27]

These 1835–44 petition controversies in Congress were critical to the expansion of antislavery sentiment. Abolitionists from across the country flooded Congress with petitions on the issues of abolition, slavery in the nation's capital, and the slave trade. The refusal to accept the petitions generated Northern sympathy for the abolitionists, amid fears that the "Gag Rule" and the restriction of abolitionist mail to the South could lead to broad curtailment of Northern civil liberties. Some historians believe that the campaign rescued the antislavery movement from the stigma of Garrisonian immediatism, others that it was a vital step in the politicization of antislavery. If so, then Benjamin Lundy and antislavery activists in Pennsylvania, including south central Pennsylvania, deserve credit for pioneering the militant petitioning tactic in 1827–29.[28]

Petitions to the Pennsylvania Legislature

Even though many historians believe that the petition campaigns were critical to the development of Northern antislavery sentiment, most still believe that the petitions themselves were ineffectual in achieving their stated goals. In this school of thought, it was the Southern political response to the petitions, and the corresponding Northern reaction, that was significant, not the petitions themselves.

Such a focus on the national government, however, only reveals part of the petition story. Pennsylvania antislavery activists, men and women, also regularly petitioned the state government in Harrisburg on slavery. They were urged to by the antislavery press. Frequently, these were the same petitions that went to Congress, decrying slavery in the District of Columbia, the annexation of Texas, or other national issues. Such issues were not always directly relevant to Pennsylvania, and while some antislavery activists hoped that Pennsylvania's Congressional delegations would be instructed to vote for such measures in Congress, such tactics almost always failed.[29]

While duplicating petitions to the national government was ineffective, what did have an impact were petitions seeking to influence Pennsylvania's own legislation on African Americans and slavery, particularly regarding fugitive slaves. Here, the petitioners could urge substantive legal changes without interfering with the laws of Southern states, as immediate abolition would do. This approach could be effective: The significant legal change in 1847 strengthening Pennsylvania's personal liberty laws may have been initiated by petitions from south central Pennsylvania. It definitely was supported by petitions from a range of southern Pennsylvanians, including Gettysburg's African Americans, during the battle for the law's passage.

Unfortunately, the holdings of petitions to the Pennsylvania state legislature in Harrisburg are not complete, making it difficult to draw definite conclusions from the number of petitions submitted in a given year.[30] This militates against attaching too much importance to an analysis of the numbers of petitions or numbers of signers. However, the surviving petitions are still valuable resources. During the last antebellum decades, the federal census was just beginning to collect useful information on wealth, occupation, place of birth, and education. Using this to analyze petition signers enables demographic profiling of those activists who signed petitions in south central Pennsylvania.[31]

Antislavery activists were not the only citizens petitioning the state legislature and the 1837–38 Constitutional Convention in regard to African Americans. Supporters of colonization also petitioned. Others asked the commonwealth to restrict the immigration of African Americans. The colonization movement received support from Gettysburg's press, and some residents of Gettysburg signed a petition urging restricted immigration of African Americans in 1832.[32]

Colonization petitions will be considered in more detail in Chapter 7. In general, however, a demographic analysis of the signers of these two types of petitions shows that these groups varied in occupation, sex, and geographic location. In south central Pennsylvania, many colonizationists were professionals and artisans and lived or worked in the major towns and county seats, while most white antislavery petitioners came from rural townships. There was, however, also a core group in Gettysburg at the seminary and college and among some of the graduates of Thaddeus Stevens' "law school," the legal training he provided at his office. In addition, by 1860, many south central Pennsylvania antislavery activists were somewhat older than the colonization supporters. If their numbers were not replenished by a substantial influx of new supporters—and the evidence suggests that they may not have been—the core of these antislavery petitioners would be at an advanced age by the start of the Civil War. Indeed, a demographic analysis of these petitions suggests that the rural middle class antislavery supporters were ill-placed to repel the colonizationists who belonged to the elites controlling the region's towns. This did not bode well for the treatment of area African Americans during the Civil War and Reconstruction period and beyond.

The evidence that exists also suggests that the white antislavery movement in Adams County was divided. The core was in the northeastern part of the county, around York Springs, where there were numerous Quakers. There was, however, a second group in Gettysburg who sent in a sarcastic petition in 1845 urging Congress to annex Africa to provide a supply of slaves for the South. Their petition apparently mocked Southern interest in annexing Texas, and their opposition appeared limited to restricting the expansion of slavery. These petitioners satirized the Southern insistence that slavery was a blessing that should be extended. They did not appear to coordinate their petition activities with the northern Adams County abolitionists, nor, it seems, did Gettysburg's African Americans, who sent in an important petition in 1847 during the campaign that successfully advocated a strengthened personal liberty law.[33]

South Central Pennsylvania Antislavery Activists

Petitioning by south central Pennsylvania antislavery activists to the state legislature offers a glimpse into the rank and file support for antislavery in the region.[34] Noteworthy petition campaigns related to African Americans and fugitive slaves occurred in 1847 and 1861, during the secession crisis.[35] In 1847, a petition campaign brought fifty-four petitions to the legislature from the eastern counties of Pennsylvania. This was a highly unusual outburst of antislavery petition activity, with important links to south central Pennsylvania.

The 1847 initiative revolved around the fugitive slave issue. Pennsylvania abolitionist J. Miller McKim was at the heart of the campaign, and he was intimately connected with south central Pennsylvania. Born in Carlisle in 1810, he had graduated from Dickinson College in 1828, and completed his studies for the ministry under the direction of Carlisle minister George Duffield. Duffield was an antislavery conservative who became a leading Northern clerical proponent of colonization at his various parishes in Carlisle, Philadelphia, and Detroit, but his younger student chose a different path. Reading Garrison's *Thoughts on African Colonization* in 1832 made McKim a committed abolitionist. In 1833, he was the youngest delegate to attend the inaugural convention of the American Anti-Slavery Society (AASS) in Philadelphia. Two years later, McKim was appointed as one of the original "Seventy" lecturers for the American Anti-Slavery Society. Later he became the secretary of the Pennsylvania Anti-Slavery Society and the publisher of the *Pennsylvania Freeman*, serving briefly as its editor after John Greenleaf Whittier resigned.[36]

McKim's advocacy of immediate emancipation and Garrisonianism made him a hated figure in parts of Pennsylvania. A handbill labeled him the "advocate of amalgamation, negro equality and subversion of the constitution." McKim took an interest in fugitive slaves over his career, and was particularly active in the Underground Railroad in the late 1840s and 1850s. Nationally, he achieved notoriety for opening the shipping crate in which escaping slave Henry "Box" Brown had sent himself to the antislavery office in Philadelphia.[37] "Box" Brown was in McKim's future, however, when he became the recipient of the fifty-four petitions in 1847.

McKim was also an active proponent of the Pennsylvania Female Anti-Slavery Society (PFASS), and about half of the petitions included the signatures of women. The petitions asked that the Pennsylvania legislature ban the holding of slaves, even by short-term Southern visitors, and repeal all laws that authorized state officials to be involved in the capture or rendition of fugitive slaves.[38] This petition, because it focused solely on modifying Pennsylvania's laws, could be strongly antislavery in tone while avoiding criticism for meddling in the institutions of other states.

This petition campaign met with unusual success. Combined with pressure from influential Quakers, the drive saw Pennsylvania pass a stringent personal liberty law in 1847. The law significantly increased the difficulty of recovering fugitive slaves in the state. Not only were all state officials forbidden from helping return fugitive slaves, but county jails could not be used to hold fugitives. The involvement of constables and jails had been a staple of fugitive slave renditions in southern Pennsylvania for decades. Both prohibitions were enabled by the tangled reasoning of the 1842 Supreme Court decision *Prigg v. Pennsylvania*. In that Supreme Court decision, based on a case arising in adjacent York County, Justice Joseph Story had ruled that states had no jurisdiction whatsoever over fugitive slaves. Story was attempting to limit state interference with the recovery of fugitive slaves. Several states, however, beginning with Massachusetts and quickly followed by Pennsylvania, passed personal liberty laws based on the decision. These laws generally forbade the involvement of any state judges, law enforcement personnel, or facilities in the rendition of fugitive slaves. Pennsylvania's legislation also addressed kidnapping, a long-standing concern of antislavery activists: Stiff penalties were levied on individuals who seized free blacks instead of runaways. Even a legitimate recapture of a fugitive could be punished if it led to riot or disorder. In addition, one clause explicitly permitted the application of *habeas corpus* to fugitive slave cases. This law would profoundly irritate Southern politicians until the Civil War.[39]

This 1847 petition campaign was supported by only one petition from south central Pennsylvania, and it was not from the York Springs (Adams County) Anti-Slavery Society or the Gettysburg critics of Southern slave owner's political power. Instead, the petition claimed to be from Gettysburg's entire adult African American population. The petition signing had been organized by Aaron Constant, a fence-maker, and bore 110 signatures, almost all in an identical hand, indicating that most of Gettysburg's black population could not write.[40] The name of at least one African American resident of the borough was not included, however: Eden Devan. Devan would later be excluded from the A.M.E. church, and area white abolitionists would claim he was in league with kidnappers.[41]

The petition (see Appendix C), using the form widely circulated by proponents of the personal liberty law, stated that the signers were "earnestly desirous to free this Commonwealth from all connection with Slavery." First, the petition requested the repeal of all laws permitting the holding of slaves for any period of time within the state, revoking the exemption for visitors who stayed less than six months. Second, the petition requested "that you will repeal all laws of this Commonwealth which direct or authorize our judges, magistrates, sheriffs, constables, jailors, or other officers, to aid in the capture and removal from this State of persons claimed as fugitive slaves." Third, the petition requested that the legislature would propose measures to the U.S. Congress to abolish slavery in the U.S. "or release this Commonwealth from the legal obligation to aid in its continuance"—such as returning escaped fugitive slaves.[42] As Stanley Harrold has insightfully pointed out, many Northerners tolerated a Virginia slaveholder's recovering a fugitive in Maryland, but not on the free soil of the North.[43]

Petitions from African Americans were rare in antebellum Pennsylvania. There were some memorials and remonstrances from Philadelphia and a few from Pittsburgh, two urban centers with substantial African American populations. Petitions from African Americans living in rural counties were almost unknown: This Gettysburg petition may be the only one. Submitting such a petition boldly proclaimed the petitioner's aspirations to equality, citizenship, and a political voice. It, and the absence of any petitions on other subjects, indicates that of all the subjects before the legislature, Gettysburg's African Americans felt particularly qualified to speak on the fugitive slave issue.

There were no comparable petitions from south central Pennsylvania's white antislavery community supporting this important legal initiative in 1847. Some of this may have stemmed from jurisdictional issues. J. Miller McKim was the executive secretary of the Eastern District of the Pennsylvania Anti-Slavery Society (PASS), and the Eastern District appears to have extended just to the Susquehanna River. The state's female antislavery society (PFASS), however, which McKim was also involved with, was active throughout the state, including the thirty-three counties of Pennsylvania that lay west of the Susquehanna. The Anti-Slavery Society of Western Pennsylvania, which had been organized by the followers of Theodore Dwight Weld, was essentially independent and did not always coordinate activities with the Eastern District.[44] South central Pennsylvania apparently fell in a "no man's land" between the two. Even during the 1828–29 petition campaign on slavery in the District of Columbia, some south central Pennsylvania abolitionists signed petitions from eastern Pennsylvania one year, and from western Pennsylvania the next.

There may have been another reason, however, why the York Springs abolitionists did not petition the state legislature in 1847. The effective 1847 campaign was preceded, and may even have been initiated, by an 1846 petition (see Appendix D), signed primarily by white residents of northern and eastern Adams County, asking that the state's laws be changed to make aiding in the recovery of a fugitive slave a penal offense. Consequently, these abolitionists may have believed that, having petitioned the legislature on the same topic in 1846, they did not need to join in the petition campaign of the following year. The 1846 petition was apparently circulated by noted activist and Underground Railroad participant William Wright and his family. Wright was the first signer, and his wife, one of his sons, and two of his daughters also signed.[45]

Of the sixty signatories to this petition, forty-one could be identified in the 1850 Adams or York County censuses. Most were from Huntingdon, Menallen, and Latimore townships or even York County, all distant from the Adams County seat at Gettysburg. At least eight and probably ten women signed this petition. (Some petitioners, especially women, signed with only their initial and last name.) Seventeen male signers were listed as farmers, three as laborers, four carpenters, two merchants, two wheelwrights, one doctor, one trader, one tanner, one teacher, and one may have worked in lumbering. Another was retired by

1850. No woman was listed in the census with an occupation, but at least seven of them lived with farmers or laborers as spouses or children. These signers were rural citizens of Adams County—farmers and farm laborers, joined by village tradesmen and merchants.

Several generations of historians have noted the rural background of many Northern antislavery activists. Gilbert Hobbs Barnes mentioned it in one of the first important monographs on the antislavery movement; David Donald argued that many key abolitionists were descended from distinguished Northeastern families who were concerned about the transfer of social and economic leadership from rural to urban areas. Indeed, some abolitionists like Theodore Weld deliberately appealed to rural areas, believing that progress would be swifter there and the "back fires" would overtake the cities. While Donald's thesis has become mired in controversy, the fundamental observation that much support of antislavery was rooted in rural areas appears to have validity in southern Pennsylvania.[46]

The fact that antislavery appealed to some rural border residents, even while many townspeople were opposed, may be explained by economic factors. Along the border, many artisans and workers in towns and cities feared competition from free blacks or fugitives. Even if a black worker could not displace an artisan from his trade, he might drive down what the market would pay, or the two might have to work together, which was closer than many border Pennsylvanians wanted to associate with African Americans. In Lancaster County, Columbia was wracked by a series of race riots in the 1830s when white laborers feared social and economic competition. In contrast, farming required land, placing a barrier to entry to many African Americans. Fugitives with farming skills could help short-term or at harvest time, but would not necessarily be considered equals with white laborers. Even antislavery leaders such as the Wrights and the Wiermans frequently used fugitive slave labor, despite the risk of recapture for the fugitives.

Information on religious affiliation is not in the census, but many signers were Quakers. Using the Menallen Meeting minutes and cemetery records as sources, the names of twenty-six signers could be identified as Friends, and ten others shared a surname (Garretson, Pearson, and so on) with a family belonging to the meeting, and also may have been Quakers.[47]

The average age of the Adams County petitioners, about forty-one years old, may have been as significant as their agrarian background. Many of the older signers had come of age politically during the Missouri crisis and the late 1820s petition campaigns. While still in their political prime in 1846, seventeen years later, during the secession crisis and outbreak of the Civil War, many would have retired from public life, left the area, or died. In 1861, when over one hundred petitions relating to African Americans and fugitive slaves poured into the Pennsylvania legislature, the highest total for such petitions ever, none were received from antislavery activists in Franklin, Adams, or Cumberland counties. This suggests that they had become enervated, discouraged, or feared invasion. In addition, if William and Phoebe Wright and many other signers of this petition were not replaced by younger activists, this aging population of rural abolitionists might have had even less energy after the war ended, when freedmen settled there and African Americans struggled not just for freedom, but full political rights.[48]

This petition, when compared with colonization petitions from 1861 (see Chapter 7), suggests that south central Pennsylvania antislavery petitioners may have been older and more rural than their colonizationist counterparts, who tended to work in trades and professions, often at the county seat. As rural areas lost power and influence statewide, so did this rurally based antislavery.

These results from a Pennsylvania border county differ greatly from Edward Magdol's analysis of antislavery petition signers in upstate New York and Massachusetts. Magdol examined county seats, manufacturing towns, and cities. Few of his petitioners were farmers. He found that anti-abolitionists tended to be nearly five years older than abolitionists. Massachusetts and upstate New York were far enough away from the South that there were fewer fears of competition from emancipated black laborers. In their labor struggle against factory owners, the rhetoric of "wage slavery" created, for some workers, a sense of solidarity with enslaved African Americans. Finally, Magdol suggests that for both Massachusetts shoe manufacturers and laborers, there was always the chance that freed African Americans would boost business by demanding higher quality footwear.[49]

Even if the antislavery activists in eastern Adams County did not submit a petition in 1847, they rejoiced over the new personal liberty law. The York Springs Anti-Slavery Society passed resolutions proclaiming it as a "triumphant refutation" of the charge that antislavery efforts "by petition and otherwise, are vain." The group celebrated that the "Slave Laws" of Pennsylvania had been abolished, and legal protections enacted for fugitives who sought refuge in the state. Clearly, they believed that their petition work in 1846 was vindicated. This was, however, the last published mention of the society.[50]

Thomas Morris, in his study of personal liberty laws, has stated that the cause of the 1847 petition flurry and the near unanimous passage of the new personal liberty law is "unknown." It was likely, as Morris suggested, that the confluence of concerns about *Prigg v. Pa.* and the acquisition of Texas played a role. The 1847 law was also rooted, however, in the 1846 petition, inspired by an important 1845 Adams County kidnapping case, the trial of Thomas Finnegan.

As a result of that case, the 1846 Adams County petition, the 1847 petition campaign, and the cooperation of legislators, the friends of the fugitive won a significant victory. Pennsylvania's legislation now posed significant barriers to the recovery of fugitive slaves. Like all new legislation, however, it would be tested when the courts applied the law and interpreted its bounds. That test, like so much else concerning fugitive slaves in Pennsylvania, came in the south central portion, where conflict between the state's legal protections and federal provisions for the return of escaped fugitives came to trial.

4 The Fugitive Slave Issue on Trial

The 1840s in South Central Pennsylvania

Stymied by entrenched opposition to their grassroots efforts, and perhaps cowed by the violent murder of Elijah Lovejoy in Ohio and the burning of Pennsylvania Hall, south central Pennsylvania's antislavery activists turned to another traditional refuge of minority groups seeking change: the court system.[1]

The courts offered opportunities to circumvent border sentiment sympathetic to the South. Convincing an entire community of a new legal perspective might be impossible, but in a legal case, only a small jury had to be persuaded, or possibly just one individual—a judge, or a jury member who could deadlock a trial. There were enough pockets of sympathy for fugitives that a jury might rule against a kidnapper if the case was properly framed.[2] An appeal to law could also marshal the power of the state behind the antislavery effort to levy punishments more effective than moral censure. The courts also offered a "bully pulpit," giving prosecutors and litigants opportunities to further publicly define the state's relationship to slavery. The decision of the state's antislavery minority, particularly in southern Pennsylvania, to adopt an aggressive legal strategy prosecuting kidnappers helped lead to Pennsylvania's 1847 personal liberty law. This in turn laid the basis for ongoing controversy over the fugitive slave issue until the Civil War. In contrast to a Garrisonian emphasis on lecturing and moral suasion, south central Pennsylvania's antislavery movement was characterized by this legal engagement and continuing partisan involvement.[3]

This mid-1840s turn to the courts occurred at an important moment in the development of antislavery ideology. With controversies over the annexation of Texas and war with Mexico looming, renewed concerns over the slavery's expansion into new territory surfaced. The cases allowed antislavery lawyers to present emerging "free soil" doctrines and to claim that Pennsylvania was historically a land of liberty. Despite significant numbers of slaves living in southern Pennsylvania just thirty years before, lawyers reached back to the American Revolution to persuade judges and the public—inaccurately—that Pennsylvania's blacks had been essentially free from the moment the 1780 Abolition act passed. Whether the appearance of nascent free soil doctrine in fugitive slave cases was a symptom of the concept's growing prominence, or a cause of it, is unclear, but it did reflect its increasing importance. This free soil interpretation of Pennsylvania's past overlooked the state's legacy of slavery and racism, but it helped define Pennsylvania as part of a "free" North set against the slave South, including its neighbors across the Mason-Dixon Line. This animosity would be new—Pennsylvania had voted with the South in most Presidential elections since 1800.[4]

Emphasizing legal action was not new. South central Pennsylvania antislavery activists built upon the older legal strategies of the Pennsylvania Abolition Society (PAS) as it sought to enforce Pennsylvania's abolition acts and protect free blacks from kidnapping and enslavement. Recent scholarship has portrayed a sharp distinction between the legalistic PAS and Garrisonian abolitionism. PAS attorneys, while personally courageous and dedicated, have been characterized as largely ineffectual, and the state organization as too determined not to upset Southern sensibilities to be effective. The PAS has been portrayed as the sort of abolition society that Southerners could tolerate, while the Garrisonians, adopting African American strategies of protest and organization, became the next wave of abolitionism.[5]

This interpretation has merit because the PAS leadership was less confrontational than the Garrisonians in the 1830s and 1840s, but it underestimates the impact of the Pennsylvania organization before Garrison's rise. It also understates the degree to which Southerners saw the PAS as a threat. During the mid-1830s controversies over immediate abolitionism, PAS president William Rawle claimed that his organization had always favored moderate, gradual approaches and had limited itself to activities within Pennsylvania.[6] This was not entirely true. At times, the rhetoric used by the PAS could be nearly as heated and stark as that of the Garrisonians. Part of the problem with understanding the PAS is that its title was misleading. Its influence was not limited to Pennsylvania; in many ways, it was the nation's first national antislavery society. Pushed by Benjamin Lundy and others, its agents actively supported emancipation societies in Virginia, Tennessee, Kentucky, and North Carolina. PAS agents also tried to persuade Southern slaveholders to voluntarily manumit their slaves in Maryland, Virginia, and elsewhere. They even purchased and freed slaves in South Carolina, the cradle of Southern slavery.[7] As a committee of the society put it, "they feel a strong solicitude that the abolition of slavery *in every part* of the United States should be favored & promoted by this Society in every practicable manner [emphasis added]."[8] Since the debates over the Missouri Compromise, Southerners had frequently complained that abolitionists were not content to work merely in the North, but actively promoted abolition in the South. The activities of the PAS gave ammunition to any suspicious Southern slaveholder looking for evidence of a Northern conspiracy against slavery. The society's tactics might have been more genteel than the American Antislavery Society, but to Southern slaveholders, many of its aims were as alarming.

As threatening as these activities could be, the PAS was primarily focused on Pennsylvania, and the legal legacy established by early PAS court cases laid the groundwork for later effective activity in the state's south central region. Their success and experience in the courtroom made an appeal to law an effective tactic for friends of the fugitive and abolitionists throughout the antebellum period, particularly in the 1840s, when a U.S. Supreme Court decision created an opportunity to divorce Pennsylvania from enforcement of the Fugitive Slave Law.

The same reasons that the courts appealed to abolitionists, however—the reliance on a potentially supportive body of law, the small number of people needing to be convinced, the publicity, and the fact that a conviction would warn others engaged in the activity—also appealed to the abolitionists' opponents. They struck back beginning in 1847. The cycle of attack and counterattack marked the 1840s. That decade alone saw the important case *Prigg vs. Pennsylvania*, two prosecutions of slave catchers for kidnapping African Americans (*Finnegan, Auld*), a prosecution for harboring fugitive slaves (*Oliver v. Kaufman*), and a slave rescue/riot case (*McClintock*), all originating in south central Pennsylvania. These legal disputes and the underlying activity that they represented contributed to Southerners' general dissatisfaction with fugitive slave renditions, leading to a new federal Fugitive Slave Law in 1850. Armed with this law, the Southern legal assault on southern Pennsylvania's Underground Railroad came to a furious crescendo in the Christiana treason trials of 1851. This antebellum legal struggle elevated the importance of the fugitive slave issue and made involvement in fugitive slave cases more dangerous for both those who captured fugitives and those who helped them.

That fugitive slaves had to be brought before a local magistrate to be legally removed from Pennsylvania created a critical bottleneck, an opportunity for friends of the fugitive. Prior to 1826, Southerners could seize a slave without legal process and carry him south, under the so-called "right of recaption." In the 1820s, Pennsylvania's law was changed to require a hearing before a judge. A Northern judge was susceptible to local community sentiment just as much as his Southern counterpart who had issued a writ for recovery of a fugitive. If judges could be convinced to rule in favor of the fugitives rather than the owners in doubtful cases, the tide of remanded fugitives could be checked legally, without tumultuous antislavery lecturing, forcible resistance, or outright violation of the law. Open resistance was anathema for many Northerners who favored law and order, and for many Quakers who made up a significant part of the core antislavery sentiment. In addition, because of the *stare decisis* basis of the Anglo-American court system, decisions by one judge could serve as precedents for successful arguments in another courtroom. Ultimately, one favorable ruling could protect many African Americans; the publicity generated by such cases could also spread the antislavery message.

Pennsylvania's gradual abolition law with its separate legal categories almost guaranteed activists would soon turn to legal action. After the passage of the law and its corollary in 1788, individuals working for the Pennsylvania Abolition Society devoted substantial time to "freedom suits" and fugitive slave cases. PAS lawyers strove to expand Pennsylvania's definition of freedom by getting judges to rule "for freedom" in doubtful cases, redefining the state's mixed legacy toward slavery.[9] In southern Pennsylvania, Benjamin Wright and Samuel B. Wright were often involved. They were the uncle and cousin, respectively, of one of the area's leading 1840s abolitionists, William Wright.[10]

Several legal avenues existed for African Americans to prove their right to freedom. The 1780 gradual abolition act stipulated that all slaves then living be registered, and that all children of slaves born after November 1, 1780 be registered at birth and freed at age twenty-eight. The 1788 act mandated that this registration include the slave owner's name and occupation; the county, township, district, or ward where the owner lived; and the slave children's age, name, and sex. Such information could only be omitted "under pain and penalty of forfeiting . . . all right to every such child . . . and of him, her, or them immediately becoming free." The registration was to be on oath and copies kept at the courthouse.[11] After 1788, if a slave child's birth was registered improperly, he or she could win freedom. If slaves were brought to Pennsylvania by a Southerner who intended to reside there, they too could sue for freedom. If they belonged to a Southern owner who was just visiting Pennsylvania, but had stayed in the state for longer than six months, they were also entitled to their freedom. This was the very issue Thaddeus Stevens litigated in the Butler case, arguing that the sojourn had to be continuous to free the slave.

In Philadelphia, Isaac Hopper and others engaged in some high profile lawsuits, including attempting to force South Carolina Congressman Langdon Cheves to free his slaves after they resided in Philadelphia when that city served as the nation's temporary capital during the War of 1812. South central Pennsylvania, however, was nearly as important as Philadelphia in defining the rights

Table 2   Slaveholding in South Central Pennsylvania as a Proportion of the Total Slave Population of Pennsylvania (1810 peak year)

Year	State	Number of Slaves / Percentage of Total Number in Pennsylvania						South Central Penn. %
		Adams		Cumberland		Franklin		
1790	3737	328	8.8	223	6.0	330	8.8	23.6
1800	1706	111	6.5	228	13.3	181	10.6	30.4
1810	795	71	8.9	307	38.6	87	10.9	58.4
1820	211	23	10.9	17	8.1	19	9.0	28.0
1830	403	45	11.2	7	1.7	13	3.2	16.1
1840	64	2	3.1	24	37.5	0	0	40.6

Source: Historical Census Data Browser
Note: The high numbers reported for the state and Adams County in 1830 and for Cumberland County in 1840 appear anomalous. In each census year, the guidance was slightly different. Census takers may have started enumerating slaves differently; perhaps they began including some indentured servants in this category.

of Pennsylvania's slaves and free blacks, and its importance increased over time. As slavery disappeared rather rapidly east of the Susquehanna River, this region was one of the few where substantial slaveholding remained—and where masters were determined to hold on to their property. Many of the cases that helped define the reach of the emancipation laws occurred there, where Pennsylvania's remaining slaves were concentrated. As Table 2 shows, in 1810 nearly sixty percent of the state's slaves lived in south central Pennsylvania; as late as 1840, nearly forty percent of the state's rapidly diminishing population of slaves resided there.

Initially, after passage of the eighteenth century gradual abolition legislation, Pennsylvania's Circuit and Supreme Courts generally ruled for the slaveholder, despite defects in the slave registry.[12] Eventually, changes in the Pennsylvania Supreme Court and the gradual diminution of slavery in Pennsylvania led to an increasing number of rulings for the slave in doubtful cases. For example, in *Wilson v. Belinda* (1817), argued in Chambersburg, a failure to register Belinda's sex resulted in freedom for her and her children.[13]

By 1820, fewer south central Pennsylvanians owned slaves, so court rulings on slaveholding did not attract as much attention. Kidnapping cases, however, could stir up a community. The seizure of free blacks as fugitives or to be sold as slaves was labeled by Pennsylvania's antislavery activists with the volatile—and accurate—description of kidnapping. Since American slavery was defined by skin color, as long as the institution existed, free African Americans could be wrongfully seized and enslaved. Although little noted at the time, Pennsylvania's gradual abolition law created a presumption of freedom for African Americans whose names had not been registered. In Pennsylvania, an unregistered black individual must be considered free unless proven otherwise. Southern jurisprudence, however, assumed that African Americans were slaves unless proven otherwise.[14] Along the critical "edge of freedom," antislavery activists could argue that a seized, unregistered African American was presumptively free, whereas Southerners assumed he or she was likely a fugitive slave.

In fact, the first national Fugitive Slave Act in 1793 grew out of a kidnapping incident in Pennsylvania. Three Virginians had captured a free black man in the state and carried him back to the Old Dominion. A flurry of correspondence resulted as Pennsylvania's governor tried to have the three men extradited for kidnapping. The governor of Virginia refused extradite the men because the Constitutional clause regarding fugitives from justice had not yet been codified. The result was the 1793 Congressional act, the first two sections of which related to fugitives from justice, the last two to fugitive slaves. As in the Constitution, these clauses concerning the renditions of criminals and escaped slaves were juxtaposed, complicating future kidnapping and fugitive slave cases.[15]

The new law did little to mollify concerns about kidnapping. Near the Mason-Dixon Line, it was easy for black Pennsylvanians to be seized and carried into the South.[16] During the 1820s, the Pennsylvania Abolition Society condemned kidnappings at the biannual American Convention of Antislavery Societies, when many other societies were content merely to report their efforts to encourage voluntary manumissions and membership and correspondence activities.[17]

The 1840s and the Adoption of a New Legal Strategy

By the 1840s, the legal situation had changed. Antislavery lawyers had previously emphasized enforcing Pennsylvania's laws to free the state's own African Americans; now the focus had shifted to using Pennsylvania's code to protect fugitives and free blacks. Fugitive slave and kidnapping cases were also used to dramatize the injustice of slavery and to strike at Southern political power.

Even among some antislavery activists, sympathies were more often on the side of free African Americans than southern fugitives. For example, Samuel Taylor was a Cumberland County resident described by a contemporary as an "original abolitionist," and he had signed two petitions in 1828 urging the abolition of slavery in the District of Columbia. In the 1840s, he once noticed an

African American headed down the road past his house, pursued, shortly afterwards, by two white men. Mounting a horse, he rode ahead and overtook the man, demanding to see his "free papers." The man refused to produce them until a bystander assured him Taylor was trustworthy. Then, in an account that may be slightly romanticized—although it is recorded in two separate manuscript accounts—Taylor and the man fought off attempts to capture him by three different slave catchers. These included Taylor's brother and J. Thompson Rippey, who would later become the sheriff of Shippensburg. Easy to overlook in this dramatic account, however, is the fact that Samuel Taylor demanded to examine the traveler's "free papers" first. What would have happened if he had not carried any is unclear.[18]

As this incident indicates, the legal basis for recapturing genuine fugitive slaves was reluctantly accepted even by some opponents of slavery. If south central Pennsylvania's abolitionists hoped to prevail legally, they needed to argue that the individuals in dispute were free, not fugitives. Consequently, in the 1840s, Quakers and antislavery attorneys brought forward kidnapping cases. These cases served not only to protect free blacks but also to discourage the capture of African Americans in general, including fugitive slaves.

As a result, the fugitive slave issue was genuinely "on trial" in south central Pennsylvania in the 1840s. Antislavery activists turned to the courts to discourage the capture of fugitives by vigorously prosecuting individuals who seized African Americans. In response, slave owners and those sympathetic to them decided to use the courts to punish those who helped fugitive slaves escape. Although the legal legacy of this period is mixed—both slaveholders and abolitionists prevailed at times—it clearly became more dangerous for slaveholders and slave catchers to try to recapture fugitives, and it was legally hazardous for those who aided fugitives as well. The risk was at the margins, for both those who tried to recover and those who tried to help fugitive slaves.

This legal evolution can be traced in a series of key cases, as described in the sections that follow.

Prigg v. Pennsylvania *(1842)*

The U.S. Supreme Court decision in the case of *Edward Prigg v. Pennsylvania* vitally affected the trajectory of the fugitive slave issue, and inspired a new set of Northern personal liberty laws. They, in turn, helped precipitate the 1850 Fugitive Slave Act. Although a titular victory for slaveholders, the decision significantly changed the balance of federal and state responsibilities regarding fugitives, enabling Northern states to essentially refuse to cooperate in the rendition process.

In 1828, a prosperous central Maryland farmer died after giving most of his property to his daughter and son-in-law, Susanna and Nathan Bemis, but leaving his slaves under the control of his widow, Margaret Ashmore. One of the slaves, also named Margaret, had lived for years in "virtual freedom" and married a free black, Jerry Morgan. She was even listed as free in the 1830 census, although she apparently did not have any emancipation papers. In 1832, Margaret and Jerry moved to York, Pennsylvania; shortly afterwards, she had her second child.[19]

Margaret's story illustrates both the risks faced by African Americans living near the Mason-Dixon Line, and broader trends in the upper South. As previously rich soils became depleted from tobacco farming, much of central Maryland and Virginia's Shenandoah Valley switched to grain cultivation. Tobacco required labor throughout the growing season, whereas raising grain could often be managed by a farm family, requiring extra labor only at the harvest. This conversion made slave labor less essential and significantly contributed to Maryland's and Virginia's transition from slave importers to slave exporters to the Deep South.[20] With fewer slaves required to run farms, they were seen as more of an investment or a source of capital.

Both trends affected Margaret Morgan and her family. Legal historian Louis M. Waddell believes that if Margaret were really free, the Ashmores may have liberated her because of the changes in Maryland's agricultural economy. Ashmore's heirs, however, were mainly interested in Margaret and her children as saleable assets.[21]

When those heirs decided to recover Margaret and her family, she was living in southern Pennsylvania, like many other manumitted or fugitive slaves from central Maryland.[22] In 1837, Margaret Ashmore authorized her son-in-law, Nathan Bemis, and three neighboring slaveholders (Jacob Forwood, Stephen Lewis, and Edward Prigg) to recover Margaret and her children. It is likely that Bemis had finally impressed on Ashmore the value of the departed slaves, even if their labor was unnecessary. He would sell Margaret as soon as she was recovered.[23]

Bemis obtained a warrant for Margaret from a Maryland magistrate and, accompanied by his neighbors and a constable, seized her in York. When they went before a local justice of the peace, however, he refused to hear the case. He cited Pennsylvania's 1826 law, which forbade lower judges from becoming involved unless the slave catchers followed a distinctive Pennsylvania practice of going to the magistrate both before and after the seizure of the fugitive. With no other court nearby—the nearest federal court was in Philadelphia—Bemis and the party took Margaret back to Maryland without legal sanction, exercising the "right of recaption." They were indicted for kidnapping in Pennsylvania and the state began the extradition process with Maryland.[24]

It was difficult for Maryland to simply refuse Pennsylvania's request for the slave catchers. In both Article IV, section 2 of the U.S. Constitution and the 1793 fugitive law, the fugitive slave clause lies directly adjacent to the clause enabling interstate extradition of "fugitives from justice."[25] This juxtaposition made it difficult for Southern states to ignore requests to extradite kidnappers. Spurning them might give abolitionists implicit justification to ignore the fugitive slave clause. As a result, Maryland Governor Thomas Veazey prevailed on Bemis to return Margaret Morgan to York. Special legislation was passed so Bemis and his party would appear before a York County grand jury. Rather than render a verdict, the jury summarized Pennsylvania's emancipation and anti-kidnapping legislation, and asked the judge to determine guilt or innocence. After more legislative maneuvering and some discussion between Prigg's counsel and Pennsylvania's attorney general, Prigg was convicted (the other defendants had been dropped), so that the case could function as a test in the federal courts. The other defendants had been dropped from the case, but Prigg appealed and the case reached the U.S. Supreme Court in 1842. The Court upheld the 1793 federal fugitive slave law and found that Pennsylvania's 1826 law unconstitutionally interfered with it.[26]

The decision was a reverse to Margaret Morgan and the friends of the fugitive involved in the case; the wording of the opinion, however, gave ammunition to both supporters and opponents of slavery. The Court was unusually divided on the basis for overturning the lower court rulings. Illustrating their diverging perspective on the fugitive slave issue, six of the nine justices delivered separate opinions.[27] The opinion of the court was written by Justice Joseph Story of Massachusetts, author of the widely cited *Commentaries on the Constitution* (1833) and one of the country's most respected legal theorists. He later claimed that he did not want to write the majority opinion, but the other justices persuaded him to, probably because they wanted his authority behind any ruling on the contentious fugitive slave issue. Story opposed slavery and the slave trade, but he despised the fanaticism of abolitionists. In the opinion, Story ruled Pennsylvania's 1826 law was unconstitutional because the power to regulate fugitive slave renditions lay exclusively with the federal government. This returned Margaret Morgan to slavery. Because the recovery of fugitive slaves was a federal matter, however, Story granted that states could prohibit their officials and facilities from being involved. In addition, he wrote that states could prosecute slaveholders if the recovery, even if legal, resulted in riot or violence.[28] Only two justices agreed with Story's argument. Chief Justice Roger B. Taney and other Southern justices particularly took issue with Story's position that states needed to render no aid to the capture or return of fugitives.[29]

Although Story would later claim that his opinion was a "triumph of freedom," one biographer, R. Kent Newmyer, believes that it was motivated more by Story's hatred of abolitionism than a desire to free fugitive slaves. It was, however, a vital step to nationalizing the fugitive slave issue. According to Newmyer, "*Prigg* set in motion forces that led directly to the [Fugitive Slave] act of 1850 and beyond it to *Dred Scott*."[30]

In the *Prigg* decision, the Court had ruled portions of Pennsylvania's 1826 personal liberty law unconstitutional. At the same time, the Supreme Court had opened the door for antislavery activists to argue that the rendition of fugitive slaves was exclusively a federal matter, in which state courts and law enforcement agencies did not have a role.[31] Story's intention may have been to shield the recovery of fugitive slaves from interfering state legislation, but the result was exactly the opposite. The *Prigg* case stood as the active federal guidance on the fugitive slave issue until the 1850 Fugitive Slave Law.

Antislavery activists were able to pass Pennsylvania's 1847 personal liberty law in response to *Prigg*. That law banned the participation of Pennsylvania law enforcement personnel, or the use of state facilities, to capture, hold, or return fugitive slaves. As there was no national police force to enforce the fugitive slave law, slave owners depended upon local law enforcement to help them recover their slaves.[32] They in turn often received part of the reward money. As in this case, it had been common for constables in south central Pennsylvania to capture suspected fugitive slaves.

The 1847 law hampered fugitive slave recovery by prohibiting slave owners from relying on constables who carried legal authority and knew the local landscape. Forbidding owners from using Pennsylvania jails and judges may have been even more significant, however. Regardless of whether a runaway had been arrested by a constable or was brought to town by a slave hunting party, fugitive slaves were typically held in the local jail while the master was notified to come and claim him or her.[33] Runaway ads from the 1820s from this area frequently mention the amount of reward if the fugitive was lodged in the Gettysburg or Carlisle jail. In addition, while Pennsylvania's 1826 act had imposed penalties for kidnapping, it had also made the state's judges an integral part of regularized fugitive slave renditions. Now Pennsylvania's constables, aldermen, and judges were forbidden to aid slave hunters.

In sum, *Prigg* and Pennsylvania's resulting 1847 personal liberty law made legal recovery of fugitives much more difficult. Rather than rely on agents, local helpers, and a constable to capture fugitive slaves and lodge them in a jail until they could be reclaimed, now in many instances a slave owner himself had to become involved in the dangerous business. With little practical recourse to federal officials in this area until the 1850s—the federal fugitive slave commissioner was an innovation of the 1850 law—those capturing runaways had to carry them back to Maryland or Virginia themselves, often passing watchful local residents. The whole slave catching party, engaged in what they believed to be a constitutionally sanctioned activity, could be placed in legal jeopardy under Pennsylvania's anti-kidnapping law. Pennsylvania's legislation was considered so obstructive that it was specifically cited as inflammatory by the Nashville Convention of 1850, which sought a unified Southern political movement. Even Southern moderates despised the law: Missouri Senator Thomas Hart Benton, no friend of John C. Calhoun and the radical Southern proslavery activists, blamed Pennsylvania in particular for exacerbating the sectional crisis through the 1847 personal liberty law.[34]

Before even the full ramifications of *Prigg* were understood and the new law was passed, Quakers and abolitionists in south central Pennsylvania determined to make recovering fugitive slaves more dangerous by zealous prosecutions under existing law. Although willing to disobey laws that conflicted with their conscience, through helping fugitive slaves or refusing to pay militia dues, Quakers also believed that the legal system could help the oppressed. The colony's founder, William Penn, had triumphed in a landmark English case establishing the right to trial by jury. Since its founding, Pennsylvania had more legal protections for defendants, such as fugitive slaves, than many states or colonies.[35] In the mid- to late 1840s, several kidnapping cases were brought in the south central region, one each in Adams, Cumberland, and Franklin County. While each case influenced the atmosphere around fugitive slave renditions, Adams County's "Kitty" Payne case is the best documented and most influential.

The "Kitty" Payne Case (1845)

This dramatic case illustrated the shift in antislavery tactics to emphasizing prosecutions of kidnappers. Prior to that point, while there had been disputes over the extent to which fugitive slaves received legal protection, there were few prosecutions in Adams County.[36] This was not as true in York County, where an attempt to prosecute a kidnapper had failed in 1822, and where in 1826, some citizens had attempted to impeach a judge for freeing a fugitive. In 1833, however, a case in eastern Pennsylvania, *Johnson v. Tompkins*, received attention. There, Quakers prosecuted several individuals as kidnappers who had seized African Americans in New Jersey and tried to carry them south under the "right of recaption." The U.S. Circuit Court ruled for the slave catchers. Justice Baldwin's charge to the jury indicated that his primary concern was maintaining the Union, and not Pennsylvania's law, which mandated a legal hearing in such a case.

Justice Baldwin may have ruled that slave catchers did not need a hearing in Pennsylvania to seize fugitives, but by 1834, an Adams County court case (*The State v. Negro Jim and Ephraim Valentine*) enters the record where a simple writ of removal would have appeared earlier. This is suggestive of legal barriers being erected to the return of fugitive slaves, but only that. It is not equivalent to prosecuting those who seized fugitives or free blacks. While Underground Railroad operatives aided fleeing fugitives, it seems few had used the courts to punish the seizure of African Americans.[37]

The Payne case changed that. Catherine "Kitty" Payne and her three children were seized early one morning in 1845 by white men who carried them to Maryland and then Virginia. The kidnapping party traveled south along the roads of Adams County, passing before houses and through villages, and were observed by local residents. The Whig paper, the *Adams Sentinel*, characterized the seizure as a "gross outrage" perpetrated by "citizens of a neighboring state assisted by others residing in the county of Franklin."[38]

Even more so than Adams County, Franklin County was a hunting ground for slave catchers. One of them, Thomas Finnegan, a Hagerstown slave hunter who roamed the area, played a key role in this case, because he knew the local geography. A warrant for him was sworn out the day after the seizure. When he traveled through Gettysburg in disguise months later, he was arrested after a lengthy chase. He was quickly implicated in other cases.[39] Even the Democratic *Republican Compiler* joined in, reporting that even while awaiting trial, he was involved in a thwarted kidnapping attempt in Emmitsburg.[40]

The seizure of the Paynes, like the *Prigg* case, stemmed from a generational conflict in border slaveholding. Aging owners had long relationships with their slaves, who they might wish to manumit as a reward for faithful service, but younger heirs saw primarily the wealth potential of their family's human property. Payne and her children had belonged to Samuel Maddox, Sr., of Rappahannock County, Virginia. Upon his death in 1837, he had willed Catherine and her children to his wife, Mary Maddox, during her lifetime. Afterward his entire estate, including the slaves, was to revert to his nephew, Samuel Maddox, Jr. In May 1843, Mary Maddox moved from Virginia to Adams County, where she rented a house. She and the Paynes lived there until March 1844, when she returned to Virginia.[41] Payne and her children remained in Adams County, living near Bendersville until July 24, 1845, when they were seized, bound and gagged by Samuel Maddox, Jr., Thomas Finnegan, and four others.[42]

Kitty Payne had been taken from the midst of an Adams County Quaker settlement. Local Quakers pursued her kidnappers to Rappahannock County, Virginia, visiting the incarcerated Payne. They were determined to see her freed and her kidnappers punished, and they worked with Quakers in Virginia to achieve her freedom.

Under more than one straightforward reading of Pennsylvania law, Kitty Payne and her children were entitled to freedom. According to the 1780 abolition act, visitors to the state could retain their slaves for only six months—and slaves brought by someone intending to become a permanent resident were freed immediately. Mary Maddox had stayed in Pennsylvania for nearly a year. In addition, in January 1844, before she returned to Virginia, Maddox had executed deeds of manumission for Kitty Payne, her two children, and several other slaves she had brought to Pennsylvania.

When Finnegan was tried for kidnapping in August 1846, the prosecution argued that he had played a leading role, "hunting up" the family and guiding the slave catchers. Perhaps because of ample witnesses to the slave hunters carrying the family from the state, the defense did not deny Finnegan's involvement. But they claimed that he was not implicated in the capture of the slaves; he had only driven the wagon that transported them.[43]

Finnegan had an unusually distinguished defense team to make this argument. Cases involving slavery usually attracted top border legal talent, with antislavery activists anxious to establish a new precedent and other area lawyers, often Democrats, wanting to reassure their Southern neighbors that the laws securing their property would be upheld. Finnegan's lawyers were John Reed and Thomas McKaig. Reed had lived in Gettysburg, had founded Dickinson College's School of Law, and was a lawyer and judge in Cumberland County. McKaig was a Maryland lawyer and legislator.

Despite the question about the extent of Finnegan's involvement, the principal legal issue debated at the trial was whether Mary Maddox could free the Paynes—whether she had received an absolute estate in the slaves or an estate for life only. Virginia's laws stated that any legatee who had slaves bequeathed to them for life forfeited them to the next owner if they were removed from the state.[44]

Finnegan's counsel argued that Maddox had been willed only a life estate in the slaves. Reed, Finnegan's lead attorney, argued for his innocence based on Virginia's limitations regarding when a slave could be manumitted. Like Thaddeus Stevens in the Charity Butler case twenty-four years previously, Reed contended that someone who was not the slave owner could not take the actions to free a slave under Pennsylvania law. He argued that the slaves were Mrs. Maddox's for life only, and she had ceased to own them when she left the state. As a result, the slaves brought into Pennsylvania belonged to Samuel Maddox, Jr., not Mary Maddox. Pennsylvania's law only conferred freedom on slaves if they were brought there by their "owner." Therefore their recapture was legal, and Finnegan, was "guilty of no crime, and must be acquitted." No kidnapping occurred helping a man reclaim his own property, even forcibly.[45]

Reed even courted local opinion by condemning kidnapping. He stated that he had no objection to Finnegan's conviction if it were proved that "Mrs. Maddox had an absolute estate." With perhaps some disdain for his client, he said, "It was the duty of the prisoner to look out before he seized on the persons of freemen," but he still expressed confidence that the jury would acquit Finnegan.

The defense also expressed fears about local antislavery sentiment. McKaig rose and described his fears that the area's "prejudices against the system of slavery" would injure his client. He stressed his local ties: He had lived in Adams County before moving to Ohio and then Maryland. Now he had returned to "restore this man to family and wife." McKaig argued that since Finnegan thought the Paynes were fugitives, he did not have the malice necessary for kidnapping. He carefully complimented the Quakers who had brought the case. Although he now owned five slaves, he praised abolitionists, believing that they lightened the burden of the slave and that public pressure was needed for "great reforms."[46]

The attorneys for Pennsylvania were also distinguished. The lead attorney, James Cooper, was Adams County's former Congressman and a future U.S. Senator. He was assisted by local lawyer Daniel Durkee, a protégé of Thaddeus Stevens. Cooper had also received training from Stevens, but Cooper was born in Maryland, and he and Stevens did not always agree on antislavery. Later they would become significant political rivals.[47]

Cooper's arguments reflected the development of antislavery and free soil concepts in border Pennsylvania. He reminded the jury that "every day" saw "attempts of slaves to escape from bondage" along the border. He invoked, as the prosecution frequently would, America's Revolutionary and Constitutional heritage. The Revolution was fought for freedom, which was now protected by the Constitution, except that "the slave interest" in the Constitutional Convention "inserted in it the article which authorized the reclamation of 'fugitives from labor,' escaping into the free States." This fugitive slave clause was part of the bargain Americans had made to ratify the Constitution. While the clause must be obeyed, Pennsylvanians must aggressively protect the liberties of all free men, lest their own freedoms be jeopardized.[48] Cooper extolled Pennsylvania's own history of emancipation; for him, the "chiefest glory" of the Pennsylvania statute book was "the [abolition] acts of 1780 and 1788." The Revolutionaries, after winning their own "redemption," passed these laws to ensure that the same blessings "might be extended to the whole brotherhood of man." Because a judge in Virginia had just declared the 1788 Pennsylvania law unconstitutional, Cooper's encomium to that law both supported his legal case and appealed to the jury's pride.[49]

Cooper was willing, however, to use that same Virginia judge's arguments when it helped his case. The issue of the Paynes' status had come before a Virginia court first after their forcible return there. That Virginia judge, while believing that Pennsylvania's 1826 legislation was unsupportable, had ruled that Mrs. Maddox had an absolute estate in the slaves and could free them if she desired. Because slave property was involved, he directed that the matter was not one for a court of law but a court of equity, where he had little doubt the Paynes would prevail. Citing his opinion, Cooper stated that "Mrs. Maddox did acquire an absolute title . . . to these slaves—a title full and ample for all purposes whatsoever—to sell, manumit, hire, or remove . . ."[50]

"Removing" was key to Cooper's concept of the case. He distinguished between the slave South and Pennsylvania's "free soil." "[H]aving removed with them [here]," he declared, "the moment [the slaves] placed foot upon our soil, the shackles fell . . . and under the operation of this great and glorious law which swept slavery from our borders, these poor victims of a miserable Institution emerged from slavish degradation and stood forth erect—free—free men and free-women as long as life shall last!"[51]

Cooper emphasized immediate liberation because of its rhetorical simplicity, and because of Mrs. Maddox's professed intention to live in Pennsylvania, not to sojourn less than six months. The argument also played well to the nascent free soil sentiment in southern Pennsylvania. Cooper could portray Pennsylvania as sacred ground, where the shackles fell off the instant a slave crossed the line, even though that was not always true.

Cooper's speech, in a local trial in border Adams County, Pennsylvania, reflects the expanding influence of what historians call "free soil" doctrines. Recent research shows that free soil ideas were arising nearly simultaneously in a number of different parts of the North, in response to local conditions. For instance, in New York, the precursors of free soil rhetoric emerged from the Anti-rent disputes against the large, absentee landlords of the state's unique and massive estates. In Pennsylvania, Cooper's argument shows that the early development of free soil concepts there emerged at least in part from the fugitive slave issue and the conception that Pennsylvania's earth did—or should—immediately unshackle bondspeople once they set foot on it.[52]

These concepts of free soil would continue to be developed in Pennsylvania politics, although James Cooper would not contribute to their maturation. After his election as Senator in 1849, Cooper moderated his position during the 1850 Congressional crisis, and he would be the Northern Senator who most consistently supported the Compromise measures. Thaddeus Stevens, however, continued to develop the free soil concept, and in 1850 the floor of the House of Representatives would ring with his fiery assertion that the instant escaping slaves touched free soil they would be free. In Stevens' case, he was referring to the western territories, but his argument, like Cooper's, had been forged from his experiences in border Pennsylvania.[53]

In his argument, Cooper reluctantly admitted that had Payne and her children been fugitive slaves, they could have been legally taken back to Virginia. He stated:

> If Mrs. Maddox had not such a right to these negroes as under the circumstances to entitle them to their freedom—if they were . . . "fugitives," then the broad wing of the Constitution, much as it might be regretted, stretched over them to reclaim them into slavery.

"Would to God," Cooper declared, the Constitution would have abolished "the shackles of servitude" and granted freedom to all—and then, he hinted, the South would have not fallen behind the North in economic development.[54]

To win their case, the prosecutors did not rely solely on legalities. In his opening argument, Cooper emphasized the heritage of Pennsylvania's Revolutionary War forefathers and their most "glorious" achievement, the abolition law. This strategy was aimed at swaying the case's presiding judge, Colonel William Irvine. Irvine was a Mercer County judge filling a temporary absence on the Adams County bench. Cooper knew that Judge Irvine was the son of a Carlisle doctor who had been a Revolutionary War companion of George Washington. William Irvine himself had served as Pennsylvania's acting Adjutant General during the War of 1812.[55] In closing, Cooper again appealed to the example of the Revolutionary Fathers:

Among all the laws of our ancestors, of those who fought the battles of the Revolution—there is no more humane, no more glorious law than that which strikes the manacles of the slave from his limbs as soon as he is brought upon our soil... I hope that this verdict may have the influence to deter men from attempting, upon our soil, to degrade the image of God into a hopeless bondage.

Despite the defense's efforts, the prosecution's arrows found their mark. Judge Irvine, the Revolutionary's son, charged the jury that "Mary Maddox took an absolute estate under the will of her husband; and that if the fact of taking and carrying away the negroes had been proved, the defendant was guilty." Whether the Paynes had been captured and carried away had not been in dispute at the trial, so this destroyed the defense's case. Even the defendant's chief counsel had stated that if Mrs. Maddox had an absolute estate, Finnegan should be convicted. After a short retirement, the jury returned a verdict of guilty. The defense immediately moved for a new trial because of the judge's charge. In November, this motion was denied, and Finnegan was sentenced to five years' imprisonment at Eastern State Penitentiary in Philadelphia. After a year and a half, he was pardoned by the governor.[56]

The Kitty Payne case in Pennsylvania was a victory for concepts of free soil and a hagiographic vision of the Pennsylvania's Revolutionary leaders as egalitarians. Finnegan was convicted, and Payne and her children returned to Adams County after a prolonged legal dispute in Virginia's courts, in which she received additional aid from Quakers in Pennsylvania and Virginia.[57]

The case did not end the efforts of area Quakers and antislavery activists to prosecute kidnappings. Both Franklin and Cumberland counties also had cases in the second half of the 1847 and an additional case was tried in Carlisle in 1850. The Finnegan/Payne case appears to have been a forerunner in a larger legal initiative by Quakers and antislavery activists to combat kidnappings in south central Pennsylvania.[58]

These cases allowed Quakers and their antislavery allies to focus attention on the fugitive slave issue and kidnapping. Kidnapping could be an even more volatile issue than the seizure of runaway slaves. A fugitive slave case concerned whether an African American would be sent back to the South; many south-central Pennsylvanians did not really care. A kidnapping case, however, could not only free a local African American family, it also could result in white perpetrators being sent to the penitentiary for extended periods. This brought additional attention to the cases and made them topics of local debate.

Consequently, kidnapping cases often struck a deeper chord with many Pennsylvanians than the fugitive slave issue. Only a few individuals outside of the African American community were willing to risk helping fugitives regularly, but kidnapping threatened the rights of all, at least as antislavery activists portrayed it. While antislavery newspapers tried to whip up fears of white slavery and the kidnapping of sunburned white farm girls (a case briefly agitated in the 1850s), most south central Pennsylvanians may have been more concerned about the Southern political power that could arbitrarily protect those who seized Pennsylvanians and carried them south without trial. That same Southern power might encroach on their rights and liberties in Pennsylvania, or in the western territories where they or their children might desire to go.[59]

Fugitive Slaves, Hot Pursuit, and the "Tragedy of the Commons"

Most area whites' response to fugitive slaves was distinctly limited. While many might spontaneously offer food or directions, only a few sympathetic abolitionists cared enough to offer sustained help. If a fugitive fled into south central Pennsylvania and was rapidly recaptured, it generally caused little concern, except among the region's African Americans, and only then in cases where they received ample warning.[60]

The Payne case, however, with its capture of individuals who had resided in the area for several years, is typical of many kidnapping cases. Along the border, some slaves were recovered "in hot pursuit," but many times it could be years before a fugitive was recaptured. This lag between escape and capture permitted a broader base of sympathy to develop for a captured fugitive than might have been the case for a newcomer. If Southerners had restricted themselves to recovering fugitives who had absconded for one year or less, then their image problems in the North might have been significantly less pronounced.[61] Of course, most slaveholders did not see it this way. They regarded escaped slaves as their lifelong chattel property, whether they had been missing for six months or six years. A delayed response sometimes reflected realities of Southern life. When a fugitive escaped, it might not be the best time to organize a pursuit. Many fugitives fled during the December holidays, or at harvest time, when it might be difficult to spare men to pursue slaves. It also could take time for Northern informers to report where the fugitives were.

When Southerners captured fugitives whose absence had been of a long duration, however, they were often seizing individuals who may have married, had children, and become part of a Northern community. In some cases, the captured fugitives were regarded as longstanding local citizens. The faceless fugitive had received an identity. It was the seizure of these individuals, such as the Paynes, which raised community ire beyond just a narrow circle of abolitionists. This reaction helped result in laws that made it more difficult for the recovery of all fugitive slaves.

It must also be admitted, however, that even if slaveholders had perceived that recovering a long-departed fugitive might turn Northern sentiment against them, it might not have changed their actions. In an innovative essay on the environment, "The Tragedy of the Commons," Garrett Hardin wrote that in many situations where individuals profit from something open to all, harmful activities are not sufficiently discouraged. This is true whether the benefit is Hardin's example of common grazing grounds, or the right to recover fugitive slaves under nineteenth century law. While everyone benefits from the property held in common (the land or the law), the costs of deleterious events that damage it are spread over all the users; they do not all accrue to the individual taking the harmful action. In Hardin's example, it was overgrazing; in this case, if a slave owner travels north and successfully recaptures his runaway slave, he has recovered his family's investment, even if the resulting outcry turns the section of the country into which he traveled even more resolutely against the further rendition of fugitive slaves. That cost is borne by future slaveholders trying to recover their slaves; he has received what he wanted.[62]

In the Kitty Payne and other kidnapping cases, we see this principle at work. Samuel Maddox briefly recovered what he maintained were his slaves, before determined Quaker legal action thwarted him; regardless of whether he had been successful or not, he may have turned many in south central Pennsylvania against the seizure of fugitives. In this environment, the legal strategy pursued by area Quakers and abolitionists showed substantial promise. Probably adopted in part because of the difficulty of building a mass antislavery organization along the border, this legal approach had seen Thomas Finnegan sentenced to the penitentiary, and his trial had generated significant publicity for antislavery opinions. This case almost certainly inspired the 1846 Adams County petition, which may have led to the successful 1847 petition campaign and the passage of the new personal liberty law. This law was then upheld in a Cumberland County case, *Pennsylvania v. Auld*, when a sixteen-year-old African American male had been drugged and carried south. It seemed as though support for the rights of Southern slave owners was declining. That was before the response, however, which would put the fugitive slave issue on trial in Pennsylvania into the 1850s.

The Fugitive Slave Issue on Trial: The Southern Response

With the ambiguous resolution of *Prigg v. Pennsylvania*, and the conviction of Finnegan, the friends of the fugitive were gaining momentum in south central Pennsylvania. When the legislature, responding to pressure from Quakers and southern Pennsylvania abolitionists, passed a strong personal liberty law in 1847, it seemed as if Pennsylvania might become a true refuge for fugitive slaves. Because the state lay just north of Virginia and Maryland, and shared a nearly 300-mile border with its slave state neighbors, this represented a threat to which Southern slave owners had to respond.

In this context, the law became a double-edged sword, which could be wielded by slave owners as much as by the friends of the fugitive. The federated system of the American judiciary created an opportunity for the Southern response. The opponents of slavery had been working on a local and state basis, in the county and state courts of Pennsylvania, as well as in the state legislature. If Southern slave owners and their allies, those who wanted to preserve sectional peace by easing recovery of fugitive slaves, could successfully win cases in the higher state and national courts, then they could trump the gains made by Quakers and antislavery activists.

This approach had several potential advantages. Advocates for fugitive slaves might be intimidated by prosecution. In addition, just as the courtroom gave antislavery supporters a prominent location to promote free soil doctrines, it gave Southerners and their supporters a place to argue that domestic slavery and the right to recover fugitive slaves should continue to be protected by the national government. As the Constitution itself contained a fugitive slave cause (Article 4, Section 2), which had been reinforced by the 1793 enabling legislation, slave owners were often able to prevail on legal grounds. The approach held risks, however. The battle for public opinion was not as successful. Some of their successes helped turn public opinion in Pennsylvania against them, souring the future social, political, and judicial environment.

Some of the first cases in this legal counteroffensive were in Cumberland County, which, like Adams and Franklin, had extensive economic and social ties to the South. Although not located directly on the Maryland border, Cumberland County was linked to the South through its military and educational institutions. A number of future high-ranking Confederate officers were instructed at the U.S. Army's Carlisle Barracks, a cavalry training school, and several at Dickinson College, which attracted the children of elite Southerners. One historian described it as a "favorite resort for young students" from "many prominent Virginia families."[63] Dickinson was also the alma mater of Marylander Roger Brooke Taney, the long-serving Chief Justice of the U.S. Supreme Court (1836–64).[64] Although twenty miles from the Mason-Dixon Line, Carlisle was a border town in spirit, with many residents anxious not to offend their Southern guests.

By 1847, however, the atmosphere was subtly changing. Dickinson was now a Methodist institution, after the disastrous disputes which had doomed its Presbyterian predecessor. Some of its faculty had been drawn into the 1840s controversy over slavery, which split the Methodist church into northern and southern wings. Because the early Methodist church had banned slave owning entirely, Northerners felt justified in insisting that church officers at least not hold slaves. This was an implied criticism of slavery, however. When a Methodist bishop in Georgia refused to free slaves he inherited, Southerners supported him. This dispute was particularly significant in the "borderlands," where church jurisdictions spanned the boundaries of Pennsylvania, Maryland, and Virginia. If a division occurred over slavery, an equitable way of parsing out church assets would have to be devised.[65]

The debate slowly turned from church governance to the morality of slavery. Dickinson College faculty made important contributions. John P. Durbin was Dickinson's president until 1845 and the editor of the *Christian Advocate and Journal* (New York). He used the pages of that national journal to promote a plan of gradual, compensated emancipation. Durbin tried to play a pacific role in the controversy, but his writings stirred up Southern resentment.[66] On the other hand, Professor John McClintock, an influential church intellectual, strongly opposed slavery and supported the Northern side of the Methodist dispute. In early 1847, he published a series of articles criticizing slavery in the *Christian Advocate*. These articles provoked a strong reaction, particularly when McClintock compared Christian slave owners who sold their slaves to Judas, who sold Jesus for thirty pieces of silver. McClintock also stated that the slave was more Christlike than the slaveholder. Controversy erupted, and the paper stopped printing McClintock's series, although it did not entirely disavow his sentiments.[67]

Into this charged environment intruded a party of fugitive slaves and their owner, bent on their recapture. He found them in the house of an African American resident of Carlisle and committed them to the county jail. When he brought them before a judge to authorize their removal, it resulted in tumult, escapes, and a near murder.

The area's African American community initiated most of this activity, but McClintock was arrested on charges of inciting the crowd to riot.[68] The riot case was noteworthy, because of McClintock's prestige. He was a nervous, excitable individual, but his colleagues regarded him as a genius. Some believed he was one of the most gifted preachers in the Methodist church.[69] He corresponded extensively with European intellectuals, especially August Comte. Later in his career, he would become the first president of Drew University. At this point, however, he was young and ardent, and the riot gave Southern slave owners the opportunity to strike back at him and intimidate those who would help fugitives.[70]

To convict McClintock of inciting to riot, the prosecution had to prove he had urged the African Americans to organized, unlawful resistance. This added to the drama, because in this case, the facts were in dispute. Unlike the Finnegan case, where both defense and prosecution basically agreed on the sequence of events and merely debated whether the individuals seized were still legally enslaved, in the McClintock riot case, the issue was whether—and how much—the professor had helped the fugitives escape.[71]

McClintock had been at the post office on June 2 when someone entered and told him that there was a party of fugitives about to be remanded south. He walked to the nearby courthouse and entered while the proceedings were in progress. He stationed himself near the defense table and conversed with one of the counsel. Soon McClintock heard Judge Samuel Hepburn rule that the sheriff had to release the African Americans on writ of habeas corpus, but since the slave hunting party had certificates of removal, they could then seize the fugitive slaves and take them south. McClintock animatedly insisted that a new law, just passed by the General Assembly, was relevant to this case. This was the 1847 personal liberty law, which forbade local constables from apprehending and holding fugitives, and judges from hearing the case. When Hepburn said he had never heard of such a law, McClintock left to retrieve a copy from his office at Dickinson a few blocks away. Some claimed, however, that first, after sparring with the prosecution, he turned to the prisoners in the dock and told them they were free to go. During the dispute between McClintock and the claimants, one fugitive escaped out of the back of the courthouse.[72]

Meanwhile, members of Carlisle's African American community had gathered outside, and when the other fugitives were brought out of the courthouse to be put in a carriage for transporting south, a rescue was attempted, enabling additional fugitives to escape. By now, McClintock had returned from his office, although he appeared as swept up in the events as everyone else. The slave owner, Thomas Kennedy, was knocked down and severely beaten. Kennedy seemed to recover after several weeks' convalescence, but then he died after eating at a Carlisle hotel. It is possible he succumbed to the lingering effects of undiagnosed internal injuries. If so, only the circumstances of his death being distant from his wounding, and the fact that the federal Fugitive Slave Act of 1850 did not yet exist, kept Carlisle from achieving as much fame in slave resistance as Christiana.[73]

At his trial, McClintock was represented by local counsel. Thaddeus Stevens had indicated a tentative willingness to defend him, but withdrew when the administration of Dickinson apologized for the incident. Stevens had wanted to try the case on his traditional antislavery issues of the human rights and the Declaration of Independence; his letter to McClintock indicates his disappointment that the administration wanted to minimize McClintock's involvement rather than defend it.[74]

The school's ambivalence stemmed from its finances. At the time, the state, as a result of budget constraints, was unable to support higher education. Robert Emory, Dickinson's president, was determined not to lose the school's Southern students, who had threatened to withdraw *en masse* over the incident.[75]

McClintock himself predicted that ample false witnesses would be found among "miserable creatures" in town, including "kidnappers &c." At the trial, many witnesses did appear against McClintock—"perjurer after perjurer" as Moncure Conway termed it—but their stories did not agree. Conway would become an abolitionist, Transcendentalist, and free thinker, but at the time, he was a Dickinson student from Virginia. The trial's transcript reveals charges and counter-charges, both damning and exculpatory evidence.[76] The defense argued that deliberate efforts were being made to drive McClintock from the town. The jury acquitted him, bringing a vigorous protest from the judge, Samuel Hepburn. Hepburn had been the judge in the Kennedy slave rendition hearing. Had it been a civil case, he said, he would have set McClintock's acquittal aside, but because it was a criminal trial, he felt he could not. The African Americans involved, however, were dealt with harshly: Ten were sentenced to the penitentiary. Many of these verdicts were later set aside or ameliorated on appeal after McClintock had been exonerated.[77]

Despite his acquittal, McClintock may have admitted there was a grain of truth behind the accusations. The next year it was rumored he would be offered the presidency of Dickinson College. McClintock demurred, insisting that the college needed someone older, less impetuous, and more sagacious. He soon left for a tour of Europe, then resigned from Dickinson and left the area, briefly returning when he purchased a house in the 1850s. If there had been a design behind the prosecutions, as some commentators allege, then the object may have been achieved by ultimately driving McClintock from the area. If the goal was to intimidate the local African American community from helping fugitive slaves, it is less clear if that was successful.[78]

The case received widespread publicity. In the North, it was followed by papers throughout south central Pennsylvania, Harrisburg, and Philadelphia. Reports of the case were also carried in leading New York papers; even just a few days before the riot, the *New York Tribune* had even labeled the curtailment of McClintock's *Christian Advocate* series the "Application of the Gag."[79]

Below the Mason-Dixon Line, the incident was characterized as an "alarming riot" as far south as South Carolina. The case especially convulsed the border. Particular interest was shown by newspapers in Baltimore, Richmond, and Kennedy's hometown of Hagerstown. In Baltimore, the *Sun* covered the case extensively and reprinted the trial transcript from the *Philadelphia Enquirer* over three separate days.[80] In Richmond, the incident caused strong reactions. The *Richmond Whig* struggled to have a measured response, but remarked that although the citizens of Carlisle condemned the "flagrant outrage," they should have done more to "*prevent*" the crime in the first place. The paper declared that through the incident Southern "rights have been attacked in the person of the murdered Kennedy."[81] The *Whig*'s correspondents were even more agitated. One letter writer asked how long such "outrages" could be borne, and is "the South to be abandoned lest the North be offended?" A correspondent from Martinsburg sent in the entire text of the 1847 personal liberty law, announcing that it had "the manifest design to *defeat the recovery* of an absconding slave." He predicted that Virginia's border counties would suffer the most from the legislation. A third correspondent urged the paper's readers to boycott Northern products and to press the legislature to exclude Northerners "from participation in our trade" through a high tariff on Northern goods. Papers in Richmond, Winchester, and Hagerstown also urged Southern students not to attend Dickinson College.[82] The animosity lingered; when Confederate forces briefly held Carlisle during the Gettysburg campaign, one Southern soldier wrote: "I wanted to see the building burned to the ground for it is one of the most intense antislavery literary institutions in the whole North."[83]

The McClintock trial represented one attempt to use the legal system to strike back at south central Pennsylvanians who helped fugitive slaves. Even though the professor was acquitted, with his refusal to be considered for Dickinson's presidency and his subsequent departure, it can be argued that those who brought the prosecution achieved their goal. This strategy of using the courts to cow area antislavery activists is illustrated by a second notable case: the Kaufman case.

The Kaufman Case (*Oliver v. Kaufman*; *Oliver v. Weakly*), 1847–52

Southern slaveholders were not merely interested in prosecuting those accused of enabling large-scale fugitive slave rescues; they also wanted to retaliate against more secretive aid to fugitives as well. The Daniel Kaufman case targeted another prominent Cumberland County resident. Kaufman had founded the little community of Boiling Springs south of Carlisle. His brother David migrated west and became a leading Texas Congressman, rising to chair the powerful House Rules Committee. Only his death in office may have prevented his rumored ascension to the U.S. Senate.[84] Like McClintock, Daniel Kaufman did not initiate the series of events that led to his arrest. Although he was a known Underground Railroad worker, he seems to have become wrapped up in this case almost by accident.

The Kaufman case unfolded several months before the McClintock riot. One night in December 1846, Robert Cole, an African American resident of Chambersburg, set out to transport ten fugitive slaves toward Harrisburg. The slaves had fled from a widow in central Maryland because they feared being sold from their late master's estate. This frequently happened to slaves when accounts were reconciled, estates divided, and debts settled. This large of a group of fugitives, including children, was hard to move surreptitiously, creating danger for everyone involved. The slaves had first gone to Chambersburg, where they stayed for several days, but that was too close to the widow's Washington County home, where a pursuit was being organized. So Cole undertook to transport them at night to the Ege iron works in Cumberland County, where there were hiding places for fugitives. Then they would be transported further.[85]

The trip was dogged by difficulties from the beginning. Cole fell behind schedule; then he had difficulty finding the paths across the South Mountain at night. As morning approached, he had not reached the ford across Yellow Breeches Creek, which led to the iron works. Traffic was increasing as laborers headed to work. How could Cole avoid detection with his conspicuous cargo?[86] With day breaking, Cole diverted to a side road. Finding Kaufman's house, he left the fugitives in his barn.

It is unclear whether the two men had ever met, or if Cole only knew of Kaufman by reputation. Presumably they knew each other, but such a link was never admitted at trial. When Kaufman came outside, Cole showed him the fugitives in the barn.

According to Cole—who testified at the trial in Kaufman's defense—Kaufman several times urged Cole to take the fugitives further. Cole said he could not, but promised to continue on to the iron furnace alone to see if he could hide them there. According to his testimony, however, he went to the furnace, ate a hearty meal, and then turned around and went back to Franklin County, after a perfunctory check on the fugitives.[87]

Kaufman did not act overly concerned, however. He fed the fugitives and made them comfortable. During the day, groups of locals came to gawk at them. Trial testimony established that Kaufman loaded up a wagon that evening— presumably with the slaves, who were never seen again—and disappeared into the gloom, returning with the wagon empty. Circumstantially, it was believed that Kaufman had carried them on.[88]

Cole and Kaufman's lack of caution came back to haunt them. Slave catchers were in pursuit, led by the widow's cousin. They arrived the next day, having been tipped off by locals that the slaves had been at Kaufman's. Failing to find Kaufman there, they warned his wife that both of them would be prosecuted for harboring the slaves. A suit was brought for the value of the fugitives, which likely also had the purpose of intimidating the Underground Railroad in south central Pennsylvania.[89]

The suit was originally argued before a Cumberland County jury. The key witness was Robert Cole, who testified that Kaufman had received the slaves very reluctantly. Kaufman's defense team argued that he had done nothing more than give the unfortunates he had found in his barn food and drink, basic humanitarian actions enjoined by the Bible; he had not "harbored" them. The judge's instructions to the jury suggested that this aid did not constitute harboring fugitive slaves, and the verdict was acquittal.[90]

The case was appealed to the state Supreme Court, which ruled that, because of *Prigg v. Pennsylvania*, it lay outside of the state's jurisdiction and should have been a federal case from the beginning. By now, the Kaufman case was increasing in prominence, and Thaddeus Stevens joined Kaufman's defense team. The case dragged on, finally being heard at federal district court in Philadelphia. Many of the original witnesses were subpoenaed, but Robert Cole did not answer his. He had moved on, probably to safer regions. Perhaps he was aided by the Underground Railroad himself.[91]

Kaufman was found guilty in federal court and fined several thousand dollars. As in the McClintock case, the Kaufman case received substantial notoriety and press. Eventually Kaufman's brother-in-law, Stephen Weakly, assumed the costs and liability.[92] Abolitionists publicized the case, with handbills circulated soliciting funds to pay the fine.[93] Philadelphia supporters reportedly gave $25 each, and even abolitionists outside of Pennsylvania became involved. New York abolitionist Samuel May contributed twice to Stephen F. Weakly's defense account, once for $200 and once for $77.98.[94]

The trial had driven Kaufman out of helping fugitive slaves, but other local Underground Railroad workers, including Weakly and Philip Brechbill, continued the operation. Kaufman's prosecution had illustrated the risks of keeping fugitives inside houses or barns, so Weakly and Brechbill started hiding fugitives on a small island in a swampy bog of Yellow Breeches Creek. This was an ideal location for all except the fugitives, who had to endure the mosquitoes and the damp. If the slaves were discovered in such a remote location, it would be harder to tie them to local abolitionists. Such a discovery would be difficult anyway—as with William Wright's home in Adams County, many of the surrounding property owners were sympathetic to antislavery.[95]

With the Kaufman and the McClintock cases, substantial energy had been devoted by Southern slaveholders and their Pennsylvania allies to retaliate against aid to fugitives in south central Pennsylvania. Had Kennedy died sooner after receiving his wounds in Carlisle, no doubt the outcry would have been even greater. These cases changed the approach of the area's Underground Railroad. Possibly on the advice of Thaddeus Stevens, one of Kaufman's counsel, south central Pennsylvania's friends of the fugitive began to alter their tactics to minimize their legal exposure. By regularly keeping outbuildings unlocked, for instance, a farmer could plausibly claim that he did not know that fugitives had slipped in.[96]

Both the McClintock and Kaufman cases were prosecuted under the 1793 Fugitive Slave Act. Although this act was national legislation, the effect of these cases was still largely regional, of greatest interest where the escapes were actually occurring. While fugitive slave escapes were troublesome to the South, most of the attention to the issue was from the border regions. Both major political parties supported the existing fugitive slave legislation, if reluctantly on the part of some Northerners.

This regional character of the fugitive slave issue would change with the passage of the federal Fugitive Slave Law of 1850. This law was part of the compromise package that was supposed to resolve sectional disputes left over from the Mexican War. Other sectional issues were added, such as the abolition of the interstate slave trade in Washington, D.C., and the fugitive slave issue. The Fugitive Slave Act was one of the few concessions to the South in the compromise. Through it, Southerners gained a tool to largely trump the personal liberty laws of Pennsylvania and other northern states. It was a Pyrrhic victory, however. Any hopes for intersectional cooperation on the return of fugitive slaves were substantially thwarted, and by making the fugitive slave issue a vital part of the compromise legislation, Southerners nationalized and politicized the fugitive slave issue to an unprecedented extent. Now federal officials would be involved; now, too, the nation's fugitive slave policies would become an integral part of the debate on the wisdom of the 1850 Compromise, the perceived rise of the Slave Power, and the sectional dispute. Northern newspapers that prior to 1850 might not have reported on a fugitive slave case in the next state or even the next county did so now because it was part of the national debate.

The Kaufman and McClintock cases were harbingers. They were about to be overshadowed by the most famous case of fugitive slave resistance in southern Pennsylvania: the Christiana Riot. Christiana would be the ultimate case of Southern slave owners striking back at those who aided fugitives, this time with charges of treason and the power of the federal government. Before Christiana, however, the Compromise of 1850 and the federal Fugitive Slave Act set the stage for the deadly confrontation.

5

Controversy and Christiana

The Fugitive Slave Issue in South Central Pennsylvania, 1850–51

The opening of the 1850s marked the beginning of a new era in Pennsylvania's protracted engagement with the fugitive slave issue. The state's new personal liberty law, passed in 1847, had largely superseded previous legislation passed in 1820 and 1826. More significant, however, was the federal Fugitive Slave Act of 1850, which gave new powers to the federal government and made new claims on ordinary citizens. As border Northerners divided on whether to help fugitive slaves or mollify Southern slaveholders by upholding federal law, the fugitive slave issue became a dynamic part of the partisan conflict of the early 1850s.

Political alignments were also shifting. The late 1840s had seen Whigs elected as President and as Pennsylvania's governor, but in 1850 the state's Democrats put the Whigs on the defensive by pushing to repeal the personal liberty law as the federal law was being debated in Congress and the press. Wary of being labeled radical, Union-splitting lawbreakers, most Whigs prevaricated. Soon most of both parties' leadership would accept the new law and the 1850 Compromise. In south central Pennsylvania, even some antislavery newspapers grudgingly adopted a "law and order" position in support of the new law. While the law did meet strong resistance from many abolitionists and African Americans, the early 1850s illustrated the difficulty of mobilizing a majority behind opposition to the fugitive slave law. At the same time, fugitives continued to flee into Pennsylvania, stirring up an issue many hoped had been resolved.

Antebellum South Central Pennsylvania Newspapers and the Fugitive Slave Issue

As a result of the increasing partisan conflict over the fugitive slave issue, in the 1850s, an important shift in source material takes place. The fugitive slave issue moves into the press much more regularly, and newspapers become increasingly important sources for examining local responses. In addition, other valuable sources were disappearing. In the aftermath of the Kaufman case, south central

Pennsylvania's Underground Railroad was becoming more careful. Court cases dry up in the region, although the Christiana riot would be extremely important and Philadelphia's Passmore Williamson case was also significant. In addition, the York Springs (Adams County) Anti-Slavery Society stopped meeting around 1847, ending pronouncements from that source.[1] Partisan newspapers, even with their distortions, become one of the best sources for insight into the fugitive slave issue in the area throughout the 1850s.

Before 1850, most fugitive slave cases were local, although a few, such as the McClintock riot and the Kaufman case, had regional significance. Perhaps only two fugitive slave cases had been nationally important: the kidnapping dispute between Pennsylvania and Virginia, which had led to the 1793 fugitive slave law, and the 1842 *Prigg* case, which further defined the operation of that law.

The Compromise of 1850, however, elevated and essentially nationalized the fugitive slave issue. The Fugitive Slave Act was the only part of the Compromise that could obligate the average Northerner. It was also the only part that Southerners saw as a vital concession, so both sections were vitally interested in its operation. A routine fugitive slave case, which before would have attracted scant attention a county away, now might be mentioned in newspapers across the country. The fugitive slave issue received a new level of publicity.

Newspapers, of course, are as much a part of the narrative of the fugitive slave issue as they are recorders of events and debates. How and why a newspaper reports a story is often as important as what it reports. Newspapers both influence, and are influenced by, public opinion. In the case of the fugitive slave issue in south central Pennsylvania, newspapers were not only chroniclers of events, but historical actors, which shaped—and were shaped by—the region's response to the controversial new law.

This was especially true because newspapers had a hybrid identity in antebellum America. They were both sources of information and partisan instruments. No paper was founded without a political purpose, and the press was critical to turning out supporters at elections. Local sentiment had to be heeded, as circulation and advertising revenue were important, but very few newspapers could survive on local revenue alone. Most newspapers were subsidized by political parties and candidates to provide favorable coverage. The truly fortunate newspaper could hope for contracts to do the government's printing if their candidates won.[2] These influences would moderate border Adams County's newspapers, which generally avoided the extremes of antislavery or Southern sympathy.

Table 3 Newspapers in Adams County, Pennsylvania, 1850–68

Name	Short Title	Editor	Perspective	Representative Political Influence
Republican Compiler	*Compiler*	Henry J. Stahle	Democrat 1850–68	James Buchanan
Adams Sentinel	*Sentinel*	Robert G. Harper	Whig 1850–56 Republican c. 1856–68	Henry Clay
Gettysburg Star & Republican Banner	*Star*	C. H. & D. A. Buehler 1850–57 J. McIlhenny 1857–68	"Conscience Whig" 1850–53 American (Nativist) 1854–58 Republican 1858–68	Thaddeus Stevens

Adams County had three significant newspapers. There was a strong Democratic paper, the *Republican Compiler*, with an important base among the county's Germans; a moderate Whig paper, the *Adams Sentinel*; and a reform paper best described at the beginning of the decade as "Conscience Whig," the *Star and Banner*. At different times, the *Compiler* and the *Sentinel* claimed to have the largest circulation in Adams County. Table 3 summarizes these papers and their positions.

The *Compiler* followed the lead of the national and state Democratic parties, which in turn were influenced by the national party's domination by Southern politicians. That meant that the ideological locus of the party lay south of the Mason-Dixon Line, and the paper generally avoided criticizing slavery, praised the execution of the fugitive slave law, and downplayed kidnapping cases. Still, the paper's viewpoint was not uniformly "pro-slavery," as its opponents would claim; occasionally the paper printed pieces critical of the extension of slavery or the domestic slave trade.[3] In the later 1850s, however, as the Democratic Party grew more defensive regarding slavery, such pieces disappeared, and the *Compiler* adopted a harsh anti-black tone.

The *Adams Sentinel* was a moderate Whig newspaper which regretted the passage of the 1850 Fugitive Slave Law, yet supported its enforcement on a "law and order" basis. The editor, Robert G. Harper, did not brook "fanatical abolitionists" and condemned any suggestion of resisting U.S. laws. The paper would later extensively publicize the disputes over Kansas, and Harper and the paper would eventually turn Republican, but his support for antislavery would be limited to free soil positions. He wanted to keep the territories free, but opposed the abolition of Southern slavery by the federal government.

The *Star and Republican Banner* was the most antislavery newspaper of the three. It had been founded in 1829 with a substantial investment by Thaddeus Stevens. The degree to which Stevens remained invested in the newspaper in the 1850s is unclear—he passed through a financial crisis and near-bankruptcy in the early 1840s—but the paper clearly had a special relationship with him and praised him frequently. In 1852, the *Star* claimed that its major priorities were "the reform movements" especially "Slavery and Temperance."[4] Still, even the *Star* could not appear to be too militant. As a rhetorical strategy, it usually offered half-apologies for running pieces on local fugitive slave hunts, and it often ostensibly differentiated its position from more extreme pieces it printed opposing slavery or the fugitive slave law. Of all the Gettysburg papers, it usually printed the most information about fugitive slave cases, and was accused of agitating the issue for political gain. There were periods, however, when the paper appeared disinterested, or grudgingly upheld the fugitive slave law on a "law and order" basis.

Why, in a bitterly disputed section of a critical electoral state, would an explosive issue like the fugitive slave issue at times be played down? Typically, antebellum newspapers ramped up the rhetoric in an effort to ensure party loyalty and high turnout on election day. Why would this volatile issue be sometimes ignored?

Such neglect of a divisive topic was likely not an attempt to attract crossover voters. Party switching, while not unheard of, was relatively rare (although the mid-to-late 1850s would be unusually volatile with the collapse of the Whigs engendering a political realignment). Instead, the answer appears to lie in the divisions in the border community over slavery. Even in the North, the Whig Party was not an antislavery party; neither were the Know Nothings, briefly ascendant in the mid-1850s. For the Whig newspapers in Gettysburg to continually agitate the fugitive slave issue risked driving away from the polls Whig voters who supported the 1850 Compromise. With the Whigs typically the minority party, this could be fatal. This was particularly true after 1851, when the national and state Whig Party reluctantly endorsed the Compromise, and even more so from 1852 on, after the resounding defeat of the antislavery governor William Johnston. The reform paper, the *Star*, would agitate the slavery issues more than the *Sentinel*, but even the *Star* would temper its criticism at times. The Democrats were less divided, but there were some in the party who strongly opposed Southern slavery or later became free soil Democrats. Their opposition in part was rooted in Democratic ideals of egalitarianism and Pennsylvania's legacy of opposition to slavery.[5] The Democrats did benefit from their ability to portray acquiescence to the fugitive slave laws as a "law and order" issue, upholding the Constitution, promoting sectional peace, and avoiding war. This was also why they opposed Pennsylvania's personal liberty laws, which interfered with federal fugitive slave laws.

The border-influenced perspectives of south central Pennsylvania's newspapers are important to consider, because an earlier generation of historians argued that the inflammatory rhetoric of newspapers, such as the *New York Tribune*, helped cause the Civil War.[6] Along the border in the early 1850s, however, local newspapers often expressed moderate positions on issues that could cause sectional rift. South central Pennsylvania's newspapers, although capable of biting invective, had to negotiate both the increasing sectional tension and residents' unease at the prospect of conflict or even war with their southern neighbors. Even with the toning down of criticism—often accounts of fugitive slave cases were printed without comment—the newspaper record still enables us to track the fugitive slave issue during the critical early years of the 1850s.

1850: The Year of the Fugitive Slave Law

In early 1850, a divided Congress confronted a sectional crisis intensified by the acquisition of territory after the Mexican War. The fugitive slave issue was rapidly injected into this debate. After Virginia Senator James Mason submitted a fugitive slave bill empowering all federal officials to hold rendition hearings, Henry Clay incorporated a new fugitive slave law into his package of compromise proposals.[7]

Daniel Webster, in his famous Seventh of March speech, supported Clay's proposals, including the proposed fugitive slave law. His endorsement ignited a firestorm of controversy among his Massachusetts constituency, but not in border Pennsylvania, where many, like Webster, supported the fugitive slave bill and sectional reconciliation.

As Congress considered the compromise proposals, Democratic-led "Union meetings" supporting it took place in Lancaster, Philadelphia, Baltimore, and New York. The fugitive slave issue was a critical point. A Democratic-dominated gathering in Philadelphia called "upon our State Legislature to repeal all laws conflicting with [the fugitive slave clause] of the Constitution . . . so that . . . the rights of our Southern brethren [may no longer be] trampled under foot."[8] In Adams County, the *Compiler* and the *Sentinel* felt that the Union was safe if radicals from both sides could be silenced. The *Star*, however, believed that threats of secession were a bluff. It criticized Mason's bill, "by which it is proposed to convert Postmasters, Deputy Marshals, and all other officers of the U. States, into supple tools of the Slave-dealers, and to compel them to assist in hunting up and sending back to chains . . . the fugitives from oppression."[9]

South central Pennsylvania's politicians also joined the debate. On June 9, 1850, James McLanahan, the Democratic Congressman from Franklin County, spoke in support of the Compromise. He said little about the proposed Fugitive Slave Act.[10] As McLanahan would later staunchly support the law, his silence here indicates an unwillingness to buck local sentiment against returning fugitives until the new law had been passed.

James Cooper responded somewhat differently. In 1837, Cooper had opposed antislavery lecturer Jonathan Blanchard on the courthouse steps in Gettysburg. In 1845, he had prosecuted Thomas Finnegan. Now, despite being just a freshman U.S. Senator from Pennsylvania, he became a significant voice of moderate, border Whiggery. He was the only Northern Whig Senator to consistently support the Compromise measures throughout the summer. Two days after McLanahan's speech, Cooper addressed the Senate in support of the Compromise. Perhaps deliberately, he ran out of time before commenting on the fugitive slave bill, but he implied that regardless of his sympathy for runaways, he did not object to the proposed law.[11]

Recently, Michael Holt, a leading scholar of the 1850 Compromise, has portrayed Cooper as an antislavery politician who altered his stance during the critical year of 1850, but Cooper was always a committed border moderate with ties on both sides of the Mason-Dixon Line.[12] He was born and would be buried in Frederick, Maryland. In 1860, he returned to Maryland to lead one of the state's Union regiments. Educated in border Pennsylvania, he lived in Adams County until the late 1840s. During election season, in antislavery areas, his supporters celebrated his defense of fugitives in Adams County.[13] Certainly, he was critical of slavery during the 1845 trial of Thomas Finnegan and in his June 11 speech. Cooper, however, was nowhere near as radical as Thaddeus Stevens, an associate in Gettysburg, and increasingly was in opposition to him. During the Christiana trial in 1851, Cooper served as prosecutor, collecting pay from the state of Maryland, while Stevens helped lead the defense. Any opposition to slavery on Cooper's part had always been measured, and mingled with his savvy as a border politician.

In February 1850, Cooper damaged his standing among his antislavery constituents by criticizing disunion petitions from Quakers and abolitionists in Delaware and Pennsylvania.[14] After his June 11 speech, Pennsylvania's antislavery Whigs wondered if Cooper was insane, but his stock was rising nationally even as it declined in Pennsylvania antislavery circles.[15] Henry Clay appointed Cooper to the Select Committee on California, the Territories, and Slavery (the Compromise Committee, or "Committee of Thirteen"). This was exalted status for a freshman Senator and explains why Holt considered Cooper one of the key Northern figures during the Compromise summer.[16]

Both the Democrat McLanahan and the Whig Cooper had supported the compromise measures and gave important expressions of south central Pennsylvania sentiment on the Compromise and fugitive slave bill. It would be the fiery explication of emerging Free Soil doctrine by the flamboyant Thaddeus Stevens, a former area resident now representing Lancaster in Congress, which would generate the most controversy.[17]

Stevens delivered his speech against the Compromise on June 10, arguing that the territories were by nature free. In an important foreshadowing of the stance he would take toward the South during Reconstruction, Stevens argued that the Constitution and its compromises did not extend to the U.S. territories, which were solely under the jurisdiction of Congress. Stevens opposed the Fugitive Slave Bill because it explicitly included the territories. He maintained that the existing fugitive slave law, which only referenced "states" and not "territories," did not extend to the latter. In regard to the lands acquired from Mexico, he held that only a treaty could extend U.S. jurisdiction there; old laws remained in force until explicitly changed. This reasoning allowed Stevens to argue that all the new western territories should be free, and that slaves escaping to the territories were instantly free.

Stevens' logic reflected his career as a border lawyer in Gettysburg and Lancaster. His legal experiences, including with the Kaufman case, made him familiar with the English 1773 *Somersett* case. There, Lord Mansfield had ruled that by general, common law, humans were free and only by explicit, special law could they be enslaved. For Stevens, this principle meant that a slave escaping to free soil was immediately liberated. In the states, Stevens explained, that legal principle was contravened by the fugitive slave clause of the U.S. Constitution, which required states to deliver up escaping slaves. But common law still extended to the territories, and a slave taken to the territories "becomes a man," with an immediate, "vested inalienable right to liberty." Stevens also warned that his constituents would never join slave posses, as called for in the bill.

Stevens' argument was based on the startling contention that the U.S. Constitution was not law in federal territories. Although the *Somersett* case had been used for decades to argue for the freedom of slaves, few had applied it to the territories in this way.[18]

The reaction to Stevens' remarks was as intense as the speech itself. The *Compiler* reprinted a piece from the Lancaster *Intelligencer*, which suggested that more speeches like Stevens' would "result in disunion." The *Star*, conversely, wished that the new Fugitive Slave Act would be stricken from the compromise.[19]

Many opponents to slavery extension would eventually adopt similar reasoning, even if they could not swallow Stevens' boldest contentions about the common law. His ideas were analogous to Salmon P. Chase's concept of freedom as national, slavery as sectional. Stevens' concepts, like Chase's, were firmly rooted in border fugitive slave cases and litigation. In his speech, Stevens cited the Kaufman case and that of another Pennsylvania farmer, Robert Mitchell, as evidence that existing fugitive slave laws were too strict, not too lax. He used his familiarity with the fugitive slave issue in border Pennsylvania to develop and articulate his free soil ideal. With Stevens' speech, and to a lesser extent Cooper's, arguments developed along the "edge of freedom" were influencing Congressional debate at a critical juncture.

Pennsylvania: The Debate over Repeal of the 1847 Personal Liberty Law

As controversy over the Fugitive Slave Bill unfolded in Congress, Pennsylvania's Democrats angled for political advantage by trying to overturn the state's 1847 personal liberty law. This repeal effort began after Governor Johnston militantly rejected resolutions by Maryland and Virginia's legislatures asking that Pennsylvania better enforce existing fugitive slave law. Johnston's special message to Pennsylvania's legislature in March complained that Virginia and Maryland had failed to extradite kidnapping suspects sought by Pennsylvania. He also favored admitting more testimony and requiring additional proof in fugitive slave cases. In a message ostensibly about fugitive slaves, he also advocated slavery's exclusion from the territories and the end of slavery in the District of Columbia, and criticized the inflated size of Southern Congressional representation because of the Three-Fifths clause of the Constitution.[20]

Johnston's statements were a bold proclamation of free soil principles by a border governor in 1850, and were published in the most antislavery paper in Adams County. The *Star* claimed Johnston had "vindicated" Pennsylvania.[21]

The Democrats felt otherwise. A week later, James Buchanan was in Harris-burg, anxious about the repeal effort. Buchanan, recently U.S. Secretary of State (1845–49), was probably the most powerful politician in Pennsylvania.[22] He, the state Democrats, and possibly even the national party were keenly interested in the repeal effort.[23]

When a partial repeal of the 1847 law did pass, Johnston vetoed it. Now Democrats could attack Johnston and the Whigs for interfering with fugitive slave laws.[24]

Fugitive Slave Cases in the South Central Pennsylvania Press in 1850

With the fugitive slave issue looming in both Congress and the state legislature, all of Gettysburg's papers began reporting more frequently on fugitive slave cases. The *Compiler* and the *Sentinel*, however, did not start intensive coverage until September, when the Fugitive Slave Law was passed. The *Star* began de-tailed reporting in June. The paper described how the pursuit of a fugitive slave from Carroll County, Maryland was thwarted near Gettysburg by a local African American. He spotted a slave catcher ordering a horse and carriage, and rode off and warned the fugitive. The *Star* crowed, "the Slave was saved!" After giving this incident unusual publicity, the paper closed with a characteristic half-apology: "Thus ended the latest slave-hunt in these parts, which, as chroniclers of passing events, we have deemed it our duty to notice."[25]

In August, both the *Star* and the *Compiler* reported on a slave hunt near Shrewsbury in adjacent York County. A gang accosted eleven fugitive slaves in a barn just north of the border and apprehended seven. Two soon escaped, but the other five may have been duped into believing that they were being helped, not captured. When they were loaded into a railroad car for Baltimore, they realized their betrayal and engaged in a shootout with their captors. Later, when this same group of slave catchers captured more fugitives, the *Star* complained, "The set of mercenary wretches around Shrewsbury are at it again. . . . Of all men, these negro catchers in free States . . . are the meanest, and they would coin their souls for dollars."[26]

Both state parties and their newspapers were trying to figure out how to han-dle the explosive Fugitive Slave Bill, and were inconsistent. Rather than agitate the issue initially, they temporized. When the Compromise agitation was ap-proaching a fever height, the *Star*, in a reprinted article, listed slavery as only number seven on a list of troubles facing the country—after the need for tariff.[27]

Similarly, messages from the state Whig Central Committee and the Lancaster Whig Committee focused mainly on the tariff also. The August letter from the Democratic State Central Committee said little about the compromise or slavery. Along the border, both major parties may have been avoiding splits in their organizations, downplaying slavery and the fugitive slave issue while waiting to appraise the political landscape.[28]

Both the Democratic *Compiler* and the Whig *Star* reported on an attempted rescue of runaways in Harrisburg. Three fugitive slaves had been charged with stealing horses as they fled. Because they had eventually released the animals, Judge John Pearson decided that they were technically innocent of horse theft, but he told the masters they could claim the slaves. When they tried to do so, a melee erupted, and the Harrisburg militia was called out. The masters, the slaves, and several others were arrested. Ultimately—and typically—the fugitives were remanded to their owners while the white captors were acquitted of riot.[29]

The Harrisburg case illustrates the development of tactics to circumvent personal liberty laws. Pennsylvania's 1847 law prohibited using state prisons and jails to hold fugitive slaves, and incarceration in a private home was very risky. Professional slave catchers, then, usually in concert with a constable, would seize fugitives, charge them with a petty crime so that they could be imprisoned, and notify the owner to come and claim the slave. Charging fugitives with a crime also enabled state officials including constables and judges to become involved in the case.[30]

The disturbance in Harrisburg was not an anomaly; resistance to the operation of the Fugitive Slave Law there was pronounced. In November, the *Star* reported on a convention of Harrisburg African Americans opposing the new law. The group announced their determination to help fugitives:

> Resolved, That we, as heretofore, will assist the flying bondmen to escape—that we will give them food and shelter—and if it be that we have to suffer, or drag out weary months in prison, and be subjected to cruel fines, for acting the part of the good Samaritan, we will cheerfully submit . . .
>
> Resolved, That as R. S. McAllister, U.S. Commissioner for Dauphin County, one of the Vestrymen of the Episcopal Church of this place, is an aspiring man, we congratulate him on his fortunate elevation as CHIEF KIDNAPPER of this County.[31]

McAllister should have heeded this warning. His tenure as Harrisburg fugitive slave commissioner would be very controversial; several area deputies and marshals would be indicted for kidnapping. McAllister himself would join a train of emigrants heading to Kansas, rather than remain in Harrisburg.[32]

In nearby Lancaster County, African Americans also determined to resist the law, with force if necessary. The county's abolitionists passed a resolution in October proclaiming that they would "harbor, feed and aid" escaping fugitives, and would "obey no such [fugitive slave] law." William Parker, who would lead the resistance, and other local African Americans organized a self-protection society to forcibly oppose both kidnappings and fugitive slave seizures.[33]

Lancaster County was the new home of Thaddeus Stevens. It had a large population of African Americans and was tied economically and socially to the state's Quakers and abolitionists in eastern Pennsylvania. No such determination to openly defy the law was evident in south central Pennsylvania in 1850.

Elsewhere, entire neighborhoods were emptying out as a result of the new law. Three hundred African Americans reportedly moved north toward Canada from Pittsburgh. The *Compiler* claimed that forty-five had passed through Erie in just one day. The *Star* reported on thirteen fugitives overtaken at Wilkes-Barre, on their way to Canada.[34]

After initial indecision, by the last quarter of the year, the Adams County newspapers had staked out varying positions on the Fugitive Slave Law. The federal law appointed independent federal Fugitive Slave Law commissioners to try fugitive slave cases, paid them double for ruling the individual was a slave ($10 vs. $5), established hefty penalties for interfering with the law's operation, and put white Northerners at risk of being summoned to help capture fugitives. The *Compiler* and the moderate Whig paper, the *Adams Sentinel*, supported the law. The *Star* opposed it, although its criticisms were sometimes muted. Only the *Star* published the actual text of the law, concluding:

Probably no law, enacted by the General Government for the last fifty years, has drawn forth a more general and decided . . . condemnation. . . . Passed as a part and parcel of the "compromise" measures which were to quiet agitation and restore peace and harmony to the country, it has most signally failed. . . . Instead . . . it . . . threatens to lash into greater fury than ever the waves of popular feeling . . .

With this editorial, the *Star* reprinted a detailed critique of the law from the *National Era*, an antislavery newspaper published by Gamaliel Bailey. Bailey was a child of the border: Born in Mount Holly, New Jersey, where Lydia Lundy Wierman had lived, and raised in Philadelphia, he had edited James Birney's antislavery publication in Cincinnati and also a newspaper in Baltimore. In July 1851, the paper began serializing *Uncle Tom's Cabin*. Here, nine months earlier, the *Era* predicted that the law would force the antislavery issue into every Northern election.[35]

This prediction was largely fulfilled, and the new law and the fall elections further politicized ongoing legal proceedings related to fugitive slaves. In late October, the appeal of the Kaufman case, now called *Oliver v. Weakly*, was heard in federal court. Stephen Weakly, Kaufman's brother-in-law, had assumed his legal liability. Thaddeus Stevens, his counsel, made a controversial closing argument. According to the unfriendly *Compiler*, Stevens had denounced the Compromise as "hateful," and urged Pennsylvanians to follow higher law, a "detestable doctrine" to the paper. Even the *Star* thought Stevens' comments extreme. (Stevens claimed to have been misquoted and threatened a libel suit.) The jury ultimately split 10–2, and Judge Robert Grier dismissed them reluctantly. The case would be tried again.[36]

Nationally, President Millard Fillmore and his attorney general affirmed the new law's constitutionality.[37] Hemmed in by a publicized escape in Boston, Fillmore, in a widely reprinted letter to a Georgia newspaper, promised that the law would be "faithfully executed," and announced that he was staking his administration's success on it. Fillmore later called the Compromise the "final settlement" of issues related to slavery.[38]

Fillmore's asserted his leadership because after Congress recessed, the initiative on the fugitive slave issue had passed briefly to the states. Vermont's state legislature passed a personal liberty law guaranteeing the writ of habeas corpus and essentially nullifying the Fugitive Slave Law. Virginia's governor John Floyd condemned the Vermont "nullifiers" and called for a Southern convention. In Georgia, a state convention warned that preserving the Union relied on the "faithful execution of the Fugitive Slave Bill." The resolution was quite similar to that passed by the Nashville Convention in the summer, which had gathered to consider secession. That body had specifically criticized Pennsylvania's personal liberty law, asking in its address to the Southern states what United States' officers could do "in such a State as Pennsylvania to recover fugitive slaves?"[39]

The Challenge to South Central Pennsylvania's Whigs

By November of 1850, Pennsylvania's Whigs were in trouble. They had lost ground in the November Congressional elections in Pennsylvania, New Jersey, Delaware, New York, and Massachusetts.[40] Adams County's Whigs were also in disarray. Daniel Smyser, a Stevens' protégé, had narrowly edged David Mellinger to become the party's 1850 Congressional candidate. Mellinger came from the local Whig stronghold of York Springs. The county's Whigs were unable to run an ally of a powerful regional politician without alienating support in their strongest region, and Smyser was defeated in November.[41]

In Pennsylvania, trouble had started several years before, with the development of a serious rivalry between two of the state's leading Whigs. James Cooper, Adams County's favorite son and the state's Attorney General, had lobbied for the Whig gubernatorial nomination in 1847. When it went to James Irvin instead, who lost to Democratic governor Francis Shunk, Cooper expected to be nominated the next time. When Shunk resigned in 1848 because of illness, under Pennsylvania's succession system, the Speaker of the Senate became governor. The Speaker, William F. Johnston, was a Whig, so the process essentially thwarted the preference of the electorate. After a brief interim, Johnston called a special election, and, with Cooper's backing, secured the Whig nomination. He then defeated Morris Longstreth (D) by a mere 302 votes in the closest gubernatorial election in state history.[42]

In exchange for supporting Johnston for governor, Cooper expected that Johnston would back him for the U.S. Senate seat coming vacant in March 1849. But there were few simple Senatorial selections in mid–nineteenth century Pennsylvania. When the legislature did convene, a number of candidates were put forward, including Thaddeus Stevens. The Philadelphia-based Native Americans, a key nativist constituency for Johnston, expressed concerns about Cooper. The governor declared his neutrality. Cooper eventually won on the third ballot, but the rift between him and Johnston would not be healed. The animosity became so bitter that several years later the Democratic papers announced, erroneously, that they would fight a duel.[43]

Johnston and Cooper's rivalry hamstrung Pennsylvania's Whigs at a critical moment. The party was struggling to define its positions on slavery and the Fugitive Slave Law, and the two politicians represented differing Whig philosophies. Johnston had supported Zachary Taylor's hard line toward the South, while Cooper was a Henry Clay moderate. Both had numerous allies, and this factionalized Pennsylvania's Whig Party, boosting the Democrats just when their hegemony in state politics was being threatened. In Gettysburg, the *Compiler* crowed over the growing split between the Silver Greys (conservative Whigs), and the Wooly Heads, a derogatory, racist term for antislavery Whigs.[44]

By the end of the 1850s, the fugitive slave issue, little noticed when the year began, had become one of the most important political issues in border Pennsylvania. As the year closed, the Adams County newspapers were following important incidents in Carlisle and Philadelphia. In fact, in this atmosphere, nearly every fugitive slave case was news: the Compromise had essentially nationalized the fugitive slave issue. This was particularly true in Pennsylvania, where the Christiana riot would explode into national and state consciousness in 1851.

1851: Preamble to Christiana

In 1850, the fugitive slave issue had reached prominence largely because of national developments—the introduction of Mason's bill, the evolution of the Compromise, and the long shadows cast by Calhoun, Webster, and Clay. Even events specific to Pennsylvania, such as the effort by Democrats to repeal the state's 1847 personal liberty law, had been sparked by the federal bill and by an appeal of Virginia and Maryland to Pennsylvania's legislature. In 1851, the situation nearly reversed. Now it would be the events inside Pennsylvania that would influence the state and the nation regarding fugitive slaves, instead of the other way around. Two significant, intersecting events contributed to this reversal: the Pennsylvania gubernatorial campaign, which stoked the controversy over the 1847 personal liberty law, and the Christiana riot in September 1851, in the midst of the hotly contested governor's race, with the resulting trial in November and December. Other events, such as two fugitive slave cases in Boston, were also important, but this year, it was events inside Pennsylvania that had the biggest effect on the course of the fugitive slave issue there.

All three Adams County newspapers gave as much or more coverage of the fugitive slave issue in this year than any other. Still, before the Christiana riot, Democrats and Whigs had gradually converged on support for the 1850 Compromise. This muted criticism of the Fugitive Slave Law, even among antislavery papers such as the *Star*. In fact, early in the year, both political events and the response of the newspapers seemed to be pushing toward a grudging acceptance of the Fugitive Slave Law.

This convergence was foreshadowed by Governor Johnston's annual message in January. He devoted thirteen full paragraphs to the fugitive slave issue. With both parties believing that most of the state's populace backed the Compromise, Johnston's rhetoric had mellowed. The governor stated that the federal law must be completely obeyed. He maintained that the 1847 personal liberty law did not interfere with fugitive slave renditions, but reiterated that states had no role in returning fugitives—had the Founders intended that, they would have put it in the Constitution. He desired that a record be made of fugitive slave hearings; that a judge, not a commissioner, preside (because a judge could be impeached); and that those who falsely claimed fugitives be chargeable with kidnapping. In sum, Johnston was trying to have it both ways, ostensibly supporting the federal law while maintaining Pennsylvania's right not to aid fugitive slave renditions.[45]

In Congress, while antislavery Congressmen such as Joshua Giddings still militated against the law, there was increasing pressure to support the Fugitive Slave Law and label the Compromise a "final settlement" of slavery issues (James McLanahan, the Democratic Congressman from Chambersburg, offered one of a number of resolutions declaring it "inexpedient" to repeal the Fugitive Slave Law).[46] In the Senate, James Cooper was involved in a sectional contretemps involving southern Pennsylvania's loyalty to the Fugitive Slave Act. When Cooper, in response to a petition urging modification of the Fugitive Slave Law, said that most Pennsylvanians wanted to follow the law, he attracted the attention of one of the South's leading legislators. South Carolina's Robert Barnwell Rhett asked Cooper if the state's personal liberty law had been repealed. Cooper said that the majority of his constituents favored carrying out the Fugitive Slave Law, but the personal liberty law had not been repealed "because of local politics, not necessary to be explained." Rhett was dubious that the Fugitive Slave Law would ever be enforced by Northerners. He pounced on Cooper's statement and declared, "The laws of Pennsylvania had not been repealed, nor would they be. The mercantile interests of Pennsylvania and New York might be in favor of executing the law, but the interior counties would never execute it." This 1851 comment by a leading Southern fire-eater is telling. Pennsylvania's south central counties were perceived to be part of a region where enforcement of the Fugitive Slave Law was very difficult.[47]

The ferment in Congress led to more "Union meetings" in York, Philadelphia, and elsewhere, typically organized by Democrats. In March, the *Star* reported on a Union meeting of Whigs for once. Showing the deep divisions in the Whig Party over the fugitive slave issue, "a large meeting" of Whigs in Philadelphia met on February 27. They passed resolutions supporting the 1850 Compromise and instructing their representatives to "use all possible diligence to secure the passage of a bill repealing the obnoxious sections of the Act of Assembly of the 3[r]d of March, 1847 [the personal liberty law]." The *Star* had campaigned in 1850 against repealing the personal liberty law; now, in a sign of shifting sentiment on the fugitive slave issue, it let stand, without comment, the "obnoxious" reference.[48] It also started publishing pieces on colonization again.[49]

Soon, the coverage of all three Adams County papers was dominated by the Shadrach fugitive slave case in Boston. Shadrach Wilkins, a waiter, had been seized as a fugitive and then rescued by a mob from a home where he was being held. (The mob was aided by the fact that Massachusetts' laws, like Pennsylvania's, forbade the use of jails to house fugitives).[50] Southern pressure forced President Fillmore to reiterate his determination to enforce the Fugitive Slave Law. The *Star*, the paper once founded and extensively bankrolled by Thaddeus Stevens, used this occasion to declare its moderation on the issue. Rather than laud the rescuers of Shadrach, the editors supported the President's proclamation, decried mob law, and opined that while the Fugitive Slave Law was flawed, it must be amended or repealed using lawful means.[51]

This shift to emphasizing obedience to the law occurred when many news reports of cases began to stress increasing violence. In one example, slave catchers near Coatesville forced their way into a house at 2:00 A.M. The residents fought them off using guns and axes.[52] In Pottsville, African Americans surrounded a fugitive's house to prevent her capture. Apparently reflecting its more conservative position, the *Star* commented inaccurately, "The matter elicited little excitement," but this may have been true: "few white persons have cared to trouble themselves about it."[53] In Columbia, abolitionist lecturer C. C. Burleigh was forcibly kept from speaking on the Fugitive Slave Law. Noted African American entrepreneur William Whipper was stoned during an attack on his house.[54]

The *Star*'s more temperate stance regarding the Fugitive Slave Law did not lessen its reporting of kidnapping, a way the paper could criticize the capture of African Americans without advocating law-breaking. An advertisement inadvertently dropped at the scene of one violent "kidnapping outrage" near Delaware indicated that the kidnappers might be from Emmitsburg, Maryland, just thirteen miles from Gettysburg.[55] In another case, Judge John J. Pearson, presiding over the case of two accused kidnappers, George Alberti and James F. Pierce, called kidnapping a "revolting" crime, "second only to homicide," and the case "the most aggravated . . . that has ever been presented to the American Court of Justice." Both defendants were fined $700 and given ten years in the penitentiary—sentences that Pearson said might err on the side of leniency.[56] This enraged supporters of close ties to Pennsylvania's southern neighbors.

In April, another fugitive slave case erupted in Boston. Despite strenuous efforts by Boston abolitionists, Anthony Sims was seized, ruled a fugitive slave, and ordered returned to his master. He was eventually marched down to the dock under U.S. military guard and sent back by ship to Georgia. There he was publicly flogged.[57]

All of the Adams County and Harrisburg newspapers reported extensively on the Sims case. The Harrisburg papers were frequently read in south central Pennsylvania, and sometimes their pieces were reprinted verbatim by local papers.

One of the papers that stirred up the Boston fugitive slave cases the most was the Harrisburg *Daily American*, where a young editor named Edward McPherson was working. He was the son of John B. McPherson, the long-standing cashier of the Gettysburg bank and business associate of Thaddeus Stevens. Some local sources claim that the McPherson farm was a station on the Adams County Underground Railroad. Edward McPherson had served an informal apprenticeship in the offices of the *Sentinel*. He claimed to favor abiding by the Fugitive Slave Law, but because he ran a daily paper, he could publicize cases to a greater extent than Adams County's weeklies. Edward McPherson later became the area's Congressman, and the Sims case may have been an important part of his early political education.[58]

Some Pennsylvania juries, like some Pennsylvania newspapers, were also trying to find a middle ground in fugitive slave and kidnapping cases. In Lebanon County, two Harrisburg men—one a constable—were charged with trying to abduct African Americans to Maryland. The jury acquitted them of kidnapping, but found them guilty of assault and battery. As this charge was not in the indictment, the *Star* noted that the conviction would be set aside at the next court. The jury's actions probably represented a backlash against Judge Pearson's harsh sentences under the 1847 law. Rather than find these men guilty of kidnapping, the crime "second only to homicide," this jury chose to convict them of lesser crimes with lighter punishments than years in the penitentiary.[59]

Renewed efforts to repeal the personal liberty law ensured that the issue stayed before the state legislature. While the *Compiler* noted approvingly that the bill to repeal the 1847 law had passed the Senate and would "doubtless" pass the House, the *Star* had a different perspective.[60] When the House bill overturning the legislation reached the Senate, all of the repealing clauses were stripped from it except for the one prohibiting the state's jails from being used to house fugitives. Even though seven Whig Senators voted against that bill, the *Star* tried to deflect Democratic criticisms that Whigs opposed the bill, claiming (based on a unanimous Whig vote to limit the repeal to just the section on jails) that all Whigs had voted for the one section that passed.[61] This was misleading and indicates the strength of the repeal movement and a desire by the *Star* to avoid having Whigs associated with a radical position on the personal liberty law. The final decision was deferred, however, because Governor Johnston pocketed the bill.[62]

This temporizing by the *Star*, the most antislavery of the Gettysburg papers, corresponded with its movement toward accepting the Fugitive Slave Law on the basis of maintaining law and order. This is illustrated by the newspaper's remarks on a Harrisburg fugitive slave case. A man, a woman, and a child had been arrested as fugitives—the man belonged to one Maryland slave owner, the woman and child to another. Despite the presence of a large group of African Americans "at every corner, in the jail, in the Court House, and in front of McAllister's office," the commissioner was not intimidated, and he "proceeded to the discharge of his onerous duty, in the most fearless and impartial manner." While commenting that the slaves were objects of "universal sympathy," the paper did not object to McAllister fulfilling his duties.[63]

The *Star* was clearly struggling with the new law. The paper reprinted a piece from the *Louisville Journal*, a major Whig border newspaper, suggesting that objectionable sections of the Fugitive Slave Law could be modified.[64] The *Star* still also highlighted provocative local cases. Under the headline "Nigger Catching," it hinted that a Gettysburg constable had become involved in slave catching. The officer had allegedly lured a black woman out of town in order to arrest her as a fugitive. The paper gave few details, but he may have wanted the woman to be seized in a remote place, away from Gettysburg's watchful African American community. The paper expressed the hope that this would be Constable Robert White's last foray into slave catching, as "there is no calling so meanly despicable as that of the professional Slave-hunter in the Free States."[65] A subsequent story suggested that White had been duped into the "dirty business," and the *Star* hoped that he would realize his error. Meanwhile, the fugitive had been sent to Maryland. The *Star* fumed that the whole episode violated the sacred right defined by Mr. Jefferson, "PERSONAL LIBERTY."[66]

If the allegation was true, White maintained a long tradition of slave catching by southern Pennsylvania lawmen. In the early 1820s, a member of York County's vigilance committee had lamented the work of "negro hunting constables." In 1837, when a Franklin County constable tried to capture a runaway, the fugitive dispatched him with a scythe. In 1844, a Gettysburg constable received a reward for helping to capture a fugitive and earned the ire of Washington, D.C. Underground Railroad worker Charles Torrey. In 1863, Shippensburg's constable was a former slave catcher who, perhaps ironically, was roughly handled by the invading Confederate army.[67]

By June, the approaching gubernatorial campaign influenced coverage of the fugitive slave issue in all of the Adams County papers. At the state convention in Reading, Democrats resolved: "That whatever may be the opinion of individuals as to the wisdom of the details of the Fugitive Slave law, it is the duty of all good citizens to conform to its requisitions." They labeled the law and the Compromise as "coeval with the Federal Government." The *Star* charged that although the people rejected the Fugitive Slave Law, the Democrats were endorsing it. At the same time, the *Star* tried to deflect criticism from Johnston for failing to sign the repeal of the 1847 act by pointing out that the Democratic candidate for governor, William F. Bigler, had voted for the personal liberty law in 1847, and a Democratic governor, Francis Shunk, had signed it.[68]

If the *Star* tried to stir up trouble over a resolution in the Democrat's Reading Convention, the Whigs faced even greater problems at their state convention. Only some Northern Whigs espoused antislavery, and condemning the Fugitive Slave Law could split the party. During the convention, a delegate offered a resolution explicitly pledging the Whigs to support the Fugitive Slave Law. John Scott lived in Huntingdon, a central county, but he had a border perspective: he had been educated in Chambersburg. His proposed plank seemed superfluous, as the platform's sixth resolution already committed the party to support the "adjustment" of the late Congress. Scott's motion was defeated 71–48. His initiative, however, enabled the *Compiler* to claim that Whigs had declined a clear-cut opportunity to support the law. The *Compiler* even labeled the resolutions that did pass as "treasonous," despite the fact that they endorsed the Compromise of 1850![69]

In his speech to the Whig convention, Governor Johnston tried to fix the damage. He claimed that since the 1847 law had existed for four years and the Union had not dissolved, it could not be as great a threat as its opponents maintained. He also argued that the Fugitive Slave Act could still be amended. It must be modified, he declared, but until then, it must be obeyed.[70]

With the Whig Party struggling, the *Star* backed both moderate (James Cooper) and free soil (William Johnston) Whig leaders. Johnston was an effective stump speaker, and he decided to tour the state to campaign. When the *Star* announced that Johnston would be stopping in Gettysburg, it also printed a letter from Senator Cooper to Whigs in Easton, deploring any sectional agitation or resistance to the Fugitive Slave Law.[71]

The stop at Gettysburg was one of Johnston's last "before the deluge." The governor's race was about to be transformed by dramatic events at Christiana. During the summer, the campaign was marked by debate over fugitive slave laws; in the fall, the campaign's direction would be largely determined by the actions of fugitives themselves.

The Christiana Riot and Its Aftermath

In Baltimore County, Maryland, in November 1849, four slaves fled from Edward Gorsuch after a theft of grain. Gorsuch was a farmer who tantalized his slaves with vague assurances of freedom that never seemed to arrive. Four male slaves in their prime were a valuable investment, and Gorsuch was determined to get them back.[72]

Once the runaways arrived in Pennsylvania, they settled near William Parker, a determined fugitive who led Lancaster's self-protection society. Parker had organized several slave rescues as well as efforts to punish African American informers. He nearly killed one, and he organized the gang that tried to burn down the house of another. When the Fugitive Slave Act was passed, Parker participated in a meeting denouncing it, and decided not to flee to Canada. Instead, he determined to fight, and he persuaded other local African Americans to resist.[73] In September 1851, Gorsuch's resolve to recover his slaves would collide with Parker's determination to stand for their freedom.

The owner was tipped off to the whereabouts of his slaves by an informant, apparently a day laborer who belonged to a gang of slave catchers who operated around Clemson's Tavern in the border town of Gap, Pennsylvania. He advised Gorsuch to travel first to Philadelphia to obtain constables, slave catchers, and warrants from Edward Ingraham, the fugitive slave commissioner. Gorsuch did, hiring several deputies and constables, including Marshal Henry H. Kline, who frequently aided in the capture of fugitive slaves.[74]

The Parkers were warned about Gorsuch's approach, but there had been so many false alarms about slave catchers that there was no mass mobilization at the house the night before. Seven African Americans did stay in the Parker house that night, however, including two of Gorsuch's fugitives. The neighborhood was in a state of readiness.[75]

On the morning of September 11, the Gorsuch party was guided to Parker's house, probably by the informant. As they moved up the lane, one of the Gorsuch fugitives, heading to work, surprised them and ran back to the house with a warning. Kline and Gorsuch went inside, but Parker's group was barricaded upstairs. After a tense confrontation and a reading of the warrant, Kline proposed burning the fugitives out.[76]

It is unclear what might have happened had the standoff continued. Despite Parker's resolve, several of his companions were weakening. Jonathan Katz, a historian of the riot, believes that the slave catchers were being reinforced by kidnappers determined to take or kill Parker after Gorsuch recovered his slaves. Parker's wife, Eliza, however, blew a horn as a signal to rally local African Americans. Accounts of what followed are confusing, but apparently Kline or Gorsuch directed their party to fire on her. This started the gunfire at Christiana; it did not silence Eliza Parker, who retreated to a more protected position but continued to blow the horn.[77]

Gorsuch's son, Dickinson, smelled danger. He urged his father to let the fugitives go, but Edward Gorsuch was resolute. What turned the tide was the arrival of reinforcements for Parker, summoned by the horn. Area African Americans converged on the Parker house, armed with scythes, hoes, and firearms. They were accompanied by several white observers who had heard that slave catchers were there. When Marshal Kline spotted these men, he tried to deputize them under the Fugitive Slave Law. They refused, and one, Castner Hanway, was later charged with inciting the riot.

With these reinforcements for Parker, the slave catchers faced the possibility of being surrounded or caught in the crossfire. Kline ordered his men back. Because of the Kaufman case, he apparently believed that Hanway and his companion could be sued for the value of the slaves if they escaped. When Kline's men began to withdraw, Gorsuch lingered. The defenders broke out and killed Edward Gorsuch, wounded Dickinson severely, and beat Joshua Gorsuch, a nephew, nearly senseless.[78] The African Americans fled, but many were soon arrested.

The Christiana riot clearly challenged the Fugitive Slave Law. The tenuous sectional truce depended on the government's reaction. It came at a critical time: In response to the Boston cases, Millard Fillmore had staked his presidential prestige on his determination to enforce the law. Some believed that the law was all that was holding the country together, and that attacks on it could rupture the nation—1850 had seen several southern states gather in Nashville and threaten to secede, and their bill of complaints included an attack on personal liberty laws, particularly Pennsylvania's. Now, newspapers from Boston to Florida carried articles and editorials about the violence. As Katz aptly termed it, "Christiana . . . became propaganda" as Southerners and Northerners sought to use the unrest for political ends. In South Carolina, there were calls for secession and denouncements of the 1850 Compromise and its seemingly ineffective Fugitive Slave Law. A newspaper in Florida stated that any new Christianas would bring civil war. Maryland's governor wrote an open letter to Fillmore, suggesting that if secession occurred over the fugitive slave issue, Maryland would lead it.[79]

In Pennsylvania, the Christiana riot was the perfect tool for Democrats to force the campaign for the governorship to turn on the Fugitive Slave Law, cementing the split between conservative Silver Greys and antislavery Whigs. Johnston did not help his cause when he passed through Lancaster while campaigning on the evening of September 11. Unlike some other passengers, he did not leave the train to see the mangled body of Gorsuch. He did not call out the militia to quell "insurrection." He also failed to issue a proclamation offering a reward for the rioters until four days later. The Whigs claimed, accurately, that by then most had been arrested, but the Democrats seized on this supposed dilatory response. One of Gorsuch's sons wrote a publicized letter in which he accused the governor of reacting tardily. The Rev. J. S. Gorsuch claimed to be a Whig, but his letter made great Democratic propaganda.[80]

The Whigs fought back. A mass meeting in Philadelphia lauded Johnston for his proclamation and quoted his last annual message which declared that "the recently enacted fugitive slave law, while it remains a statute, demands the support of all the citizens."[81]

Christiana, however, destroyed any lingering ability for Pennsylvania Whig politicians to mask their sentiments on the fugitive slave laws. Until the riot, the dichotomy between Pennsylvania's 1847 personal liberty law and the Fugitive Slave Law had offered political refuge. Like Johnston in his annual message, Whig politicians could proclaim their support for the federal Fugitive Slave Law, grudgingly or otherwise, knowing that Pennsylvania's state legislation made the rendition of fugitives cumbersome. The Democrats, by forcing the repeal issue, made such subterfuge difficult. By combining their repeal efforts with proclamations that the Union was in danger, they split the Whig Party between antislavery Whigs who condemned the Fugitive Slave Law and Silver Greys who wanted to maintain sectional harmony and good business relations with the South. As Katz points out, the Christiana riot and the resulting firestorm of publicity pushed the Silver Greys over the edge.[82] The *Star* tried to keep the conservative Whigs by attaching blame for the riot to the national Fugitive Slave Law, passed mainly by Democrats, and not Pennsylvania's 1847 personal liberty law, passed by state Whigs. It did not work. Johnston was soundly defeated by William Bigler in 1851.[83]

As the Christiana riot thrust fugitive slaves and issues of race into the forefront of the governor's campaign, the state's Democrats exploited those issues in south central Pennsylvania in particular. One of the major electoral events in the region was a pro-Bigler rally in Hanover, a town just east of Adams County. One speaker was Reah Frazer, the "War-Horse" of the Democracy, a prominent Lancaster lawyer. While many future Republicans such as Abraham Lincoln, Thaddeus Stevens, and Salmon P. Chase had represented fugitive slaves early in their careers, the reverse was also true: Some leading Democrats had prosecuted Underground Railroad workers. Frazer had prosecuted Samuel and Daniel Gibbons for harboring fugitive slaves in 1830.[84] According to the unfriendly *Star*, at the

1851 rally, Frazer declared that the United States was for whites only, maintaining that "niggers had no rights to be in the country except as slaves." While many border states considered banning the immigration of African Americans, Frazer went further, suggesting that if Bigler were elected, legislation should be passed driving all African Americans out of the state, and then a "big wall" should be erected to prevent communication between the slave and free states. The *Star*, while admitting that it was not completely certain that Frazer's remarks were serious, remarked drily that a few more such meetings and the election would be theirs—i.e., they regarded them as so extreme they would drive voters to the Whigs.[85]

Frazer's remarks, however, were a harbinger of the future. Pennsylvania's Democrats would employ racial rhetoric in political campaigns for at least the next twenty years.

Meanwhile the *Star* continued to maintain that slave catching was abominable. It reprinted a letter from Frederick Douglass in which he remarked:

> I do not believe that slave-catching is . . . a Christian duty. . . . I do not believe that he who breaks the arm of the kidnapper, or wrests the trembling captive from his grasp, is a "traitor." I do not believe that Daniel Webster is the Savior of the Union, or that the Union stands in need of such a Savior. I do not believe that human enactments are to be obeyed when they are point blank against the law of the living God.

Perhaps tellingly, however, immediately after the election ended with the defeat of Johnston and Daniel Durkee, a local antislavery Whig candidate, the paper published a sizable piece on the colonization of African Americans to Africa.[86]

The Trial of the Christiana Rioters

What southern Pennsylvanians believed concerning resisting the Fugitive Slave Law, as opposed to Frederick Douglass or abolitionists in upstate New York or Massachusetts, would be put to the test in the treason trial of the Christiana rioters. Adams County in particular had significant ties to the case: Former residents Thaddeus Stevens and James Cooper were counsel for the defense and the prosecution, respectively, and three Adams County residents were chosen for the jury, including William R. Sadler, who had led a Whig meeting in June![87]

The *Star* accurately predicted that the treason charges would not stick, but it was widely expected that if those charges were not sustained, the defendants would be tried in state court for Gorsuch's murder. If that also failed, they would be charged again in federal court, this time with obstructing the operation of the Fugitive Slave Law.[88]

With such grim prospects, the defendants needed good legal counsel, and they received it from Stevens, assisted by John M. Read, a Democrat. The first trial was that of Castner Hanway, the white miller accused of masterminding the riot. Stevens did not lead the defense, perhaps because he recognized how controversial he was, or perhaps because he knew he might have to be absent for the opening of Congress. He did take a strong role in cross-examination, legal motions, and courtroom arguments and strategy.[89]

The summations and final arguments illustrated diverging opinions on both sides of the border. Maryland's Attorney General Robert Brent, one of the prosecutors, blasted Northerners and abolitionists, stating that they were constitutionally bound by the Constitution to help recapture fugitive slaves. Read summed up for the defense and stated that Pennsylvania would not tolerate kidnappings of its citizens. Senator James Cooper closed for the prosecution, arguing that since fugitive slaves were unready for freedom, the Union should not be torn apart to grant them an abstract right. After the closing arguments, Judge Robert Grier suggested to the jury that the treason charge was unsustainable. Grier pointed out that what was considered treason in older law was now considered aggravated or felonious riot. Proving treason required an intent to overthrow the government or to completely nullify its laws. Simply breaking laws, like a smuggler's evasion of the revenue acts, did not constitute treason. Here Grier was following recent American jurisprudence. In the Constitution, treason had been narrowly defined, and in the Burr conspiracy trail, Chief Justice Marshall required an overt act to prove treason.[90]

The treason charges proved to be an overreach. The jury brought in a verdict "in accordance with its instructions" and acquitted Hanway. Soon the cases against the other defendants also lost momentum.[91] The U.S. government may have mollified Southern anger by trying the rioters for treason, but the charge implied that all who helped fugitives were traitors and that even just criticizing the new law was disloyal.

The treason trial helped shift the mood in the border North. Public opinion had initially been sympathetic to the Gorsuch family after the tragedy, but it turned as the trial continued. The able arguments of Hanway's counsel spread the realization that widespread kidnappings were occurring in Lancaster County, that those who helped fugitives could be charged with a capital crime, and that almost any innocent bystander could be swept up by the law. The trial reinforced to Northerners the onerous extent of the law, just as the Southern press was demanding full and energetic enforcement.

Despite overreaching on the treason charge, Pennsylvania's Democratic Party had used the fugitive slave issue very effectively in the first year since its passage. It split the Whig Party and helped the Democrats defeat the sitting Whig governor. Even the border antislavery Whig press, such as the *Star*, moderated its criticisms and admitted that the law must be enforced. With a national election looming, and with Pennsylvania—the "maker of Presidents"—firmly in their hands, Democrats had every right to be optimistic.

The Democratic Party appeared to be on the winning side of the fugitive slave question, at least in south central Pennsylvania. After protests in 1850, both the Whig and Democratic parties declared acceptance of the Compromise of 1850, but the Democratic support was firmer. With diminishing opportunities to resist the law itself either politically or physically, as in the case of Christiana, opponents of the Fugitive Slave Law would have to resort to new tactics to increase outrage over the issue.

6

Interlude: Kidnapping, Kansas, and the Rise of Race-Based Partisanship

The Decline of the Fugitive Slave Issue in South Central Pennsylvania, 1852–57

The explosive Christiana riot and trial brought the fugitive slave issue to the forefront of national attention, and highlighted deep divisions within Pennsylvania. So did the defeat of Governor Johnston. The fugitive slave issue seemed poised to usher in significant political change, possibly even to split the Union. Facing this prospect, many white Pennsylvanians flinched. In the border regions, many in the two major political parties already accepted the 1850 Compromise, some Whigs more reluctantly than most Democrats. Maintaining peace along the border and honoring each other's laws ("comity") was essential for arresting cross-border criminals such as counterfeiters and horse thieves as well as recovering fugitives. In addition, many jurists believed that because the Constitution's privileges and immunities clauses required states to recognize each others' laws, this mandated permitting the recovery of fugitives.[1] Southern Pennsylvania's economy benefitted from Southern trade, and this also led many inhabitants away from open conflict with Southern states over slavery or fugitives.

Sensing retrenchment in popular mood, abolitionists tried to regain momentum by repeating the formula that won Castner Hanway's acquittal: emphasizing the innocents swept up in seemingly arbitrary Southern efforts to recover fugitives. The capture of free blacks as alleged fugitives would be opposed in kidnapping cases. If some of the innocents were white, like Hanway, it would be even better. Several notable cases resulted, including southern Pennsylvania's Parker/Miller case. A white farmer, Joseph Miller, was murdered after he pursued a party of slave catchers to Baltimore. They had taken a young black woman, Rachel Parker, from his farm as a fugitive. Rather than risk open breach, many politicians and judges accepted compromises to keep the peace along the border. In this case, Rachel Parker, was ultimately released, along with her sister, but the individuals who had seized her and possibly murdered Joseph Miller were not prosecuted.[2] In a related *quid pro quo*, Pennsylvania's Democratic governor, William Bigler, had released an incarcerated kidnapper from prison in an attempt to get the case against Miller's murderers moving forward. In Gettysburg, the *Star* questioned whether "Mr. Bigler designs by this pardon to show Maryland that her agents can hereafter invade our soil and kidnap our free colored people with impunity," but other notable cases used these kind of informal border *quid pro quo*'s as well.[3] One such example occurred when a Baltimore police officer (accompanied by a Harrisburg constable) shot and killed a fugitive slave named Ridgeley while attempting to capture him. The officer was not extradited, but authorities from Maryland sent back a black man from Harrisburg named James Johnson, who, after having traveled to Baltimore without a pass, had been bound out to labor there.[4]

In this case, southern Pennsylvania's Whig and antislavery newspapers smelled a rat. The York *Republican* fumed that the return of Johnson was "one of the richest attempts at diverting public attention from the violation of the law by the murder of a man, that we have ever seen." The paper went on:

> These Locofoco Grand Inquisitors . . . find out that a little negro boy, who had strayed into Maryland, ignorant of her *humane* laws, had been . . . sold as a slave. Here was a chance to . . . furnish a set-off to Ridgely's homicide! They . . . send him back with a grand flourish . . . and in effect say, take your free boy, but don't ask us to give up our shooting officer.[5]

This was one *quid pro quo* that the *Star* would not tolerate. The following week, it reprinted an ad from a Frederick paper from an enterprise offering to purchase "one hundred negroes" for New Orleans. The *Star*, still seething over violent seizures of fugitives in the state, sneered: "We are surprised at [someone] offering to buy negroes in Maryland, when they can be knocked down and dragged out for a mere song in Pennsylvania."[6] Soon the *Star* would become an anti-immigrant, Know Nothing newspaper, however, and the attention it gave to fugitive slave cases would diminish for several years.

Even before the *Star*'s conversion to Know Nothingism, the "kidnapping" controversies failed to gain the desired traction. The slow decline of the Whigs, and the rise of the nativist Know Nothings, slowly pushed the fugitive slave issue to the background in the public sphere. The issue was still present in politics, but its role was diminished except in spectacular cases. In one such example, in Harrisburg in 1854, the uncovering of a mendacious, slave hunting constabulary contributed to significant local reverses for the Democrats. That year's Whig platform, while not mentioning fugitive slaves, supported the writ of habeas corpus and the right to trial by jury (both positions, by implication, including fugitive slave cases). In his successful 1854 campaign for governor, James Pollock, a Whig, highlighted the inequities of Fugitive Slave Law, but only when he felt he was in antislavery areas. In part, he was trying to attract Free Soil Democrats. The summer of 1855 saw an officer of the Pennsylvania Antislavery Society, Passmore Williamson, arrested in Philadelphia as he tried to persuade the shipborne slaves of the U.S. ambassador to Nicaragua that they were free because they were inside the bounds of Pennsylvania. This resulted in the spectacle of Williamson being nominated, from jail, for canal commissioner (the highest state office being contested that year) by the new Republican Party.[7]

In 1855, an Adams County resident, perhaps Lydia Lundy Wierman, tried to stir up controversy over the capture of a fugitive slave from her family's farm, but the incident appears to have had no lasting impact. In 1856, the Democratic *Republican Compiler* accused antislavery forces friendly to the first Republican presidential candidate, John C. Fremont, of mounting an abortive effort to capitalize on a fugitive slave case in Carlisle to benefit his candidacy.[8] It was the conflict over Kansas, however, that truly eclipsed the fugitive slave issue until John Brown's raid and secession. Diminishing interest in the fugitive slave issue until 1859, at least in south central Pennsylvania's newspapers, did not signify reduced attention to issues of race, however. In fact, the Democratic Party responded to the Republicans' rise with race-based attacks that would last for decades and profoundly affect area African Americans during the Civil War and Reconstruction.

This decline in interest in the fugitive slave issue by local newspapers is reflected in Table 4. After the Boston cases and the Christiana riot in 1851, coverage of the fugitive slave issue steadily declines until the attack at Harpers Ferry. In south central Pennsylvania, where newspaper space was strictly limited, space that might have been given up to the fugitive slave issue was now devoted to nativist topics (public school controversies, papal plots, foreign influence, and so on) or, increasingly, the controversy over Kansas.

The Kansas controversy stemmed from Western expansion and Congressional politics. In 1854, Stephen Douglas pushed the Kansas-Nebraska act through Congress, invalidating both the Missouri Compromise and the "final settlement" of the 1850 Compromise. As Kansas settlers would decide whether the territory would become a slave state or free state, immigrants surged into the area from both the South and the North. Many who supported slavery were pro-Southern Missourians; many of the Northerners were from Pennsylvania and New England.

Table 4   Number of Articles Mentioning Fugitive Slaves, the Fugitive Slave Issue, or Kidnapping in Adams County Newspapers, 1849–April 15, 1861

Newspaper	1849	1850	1851	1852	1853	1854	1855	1856	1857	1858	1859	1860	1861*
Compiler (D)	2	36	48	22	12	13	11	11	7	2	40	41	22
Sentinel (W/R)	X	50	49	23	24	16	22	8	4	11	20	19	10
Star (W/A/R)	X	72	114	38	26	16	28	10	4[†]	—	—	—	—

LEGEND: X = Data not gathered; — = Extant continuous newspaper files not available for this year; [†] = To May 8, 1857 only; * = Issues from January 1, 1861–April 15, 1861 only; D = Democrat; W = Whig; A = American (Know Nothing); R = Republican

The Kansas controversy allowed many of the essentials of the fugitive slave issue to be recast in compelling terms affecting white people. South central Pennsylvania's newspapers were quick to see the possibilities. The suspension of habeas corpus and execution of summary justice concerned abolitionists and humanitarians when applied to fugitive slaves; when the same things happened to white settlers in Kansas, the range of interest was potentially greater. Even the fugitive slave issue itself was recast in a way subsidiary to Kansas. "Negro Dogs" used to hunt fugitives, often a staple in complaints against the Fugitive Slave Law, were now particularly reprehensible in the eyes of one newspaper because they would hunt slaves *in Kansas*. Kansas's territorial legislature threatened to execute white settlers who helped fugitives, which only served to make the issue more inflammatory for Pennsylvania's antislavery newspapers. In addition, in an updating of the 1830s concern about Gag Rules and free expression, now a Kansas settler who spoke out against the territory's draconian laws on slavery and fugitive slaves could be jailed.[9] Some undoubtedly saw a slippery slope descending from the habitual abridgement of rights for African Americans to a voracious Slave Power now curtailing those rights for white settlers. Others may have simply cared more now that white immigrants and not blacks were the victims.

The decline of the fugitive slave issue in south central Pennsylvania did not, however, end partisan struggle over issues of race and slavery. Northern outrage over the Kansas-Nebraska act had led to the founding of the Republican Party, set firmly against the extension of slavery. Democrats tried to counter the new party's rapid rise, by tying Pennsylvania's Republicans to African Americans. They did this by crudely exploiting racial stereotypes and prejudices. This was an important sea change in south central Pennsylvania, the state, and nation. These tactics would be used by the Democrats to oppose the Republicans in the 1856 Presidential campaign, in the 1857 gubernatorial campaign, and in 1858 and 1860 against the resurgent Republican Party. In fact, this change in political rhetoric would last through the disputes over contrabands, the Emancipation Proclamation, and into the post-war years. It was a decidedly significant shift.[10]

In response to Fremont's 1856 candidacy—which looked like it might ride a wave of outrage from "Bleeding Kansas" and "Bleeding Sumner" into the White House—Democrats wielded an aggressive, mud-slinging campaign. They accused Fremont of financial dishonesty and of being a secret Catholic, a potent accusation at a time when anti-Catholicism was at its peak. They also employed a new level of anti–African American invective, charging that the Republicans were allied with African Americans against immigrants and white workers. Democrats also resorted to an old standby and accused the Republicans of promoting amalgamation, technically sexual relations between black and white producing mixed race children, but generally used to cover all interracial sex. Prior to 1856, the *Compiler's* editor, although undoubtedly imbued with the casual racism characteristic of many Northerners, had rarely, outside of the joke section, let anti-black sentiments slip through to its pages. Now, during the first Republican campaign for President, racist rhetoric was deliberately wielded. Fremont was ridiculed as a "Wooly Head," a derogatory term first applied to antislavery Whigs.

Instead of winning the Presidency, Fremont was defeated in Pennsylvania, thwarting the Republican strategy of winning the Presidency by carrying the entire North. Pennsylvanian James Buchanan, a Democrat, took office promising to pacify the Kansas violence, but he was no more successful than his predecessor. The Kansas issue was drawing into the opposition tent a large group of people who were not necessarily sympathetic to abolition or even fugitive slaves.[11]

Republicans deliberately stirred the Kansas pot. Even the *Sentinel*, the moderate opposition paper in Gettysburg, took a strong position for free Kansas. The *Star* reprinted a piece from the *Erie True American*, which suggested that uncompassionate individuals who minimized the suffering of Kansas settlers or the "wrongs of the poor crushed slave" (it is significant which oppressed group was listed first) "hath a devil."[12]

The Supreme Court stoked the dispute in early 1857 in the *Dred Scott* decision, declaring that the Missouri Compromise unconstitutional. This also abrogated the 1850 Compromise and the Kansas-Nebraska act and permitted slavery anywhere in the territories. With thousands of free soil and proslavery settlers now in Kansas, the decision threatened to unleash more violence. That Kansas concerned residents of south central Pennsylvania no local paper doubted. Even before the Civil War, many south central Pennsylvanians migrated west for better opportunities. These included antislavery supporters such as Benjamin Lundy's children and, in the late 1850s, Joel and Lydia Wierman. So had anti-abolitionists such as the Rev. Richard Bond and Andrew G. Miller, both of whom had opposed antislavery in the 1830s debates in Gettysburg. Even the Harrisburg fugitive slave commissioner, Richard McAllister, migrated to Kansas in the 1850s, where, according to one observer, some suspected he was a "rank Abolitionist" because of his state of origin! Area newspapers frequently ran pieces about the increasing "mania for 'going west.'"[13] This westward migration kept many Pennsylvanians keenly interested in Kansas's fate.

Soon after *Dred Scott*, Pennsylvania's opposition parties met in a Union convention on March 22, 1857. After recent defeats, they realized that close political cooperation was needed between the Republicans, Americans, Free Soilers, antislavery Democrats, and the old Whigs.[14] With the Republicans ascendant, the various groups closed ranks and nominated David Wilmot for governor. He would prove a poor choice.[15] The Democratic *Compiler* condemned Wilmot as a "sectional agitator," and correctly predicted that Pennsylvanians, "slow to follow after strange gods," would shun divisive abolitionism.[16]

The 1857 gubernatorial campaign was largely contested over slavery. The Republican Party had been founded in 1854 to oppose the Kansas-Nebraska act, and was determined to fight out the 1857 election on its antislavery principles. Not only did they nominate Wilmot, the militant free soiler who forever would be linked to his Proviso to exclude slavery from the territories acquired from Mexico, but they also adopted a strong antislavery platform.[17]

Vulnerable on the Kansas issue, the *Compiler* increased its level of race baiting as the election approached. The paper began to highlight calls from Republican leaders such as Salmon Chase for black suffrage, which the *Compiler* said, was a small step to "NEGRO EQUALITY."[18] Pennsylvanians could prevent it by defeating Wilmot.[19]

The issue that may have decided the 1857 election, however, arrived unanticipated by either party. In August, a panic began on Wall Street, wiping out investors and companies, and plunging the country into a sharp depression. Eventually, even the normally strong Bank of Gettysburg had to suspend specie payments larger than $5.[20]

The panic of 1857 doomed Wilmot. He had already alienated part of his base because he had supported the unpopular, lower Tariff of 1846. Aside from supporting free trade, however, Wilmot's lack of interest in fiscal issues gave voters little confidence he would be able to lift the state quickly out of the depression. As the panic deepened, his speeches and meetings were greeted with diminishing enthusiasm. When he arrived in Gettysburg late in the campaign, the *Com-*

piler mocked the affair as a "One-Horse Mass Meeting!" It remarked that despite the fusion of Know Nothings and Republicans—"Sam" and "Sambo" as it derogatorily called them—the meeting had little energy. "No crowd," the *Compiler* snickered, "no flags—no enthusiasm—Know Nothing." When Wilmot closed his speech with opposition to slavery extension, the *Compiler* sneered, "his speech was little less than Abolitionism of the darkest dye."[21]

The Democratic attacks and Wilmot's apparent financial incompetence cost him. General William F. Packer, the Democratic candidate, won by a substantial majority.[22] The Republicans saw that they had to broaden their appeal. The consecutive defeats of Fremont and Wilmot in Pennsylvania made it clear that an antislavery platform alone could not prevail there. In 1860, militant antislavery statements would be toned down, and the party would adopt strong support for a protective tariff.[23]

Despite the rise of a party formed around opposition to slavery extension and the Kansas-Nebraska act—or perhaps because of it—the fugitive slave issue was still eclipsed. Resistance to the Fugitive Slave Law could be stigmatized as illegal extremism, distancing moderates from the issue, and controversies over Kansas proved more effective tools for keeping old Whigs, Free Soilers, and Know Nothings in the Republican camp. In many Adams County newspapers, space that might have gone to cover fugitive slave cases before now went to material about Kansas. Notable local or regional cases were still covered, but the fugitive slave issue itself seemed mostly dead as a political topic, largely killed by the requirements of fusion.

Instead, Kansas had displaced the fugitive slave issue as the leading way agitation against the "Slave Power" was maintained. Thousands of citizens migrated west from border Pennsylvania each year, and defending the rights of white settlers was more compelling then defending African American fugitives. It seemed that the rest of the decade would consist of Democrats throwing water on the Kansas fire and Republicans throwing oil. Or so it appeared until a Kansas settler, operating in part from south central Pennsylvania, explosively returned the fugitive slave issue to center stage.

7

Revival of the Fugitive Slave Issue, 1858–61

As a result of the pressures of the border political environment and the salience of Kansas, the fugitive slave issue appeared quiescent in 1858. Neither the 1855 case involving the Wiermans nor the 1856 Carlisle case seemed to engage the populace. Despite statewide defeats in the 1856 presidential election and the 1857 Pennsylvania governor's race, the Republican Party grew stronger. The fugitive slave issue did not rise with them, however. Although the Republicans were perceived as antislavery, the party had been founded on opposition to the Kansas-Nebraska Act and the extension of slavery, not on resistance to the Fugitive Slave Law or immediate abolition. In fact, any new political party wishing to succeed along the border or even in the North would usually shrink from urging defiance of the law and the Constitution, particularly when the Democrats presented themselves as the party of Union and law during the 1850s. Instead, the Republicans would emphasize a new interpretation of the Constitution, advanced by Salmon Chase and others, in which freedom was national and slavery had to be established by special legislation. (Thaddeus Stevens, who corresponded with Chase, had a similar conception.) Elsewhere, noteworthy fugitive slave cases such as the Glover case in Wisconsin, the Passmore Williamson case, and the Oberlin rescue cases would be agitated by some Republicans, but threatened to cause a rift with more moderate members of the party.[1]

Even without Democratic pressure and concerns about respect for the laws, Pennsylvania Republicans' uneasy alliance with the Whigs and Know Nothings led them to emphasize Kansas and the tariff. The fugitive slave issue did not reappear significantly until after the explosive 1859 Harpers Ferry raid, and again on the very eve of secession and war. When it did, in the most meaningful way since the Christiana riots, it was actually the Democrats who raised the issue, seeking to forestall Republican momentum.[2]

In the 1850s, Republicans knew that they needed only to carry the entire North to win the Presidency. As weak a candidate as he had proved to be, even John C. Fremont carried most of the North in 1856, and he would have been elected had he won Pennsylvania and Illinois or Indiana. In 1860, then, along with nominating a better candidate, the Republicans would have to develop a platform and party to carry the border North.

Swinging Pennsylvania to the Republicans was critical to the strategy. This necessitated improving on the cumbersome coalitions, fusion movements, People's parties, and Union parties of the 1850s, while retaining the support of the state's dwindling Know Nothings. This approach, which did not emphasize fugitive slaves, would be the basis for the Republicans' 1860 campaign. To the painstaking Republican plans, however, would be added John Brown's dramatic actions. His raid ensured that the fugitive slave issue would be a dramatic part of the political debate at the decade's end.

1858–59: Republican Revival, Racial Counterattacks, and Shifting Sentiments

By 1858, the Kansas controversies had cost Northern Democrats and helped Republicans prepare for 1860. Debate raged over the Lecompton Constitution, a new Kansas constitution drafted in September 1857 by the pro-slavery territorial legislature after free state supporters boycotted the meeting. While some south central Pennsylvania Democratic politicians urged acceptance of it, other Northern Democrats wearied of supporting pro-Southern positions. Some joined "free soil" Democrats or even the Republicans. Others fervently hoped that "the wounds of bleeding Kansas were being healed" and that controversy would subside.[3]

Since the mid-1850s, the Kansas issue had featured more prominently in the local papers than fugitive slave or kidnapping cases. The newspapers targeted white readers; for African Americans, of course, there was no comparison, as kidnapping threatened immediate enslavement. One such attempt momentarily grabbed the attention of the Adams County newspapers early in 1858. Mag Palm, a Gettysburg African American, had been doing laundry for a local family. Waiting for her pay delayed her departure until after twilight. Crossing an alley near the house in darkness, she was seized by men who tried to push her into a carriage. They had picked the wrong victim, however. Palm was a large woman, and strong from years of wearying labor. "Possessing more than ordinary muscular power," the *Compiler* commented, Palm drove off the kidnappers. She then swore out a warrant before the magistrate, implicating her employer and two others.

This incident illustrated the continual danger along the border. Palm was reputed to be an important member of the Underground Railroad, escorting fugitives from McAllister's Mill around Gettysburg. But networks of informers and

Figure 3. Mag Palm, demonstrating how kidnappers attempted to bind her hands.
(Adams County Historical Society)

slave catchers coexisted with the Underground Railroad. In southern Pennsylvania, it was difficult to determine loyalties. Slave catchers often posed as the fugitive's friend.

The Palm case briefly exposed this subterfuge. According to the *Compiler*, "the affair caused considerable excitement" among Gettysburg's blacks. One of them, Jacob Jones, was beaten by several African American women and their children because they believed that he had "some hand" in Palm's seizure. Jones went to a Mummasburg magistrate and swore out a warrant for assault and battery against several of the women, including Milly Magee. When the women learned this, they posted bail before the magistrate in Gettysburg, and then swore out a warrant on Jones, for attempting to kidnap two of Milly's children. The *Compiler* commented dryly, "Jones, not having as good luck as Milly in getting security, was compelled to take up quarters under Sheriff Lightner."[4]

Although a fictionalized version of the Mag Palm attack survives in Elsie Singmaster's novel *A Boy at Gettysburg*, this kidnapping attempt was more than just a local interest story. Parts of Gettysburg's divided African American community utilized not only collective action and resistance, but showed that they, and not just white abolitionists, knew how to appeal to the legal system to stop kidnappings.[5]

The momentary interest in kidnapping stirred up by the Palm incident soon faded from the politically attuned newspapers; what persisted was the need for the Democrats to find an issue to beat back the Republicans. Democrats applied to the Kansas issue the virulent racial rhetoric they were developing to combat the Republicans.

This race baiting intensified as the 1858 campaign heated up. The Democratic press appealed to their foreign-born constituencies by proclaiming that Know Nothings blocked citizenship for immigrants while the Republicans were easing it for fugitive slaves and blacks. In July, in an article entitled "The Union of Sam and Sambo" ("Sam" was a pejorative term for Know Nothings, "Sambo" of course the same for African Americans), the *Compiler* claimed that the fusion movement between the Republicans and Know Nothings had two major principles:

1. All white men born outside of U.S. to be disfranchised and proscribed from political rights. Assented to by Sambo on condition:
2. Negroes have same political and social rights as native born Americans and in all respects. Vote and hold office while the white European is to be denied these privileges.[6]

The paper accused those attending the recent Union convention of Republicans and Americans—which it labeled the "Mulatto State Convention"—of "laying down in the bed of niggerism." It predicted the movement would fail, because, "White men cannot be got to proscribe each other that negroes may profit by it."[7]

This vociferous racist critique stemmed from the *Compiler*'s deep concern over the fall elections. The Democrats' Kansas position was unpopular, and the lingering effects of the Panic of 1857 threatened anti-protectionist Democrats. In August, the paper tried to stop defections by warning its readers that Republican congressional gains could decide the Presidency if the 1860 election was thrown to the House of Representatives—regarded as a very real possibility in a race that was predicted to be very tight.[8]

While the Democrats were on the defensive, the opposition parties in Adams County saw an opportunity to recapture a seat in Congress. In Adams County, Edward McPherson was advanced for Congress. This choice was soon ratified by a mass meeting, which included representatives from both Adams and Franklin counties. McPherson was the son of John B. McPherson, who was an intimate of Thaddeus Stevens and the longtime cashier of the Gettysburg bank. The younger McPherson worked as a journalist and had mastered the slash and burn style of the day. After an apprenticeship at the *Adams Sentinel*, he edited papers in Harrisburg and Pittsburgh, and also contributed to the Philadelphia *Bulletin*.[9] The McPherson farm near Gettysburg College was reputed to be a stop on the Underground Railroad, and self-proclaimed conductor Basil Biggs lived there briefly.

Gettysburg's Democratic paper, the *Compiler*, criticized McPherson's youth, his peripatetic journalistic career, and his association with the failed free trader and defeated gubernatorial candidate David Wilmot.[10] McPherson still triumphed. This was a noticeable shift from the Congressional district's recent Democratic turn, although his margin was just 300 votes. Franklin County, the home of the young Republican power broker A. K. McClure, was the key; McPherson won it by about 500 votes. The district had given a nearly 1,700 vote margin to Democrat William Packer over Wilmot for governor the previous fall, with Adams and Franklin counties accounting for nearly 500 of the majority. So the shift to the local Republican was significant, although Adams County remained very competitive.[11]

The Republicans had also made a rapid recovery across the state and the nation. In Pennsylvania, McPherson's victory was matched by many other Republican–Know Nothing fusion candidates. In border Pennsylvania, after

the 1858 elections, Kansas stayed in the forefront and the fugitive slave issue remained largely eclipsed. The tumultuous events of late 1859 would change that,
especially along the border.[12]

To stem the Republican tide, the *Compiler* kept up racial attacks against the
"black Republicans," and tried to pin the more overt antislavery actions of their
colleagues elsewhere on Pennsylvania's Republicans, including those related to
the fugitive slave issue.[13] For example, the *Compiler* complained when a bill in
the Massachusetts legislature proposed a two-year residency requirement for immigrants to be eligible to vote, yet African Americans who moved into the state
were allowed to vote after one year's residence. "A runaway slave from a Southern
State becomes a voter there after one year's residence, immeasurably above white
foreigners," the paper sniffed.[14] In short, it claimed that Republicanism was just
abolitionism in a new guise.[15]

The *Compiler* continued to strongly support the Fugitive Slave Law. When
the U.S. Supreme Court ruled against the state of Wisconsin's actions in nullifying the Fugitive Slave Law in the Booth case, the *Compiler* expressed the hope
that the decision would "end . . . all contests . . . as to the constitutionality of the
fugitive slave law."[16] Consequently, the paper was pleased when a new case arose
in Harrisburg. A fugitive slave was arrested there and taken before the commissioner in Philadelphia. This change of venue would have been highly unusual
several years before, but the Harrisburg commissioner's job had not been filled
after Richard McAllister had moved west. Also, unlike several years before, what
changed was the degree of political attention this case received at the state legislature. One member even proposed moving the state capital from Harrisburg, because he did not want to remain in a town "where such outrages were permitted."
Some legislators also made "the 'Personal Liberty Bill' the special order for some
evening this week." The paper approved that there was no rescue attempted, but
noted that "the circumstance aroused the 'colored' element [i.e. Republicans] in
the House of Representatives."[17]

Even while the *Compiler* agitated the fugitive slave issue, there were signs
that tolerance for slave catching was diminishing in south central Pennsylvania. John Butler and his wife and children had lived for years in Adams County
and Cumberland County before being seized. This time, rather than aiding slave
catchers, as many constables had previously done, the local sheriff devised an
ingenious stratagem to catch one. Sheriff John Harder was a free soil Democrat
who local historians later claimed had transported fugitive slaves in his market
wagon. His colleagues in Cumberland County's Underground Railroad figured
that his role in local Democratic politics would lessen suspicions. To solve the

Butler case, Harder arrested an accomplice who implicated Emmanuel Myers, a "noted negro catcher," as the ringleader. Myers lived literally just across the Maryland state line, outside of Pennsylvania's jurisdiction. With the poisoned relations between the two states over fugitive slaves, it was highly unlikely that Maryland's governor would ever extradite him. So Harder hitched a ride in the mail coach and directed it to pass Myers's house, as if by accident. Seemingly reluctant to labor at turning the horses around, the driver held a packet of letters out of the carriage window and waved it at Myers's house. When Myers walked up to claim his mail, he inadvertently crossed the Pennsylvania line and Harder arrested him. The lengths to which the sheriff was willing to go for this arrest illustrates changing sentiment in south central Pennsylvania. For years, constables had been a primary tool slave holders used to recover fugitive slaves; now they arrested kidnappers instead.

This case caused an uproar on both sides of the Mason-Dixon Line. Abolitionists insisted that the Butlers had been manumitted fifteen years earlier by a Maryland widow.[18] Many Marylanders seethed because they felt that Myers had been duped. At his trial, the state's prosecution was handled by A. Brady Sharpe and Frederick Watts, distinguished members of the Carlisle bar, indicating the continued involvement of leading lawyers in fugitive slave and kidnapping cases. Myers was convicted, but in another border *quid pro quo*, he promised to return the Butlers if he were freed. The state dropped the case when the family reappeared in Cumberland County.[19]

While Pennsylvania's Republicans downplayed controversial racial issues to maintain coalition unity, the Democrats sought to stir them up. Pennsylvania was critical in 1860. With the Democrats nearly certain to carry every southern state, Pennsylvania's electoral votes could give them the presidency. The *Compiler* insisted that the Republicans wanted "NEGRO EQUALITY" (almost always printed in capitals) or, as it crudely distorted the Republican position, "Up with the black man and down with the white!" The paper also claimed that the Republicans had "taken open ground against the fugitive slave law," exploiting rhetoric from an Ohio Republican convention superheated by the Oberlin slave rescue case, when abolitionists had freed a fugitive, and a marshal and three others were indicted for kidnapping. The newspaper also appealed to traditional, law-and-order Whigs, as any attempt to reach out to former Know Nothings could alienate the Democrats' immigrant constituency. It urged former old-line Whigs to abandon the Republicans and give the Democrats a majority in Pennsylvania in 1860, but these Whigs had been carefully wooed by the Republicans for years. They would largely stand with the new party.[20]

The Oberlin case was a portent; events of the fall of 1859 would force partisan political debates about Kansas, immigrants, and equality to take a back burner to the issue of escaping slaves and insurrections. John Brown's raid shook south central Pennsylvania out of any complacency regarding fugitive slaves.

The Harpers Ferry Raid

John Brown was a volatile mix of the militancy of a Kansas Free Soiler with the willingness to disregard the law of a nonresistant Quaker. Fugitive slaves were close to Brown's heart. His father had helped them, and early in his career, Brown tried to start a school for the children of fugitives and free blacks. He also engineered several expeditions to liberate slaves, one that covered 1,100 miles. This interest led Brown to plan a way to enable large-scale escapes from the Upper South. Brown wanted to exploit the Allegheny Mountains as a pathway for fugitives heading north, sort of a "super Underground Railroad"; later he decided to make the mountains a redoubt.

Turning locations in the Alleghenies into fortresses required arms, which directed Brown's attention to Harpers Ferry. Once the decision to attack the armory was made, geography ensured that south central Pennsylvania played an extensive role in the raid and its aftermath. It was the closest region to Brown's target that was still in a Northern state. Brown based his operations out of Chambersburg for several months before moving his headquarters to a Maryland farm. Even then, he or his men returned to Chambersburg multiple times to pick up shipments, supplies, and recruits. Almost no one recognized the old man, who claimed he was a prospector named Smith. Some area blacks knew of Brown's identity, but whether they recognized him or he revealed himself is not clear. One such individual, local barber Henry Watson, helped arrange Frederick Douglass's meeting with Brown at an abandoned quarry near town. Brown wanted Douglass to lend his considerable prestige to the effort. They conversed several times over a day and a half; in the end, Douglass, fearing disaster, refused to join the undertaking. Brown's new project of armed insurrection varied substantially from what Douglass had last heard described. Then the plan had been to melt into the rugged mountains and entice slaves from Virginia, Kentucky, and elsewhere to join them. A network of fortified safe houses would be created to rapidly move fugitives to Canada, with weapons used only for self-defense. Now, Brown's plan involved an armed attack on a federal armory and insurrection. Douglass doubted whether this could succeed. As a former slave, he was particularly dubious that Virginia slaves would spontaneously join an attack about which they had no prior knowledge.[21]

Douglass stayed to give a speech at the Chambersburg Town Hall after his meeting with Brown, essentially as a cover for why he was in the area. The unannounced appearance of the nation's most famous former fugitive slave caught the town by surprise, although the local press attended. The Chambersburg *Valley Spirit*, a Democratic paper, admitted that Douglass was personally impressive, but said that he spurned the judgment of the Almighty Himself when he ignored the immutable difference between the races. The Republican paper, the *Repository and Transcript*, was more visibly conservative than Adams County's *Star* or the *Sentinel*, and stated that Douglass went too far in advocating immediate emancipation—any efforts at abolition would have to be accompanied by colonization. According to the *Baltimore American*, many of the town's residents believed "that he came solely for the purpose of delivering a lecture and pocketing the profits"—very opposite from his true purpose.[22]

Douglass's mission had serious consequences. While he did not join Brown, his companion did. Shields Green was a fugitive slave from South Carolina. Brown's group of about twenty volunteers also included Osborne Perry Anderson, a free African American from Chester County, Pennsylvania. Anderson's involvement proved that William Parker's spirit still remained after Parker's flight to Canada; at least one southern Pennsylvania African American had decided it was time to resist slavery by force.[23]

The story of the raid is well known and will not be repeated here. Part of the dramatic aftermath played out in south central Pennsylvania. Only a few conspirators evaded immediate capture and fled. Osborne Perry Anderson reached Canada, aided by the Underground Railroad. Two others were seized in south central Pennsylvania. Albert Hazlett nearly reached Carlisle before being captured and extradited. John Cook was captured near Mont Alto by Dan Logan, one of Franklin County's notorious slave catchers. Logan turned Cook over to A. K. McClure, a lawyer and politician who occasionally helped him out of legal difficulties from his activities. The slave catcher was even a Republican, having supported McClure's 1858 State Senate campaign. A plan to free Cook from the Chambersburg jail failed when an officer from Virginia showed up early the next day with a warrant. Both Hazlett and Cook would hang. Although few wanted them executed, many around Chambersburg were mortified that Brown had lived in their midst and feared Southern economic reprisal.[24]

Although Brown sought an insurrection, enticing slaves to flee from their masters was a critical part of his plan. His raid pushed the fugitive slave issue and border slavery to the forefront of national consciousness. The immediate Southern response was to organize militarily to oppose insurrection and abolitionist invasion. African Americans in northwest Virginia suffered greatly during the winter, as numerous "plots" were ferreted out. With militias drilling regularly throughout the upper South, war was possible. In the North, and certainly in border Pennsylvania, anyone not dedicated to the fugitive's cause reexamined the issue to see if the South could be mollified.[25]

Republicans in particular engaged in this introspection. They struggled to avoid endorsing Brown's lawlessness while not alienating their key antislavery constituency. Despite the violence of John Brown's raid, many south central Pennsylvanians continued to move toward the Republican Party. With the decline of the Know Nothings and the failure of the Free Soil and Liberty parties, there was really no place else for those who opposed the Southern-leaning Democrats. Old-line Whigs, who had been able to hold out for some time due to that party's persistence in some pockets of Pennsylvania, now had to choose between their traditional hatred of the Democrats and their dislike for the Republicans. For many of them, the move to the Republicans was made more palatable by the presence within the new party of champions of business and industry, including Thaddeus Stevens, William "Pig-Iron" Kelly, Andrew Curtin, and Simon Cameron.

Emblematic of this gradual swing of the Whigs into the Republican Party was Adams County's Robert G. Harper. Harper, a committed Clay and Webster Whig, had edited the *Adams Sentinel* for decades.[26] He despised "fanatical" abolitionists, but with the Whig Party gone, he had limited options for continued political leadership. After thirty years of opposition to the Democrats, joining them was inconceivable. The bigoted Know Nothings violated his sensibilities, and he had a running feud with the Know Nothing editors, Charles and David Buehler, who were trying to supplant his paper for opposition leadership in Adams County. During the 1850s, Harper strongly supported a free Kansas and colonization for Pennsylvania's African Americans. Eventually, he turned to the Republicans, sealing his commitment by attending the 1860 Republican convention in Chicago. When Lincoln was nominated, he was enthusiastic—largely because Lincoln was perceived as an antislavery moderate.[27]

If conservative Whigs like Harper were turning into Republicans, the Democrats were in danger. Adams County, which often voted Whig until Scott's defeat in 1852, had become quite competitive because of the strong Democratic base among the county's Germans, and within Gettysburg's professionals and artisans. In 1858, Edward McPherson broke an eight-year Democratic hold on the Congressional seat from Adams and Franklin, but the county's Democrats were still optimistic for recovery. Most of McPherson's winning margin came from

Franklin County, despite his descent from a prominent Adams County family. To prevail in 1860, however, the Democrats had to ensure their position did not further erode.

The 1860 Election and the Fugitive Slave Issue

In 1858, Republicans had done well across the North. Their strong showing had revived the hopes of 1856—that by carrying all the Northern states, the Republican Party would control the electoral college and elect the next President. In Pennsylvania, the possibilities for success had been improved by the national party's decision to support a strong tariff, winning support in vital manufacturing and coal mining districts. The party leadership also was determined to maintain unity among the varied parts of the statewide fusion coalition. In particular, if former Know Nothings could be persuaded to vote Republican instead of Democratic, success would be almost assured. Here is where the difficult Republican–Whig–Know Nothing fusion politics of the 1850s paid off. By 1860, most Know Nothings were already in the Republican fold, having voted for candidates supported by Republicans in fusion elections. The trick would be to keep them voting Republican, despite determined Democratic efforts to pry them away.[28]

Perceptive Democrats realized that defeat in 1860 was likely, with secession after that a possibility. During the 1850s, Northerners had been president, but many Southerners had felt protected by Millard Fillmore, Franklin Pierce, and James Buchanan, Northern Democratic "doughfaces" who relied on Southern support. Abraham Lincoln was a different kind of Northern politician, running on a platform opposed to slavery extension. The Democratic Party split at the Charleston convention. When the party reconvened in Baltimore, Deep South delegates nominated John C. Breckenridge, while most Northern Democrats supported Stephen Douglas at a second convention in Baltimore. A third candidate, John Bell, a Constitutional Unionist and former Whig, appealed to the Upper South. The platform adopted at Charleston had specifically endorsed the Fugitive Slave Law, arguing that because it was "designed to carry out an express provision of the Constitution, [it] cannot with fidelity therefore be repealed." Most of the platform, however, was concerned with slavery, the territories, and states' rights. These were the critical issues for 1860. Both Douglas's and Breckenridge's acceptance letters emphasized the territorial issue, and neither mentioned fugitive slaves.[29]

Douglas campaigned extensively, warning of war if the Republicans won. He attracted many Pennsylvania Democrats, and the *Compiler* prominently published his June 1859 speech in Philadelphia. Along the border, however, even John C. Breckenridge had support, particularly among Democrats who realized that as the candidate most acceptable to the South, he had the best chance to win. The split between the two Democrats was contentious, but a letter writer to the *Compiler* warned that either one must be preferred over the Republican: "Douglas or Breckenridge before Lincoln."[30]

Regardless of which Democrat was preferred, the Republicans were attacked with the now common tactic of racist smears. The *Compiler* summed up the difference in the Pennsylvania governor's race: "[Democrat] Gen. Foster is advocating the passage of the tariff bill and the interests of the white people of Pennsylvania; [Republican] Col. Curtin is stumping it in Pennsylvania in behalf of niggerism and the 'Nigger.'"[31]

Enthusiasm for Lincoln and the Republicans, however, was palpable in some parts of Adams County. In York Springs, a traditional area of opposition strength and antislavery sentiment, volunteers raised an eleven-foot flagpole topped by a Republican campaign flag. The "Wide Awakes," young Republican men who paraded in oilskin cloaks and carried lighted torches, demonstrated frequently. They were mocked by the *Compiler*, which reported (ironically, in view of later events) that their favorite marching song was a ditty suited to Gettysburg's border location—"Dixey's Land."[32]

As it became clearer that Lincoln could win and that the nation could fracture, Pennsylvania Democrats developed a "Plan of Union." Voters could select electors who would choose either Douglas or Breckenridge if either could win the Presidency with the support of Pennsylvania's Democratic vote. After the Democrat's defeat in the October statewide elections, this plan was largely moot. Andrew Curtin routed Henry Foster by 32,000 votes, and in south central Pennsylvania, Edward McPherson won reelection to Congress, although Foster outpolled Curtin in both Adams and Cumberland counties. Because Pennsylvania's October elections were seen as a harbinger of November's results, the Democrats grew desperate. The fugitive slave issue reappeared, this time raised not by abolitionists, Free Soilers, or Republicans, but by the Democrats. In a prominent, front-page article reprinted from the *Cincinnati Enquirer*, the *Compiler* warned that Republican defiance of the Fugitive Slave Law meant that they had little regard for the U.S. Constitution. According to the Cincinnati paper's accounting, ten Northern states prohibited their officers from arresting fugitive slaves; five forbade the use of jails in renditions; seven provided legal defense for fugitives; and three declared slaves free if their master brought them into the state. New Hampshire even recognized a slave as free if he escaped to the state on his own.

Pennsylvania and eight other states imposed sizable fines or prison terms if the slave owner violated these personal liberty laws.[33]

This last-minute agitation of the fugitive slave issue failed to sway the election, but it was an omen of what would come. Lincoln won in Pennsylvania and carried the North. Across the state, although 16,000 fewer voters participated in the November elections than in October, Lincoln won 5,640 more votes than Curtin—a sure sign that the Democrats had become demoralized after their October defeat. Lincoln also carried Adams County, although all of the Democratic votes, including "straight out" votes as well as votes for the "Union ticket" of Breckenridge and Douglas electors, amounted to three more than Lincoln's total. Lincoln's plurality in the county should not be interpreted as a strong turn to the Republican Party.

The Fugitive Slave Issue, the Secession Crisis, and Pennsylvania's Petition Campaign

Statewide, the Democratic reaction to Lincoln's election was so immediate that it was probably pre-planned. In their moment of crisis, Pennsylvania's Democrats seized on the fugitive slave issue. Repealing personal liberty laws would harm no white Pennsylvanians, and it could be portrayed as respect for the Constitution, law and order, and comity. Almost immediately, the *Compiler* highlighted a fugitive slave rescue in Chicago. The paper warned that the rescue, occurring as South Carolina was sliding toward secession, marked "the beginning of the end." A week later, it printed remarks from the *Journal of Commerce*, which, like the *Cincinnati Enquirer*, had published a summary of how the North had "broken faith" through its personal liberty laws. The national journal opined that "Northern thieves steal great numbers of slaves in the border slave States, and . . . harbor them . . . or send them off to Canada." The solution to the disruption of relations was for the North to *"fulfil the stipulations of the Constitution."*[34]

Recognizing the risk to national unity posed by Lincoln's triumph, Pennsylvania's Democratic leaders and newspapers called for a petition campaign urging repeal of Pennsylvania's obstructive law to preserve sectional peace. The *Harrisburg Patriot and Union*, a statewide Democratic journal, called for the Republicans to "at once repeal their Personal Liberty bills."[35]

This movement to repeal the personal liberty laws was very shrewd: Whether it held promise to avert war, as many hoped, if war came, it created a way to blame Republicans for it. This approach could generate a groundswell to blunt Republican gains in Pennsylvania and elsewhere. It was also a tactic being adopted in legislatures across the South because it created a powerful argument that Northerners had breached their constitutional responsibilities, and essentially had seceded first. This approach was vital to binding moderate and conservative Southerners to secession, and even during the Civil War, Confederate soldiers' diaries would contain angry entries that Northern failures to return fugitives had helped cause the war.[36] In the North, this approach angered a constituency that the race-baiting Democrats cared little about: Pennsylvania's disfranchised African Americans and their committed abolitionist allies, who were not likely to vote Democratic anyway.

By December, accounts were pouring in to Democratic newspapers from Southern mass meetings. One in South Carolina denounced the "unfriendly legislation" of many Northern states as an "outrage" which was "demanding resistance." In an editorial, the *Compiler* remarked that the Democratic press was unanimous in demanding "speedy repeal of the nullifying acts" of Northern state legislatures. As soon as the new Congress opened, Stephen Douglas was expected to introduce a bill to make it a penal offense to obstruct U.S. officers from carrying out the Fugitive Slave Law.[37]

In Pennsylvania, the campaign to repeal the personal liberty law emanated from Philadelphia, the state's traditional Democratic stronghold. The city's mercantile community was strongly tied to Southern commerce. In 1859, some Philadelphia merchants had even proposed resuming the slave trade, as a way of meeting—and profiting from—the rising demand for slaves in the cotton South. Philadelphia's Democratic Party was led by Robert Tyler, a former chairman of the Democratic State Central Committee, and the brother of John Tyler, the Virginia planter and former Democrat chosen to be the Whig Vice Presidential Candidate in 1840. When William Henry Harrison died suddenly, and Tyler became president, he had supported Southern positions. Robert Tyler, too, had pro-Southern leanings and was accused of urging Pennsylvania to join the Confederacy. His views were sufficiently extreme that he was forced to leave Philadelphia for the South once the Civil War began.[38]

That city's Democrats, led by the mayor, turned out in early December for a massive Union meeting in Independence Square. It urged repeal of the personal liberty laws and compensation for owners of rescued slaves. Judge George Woodward, a leading Democrat who would run for governor in 1863, addressed the gathering. Woodward decried "[the] Liberty bills," and asked, "What part of the purposes of the founders are the underground railroads intended to promote?"[39] The repeal movement was also supported by the Pennsylvanian in the White House. In his December 3 message on the crisis, Buchanan urged repeal of Northern personal liberty laws and suggested Congress pass a Constitutional amendment to nullify them.[40]

Pennsylvania's petition campaign and the Union meetings were parts of a concerted effort to mollify Southern anger over Lincoln's election. Printed literature was a third ingredient. Joshua Fisher, the likely author of "Concession and Compromise," a pamphlet published in Philadelphia and intended for wide circulation, proposed a number of ingenious constitutional modifications to preserve national unity. He urged that all state laws obstructing the return of fugitive slaves be immediately repealed and that "suitable penalties" be applied to individuals who interfere with the Fugitive Slave Law. The author also argued that in case of a slave rescue, the county where it occurred should be liable for the slave owner's loss. In return for these concessions, the author proposed that the Fugitive Slave Law should be modified to have a five-year statute of limitations, and to guarantee a jury trial, albeit in the Southern county from which the slave was said to have escaped. He also argued for a right of transit for slave owners visiting free states.[41]

Fisher saw Pennsylvania as the key locale: If the Northern border states could compromise with the Southern states, "the crusade against slavery will end" and "the political philanthropists of New England must seek some new field for their labors."[42]

This pamphlet explicitly supported the petition drive on these topics. This campaign was more than just a reprise of the 1851–53 statewide contention over Pennsylvania's personal liberty laws. This time, similar concerns were expressed across the nation. Kentucky Senator John J. Crittenden made the fugitive slave issue an integral part of his proposals to end the sectional crisis. After resolutions to extend the Missouri Compromise line, guaranteeing the right of transit and forbidding Congress from abolishing slavery (including in the District of Columbia), Crittenden's fifth resolution called for Congress to compensate the owners of fugitive slaves who were rescued. The United States also would gain the right to sue the county where the rescue occurred for reimbursement. Crittenden's bill was accompanied by resolutions calling for the repeal of personal liberty laws. Even William Seward, the militant Republican governor of New York, experienced an eleventh-hour conversion on the fugitive slave issue that made the friends of noted Underground Railroad conductor Harriet Tubman fear for her personal safety. (Tubman lived in a house she was buying from Seward.) In 1850, Seward had electrified the country by advocating a "higher law" than the U.S. Constitution and the Fugitive Slave Law, and the American Anti-Slavery Society had printed 10,000 copies of his speech. In 1857, he had proclaimed an "irreconcilable conflict" between free and slave labor societies. Now, Seward too began to advocate enforcement of the Fugitive Slave Law as a way to preserve the Union.[43]

In the last thirty years, historians have recognized the importance of the critical issue of slavery extension to the territories to the Northern electorate, and highlighted its pivotal role in the 1860 presidential campaign.[44] If this issue was so important, why, on the eve of the Civil War, was there a massive petition campaign focused on the fugitive slave issue, not slavery extension? One reason was political: Antislavery Republicans could be placed on the defensive through attacks on the fugitive slave issue. Aside from that, the petition campaign appears to have been rooted in a genuine perception that Southern states were angry, fearful of the safety of their slave property, and likely to secede. One of the issues Southern statesmen fulminated over in their public statements was the fugitive slave question—in part to attract slave owners and citizens undecided about secession in the Border States and elsewhere to their cause.[45] Finally, and this should not be discounted, the fugitive slave issue, through the repeal of the personal liberty laws, was one of the few points that could be effectively addressed by Northern states.

Undoubtedly, many Southerners were angry that Northerners failed to return fugitives.[46] Pennsylvania's reluctance to remand fugitives had caused disputes between the Pennsylvania legislature and those of Maryland and Virginia for three decades. In the 1840s, some Virginians had urged an embargo on Northern goods over the fugitive slave issue. Complaints about Northern failures—particularly Pennsylvania's—to enforce fugitive slave laws had marked the Nashville Convention in 1850, the Georgia resolutions in 1850 and 1851, and Missouri Senator Thomas Hart Benton's published comments in 1856. A Pittsburgh fugitive slave case also caused an eruption of anger in Virginia in 1856. After a mob prevented the owner, James Parsons, from capturing his slave, and he was indicted on kidnapping charges, some Virginia legislators called for retaliation on Pennsylvanians and their property in Virginia. Others warned that if abolitionists were not stopped, they would actually invade Virginia to free fugitive slaves—a dark dream that came true at Harpers Ferry.[47] In the late 1850s, Southern anger was compounded by a Republican campaign to repeal the Fugitive Slave Law in Ohio, Wisconsin, Massachusetts, and other Northern states. When South Carolina seceded in November 1860, its "Declaration of the Immediate Causes" complained prominently about Northern states' failure to meet their obligations under the Fugitive Slave Law. Pennsylvania was mentioned specifically. Georgia also highlighted the Fugitive Slave Law in its secession convention and documents.[48]

While the anger was genuine, by 1860 the focus had subtly shifted. Many Southern leaders were not as vexed about the fugitive slave issue as they were about the restrictions on extending slavery to the territories, which was feared would lead to the extinction of slavery. This was where the Republicans and the new president represented a fundamental threat to the South. It was Lincoln's refusal to concede this point that defeated efforts such as the Crittenden Compromise, not the fugitive slave issue.[49]

Still, in Pennsylvania, short of instructing Congressional representatives how to vote—and that was difficult, because outside of the compromise proposals, there was no pending legislation before Congress on the territories—the only accessible way to ease the crisis seemed to be repealing the restrictive 1847 law, now codified into the new state penal code in 1860. The pro-compromise petitioners also sought to allow slaves to be brought into the state by Southern visitors (abolitionists feared that this would ultimately subvert Northern personal liberty laws). In addition, the Pennsylvania Colonization Society took advantage of the political situation to start its own campaign, urging state funding of the society as a solution to the unrest regarding African Americans.

War of Words: The Petition Campaign Against the Personal Liberty Law

The petition campaign to repeal Pennsylvania's personal liberty laws, and a counter-campaign by abolitionists to maintain them, was truly extraordinary. Petitioning was a sacred right to antebellum Americans, and petitions concerning slavery, fugitive slaves, African American immigration, and colonization had been received by the Pennsylvania legislature since the 1820s. Generally, however, there were only a few such petitions a year. Carl Oblinger claims that numerous petitions urging financial support for colonization were sent to the legislature in the late 1820s, but after that, the number drops off considerably.[50] There was a brief flurry of petitions to the 1837–38 state constitutional convention over issues of African American suffrage and immigration. During most of the later antebellum period and the war, the Pennsylvania Senate annually received six or fewer petitions or memorials relating to slavery or colonization, out of a total number typically ranging between three and six hundred. The exception was 1847, when an orchestrated campaign of over fifty petitions pressured the state legislature to pass the personal liberty law. In 1861, a record year for petitions in general, nearly one hundred were received relating to Pennsylvania's personal liberty laws, the right of transit, African American immigration, colonization, and equal rights for African Americans. After 1861, the number of petitions on topics relating to

African Americans precipitously declined to an average of two a year, even during post-war campaigns for equal treatment for African Americans on Philadelphia's public transportation.

There was another reason 1861 was unique. The previous peak year for petitions relating to slavery, fugitive slaves, and African Americans, 1847, had been a coup by antislavery forces to put pressure on the legislature to pass a new personal liberty law. The eve of the Civil War represented the only time when both abolitionists and colonizationists, Democrats and Republicans, Unionists, militants, and pacifists had flooded the legislature with petitions, making the contest truly a "war of words." The political crisis restored the fugitive slave issue to burning importance.

Many of the petitions urging repeal of the state's personal liberty law or concessions to Southern slave owners came from Democratic-led "Union Meetings" being conducted around the state. These meetings typically passed resolutions urging restored relations with the South and removal of all barriers to the rendition of fugitive slaves. At a Union meeting in Carlisle in December, many of the county's luminaries, including much of the local bar, had signed a petition to repeal the personal liberty law. The meeting was chaired by Frederick Watts, a leading lawyer who had prosecuted slave catcher Emmanuel Myers; as a judge, he had sent kidnapper Martin Auld to jail. He was also a former president of the state's Agricultural Society.

The Union meetings and the petition campaigns reveal the importance of the border in the sectional crisis. Pennsylvanians believed that their state should play a key role and that sectional reconciliation could lie in their hands. Most escaping fugitive slaves on the Eastern Seaboard had to pass through Pennsylvania, which had passed some of the first effective personal liberty laws interfering with the recovery of fugitive slaves. If issues regarding fugitive slaves could be resolved, perhaps war could be averted.

For the historian, the explosion of petitions offers a rare glimpse of antislavery and pro-colonization support at something approximating the grassroots. While some antislavery petitions were signed by influential, socially prominent individuals, or, more rarely, low status individuals (such as the 1847 Gettysburg petition of African Americans), in most cases, petitioners represented the emerging middle class. These were the middling ranks of the "antislavery rank and file," to use historian Edward Magdol's expression. Because both sides were petitioning the legislature in 1860, analyzing these petitions also gives us insight into the "pro-colonization or pro-compromise rank and file." Examining the petition signers gives us insight into the political and social divisions over fugitive slaves, African Americans, and slavery in Pennsylvania on the eve of the Civil War.[51]

In the 1860–61 Pennsylvania campaign, petitions supporting colonization, repeal of the personal liberty law, and restrictions on African Americans outnumbered by nearly four to one petitions supporting the personal liberty law and African American rights. Several of these came from south central Pennsylvania. One late-arriving pro-colonization petition was sent from Chambersburg, the county seat of Franklin County, in south central Pennsylvania (Appendix E). It was submitted with a similar petition from adjacent Adams County. These petitions sought to defuse sectional tensions by pointing a way forward to the ultimate resolution of the nation's dilemma by colonizing its African Americans. The Pennsylvania Colonization Society also hoped for state funding for its ventures.

The Chambersburg petition, which urged that the legislature appropriate money to the Pennsylvania Colonization Society (PCS), was signed by twenty-nine individuals; of these, sixteen could be clearly identified in the 1860 census records. Most of these were part of the rising town elites or middle class. All sixteen were from the Chambersburg area; three were wealthy "gentlemen," five were urban professionals (two attorneys, one physician, one clergyman, and one school teacher), and two were from the Chambersburg mercantile community (one merchant, one clerk). The rest were artisans: a printer, a machinist, a tanner, a bookbinder, a stone cutter, and a silver plater. All owned real estate as well as personal property, except for the clerk, the physician, and the school teacher. All of the signers who could be located in the census were born in Pennsylvania except for a German school teacher, a stone cutter from Scotland, and the printer, who was born in Maryland. Professionally, all of them could benefit from not offending southern clients in a border area. The signatories included B. S. Schneck, a theological professor at the Mercersburg Seminary, and William Heyser, a Chambersburg businessman and champion of the Cumberland Valley Railroad. Heyser's diary of the Civil War period has been preserved, and from it, we know that he had several African American servants. Only three signers of this petition were fifty or above, with only Heyser being above sixty (he was sixty-four). Three signers were in their twenties, three in their thirties, and six in their forties.[52]

Similar demographics can be observed in the Adams County colonization petition sent in with the Franklin County one (Appendix F). This petition had thirty-seven signers, thirty-two of which could be identified in the 1860 census. In addition, a third petition of twelve names arrived later from Adams, with identical language, requesting support for the PCS (Appendix G). Combining these petitions—seven individuals signed both—offers a slightly larger sample set to appraise Adams County's pro-colonization population. The signers were largely professionals and merchants in Gettysburg: seven merchants, seven attorneys, two, possibly three coach makers, two college professors, two physicians, a bank clerk, clergyman, clerk, clothier, confectioner, druggist, furniture dealer, hatter, printer, salesman, and saddle maker. (Two individuals of means had no listed occupation and nine others could not be found in the census.) Gettysburg's coach-making industry in particular was dependent on wealthy Southern customers from Virginia and Maryland. Most of these signers were between twenty and thirty-nine years of age, with significant numbers in their forties and fifties. The approximate average age in 1861 was 40.5.[53]

This pattern of town professionals and artisans expressing their support of the colonization society at this moment of crisis was not limited to south central Pennsylvania. A petition from Bucks County, in the southeastern corner of the state, supports this trend. In Bucks County, one petition supporting the PCS came in from Doylestown, the county seat (Appendix H). Of the thirty-one signers, twenty-four could be confidently identified in the 1860 census. While some had traditional rural occupations—three were farmers, one a drover, and one a laborer—most fit into the town professions. Five of the signers were lawyers, and one a law student. One was an Episcopal clergyman, one was a merchant, one a bank clerk, one a store clerk, one was a gentleman, and another had no occupation listed. Town artisans and craft professionals were represented as well: One signer was a butcher, one was a machinist, one made furniture for cars, and another made or operated "conveyances" (carriages). Only six of the signers were over forty, and the two oldest were sixty. The average age in 1861 was thirty-nine.[54]

Petitions supporting colonization or compromise on the fugitive slave issue greatly outnumbered petitions supporting African American rights or a standfast approach urging no change in Pennsylvania's legal code (the 1847 personal liberty law had been codified in 1860). Still, twenty-one of those types of petitions were sent in to the legislature, the largest number since the 1847 campaign for a strengthened personal liberty law. Not one of these petitions came from south central Pennsylvania—Adams, Cumberland, or Franklin counties. There are several possible reasons for which this. According to Ed Ayers, Franklin County had no organized antislavery society, although there was a strong Underground Railroad in the county. The antislavery society in Carlisle was shunned by white abolitionists; African Americans in the county seats of rural counties generally did not petition the state legislature, Gettysburg's in 1847 being a notable exception. Adams County, however, had both a functioning Underground Railroad, with both white and black participants, and an antislavery society, at least until 1847.[55] In addition, Adams County's antislavery activists had petitioned the state legislature before: Both white and black abolitionists had campaigned for a stronger personal liberty law in 1846–47.

Why, at this moment of supreme crisis and risk for fugitive slaves, did Adams County's antislavery activists not send a memorial to Harrisburg? We can only speculate, but at least three possibilities suggest themselves. First, the core activists involved in petitioning the legislature in 1846 had aged significantly. The average age of white Adams County petitioners urging a personal liberty law had been about forty-two in 1846. If new blood had not entered their ranks, the average age of these same individuals would have been about fifty-seven in 1861—and some probably would have died. Those remaining may not have had the drive and determination to mount a petition campaign. Westward migration had also reduced Adams County's antislavery community; even stalwarts like Joel and Lydia Wierman had left—Joel had been an active petitioner in the 1830s. Finally, and perhaps most significantly, Adams County and Franklin County were on the southern border of Pennsylvania. If war came, they would be on a prime invasion route. This might diminish the enthusiasm of both petition circulators and signers for a campaign that could risk rupture with Southern neighbors.[56]

To get a sense of the demographic makeup of antislavery supporters in Adams County, then, requires reexamining the 1846 petition discussed earlier. That petition showed strong support for protecting fugitives in the eastern part of the county, closer to Carlisle and York than Gettysburg. Almost all of the signers were farmers, although there were a few in rural artisanal occupations. A sarcastic petition sent in 1845 to Congress from Gettysburg suggests that there was antislavery support there as well, but in general the picture that emerges is a concentration of antislavery support among the rural populace. Many of the elites in the county seats supported colonization, and while opposition to slavery and support for colonization were not always diametrically opposed, by 1861 committed abolitionists and many antislavery supporters no longer supported colonization.

The picture emerging from Adams County, of antislavery support in southern Pennsylvania centered in rural areas and market towns not including the county seat, is supported by another 1861 petition from Bucks County. This Bucks County petition (Appendix I) asked that no change be made to the state's personal liberty laws and that an old law not be reinstated permitting Southerners to travel through or live in the state for up to six months without losing their slaves.[57] This Bucks County petition was signed by thirty-eight individuals, thirty-one of whom could be identified in the 1860 census; two others were identified by genealogical research. These petitioners generally lived near the village of Newtown; almost all worked in rural, non-professional occupations. At least fifteen signers were women; eastern Pennsylvania abolitionists and Quakers and the Pennsylvania Female Anti-Slavery Society eagerly recruited female signers in many petition campaigns.[58] Only four woman had a listed occupation, working as domestics, but eight others were married to farmers or lived with them and would be termed farmers today. Among the men, twenty-one signers were farmers, one an "assistant farmer," one was a farmhand, one with no listed occupation lived with a farmer, and one was a prosperous landlord. Another petitioner was listed as a gentleman. The only artisan identified was a "master wheelwright." Despite the presence of ten signers over the age of fifty, the average age of the signers in 1861 was about forty-one years old. The average age of the male signers was forty-seven (a number of the women signers were under twenty-five). Many of the signers had common Quaker last names, and the Quakers had a strong presence in rural Bucks County. At a time when the Keystone state was industrializing, then, committed antislavery support for Africans Americans in southern Pennsylvania appears to have bèen concentrated in rural enclaves, often around Quaker meetings. This demographic profile would seem to support David Donald's controversial contention that many antislavery advocates were from the agricultural classes, and felt displaced by the changes being brought by rapid industrialization. Donald has been criticized for the representativeness of his sample, but his model appears to hold true in at least the eastern part of Adams County. This constituency was aging or migrating westward in the last decades before the Civil War. At the same time, many of the professionals and artisans in larger towns, particularly county seats, supported colonization or the repeal of Personal Liberty laws. Even Thaddeus Stevens, as we have seen, was a sometime colonizationist before converting to abolitionism; his radical abolitionism may not have been sealed until he moved out of south central Pennsylvania. This long-term trend of an aging rural antislavery constituency and a rising class in county seats who wanted to be rid of African Americans did not bode well for any significant postwar advances in African American rights in rural Pennsylvania.[59]

In addition, this analysis suggests that Hal Barron's cogent observation regarding Antimasonry may be applicable to rural antislavery as well. He argued that Antimasonry may have been "an attack on local privilege and a home-grown aristocracy centered in the village instead of the countryside." In south central Pennsylvania, antislavery rose from Antimasonry's dying embers; perhaps it, too, appealed to a rural constituency concerned about arrogant local elites willing to compromise on slavery.[60]

1861: Denouement

As the new year opened with the petition campaigns underway, Democrat William F. Packer, the outgoing governor, discussed the fugitive slave issue extensively in his annual address to the legislature. In the previous session, the 1847 law had been codified as part of Pennsylvania's revised penal code, but Packer considered it to be a dead letter. He urged return, if possible, to the 1826 anti-kidnapping act. Packer also favored a right of transit for Southerners to bring their slaves through the state.[61]

Virginia's governor, John Letcher, expressed similar sentiments. In January, he had called "unconditional repeal" of the North's personal liberty laws his primary demand. He also insisted on continued slavery in the District of Columbia; equality for Southerners in the territories; the right of transit through Northern states, with compensation if slaves were lost; the maintenance of the internal slave trade; and the stipulation that "Government cannot appoint office holders hostile" to Southern rights. Letcher urged that commissioners visit the legislatures of each state with a personal liberty law to urge its repeal, except the New England states, which he believed were too far down the path of resistance to the Fugitive Slave Law and slavery extension to be worth visiting. Letcher's pragmatism reflected the reality that Pennsylvania and Ohio were much more significant in terms of the fugitive slave issue. The Virginia governor felt that the crisis could be resolved if border moderates could be allowed to reach an understanding. He suggested that New England and western New York should secede and join Canada.[62]

These proposals swirled around Congress while a committee of fourteen "border states" met and recommended a repeal of all personal liberty laws. The committee members tried to address Northern concerns by also suggesting amending the Fugitive Slave Law to protect against kidnapping and eliminating financial incentive to rule for the owner by equalizing the fugitive slave commissioner's fees. The committee also proposed extending the Missouri Compromise line to the Pacific, which doomed their proposals, as the Republicans would not permit further extension of slavery.[63]

To pressure Republicans in Congress, throughout Pennsylvania citizens gathered to support the Crittenden Compromise. There were large meetings in York and Carlisle—the Carlisle meeting being at least the second Union Meeting of the crisis in that town. The renowned jurist Frederick Watts, whom the *Compiler* claimed was a Republican, chaired the meeting and "nobly" supported compromise over his party's divisive positions. The paper crowed, "It was a complete triumph of the friends of our country—a triumph of patriotism over Abolitionism—a triumph of reason over fanaticism and hatred."[64]

In Congress, Pennsylvanians continued to be at the heart of the compromise efforts. Former governor William Bigler, now a U.S. Senator, introduced a measure for a national referendum on the Crittenden Compromise. This would circumvent Republican obstructionists, and the Democrats were confident—perhaps rightly so—that many people had voted Republican in the fall thinking that Southern threats of disunion were a bluff. In Bigler's proposition, the U.S. government would pay slave owners full value for their slaves if intimidation or force prevented the U.S. marshal from successfully returning them. Then the U.S. government would sue the county where the rescue or intimidation had taken place for the value of the slave. The county could then sue the individuals involved.[65]

At the same time Bigler was promoting the Crittenden Compromise, petitions in support of it continued to flow into Congress. One Pennsylvania petition was supposedly 500 feet long. A petition from Maryland reportedly contained 17,000 signatures favoring the compromise; a New York petition claimed 63,000 signatures; one from Lancaster a thousand; one from rural Massachusetts contained nearly 27,000. Fourteen thousand women, from various states, signed another. The Democratic press, including the *Compiler*, promoted the pro-compromise movement. At no time in the previous forty years had an Adams County newspaper so directly supported a petition campaign, with the *Compiler* urging "Let the good work go on." It even printed a sample form for petitions in the paper, urging for them to be circulated and sent to McPherson, Bigler, and Cameron. The paper reported that five similar petitions had been sent to Congress from Littlestown and Hanover. The *Compiler* argued that the Crittenden Compromise was eminently fair—by extending the Missouri Compromise line to the Pacific, the North would be receiving three times more territory than the South. It urged the people to agitate for compromise until there was no hope left.[66]

The people tried, but the partisan battle lines were being drawn, as illustrated by another massive pro-compromise meeting in Philadelphia on January 16. Early in the repeal movement, published calls had gone out to "all men irrespective of party," even though most state Union meetings had been controlled by Democrats. Now that fiction was ended. This invitation went to "all men of all parties in opposition to the Republicans." The meeting proclaimed that the "Democrats are the true friends of the Union," and called for repeal of all legislation "unfriendly" to Southern "brethren." In particular, it urged the legislature to secure Southerners' slave property while they traveled through Pennsylvania.[67] The meeting hinted that if war could not be prevented, Pennsylvania should secede and declare neutrality.[68]

Pennsylvania's Democratic press warned that even a successful civil war would destroy Southern markets and ruin Northern manufacturers. In the Senate, Bigler stated that while zealots in Maine, Vermont, and Florida might be anxious to fight, this was not the case along the border, where there were no geographical barriers between North and South. Instead, there were abundant social, economic, and kinship ties. "All along this line there has been marrying and giving in marriage," Bigler intoned biblically. He declared, "Pennsylvania will never become the enemy of Virginia."[69]

In February, the Union meeting movement finally reached Adams County. One in Mountpleasant resolved to "take prompt and decided steps 'clearing our skirts' . . . by repealing all laws that . . . tend to impede the recovery of fugitives from service on the part of our brethren of the South." This meeting endorsed the Crittenden Compromise, opposed coercing the South, and applauded Bigler and Cameron. One speaker introduced an additional resolution implicitly criticizing the local Underground Railroad. It stated that the meeting was "not insensible of the many great wrongs perpetrated against [Southern] local institutions by the people of our section of the Union," and pledged to remove from the books all state laws that interfered with the Constitution.[70]

In mid-February the Harrisburg *Patriot and Union*, a Democratic paper, summarized the situation. Republicans blocked compromise, national unity, and peace. Southern demands were eminently reasonable:

> The first demand of the South is, that the provision of the Constitution requiring the return of fugitives from labor shall be faithfully executed, and that all State laws which embarrass, conflict with, retard, or obstruct the peaceful enforcement of the fugitive slave law shall be repealed. There is nothing unreasonable in this demand.—The South has a right to its runaway slaves, and the North has no right to protect them. . . .

The second Southern demand, the paper stated, was equal access for slaveholders to the territories. On the eve of war, border Pennsylvania's Democratic press portrayed its perspective of the secession crisis: The fugitive slave issue was the primary barrier to reunion and peace, with the issue of slavery in the territories second.[71]

After the Crittenden Compromise did not pass, Democratic anger mounted as it became clear that Congressional Republicans would not yield. The Peace Congress meeting at Washington's Willard Hotel adopted a modified version of a proposal by James Guthrie of Kentucky. Representatives from Pennsylvania, Rhode Island, Illinois, New Jersey, Delaware, and Maryland voted for the plan, but this initiative also failed.[72]

As the crisis worsened, the conflict between Gettysburg's papers heated up. The *Star* urged the *Compiler's* editors to "move down South," where their views would be welcomed. The *Compiler's* editor, Henry Stahle, replied, "We will not retort by advising the *Star* folks to take the underground railroad for Canada, where so many of their friends have gone. But that region will ere long be more congenial to their feelings than this . . ."[73]

While there is no evidence of petitions to the state legislature from Adams County residents supporting the personal liberty law, the *Star* reported that one petition with 106 signatures had been sent to Representative McPherson, opposing the Crittenden Compromise. It asked that Congress stand by the Constitution, the Union, and the laws. The law and order sentiments used by Democrats in the mid-1850s to support the Fugitive Slave Law were now being invoked by their opponents to forestall concessions to the South.[74]

The Democratic paper clung to its slim hopes for averting disaster. In late March, it reported that the Rhode Island legislature had repealed its personal liberty law and that Maine was expected to do the same. In April, it declared that "The Constitution as It Is":

—Is against all Personal Liberty Bills in the States that conflict with the authority of the Federal Government.
—Against all Underground Railroads that run off servants from their masters South, to Canada or elsewhere, North.
—Against all mobbing of U.S. Marshals that in the line of duty execute Federal laws.
—Against the denial of all right of transit North for servants as well as masters.[75]

The fugitive slave issue, then, which by mid-decade had been eclipsed in Pennsylvania by Know Nothingism and Kansas, now appeared to be critical to resolving the sectional crisis. How much of this revival of interest was the result of the desperate raid at Harpers Ferry cannot be definitely determined. Certainly, the actions and responses of John Brown, abolitionists, and the party of Lincoln revived national interest in a political issue that had been largely an afterthought along the border in the aftermath of the Kansas-Nebraska act, at least in the press. South Carolina's Declaration of Causes had featured the fugitive slave issue prominently, and named Pennsylvania as a principal offender; and at least three of the major compromise proposals in Congress had made an improved rendition process a key to sectional reconciliation. In Pennsylvania, a massive campaign of petitions, meetings, and literature had tried to place pressure for compromise on both the state legislature and the state's delegation to Congress. All of these efforts had failed. From December to February, seven Deep South states had seceded, and the slave states closer to the border hung in the balance. War and national rupture were at stake.

The key to the crisis would be the decisions of these Southern border states, especially Virginia, the state with the most slaves. Whether Virginia seceded would determine the safety of south central Pennsylvania, which lay disquietingly close to the Old Dominion. Virginia's decision, however, would largely be determined by men pulling lanyards in Charleston Harbor and by Lincoln in the White House, calling for volunteers. Lincoln's call would chase Virginia, North Carolina, Tennessee, and Arkansas out of the Union. The resulting war would also transform the fugitive slave issue from concerns about individual fugitives to deep apprehensions about a mass movement north by southern African Americans.

8

Contrabands, "White Victories," and the Ultimate Slave Hunt

Recasting the Fugitive Slave Issue in Civil War South Central Pennsylvania

All hopes for peaceful reunion exploded at Fort Sumter. Then Lincoln's call for volunteers pushed most of the Upper South to secede. Where the Potomac River bent closest, south central Pennsylvania lay less than five miles from Virginia, and the possibility of Maryland joining Virginia in the new Confederacy gravely endangered the region. Anger over secession and concerns about recruitment and local defense overshadowed the fugitive slave controversy, which some saw as largely moot. The issue, however, was only pushed to the background, soon reemerging in the form of bitter partisan conflict over African American refugees. These fugitives, who clustered in southern Pennsylvania, especially in Franklin County, had a new name, "contrabands," because of their potential military value.[1] Later, a vengeful Confederate army captured hundreds of African Americans during its invasion of the region in 1863.

The war's commencement, then, temporarily eclipsed but did not end the focus on the fugitive slave issue. Instead, over time, the issue's scope and impact grew. Through the "contrabands" issue—the controversy over the movement of African American slaves to Northern states and U.S. military camps—the issue was transformed into a vital part of the debate about the meaning and extent of the war.[2]

The debate over secession had been highly politicized and so was the war, especially along the Pennsylvania border, where concerns for sectional amity had been pronounced, and an influx of African Americans was expected. The Democratic Party, whose national power relied heavily on support from its Southern wing, had the most to lose from a permanent rupture. The party and its press were determined to limit the war effort to restoring the Union. The intensity of their racially charged rhetoric actually increased during the war.[3] They opposed leniency toward runaway slaves, emancipation of Southern slaves, and particularly African American military participation, because they would all make a quick reunion difficult. The party's bills to restrict African American immigration into the state also attracted substantial support.

Even with the start of the war, Pennsylvania's Democrats refused to relinquish the fugitive slave issue. Less than two weeks after the bombardment of Fort Sumter, the *Republican Compiler*, Gettysburg's Democratic paper, printed a rumor that John Brown, Jr. was training 400 African American soldiers in western Pennsylvania. The paper urged Governor Curtin to disperse the gathering, if it existed, and to assure "these negroes" that "white men will attend to this war." Rebellion must be punished without the Government encouraging "another John Brown to gratify the vengeance of runaway negroes."[4]

The war had forced the Democrats to recycle material; this piece was actually an update of a similar rumor, which had circulated in the state's Democratic press in the aftermath of John Brown's raid. This reuse seems appropriate, however, as much of the Democratic critique of the war, including the contrabands issue, was also an updating of familiar themes from the late antebellum period.

Politically, south central Pennsylvania's 1850s turn toward the Democratic Party, Edward McPherson excepted, continued during the war, even as the state was trending Republican. Adams County followed the call of its leading Democratic newspaper to vote for the "white man's ticket" and supported both Democratic gubernatorial candidate George Woodward in 1863 and presidential nominee George B. McClellan in 1864. In response, the region's embattled Republicans labeled any attacks on war policy as dangerously pro-Southern and potentially treasonous. The bitter partisan conflict was exemplified in the multiple arrests of Gettysburg's Democratic editor, Henry J. Stahle, for sedition and suspected disloyalty during the turbulent summer of 1863.

Not only did the war keep partisan conflict white-hot, it substantially disrupted the area's communities to an extent unparalleled elsewhere in the North. In addition to the universal experience of young men enlisting, south central Pennsylvania also suffered substantial physical and social devastation. Chambersburg in Franklin County burned in 1864, and Gettysburg, in adjacent Adams County, experienced a massive three-day battle, accompanied by the burden of burying the dead and caring for thousands of wounded. Most pronounced, however, was the disruption brought to the area's African American community. Robert E. Lee's 1863 invasion caused a massive flight of refugees and free blacks from Maryland and the south central Pennsylvania counties to Harrisburg and Philadelphia, and many of those unable to flee or hide were captured by Lee's soldiers as potential fugitives and re-enslaved or imprisoned. This left the area's African American communities disrupted just as citizens in Pennsylvania and, indeed, the North were contesting the role of African Americans in the war, and, by implication, in post-war society. The region's Civil War experience would influence the atmosphere of early Reconstruction in the region. The irony was that, as the war brought freedom to millions south of the Mason-Dixon Line, Pennsylvania's blacks would not win the full equality they sought from the war.

The attack on Fort Sumter and Lincoln's call for volunteers pushed the fugitive slave issue, such a consuming political topic in February 1861, briefly into the background. In its place was a deep, palpable anger toward the South among many Pennsylvanians who had tried so hard to preserve the Union. Republicans tried to stoke anger at Southern secession to increase support for the new administration. Having been criticized for months for their obduracy, Republicans jumped at the chance to label Southern secessionists traitorous villains. Democrats responded by using the suspension of habeas corpus, the contrabands issue, the Emancipation Proclamation, and wartime losses to make the war seem unnecessary, unconstitutional, and unworthy of support.

The rhetorical battle commenced even more quickly than the military ones. In Chambersburg, citizens gathered on April 18, 1861, just four days after the surrender of Fort Sumter. They passed resolutions blasting the "band of traitorous spirits" that had plotted the dismemberment of the Union. Jefferson Davis was labeled "the Arch traitor of all," but the resolutions also warned against the traitors in their midst.[5] This practice of implying that Northern Democrats were as dangerous as their seceding Southern counterparts began with the war's commencement and continued into Reconstruction.[6]

As the John Brown story illustrates, fears of violence by and concerning African Americans had particular resonance in wartime south central Pennsylvania. Some blamed African Americans for the war. On June 1, 1861, troops gathering in Chambersburg killed a local African American after he had tried to protect himself and his wife from a beating at their hands.[7] On June 3, 1861, as troops were about to move south into Virginia, their commander, General Robert Patterson, warned them that one of their responsibilities would be to "suppress servile insurrection."[8]

Most Union generals followed similar policies early in the war. Retaining support of the Border States was critical to the Union war effort, and Kentucky, Maryland, Delaware, and Missouri all included slaveholders. In addition, much of the Union leadership believed there was also a potentially large body of Unionist Southerners in the Confederacy, whose allegiance could be regained if the war effort was limited and did not disturb them or their property, including their slaves. These Unionist Southerners supposedly had been silenced by a few large slaveholders who would not let the true sentiments of the South be expressed.

This concept, known as the "Slave Power Conspiracy," was widespread among the Union leadership early in the Civil War.[9]

These views began to change after the debacle at Bull Run in the first battle of the war. This defeat was partly blamed on slave-built fortifications, and some troops and commanders thought seizing slaves would be the best approach to punishing secession and winning the war. Union troops securing the defenses of Harpers Ferry fashioned a labor force from escaping slaves from Virginia's Loudoun and Jefferson counties.[10]

At first, Pennsylvania's Democratic papers were undecided regarding the military use of fugitive slaves. The state organ, the *Harrisburg Patriot and Union*, in a piece reprinted by the *Compiler*, stated, "We are not prepared to indicate what disposition should be made of fugitives when they flock in great numbers to our camps. . . . But one thing is clear—our army cannot be diverted from the great purpose of putting down rebellion, either to protect fugitives or restore them to their masters." The papers opposed slaves escaping north, as they believed that they would congregate on the border. Adding to "the vagabond free negro population of Pennsylvania would be a calamity." They complained that the fugitive slaves already in the state were "non-producing" and recommended that all abolitionists be taxed to send them to Liberia. Variations of the "tax the abolitionists to pay for the cost of freed slaves" argument would continue throughout the war.[11]

Perhaps sensing a political vulnerability for the Republicans, the *Adams Sentinel* tried to defuse criticisms on the contraband issue and the abolition of slavery in Washington, D.C.[12] In general, however, it studiously avoided the issues. In Gettysburg, John T. McIlhenny's *Star* was reportedly ruthless toward Democrats and "Copperheads," but its positions on African Americans and fugitive slaves are difficult to divine, as only scattered issues are available.[13]

The "contrabands" dispute over wartime refugees was an extension of the pre-war debate over the fugitive slaves. The Democrats favored speedy rendition of fugitive slaves before the war and continued that position during it. They opposed permitting escaping Southern slaves to flee to protection behind federal lines. Some Republicans tried to protect fugitives before the war and, during the war, welcomed fugitive slaves from the Confederacy as sources of information, military labor, and a way of weakening the South. What the war changed was the scope and the number of fugitives under discussion.[14]

The orders to suppress insurrection, the controversy over "contrabands," and the riot in Chambersburg illustrate that by July 1861, tensions were emerging that would affect the partisan debate about African Americans and the nature of the war. Some area Democrats deplored the war; most wanted to punish the rebellious seceders but limit the war to restoring the Union "as it was," including retaining Southern slavery. Some Democrats believed in the "Slave Power" conspiracy, but almost all of them blamed the war at least partially on the Republican refusal to compromise their Chicago platform opposing the extension of slavery. They hinted that Republicans had an agenda to abolish slavery throughout the South, citing as evidence every effort made to harbor fugitive slaves, help the contrabands, or end slavery in the District of Columbia. Abolition would jeopardize a quick end to the war and jeopardize the position of the Democratic Party. It also threatened to flood Pennsylvania with African Americans, who, in the long run, could become Republican voters. To forestall this, the Democratic press intensified its race-baiting assaults on the Republicans to levels that exceeded the rhetoric of even the late 1850s.[15]

At the same time that some Democrats were criticizing the early war effort, the outbreak of the war solidified antislavery opinion along the border. During much of the 1850s, active resistance to federal legislation, such as the Fugitive Slave Law, had for some been tempered by the need to maintain the Constitution and preserve "law and order." The outbreak of war, however, removed this consideration and provided an opportunity for opponents of slavery to converge. By seceding, Southerners, already guilty of holding slaves, had created a colossal breach of law, order, and polity in Northern eyes. Now border politicians and journalists who opposed slavery but supported law and order could unite with radicals and let their anger rise. The animosity secession generated is illustrated in an 1861 address by Henry L. Baugher, the president of Pennsylvania (Gettysburg) College.

Like his colleague Samuel Schmucker, Baugher was a child of the border. One Southern student accused him of being "in sympathy with . . . Garrison and Phillips," but, based on limited evidence, it appears he actually was an antislavery moderate, as were many faculty at the college and seminary. Baugher had supported colonization in the mid-1830s, and he did not write letters to the *Liberator* or take a leading role in the Adams County Anti-Slavery Society, as Professor William L. Reynolds did. What Baugher did share with radicals like Garrison was a commitment to an egalitarian, color-blind society. His addresses and speeches throughout the 1850s, however, suggest that he supported preservation of the Union through compromise. He believed that slavery, while terrible, could be tolerated while political solutions for its extinction were pursued.[16]

Secession and war changed his attitude. In April 1861, Baugher had helped write the resolutions denouncing "treason," which were presented at the April 18 meeting in Adams County. His anger at secession was still pronounced five months later. In his address to the college's entering senior class, a group of young men of prime military age, he combined an opposition to slavery with a sense of the sacredness of law and the egregiousness of secession. Baugher believed that if the American polity were destroyed, anarchy would result because America did not have a monarchy or nobility to support social stability.[17] Therefore, he urged his students to enlist to fight and die, if need be, for their country. Those who could not enlist should support the government and pay the higher taxes that would be needed for victory. Failure to prevail would be a disastrous collapse of majority rule because successful secession would mean the triumph of a minority over a majority. For Baugher, majority rule was a logical extension of his belief in the political equality of all races and ethnicities. Legislative enactments that were unjust to one section should be remedied through political action, not secession and war. In this way, even unjust laws, properly rectified, could be part of God's plan.[18]

The address discussed the Buchanan Administration's controversial final actions and made no mention of the battle of Manassas or any other military events, suggesting that Baugher was reprising a message he wrote several months before the war's costs began to be apparent. About halfway through, however, he issued a chilling lament:

> Oh it is dreadful . . . that this government should be assailed by her own children, her plains covered with blood, her towns burned, her households made desolate, and her sons slain for the purpose of establishing the dominion of the few upon the ruins of the many.[19]

When Baugher made this grim prophecy, no one knew how much death and destruction would visit south central Pennsylvania in particular. A few months after this address was printed, Baugher's own household would be desolated by the death of his son from war wounds in May 1862.[20] Homes, businesses, and farms in Franklin and Adams counties would be damaged by Confederate invasion. The African American community would be devastated. Central Chambersburg would burn in 1864.

Baugher's address illustrates the animosity that resulted from combining resentment of an encroaching Slave Power with fury over the Southern states' significant breach of the Constitution. This anger would sustain many area Republicans and abolitionists throughout the war. It also fueled their repeated invocation of "treason" during—and after—the conflict.[21]

But while this convergence appears to have strengthened the convictions of those who were already opposed to slavery, given Adams County's consistent support for the Democrats during the war, it does not appear that antislavery supporters of the Union were able to substantially broaden their appeal there. The loss and potential loss—the death and desolation mentioned by Baugher— may have worked against them.

The Democratic Critique of the War Effort

For their part, the Democrats hoped that a short, limited war would spare the country the atrocities that Baugher feared. The principal obstacle Democrats saw to limited war was any effort to free the slaves. The *Republican Compiler* warned that the Administration would try to turn the conflict into a war of emancipation, and it strongly opposed an early proclamation by former Republican presidential candidate John C. Fremont, now a Union general, freeing the slaves of Missouri. The paper also published the "Ohio Resolutions," praising the soldiery but deploring abuse of *habeas corpus* and calling for a national convention to end the war.[22] (The *Compiler* would publish extensive material about the Ohio peace movement and the noted Peace Democrat Clement Vallandigham throughout the war.)[23] Because Republicans in Congress had blocked the Crittenden Compromise during the secession winter, the paper also supported the states calling a convention to ratify it as an amendment to the Constitution, outside of Congress.[24]

The Democratic vision of the war had appeal in southern Pennsylvania. The October 1861 elections in Adams County were extremely close, with the Republican candidate for the state legislature only triumphing by three votes—after months of dispute—as a result of the soldiers' vote. The Democrats gained a majority in the state House of Representatives, although the Republicans still controlled the state Senate.[25]

Emboldened by their victories, encouraged by their close defeats, south central Pennsylvania's Democrats extended their critique. They also attacked efforts by Union General David Hunter to free Southern slaves. The *Compiler* worried, in particular, about former slaves moving north into Pennsylvania. Warning that emancipation would mean the loss of a cotton crop that clothed millions, the paper opposed Hunter's efforts to free and arm slaves in areas along the South Carolina coast. The *Compiler* fumed: "The idea of putting muskets into the hands of such men as the slaves at Port Royal is . . . ridiculous."[26]

In June 1861, the state's Democratic press had been ambivalent about the military seizing fugitive slaves; by November, it was not. Union General Henry

Halleck had banned escaping slaves from military camps in his Ohio district, a decision praised by the *Compiler* on the grounds of stopping leaks of military information. The paper contrasted Halleck's policy of treating fugitive slaves as potential spies with that of the abolitionists who wanted to arm them. It also applauded General John Dix's proclamation that the U.S. Army would "have nothing to do with the slaves in any manner, shape or form."[27]

As 1862 opened, the Democrats seemed poised to advance politically in the North just over a year after their defeat at the hands of Abraham Lincoln. After initial reverses at Manassas, Ball's Bluff, and Wilson's Creek, Union military fortunes were now advancing, raising hopes of a short war, followed by a possible return to the *status quo ante bellum*. The U.S. Navy was blockading the Southern coastline, and amphibious operations were making incursions along the coast in the Carolinas and Florida. In the west, U.S. armies were preparing to move south into Tennessee. When Ulysses S. Grant delivered significant victories at Forts Henry and Donelson, and U.S. Marines captured Roanoke Island, the *Compiler* proclaimed that these were "white victories," because they could enable a rapid end to the war without emancipation.[28]

Although content with the progress of the war, the Democratic press was concerned about Administration policy. Particularly troubling was Lincoln's offer of compensated emancipation to the border states and bans on military officers returning fugitives. Soon, the *Compiler* predicted, Congress would "open up black Pandora's box as wide as possible" by amending the Fugitive Slave Law to permit trial by jury. Along with Harrisburg's *Patriot and Union* (Democrat), the paper feared that wages would be depressed by hordes of contrabands passing flooding into southern Pennsylvania, and agreed with it on "The Necessity for a White Man's Party," which would "hurl from power the black man's [Republican] party."[29]

The Wartime Movement of African Americans to South Central Pennsylvania

As the bloody fighting at Shiloh and elsewhere made clear that the "white victories" were not going to quickly end the war, resistance to liberated African Americans and escaped slaves moving north increased. During the war, thousands of escaped slaves fled to south central Pennsylvania and other locations in the southern part of the state. The *Carlisle Volunteer* proposed that every Lincoln voter be required to compensate border state slave owners for their runaways, and to post bond as surety against damages as fugitives moved north. Soon, however, Pennsylvania Democrats would be advocating an outright ban of African American immigration to remedy the "curse" of a flood of "runaway blacks" threatening to form a "degraded caste" to compete with white labor.[30]

At least some Pennsylvania Democrats saw the problem of African American slaves moving north as forming a continuum with pre-war concerns about fugitives, and not as a special wartime circumstance. In October 1861, the *Compiler* printed a notice from the Rockville (Md.) *Sentinel*, which described how one African American, Charles Johnson, had been apprehended as a fugitive by Maryland authorities near Frederick. Johnson, who claimed to be free, was found dressed in a military uniform and with a pass to Gettysburg. The paper published it "for the information of the public as to one of the ways and modes by which our negroes are enabled to escape to the North." The document, signed by an Assistant Adjutant General, asked that Johnson be passed to Gettysburg. At the bottom were listed the military commands with which he might come into contact, including Rockville, Westminster, Gettysburg, Chambersburg, and Philadelphia. By naming the individual and publicizing his intended routes, the article was remarkably reminiscent of the runaway ads of the 1820s.[31]

While the Democratic press rejoiced in the enforcement of the Fugitive Slave Act in Maryland in Charles Johnson's case, they regretted that the law was not as effectively implemented in Pennsylvania. In April 1862, the *Bedford Gazette* lamented that four runaway slaves had passed through that county in April. They were overtaken in Altoona, but, "as usual, the master was denied his property." "Such work," the paper remarked, "is, no doubt, very efficient in restoring the Union."[32]

The unwillingness of some Pennsylvania authorities to enforce the Fugitive Slave Law partly reflected a changing attitude among part of the populace. With secession and war, many Northerners felt liberated from complying with the onerous law. Anger toward secession appears to have translated into a rapid decline in public support for fugitive slave catching. O.P.M., an informant of a local Cumberland County historian at the turn of the twentieth century, reported that at least one Maryland slave catcher tried to continue his activities in the area until the Civil War. Not realizing "that the business of slave hunting in Pennsylvania had ended," he was summarily run out of Chambersburg on the eve of war and never returned. A populace that had tolerated him, or even collaborated with him, before had now, in the aftermath of secession, turned against him.[33]

As the summer moved into the fall campaign season, much of the local Democratic criticism of Republican policy centered on Edward McPherson, Adams County's Congressman, and the scion of one the county's antislavery families.

Democrats tried to portray McPherson, a protégé of Thaddeus Stevens, as a consistent Radical.[34] This was not true. For example, in the aftermath of the defeat at Bull Run, where the defeat was partially blamed on slave-built fortifications, a bill was placed before Congress to emancipate slaves used for insurrectionary and military purposes, including building fortifications and trenches. This was the first of a long line of emancipatory and confiscatory actions by the wartime Congress. McPherson, in contrast to Thaddeus Stevens and other Republicans, asked that this bill be tabled, so that he could move to postpone consideration until December—which would have been after the elections. When McPherson's efforts were not successful, he voted against the bill, which passed anyway. McPherson did vote for Lincoln's proposal for compensated emancipation in the border states. In light of what came later, this was a mild antislavery measure, but to border Democrats, it appeared to be a massive taxpayer-funded bribe to the border states to start emancipation.[35]

The *Compiler* tried to link McPherson with Stevens because Stevens was leading many of the initiatives the Democrats hated. He was one of the most powerful and radical Republicans in the wartime Congress. In 1861, Stevens had wholeheartedly endorsed the confiscation of slaves used by the Confederate military and even predicted that soon freed slaves would be needed to wage war on the South. In 1862, he managed the passage of the bill to abolish slavery in the District of Columbia. He also introduced Lincoln's proposal for compensated emancipation of the slaves of the border states.[36] In short, it was Stevens who wanted to confiscate the slave property of Southerners, who wanted to arm the slaves, who proposed military colonies of Union soldiers in the South, who argued that the war had made fundamental changes in the constitutional polity, and who refused to return to the Union "as it was" with slavery intact.[37] In contrast, the prevailing Democratic position was succinctly stated by General William Miller, a Pennsylvania congressional candidate. According to the *Compiler*, he "was for the Constitution as it is, the Union as it was, and the niggers where they are."[38]

General Miller's succinct summary of the Democratic program was just one example of the Democrats' attempts to use racial demagoguery to solidify their core and broaden their appeal. In the last issue before the October 1862 elections, the *Compiler's* editor defined for its readers the critical question of the local Congressional election: "if you desire confiscation, emancipation, and free negro immigration into Pennsylvania—then vote for MCPHERSON and elect an Abolition Congress . . . If you wish the Constitution maintained, the negro let alone. . . . the interests of the WHITE MAN respected and maintained—then vote for COFFROTH![39]

General A. H. Coffroth did defeat McPherson handily, including besting him by 450 votes in McPherson's native Adams County (Coffroth had also once lived in Adams County). The Democrats also carried York and Cumberland counties, with the Republicans maintaining a narrow margin in Franklin County. Nationally, Democratic victories in Pennsylvania, Ohio, and Indiana, and electoral gains in New York and New Jersey, were widely interpreted as a significant midterm rebuke to President Lincoln and the Republican Party. In reality, in some regards, the Republican performance was quite good. As James McPherson has pointed out, the Democratic margins in Pennsylvania, Ohio, and Indiana were small. Had absentee soldier voting been permitted, the results could have been reversed. The Republicans actually gained in the U.S. Senate and still held a significant majority in the U.S. House of Representatives.[40]

Still, while the results cannot be interpreted as a crushing defeat for the Republicans, they indicated substantial anxiety over the progress of the war, particularly among lower North voters from New York to Illinois. Along the border, residents recognized that their local economies were likely to suffer from continued rupture with the South, and many feared economic competition with freed slaves (Lincoln's preliminary Emancipation Proclamation was issued on September 22, 1862). They also knew that they could lie on an invasion path if Confederate forces again moved north, as they had in the September Antietam campaign, and, just before the election, J. E. B. Stuart's raid on Chambersburg. For Adams County, where a native son incumbent Republican congressman had been defeated, the election was another step in the transition to becoming a traditionally Democratic county. Republicans were still competitive in some local races, but the county as a whole was shifting away from the Republican Party just as the Republicans were preparing to hold the state as a whole through much of the Reconstruction period.[41] Certainly, there was nothing in the election results to persuade Democrats to slacken their assault on emancipation, contrabands, and the direction of the war.

The Debate over Emancipation and African Americans

The war's middle year, 1863, opened in this intense political atmosphere. It would be an extremely significant year for south central Pennsylvania's inhabitants, white and black. The invasion by General Robert E. Lee's Army of Northern Virginia during the Gettysburg campaign would devastate families, homesteads, and especially the African American community. Most of the region's blacks fled the Confederate advance, and hundreds were captured by the invading Confederate army, resulting in massive displacement. For many south central Pennsylvanians, especially African Americans, life would never be the same after the Confederate invasion.

The year dawned, however, with few portents that anything would be remarkably different. J. E. B. Stuart's October 1862 raid had affected Chambersburg and Franklin counties, but had touched only the edge of Adams County and left Cumberland County unscathed. It probably had not escaped the attention of the area's black community, however, that the troopers had taken a number of African American captives from Franklin County when they decamped. Except for African Americans, many people just learned to ignore continual rumors of Confederate invasion. A local judge even refused to adjourn court to respond to one rumored advance.[42]

On January 1, 1863, President Lincoln signed the final Emancipation Proclamation. This could make any Confederate invasion even more dangerous for the region's African Americans. Lincoln's action dominated much of the discussion of the war for the first few weeks of 1863. The *Sentinel*, the county's moderate Republican paper, supported the proclamation, although only tepidly. The Democrats used the occasion to revisit the "contrabands" issue, as the movement of freed slaves north thus far in the war suggested that thousands more might migrate in the aftermath of emancipation.[43] The *Compiler* even printed a satirical anti-black ditty about the "contrabands," a biting parody of James S. Gibbon's popular recruiting song, "We are coming, Father Abraham, Three Hundred Thousand More." Although originally published in Cincinnati, this satire referred to southern Pennsylvania as a potential destination for emancipated slaves:

> They [freed slaves] come, they come in multitudes,
> Along Ohio's tide;
> The "shucking tramp" of their brogans
> By Susquehanna's side. . . .
> And though the country may be poor,
> And labor be oppressed
> And white men starve and die in want,
> You surely will be blessed;
> For fools, in ages yet to come,
> Will sing your praises long:
> They are coming Father Abraham,
> About four millions strong.[44]

The Proclamation also led the Democrats to renew their efforts to ban newly emancipated blacks from migrating to Pennsylvania.[45] At first this began as simple exclusionary legislation against black and mulatto immigration, but then the bill's sponsor recast it as an amendment to the state constitution. This would make it harder to reverse, and it also now included a provision to colonize African Americans who were "already here, who may be willing to go." The exception was for fugitive slaves: They were to be returned to their masters. In support, Democratic legislators introduced petitions from Adams, York, and Lancaster counties. The bill passed the Democratic-dominated House but not the Republican-controlled Senate.[46]

The Democrats were unable to push through the immigration ban, but they did so well in local spring elections, on top of their congressional victory the previous year, that some area Republicans began to waver. Alexander K. McClure, the Republican power broker, editor, and Speaker of the Pennsylvania Senate, reportedly began to temporize and voice reservations about the Emancipation Proclamation.[47]

The Democrats were determined to exploit any advantage, and for the next several months, the topics of emancipation, African Americans, and immigration restrictions featured prominently in the *Compiler*. The unfairness of placing the cost of emancipation on taxpayers who had already paid heavily for the war was emphasized. The paper suggested that the government was neglecting white soldiers and focusing on African Americans. Published letters from Adams County's 165th Pennsylvania Regiment, which had strong representation from the county's German community, expressed anti-black sentiments. The *Compiler* also returned to sympathetic coverage of leading anti-war dissident Democrat Clement Vallandigham after his arrest for sedition.[48]

While Democrats criticized emancipation and laid plans for excluding or returning contrabands, abolitionists hoped to arm some of them, if they could succeed in creating African American military regiments. Massachusetts had already done this on a small scale; contrabands from south central Pennsylvania had filled out the ranks. Gettysburg's *Compiler* opposed the arming of African Americans; it was antithetical to the Democratic objective of a short, limited war with a return to the status quo, and it set a potentially troublesome precedent for arguments of African American equality and citizenship. The paper condemned Thaddeus Stevens and lame duck Edward McPherson for supporting the "negro soldier bill." "Is it not time," the paper asked, "to drop niggerism, and think and act for the country and its white taxpayers?" The Democratic critique of the Republican Party was becoming increasingly centered on issues of race, and the race-baiting was intensifying: In a reprint from another paper, the *Compiler* labeled the Republican press the "Kinkyhead" newspapers.[49]

Beyond their insidious racism, the Democratic press's slurs were deliberately political in intent. A significant portion of their constituency in southern Pennsylvania was among German and Irish immigrants, who themselves were struggling to be fully accepted by society as "white."[50] The response of the Democratic press to the rise of the Republican Party and the racial issues of the Civil War could be considered an example of "herrenvolk" democracy, the concept that the interests all whites had in maintaining their position atop the racial hierarchy should override political disputes within them. This concept was rarely made explicit, but it permeated the paper's appeal to the immigrants who were at the core of the party. Before and during the war, the *Compiler* hinted several times that Republicans had deliberately insulted immigrants by insinuating that African Americans were more intelligent.[51]

Despite Democratic opposition, the drive to recruit African Americans continued. Recruiters canvassed the state to enlist Pennsylvania's free blacks and contrabands into African American military units, especially the storied Massachusetts 54th and 55th Colored Infantry regiments. Because Pennsylvania did not permit the enlistment of African Americans into its own units, this was the only way the state's blacks could serve. Noted African American leaders including James Loguen and T. Morris Chester served as effective recruiting agents. Nearly one hundred African Americans from around Mercersburg in Franklin County volunteered for military service during the war, many with out-of-state units. Others came from Chambersburg, Shippensburg, and Carlisle.[52] By 1863, the Democratic press noted this activity. One of the state organs, Harrisburg's *Patriot and Union*, remarked that "The State is overrun with agents from Massachusetts seeking negro recruits for her unfilled quota of the army. . . . Massachusetts may have all the negroes she can raise from this quarter."[53] That last remark may have been facetious; several months later, the paper made the incendiary claim that black troops would be used to track down white deserters. By June, the *Patriot* reported that 1,155 African Americans had been recruited from Pennsylvania for Massachusetts's colored infantry regiments.[54] At the same time, Governor Curtin refused to receive African American troops as volunteers or militias, even during the invasion. This included a company offered under the leadership of Randolph Johnston, a Gettysburg African American.[55]

Democratic criticism of Republican policies and expressions of virulent anti-Republican sentiment amid the tenuous military situation concerned Republicans and Union military officials throughout the border North. In March, several Democratic newspaper offices in Ohio were raided. The brigadier general in charge of the Columbus district called for calm and conciliation. It was James Cooper's last act of public service. The former Adams County resident and one-time U.S. Senator died of illness soon afterwards.[56]

Also in Ohio, Democratic peace advocate Clement Vallandigham was arrested in May. So were five Adams County residents in Pennsylvania. The Provost Guard from Westminster, Maryland seized them in Littlestown, a mostly German community located almost on the Mason-Dixon Line. They were questioned about the secretive, putatively pro-Confederate organization the Knights of the Golden Circle. Another was arrested over a week later.[57] In the summer of 1863, during and after the battle of Gettysburg, Henry Stahle, editor of the *Compiler*, was arrested three times for suspected disloyalty.[58] A Democratic editor in Harrisburg was also arrested. Along with border Ohio, southern Pennsylvania was one of the areas where the populace's loyalties concerned Union leadership the most. They feared the peace movement taking hold in an area that lay directly on any Confederate invasion path toward the heart of Pennsylvania.

The Ultimate Slave Hunt: The Confederate Invasion of Pennsylvania

Soon Adams County residents would wish for a larger Union army presence than just the provost guard. In May 1863, Confederate forces had defeated the Union Army of the Potomac near the crossroads of Chancellorsville, Virginia. By mid-June 1863, the long rumored Confederate invasion of south central Pennsylvania began. On June 16, white residents greeted with dread the news of the advance of the leading elements of Lee's army to Chambersburg and took precautions by hiding livestock and family valuables. Many of the men disappeared as well. Most of south central Pennsylvania's black population fled for their lives, as had African Americans in the path of the Confederate army from Virginia to Harrisonburg, Pennsylvania. Contemporary observers described the frantic flight of exhausted families, sometimes with the children being urged on with threats of the seizure by the Confederate army. Others went into hiding, sometimes protected by white families.[59]

There were good reasons to fear: African Americans had already been captured in 1862 in the Shenandoah Valley, at Harpers Ferry, at Cedar Mountain, and near Chambersburg. So many were seized at Harpers Ferry during the Antietam campaign that a disgusted Massachusetts chaplain, also captured there, wrote that the Confederate actions "seemed more like a negro hunt than a fight for right and country to me." In the aftermath of that campaign, estimates of the number of seized African Americans were as high as 2,000.[60]

As soon as Lee's army entered Pennsylvania in mid-June of 1863, African Americans were rounded up, bound, and sent south. This activity continued until the battle of Gettysburg in July. For generations, this activity was largely overlooked by American historians, but recently increasing attention has been placed on these events.[61]

The evidence of the captures and the resulting disruption of the African American community comes from Northern and Southern newspaper accounts, soldiers' letters, diaries of Pennsylvania townspeople, military orders, and prison records. It can also be seen in the effects caused by the absence of a large number of people. Gettysburg's Pennsylvania College had to get someone else to ring the college bell when their African American janitor, Jack Hopkins, fled. A South Carolina soldier remarked "it is strange to see no negroes" as he stayed at Chambersburg, home to hundreds of African Americans in 1860 and the destination of many contrabands since. A Gettysburg woman made the same observation of her hometown.[62]

Some African Americans fled to Harrisburg, where many of the men were impressed to build entrenchments and pump water for the endangered city. Perhaps it is not surprising that when emergency calls were issued for a volunteer militia to meet the Confederate threat to Harrisburg, a number of African American laborers answered. Some were mustered into an emergency company, which fought bravely in a skirmish at Wrightsville Bridge, protecting Harrisburg by keeping that critical bridge from falling into Confederate hands before it could be burned.

Not all of Harrisburg's residents were grateful for this protection, however. A Democratic paper suggested that the Confederates would sack and burn the city if African American soldiers had killed Confederates in its defense.[63]

Many did not escape. Rachel Cormany, the Chambersburg wife of a Union cavalryman, reported that it saddened her heart to watch Confederate troops "hunting up contrabands and driving them off in droves." Another Chambersburg woman intervened to save a woman she knew, but she was rebuffed, and had to watch her being led away. Had the Confederate forces been able to remain in south central Pennsylvania all summer, the local African American population might have been eliminated. Some African Americans in Greencastle claimed that a Confederate officer, after seizing two African Americans from a house, said, "When they had destroyed Penn[sylvania] they would return that way and take off every neager."[64]

Most of the seizures occurred in Franklin County, which was occupied by the Confederate army for two weeks. A number were also seized around Gettysburg, although some were able to escape in the confusion around the battle. One woman eluded her captors and hid in the bell tower of a church for several days.[65]

The total number of African Americans captured by the Confederate army may never be known. One Chambersburg resident recorded in his diary that the Confederate army had taken 250 African Americans from there alone, but he had been absent from the town briefly and appears to have been citing a local newspaper, not making a firsthand observation. From Franklin and Adams counties, however, it does appear that scores, if not hundreds were taken. During the entire 1863 campaign from Winchester to Gettysburg, over a thousand African Americans may have been seized in Virginia, Maryland, and Pennsylvania. One Confederate soldier in Staunton reported that they had received nearly a thousand prisoners "in all colors, ages, sizes, sexes and from all nations." Because fewer than one hundred white civilians were captured as hostages during the campaign, this statement indicates the capture of a large number of African Americans, almost certainly beginning with the fall of Winchester. Confederate prison records are ambiguous, but would seem to indicate between ten and forty African Americans from Pennsylvania wound up in Confederate prisons in Richmond—mainly African Americans who could plausibly claim that they were free. Hundreds more were sent to depots at Winchester, Staunton, and elsewhere to be reclaimed as fugitive slaves; others were sold to slave traders near the front, and some may have been detailed to labor on Richmond's fortifications. Regardless of the precise numbers involved, the Confederate invasion inflicted substantial disruption on the African American community in south central Pennsylvania just a few years before the critical Reconstruction period.[66]

No order has been located mandating the captures, although Lieutenant General James Longstreet's adjutant did direct Major General George Pickett to bring the "captured contrabands . . . with you for further disposition" as he moved his division to Gettysburg and its appointment with history.[67] Longstreet functioned as Lee's second-in-command, and this order indicates that the highest ranks of the Confederate command were aware of the captures and at least acquiesced in them. While direct documentary evidence is lacking, some surmises may be made about the motivations of Confederate soldiers and leadership. A primary purpose of the Gettysburg campaign was to provision Lee's army and relieve pressure on the Shenandoah Valley, a vital Confederate breadbasket, during the growing season. Many citizens of the Valley had been complaining to James Seddon, the new Confederate Secretary of War, about their loss of slaves and asking him to appoint an "accomplished general" to drive out the enemy. Seddon had made Lee aware of these sentiments. It seems logical that one ancillary purpose of the invasion could have been to restore a critically needed labor force to that region.[68] Certainly, one soldier in Jubal Early's Confederate division thought so, writing: "I do not think our generals intend[ed] to invade, except to get some of our Negros [sic] back which the Yankees have stolen and to let them [Pennsylvanians] know something about the hardships of war."[69]

Race and Retaliation: Lee's Army and African Americans

In addition to restoring a labor force to the vital Shenandoah Valley region, retaliation was another powerful factor motivating the Confederates. Union troops had inflicted grave damage to civilian homesteads and towns in northern Virginia, in particular the lower Shenandoah Valley, which Confederate soldiers passing through frequently described as desolated. In December 1862, Union forces had deliberately shelled the town of Fredericksburg, after warning the town's inhabitants. In June 1863, a group of invading Confederates specifically told a Mercersburg professor that they were retaliating "especially for Fredericksburg," and, in seizing African Americans, "they were only reclaiming their property which we had stolen and harbored." In addition to anger over perceived Yankee violations of the laws of war, the Confederates were influenced by the war's increasingly racialized nature and the deep Southern rage over the Emancipation Proclamation and the arming of African American soldiers. These awakened Southern fears of slave insurrections and atrocities. Many Southern soldiers had served on pre-war militias and slave patrols, slaveholder and non-slaveholder alike. The Gettysburg campaign was the first opportunity for many Confederate soldiers to retaliate, and they did so against the African American population.[70]

As early as September 1862, when Confederate forces seemed first poised to invade the North before being stopped at the battle of Antietam, the Richmond press suggested that Pennsylvanians feel the wrath of the Confederate army. One paper, fuming at the loss of "at least 30,000 negroes," urged Lee's army to "turn the whole country into a desert," stating, inaccurately, that because "[t]hey have no negroes in Pennsylvania," then "[r]etaliation must therefore fall upon something else." There were actually many African Americans in southern Pennsylvania in 1862, and because of the flight of refugees, there would be even more to experience Confederate retaliation when Lee's army invaded in 1863.[71]

In fact, even before the Gettysburg campaign, captures of African Americans were frequent enough that Lee's Army of Northern Virginia needed a policy to handle them. In an order from Lee's adjutant, the army's commanders were instructed that "arrested" fugitives were to be sent back to several "Camps of Instruction" near Richmond and Petersburg.[72] (The term "arrested" is another indication of the continuum with pre-war fugitive slave policy.) Some Confederate soldiers complied with this during the invasion, sending African American captives back to the rear.[73] As Lucy Buck, the daughter of a slave-owning family in Winchester put it, captured African Americans were to be sent to the jail in Winchester, where the women and children could be reclaimed by their owners if they were fugitives. Male slaves would be sent to Richmond to work on fortifications.[74]

The Fate of Captured African Americans

Buck's understanding of the policy for captured African Americans is supported by the experiences of one of the best documented captives from the area. Amos Barnes was captured by the Confederate army in Franklin County, sent to Winchester, and then from Winchester to Castle Thunder prison in Richmond. In an attempt to win his release, Barnes, who claimed to be free, asserted that he had actually helped the Confederate army locate the hiding places of other African Americans. He and another captive wrote to some merchants and ministers in Chambersburg and Mercersburg, including William McKinstry and Rev. Thomas Creigh, asking them to corroborate that they were free blacks. The Pennsylvanians wrote back, verifying that they believed Barnes to be free. They also asked the Reverend T. V. Moore, a noted Richmond minister, to investigate. Moore had gone to school in Mercersburg, and before the Civil War, had been offered the presidency of Lafayette College.[75] The minister visited Barnes in prison and reported that his account was credible. Before the end of the year, the Confederate Assistant Secretary of War ordered the general in charge of Confederate prisons to deliver "Amos Bar[n]es, a free negro from Pennsylvania, whose release is applied for by Rev. T. V. Moore, of this city, upon grounds which appear to the Department sufficient to justify an exceptional policy with regard to him."[76]

Such an "exceptional policy" apparently was not applied to any of the other free blacks captured in Pennsylvania.[77] Their incarceration occurred when attitudes on both sides were hardening toward prisoner exchanges and releases. With African American soldiers now being captured, the Union army insisted that they be exchanged as well as white soldiers and officers. The Confederates refused—as Northern authorities knew they would—and the prisoner exchanges stopped.[78] The captured African Americans from Pennsylvania were civilians, not soldiers, but Confederate authorities may have hoped that they could be exchanged for Confederate civilians or runaway slaves. For the most part, however, they fell through the cracks of the Confederate prison system. Major General Isaac Carrington, the Confederate inspector of the prisons, recommended that the men be placed out to work and the women to labor in hospitals and laundries. Alexander Lewis, a captured African American from Chambersburg, eventually became the *de facto* head of the culinary department in Castle Thunder. A young African American from York was used as a prison messenger and errand boy.[79]

The records in the Department of the Henrico, which had jurisdiction over the network of Richmond area prisons, are somewhat ambiguous regarding the number incarcerated; some prisoner lists from the summer of 1863 include notations, "Free negro captured in Pennsylvania" or "Negro captured in Pennsylvania claiming to be free." Often, they are at the top of a list with a number of other African American names, the status of which is not indicated. Some of these names are identical to names in the 1860 Franklin County census, suggesting that these individuals, too, may have been captured in Pennsylvania.[80] Depending on how many of these individuals, who have no descriptor next to them, were from Pennsylvania, the number of African Americans seized there and making it to Richmond appears to be between ten and forty. Many more may have been claimed, put to work on fortifications in the Valley or at Richmond, or possibly sold. Some of these Richmond prisoners likely were hired out to the railroad or to also build fortifications, as were captured slaves held in other prisons.[81]

Even if they appear to have been largely forgotten, Pennsylvania's captured African Americans had value to the Confederate hierarchy. As the Union army pushed closer to Richmond in the summer of 1864, and the prisons experienced gross overcrowding, some of the African American captives were sent to a new prison in Salisbury, North Carolina. By November, that prison's commandant was asking what could be done with the "negroes confined at Salisbury." Robert Ould, the Confederacy's agent for prisoner exchanges, noted on an endorsement to this message that he could put them to use if permitted. He probably meant he would offer to trade them for captured Confederate civilians or soldiers. A footnote identified these African American prisoners as "Brought from Pennsylvania by C. S. Army." After that, it becomes difficult to track them in the confusion of the Confederate prison system in the last days of the war. Some may have been sent to Camp Maxcy Gregg in South Carolina, where a large number of African American prisoners were sent from Salisbury in January 1865.[82]

When the war ended, it was unclear where most of the captured African Americans were and if they were still alive. Their capture and incarceration, like the flight of many others, contributed to the disruption of African American community in south central Pennsylvania.

The white communities of the area were also substantially disturbed. Houses were damaged, stores cleaned out, fences burned. Compensation from the state and federal government would be delayed for years, as Republicans and Democrats battled over who deserved it. Two fine local historians, W. P. Conrad and Ted Alexander, suggest that in Franklin County, many families simply chose to move west rather than begin again in Pennsylvania. In Gettysburg, not only was there the battle's carnage to clean up—contractor teams led by local African American Basil Biggs disposed of the thousands of human and animal bodies—but the suffering extended for months in the dozens of hospitals surrounding the town.[83]

One unexpected impact of the invasion was to change the state's position on the recruitment of African American soldiers. During the campaign, Pennsylvania's state government yielded to federal pressure and the demands of the emergency and began to allow recruitment of African Americans for state units. Once the crisis had passed, the state realized that a black volunteer could take the place of a drafted white man, and began allowing the recruiting of African American soldiers to fill up U.S. Colored Troops units and count against Pennsylvania's draft quota. Scores of African American men volunteered, particularly from counties like Adams, which had not been extensively visited by the earlier Massachusetts recruiters. At least fifty-three African Americans from Adams County volunteered to serve in ten different U.S. Colored Infantry regiments.[84]

The Invasion and the 1863 Pennsylvania Gubernatorial Election

The political struggle between Democrats and Republicans did not cease during the invasion crisis. Elections continued during the Civil War, and the Gettysburg campaign took place during a heated battle for Pennsylvania's governorship. The Democrats, wanting to expand their gains from the previous fall and conduct a referendum on the conduct of the war, nominated George Woodward, a Pennsylvania Supreme Court Justice. He was a leading figure among the state's Democrats, and had urged conciliation during the secession crisis, but he was not a strong orator.[85]

In addition to nominating a candidate who was not very charismatic, the Democrats hamstrung themselves by not postponing their convention, which began on June 17, the day after Confederate forces had moved into the state. The convention was held in Harrisburg, which lay within reach of the invading army. Without knowing whether disaster would be avoided, the convention nominated Woodward. He was believed to favor a quick end to the war and had ruled that "soldier voting" in the field was unconstitutional.[86] In the end, despite a last minute, unsuccessful attempt to have Major General George McClellan intervene on Woodward's side, the Republican Andrew Curtin defeated Woodward by about 15,000 votes, or about three percent of the vote cast.[87]

In south central Pennsylvania, however, Curtin was unpopular because he was titularly the commander of Pennsylvania's militia, which could not slow the Confederate advance before the battle of Gettysburg. Also, Democrats blamed him for delaying compensation to the farmers whose property had been damaged by J. E. B. Stuart's 1862 raid. The implication was that he might do so again in the face of the much greater losses from Lee's invasion. As the campaign became desperate, the *Compiler* resorted to its typical election tactics of race baiting. Voters were urged to "remember" that it was Woodward who had moved for the insertion of the word "WHITE" in the qualifications for voting in the 1838 constitution, so that now "WHITE MEN DO THE VOTING!" The paper maintained that, "Woodward is the white man's friend and belongs to the party that believes that this Government was made for WHITE MEN," and a vote for Woodward was a vote for "WHITE FREEDOM."[88]

Despite losing statewide, Woodward carried all three south central Pennsylvania counties by 703 votes, even Franklin County, where the Republican Party was led by the energetic A. K. McClure. Woodward also carried York County, adjacent to Adams and Cumberland, by over 2,500 votes, but in Thaddeus Stevens' Lancaster County, Curtin had a nearly 6,000-vote majority. This election continued the trend of south central Pennsylvania turning Democratic while Republicans were strengthening their position in the state as a whole.[89]

When This Cruel War Is Over: South Central Pennsylvania and the End of the Civil War

In November, President Lincoln visited Gettysburg to speak at the dedication of the National Cemetery. The *Sentinel* covered the events and minutiae of the day in an entire page of newsprint. The *Compiler* barely took notice of the visit of the sitting president to the little borough, devoting more attention to the declaration of Judge Woodward, who was still on Pennsylvania's Supreme Court, that Congress's draft law was unconstitutional.

The long war was hardening hearts. In 1864, the Republicans continued to try to pin the "traitor" label on the opposition, while war weary Democrats hammered away on their themes, criticizing the administration's conduct of the war and positions on race. Since the nation had existed with slavery for many years, and "happily," the *Compiler* believed that abolition was not necessary. The paper maintained that African Americans were inferior and not suited for freedom. Besides, Southern whites would not accept abolition in "black majority" districts; it would guarantee the resistance of 12 million white Southerners to any postwar settlement. Later in the year, south central Pennsylvania's Democratic Congressman, A. H. Coffroth, openly opposed the Thirteenth Amendment banning slavery. According to Coffroth, only the states could end slavery, and to do so would unleash the "pestilential" effect of 4 million "ignorant and debased" African Americans "swarming the country." Even more than a year after Lincoln's final emancipation proclamation, south central Pennsylvania's Democratic papers and politicians opposed the abolition of slavery.[90]

Of course, the *Compiler* also opposed any steps toward African American equality. The *Compiler* bluntly stated that it would be "vitiating the purity of the suffrage" to allow "an inferior and degraded race to partake equally with whites in that and also in all social rights and benefits."[91] Radical Republicans were labeled "miscegenation agitators," and the paper bemoaned the fact that African Americans were being "voted into railroad cars" (i.e., being granted equal access to public transit).[92]

The Democratic critique of the war gained momentum from the swelling casualty lists. The spring offensives at the Wilderness, Spotsylvania, and Cold Harbor, and the defensive stand at the battle of the Monocacy all cost the lives of Adams County soldiers. Even after that last battle, when troops under General Lew Wallace fatally slowed Jubal Early's advance toward Washington, the *Compiler* still demanded an immediate armistice.[93] To try to slow the push for peace, Union General Ulysses S. Grant warned that the South would require all contrabands and emancipated slaves to be returned and re-enslaved, and "would demand a treaty which would make the North slave-hunters for the South," as well as compensation for slaves who had escaped and could not be recaptured.[94]

During the 1864 presidential campaign, south central Pennsylvania was invaded again. Confederate cavalry led by General John McCausland burned central Chambersburg in retaliation for buildings burned by Union General David Hunter in the Shenandoah Valley. As in 1863, African Americans were particularly vulnerable. Confederates, learning that one town resident was a teacher, asked him if he taught African Americans. When he said yes, they torched his home. The *Franklin Repository* (Republican) stated that a former fugitive slave, Daniel Parker, was the only fatality in the burnings. He died when soldiers burned his house down around him.[95]

The *Compiler* suggested that, in addition to the scorched earth policies of the Union army in Virginia, it was escaping slaves and the arming of African Americans that lay at the root of the retaliation. There could be merit to this claim. David Hunter was the general who, early in the war, tried to free the slaves of South Carolina, Georgia, and Florida, only to have his edict reversed by President Lincoln. Hunter was also involved in an early effort to arm "contrabands" who came into federal lines. McCausland's commander, General Early, reportedly justified the burning by remarking that his soldiers had captured a man within Confederate lines with authority from Maryland's Union Provost Marshal to "decoy Negroes from Virginia" to be used as draft substitutes. Both the Provost Marshal and the man were to profit from the scheme. This incident, while strongly suggestive of the fugitive slave issue, had occurred months before Early's invasion, however.[96]

With the burning of Chambersburg, all the destruction the war had brought to the region, and repeated draft calls in 1864, in August the *Compiler* warned that voting for the Republican ticket was voting for "war and bloodshed, drafts and taxes" until total abolition was complete. "No more insane Abolition rule," the paper demanded. It changed its masthead to read "Peace and Union," and strongly supported the efforts to negotiate peace. The paper rejoiced when Major General George McClellan was nominated on the first ballot at the national Democratic convention. Similarly, the Adams County Democratic convention, meeting in September, condemned the Administration for having "changed the policy of this war from that of restoring the Union to a war of subjugation, abolition and extinction of slavery."[97]

The 1864 presidential election became another referendum on the war and Lincoln's leadership. In south central Pennsylvania, partisanship and race featured prominently. The *Compiler* deliberately omitted mention of significant Union victories in the Shenandoah Valley and Atlanta. It also complained that Republicans had promised that freed slaves would remain in the South—but instead, they were migrating north, taking jobs from white laborers, and being treated preferentially over white widows and orphans. The paper urged voters who wanted a "white man's Government" to "vote for McClellan and Pendleton, on the white man's ticket."[98]

Either the *Compiler*'s arrows hit their mark, or sentiment was shifting, or both. In November, although McClellan lost in Pennsylvania and nationally, he defeated

Lincoln in Adams County by over 500 votes—a large majority for a small county. This was an increase of over 100 from the Democratic majority in the gubernatorial race the year before; of course, turnout increased in the Presidential election.[99]

As Union military victory became increasingly certain, attention shifted to postwar policy, with issues of race at the center. In February 1865, the Thirteenth Amendment abolishing slavery came up again for Congressional vote. It passed 119–56, although when the same measure had come up in June of 1864, it failed to achieve the necessary two-thirds majority, 96–65. Two Pennsylvania representatives, including Adams County's A. H. Coffroth, "switched votes" from June to February. In 1862, the *Compiler* had hailed Coffroth as the "white man's candidate"; now, it expressed surprise that Coffroth had "allowed himself to stray" from the "conservative" policy of "NON-INTERVENTION." The paper predicted that Coffroth "will have no little difficulty in explaining it to the satisfaction of those to whose efforts and votes he was indebted for the seat."[100] Until the end of the war, the *Compiler* opposed any efforts aimed at equality for African Americans, or even to end slavery.

The war ended with rejoicing as Confederate troops laid down their arms, but sorrow over Lincoln's assassination. Many in south central Pennsylvania mourned. There, as in communities throughout the North, local papers filled black-bordered pages with details of the assassination, the pursuit of Booth, his death, and the trial of the conspirators. With no indication that they noticed the irony, the *Compiler* printed an "important letter" from John Wilkes Booth in which the assassin repeated a slogan used widely by border Northern Democrats: "This country was formed for the white not for the black man."[101]

For more than four years, the *Compiler* had fought Lincoln's policies; now that he was dead, it reversed course. It hoped that Lincoln's assassination would not stop his plan for reconciliation. It also noted approvingly that the new President Andrew Johnson had told freed African Americans he preferred them to live elsewhere than in America.[102]

The bitter partisan rancor evidenced in south central Pennsylvania during the four years of war did not bode well for postwar efforts to for African American equality. The war years in south central Pennsylvania had seen an escalating use of racialist rhetoric, a turn by the electorate toward the race-baiting Democratic Party, increasing concern over fugitive slaves in the guise of "contrabands," and significant disruption of the white and especially the black communities as a result of wartime invasion and military service. The ramifications of these changes would play out in the Reconstruction period and leave the area's African American residents on the edge of freedom, rather than fully within its confines.

9   After the Shooting

South Central Pennsylvania
after the Civil War

I n April 1865, the long war ended. Vacant chairs and empty sleeves across the North testified to loss; south central Pennsylvania had suffered especially. Three times the region had been invaded, including in 1863, when two large armies camped, looted, and fought within it. In 1864, Chambersburg burned.[1]

Having suffered extensively, how would the end of the Civil War affect these Pennsylvania communities' response to the African Americans among them, whether former fugitives, former soldiers, emancipated slaves, or free blacks? Would abolitionists' and African Americans' prewar focus on legal and political change result in advancement for African Americans after the war, or would the anti-black vision of a Democratic Party that used race to rally its constituency impede it? Put another way, why did not the prewar abolition organizations, Underground Railroad activity, and antislavery sentiment result in a greater role and freedoms for African Americans after the war? Similar questions can be asked across much of the North regarding the failure of African Americans to win greater equality after the war. South central Pennsylvania was a distinctive border region and the only part of the North that served several times as a battleground. Still, a brief examination of the postwar experience of its African American residents suggests why the push for equal rights, such as it existed, generally failed in the North. In south central Pennsylvania, African American aspirations for equality were stymied by conservatism, war weariness, racism and anti-black rhetoric, significant demographic shifts, and the effects of wartime dislocations.[2]

The fugitive slave issue had been particularly relevant to these communities along the border before and during the war. In Chambersburg, soldiers massing to march south in 1861 had been instructed to return fugitive slaves to their masters. During the war, despite resistance from some area residents, the region became a wartime place of refuge for fleeing contrabands, many of whom eventually volunteered for the Union army. Those that remained behind risked organized, systematic efforts at recapture. Instead of kidnappers with a wagon, however, in June 1863 a determined, destructive army was in pursuit. When area white residents saw first-hand the treatment of fugitive slaves and free blacks by Confederate troops during this campaign, it caused a brief outburst of sympathy and solidarity. The *Mercersburg Journal* called the region's African Americans "free colored citizens," and the Gettysburg *Star* had labeled Lee's invading forces "an army of kidnappers and horse thieves."[3] This brief solidarity, however, would not result in a sustained press for full rights for these "colored citizens" for several reasons. Both the African American and the abolitionist community in south central Pennsylvania were significantly affected by social and demographic changes throughout the region. In addition, this border region's continued ties to the South, which were so significant to the area's antebellum identity, also affected the postwar experience. The net effect, both what changed and what did not, severely limited any opportunity for significant advancements in African American civil rights and equality after the war.

Many key members of south central Pennsylvania's antislavery constituency had moved on. Some reformers who desired to help African Americans traveled to former Southern states such as Tennessee, Virginia, South Carolina, and Georgia. Most of the publicized opportunities to help "freedmen" were there—in Virginia's Shenandoah Valley, or in the Sea Islands project led by former south central Pennsylvania resident J. Miller McKim. Even geographically distant work such as this did not always meet with approval of conservatives back home. Rev. Thomas Agnew had moved from Mercersburg to Tennessee to work with freedpeople. In 1868, he received death threats from the Ku Klux Klan, which won him some sympathy from the Republican papers in Mercersburg. In contrast, a Democratic paper, the Chambersburg *Valley Spirit* wrote, "if such an order [the KKK] does exist in Tennessee, that they will vastly neglect their calling if they fail to wait on this old sinner—he deserves to be quietly sent home to glory." One can only hope that there was some element of humor intended in this chilling advice.[4]

These efforts to help Southern freedpeople took away some of Pennsylvania's abolitionists and reformers who otherwise might have worked to ameliorate the condition of local blacks. In border areas such as south central Pennsylvania, there would be an influx of freedpeople who might need assistance and support as much as emancipated slaves on the Southern plantations. Some did try to help freedpeople relocating to the area. A school for African Americans was started in Adams County by J. Howard Wert; his father, Adam Wert; and a local female teacher, Sallie Broadhead. This rural county could not retain many of its ambitious young men, however, and ultimately J. Howard Wert moved to Harrisburg, where he desegregated that city's school system in 1898.[5]

Emigration was a regional trend that affected the abolitionist community. As a result of the war and a prolonged recession that struck the area from 1867 to 1868, numerous merchants and businesses in the region were devastated, and many farmers on marginal lands simply gave up. Because of political squabbles over who should be considered "loyal," few local residents received compensation for their claims for wartime losses until 1870.[6] Many could not wait that long, and farmers, merchants, artisans, and town professionals all moved west to make a fresh start, following a prewar emigration trend to the west, which preceded interest from much of the rest of the state.[7] As was the case in many rural areas, the need for land to establish children on their own farms was a significant motivator, and south central Pennsylvanians had easy access to routes west.[8]

The war had increased this outflow. Perhaps emblematic of the region as a whole, Emmitsburg, Maryland, just south of Adams County, Pennsylvania, experienced a 27 percent loss in population between 1860 and 1870—and only a small percentage of that was the result of forced relocation from an 1863 fire. Most was voluntary migration. In the early 1870s, there was a massive move west from Cumberland County.[9] As very wealthy, prospering businessmen and farmers might have few reasons to move, and the poor probably could not afford it, this migration was mainly made up of middle class families. This is the class from which came many abolitionists and much Republican Party support. The migration likely sapped energy from local relief for freedpeople and any drive for African American equal rights. Joel and Lydia Wierman, stalwarts of the region's Underground Railroad, migrated to Illinois shortly before the Civil War. William H. Wright, a Quaker who helped rescue the Payne family and prosecute Thomas Finnegan, moved to Nebraska in 1857. The descendants of Thomas Creigh, the Franklin County minister who helped win the release of Amos Barnes, a captured Mercersburg free black, also migrated to Nebraska.[10] Meanwhile, it appears that southern Pennsylvania families of German descent, who often resisted antislavery and were a source of strength for the Democratic Party, tended to stay to a greater extent than some other rural ethnic groups.[11]

Recently, historian Bruce Laurie has identified rural conservatism and responsiveness to racist appeals as a factor working against long-term growth of the Free Soil Party in Massachusetts. Such conservatism is not a given, however, but a product of historical circumstances. The migration of ambitious, educated rural Pennsylvanians to larger cities and to the West may have had a significant impact on turning the social environment more conservative in rural south central Pennsylvania from 1850 to 1875.[12]

In addition to the local residents who sought opportunities elsewhere were the veterans. The war had opened up a whole new realm of experience for rural Northern soldiers. Many of these men may not have traveled further than thirty miles from home as a boy, and they had now seen thousands of miles of America. One area regiment, the 77th Pennsylvania, had fought in Tennessee, Georgia, Louisiana, and Texas.[13] Now many veterans wanted to move elsewhere instead of return home permanently. Sometimes their land had lain fallow for years. Rather than undertake the difficult task of restoring to productivity land that may have been marginal to begin with, many soldiers determined to move west and expend that same effort on "virgin lands" with sod-busting plows and mechanical reapers, if necessary. Others moved south to buy distressed land at low prices, or sought the opportunities of the larger cities. War bounties gave these soldiers the cash to get started. This class of migrants undoubtedly included some south central Pennsylvanians who had enlisted with antislavery sentiments.[14]

In addition to the departure of zealous friends of the fugitive and the migration of a significant part of the rural middle class, other changes were at work. Nationally, there was a split between the followers of William Lloyd Garrison, who considered the work of the American Antislavery Society finished with the war's successful conclusion, and those of Wendell Philips and Frederick Douglass, who considered it imperative to strive for African Americans to receive full citizenship. Garrison was a tired sixty when the Civil War ended, and other abolitionist leaders were aging as well. Garrison's latest biographer has called the 1870s "the decade of funerals" for the movement. Some had burned out even earlier. Theodore Dwight Weld and Angelina Grimké Weld, who had done so much to inspire antislavery in Ohio, Pennsylvania, Massachusetts, and throughout the North, told Henry Blackwell in 1843, "There is a fighting era in everyone's life. . . . But when your work in that line is done, you will reach another and higher view."[15] With the loss of the clear-cut goal of abolition, and the aging of the leadership, the drive for abolitionists to fight for equal rights was losing momentum.

Death and aging were laying their hand on south central Pennsylvania abolitionists as well. Most of the leading antislavery activists and figures in the Underground Railroad were dying or approaching late middle age or older. For decades, perceptive historians have suggested that considering the impact of aging may help illuminate our understanding of political, social, or military leadership.[16] Different stages in life bring different concerns and energy levels. With the westward migration of many younger abolitionists, the core of abolitionists in Adams County was dwindling and aging. William Wright and Cyrus Griest died in 1865, and Wright's widow, Phoebe Wright, was eighty at the time of the

1870 census. Most of their daughters had married or moved away as well; one had divorced and married a non-Quaker. One son, Isaac, had died in 1850 in his early twenties, and the other, a noted general of the engineers, would die an alcoholic in Philadelphia in 1882. While the Wrights tried to do their part—shortly after the war, they had reportedly rehired a former fugitive who had worked for them, at her request—they would not have had the energy to lead a new crusade after seeing their lifelong battle against slavery successful.[17] Benjamin Lundy, a leading light to many abolitionists in south central Pennsylvania, had died in 1839; his sons had moved west from Adams County in the 1830s. John B. McPherson, a key local ally of Thaddeus Stevens, and a man whose farm was reportedly a stop on the Underground Railroad, died shortly before the war. His son, Republican Congressman Edward McPherson, agitator of the fugitive slave issue in the Harrisburg papers, never moved back to Adams County after he was voted out of office in 1862. Mill owner James McAllister, another abolitionist and Underground Railroad worker, had also died. James Cooper was a moderate antislavery figure at best, but he had prosecuted kidnappers in Adams County courts. He died in Ohio in 1863. Warner Townsend, one of the youngest members of the Adams County Antislavery Society to have his name frequently appear on documents and in the press, had gone through a difficult divorce from William and Phoebe Wright's daughter, Rachel. He was ultimately disowned by the Quaker meeting, and may not have remained involved in the antislavery movement.[18]

This impact of migration and death on the abolitionist community is reflected by John G. Brinkerhoff's 1891 response to C. W. Griest, who wrote to him, inquiring after his old antislavery companions. Brinkerhoff's reply is telling:

I have made inquiry in regard to the names of your old Antislavery friends . . . Josiah Benner was one of your party then, and his son William Benner . . . now resides in Gettysburg. The others [of] his family have all removed West, so I have lost all sight of them. Robert Youngs [family], from inquiry, have all left. One of his sons left Gettysburg about two years ago and [I] was unable to learn where he went, him to[o] I was acquainted with, Michael G. Clarkson, left Gettysburg many years [ago] . . . R. W. Middleton I also knew, he too left Gettysburg many years ago, and my impression is he removed to Harrisburg Pa [the former editor of the *Star* had first gone to Lancaster], Charles Epley I know nothing about, H. Denwiddies son Hugh, left Gettysburg years ago for the west and none of the name left here that I can learn, William A. Wadsworth, I can learn nothing of any of them left here, W. J. Sloan . . . I have not seen or heard any thing about . . . for several years. Adam Werts who was also one of your party then is now deceased, his widow is living in Gettysburg. They had one son, Professor John [Howard] Werts, who resides in Harrisburg, Pa. . . . Some of Josiah Benner's sons and one Daughter went I think to Kansas, but I do not know their Post Office address . . .

Granted, this letter was written many years after the antislavery agitation, and only covered some of the movement in Adams County. Still, it shows how not just single individuals, but entire families moved to the west or to larger cities.[19]

There had also been a significant outmigration of African Americans during the Civil War. Hundreds of African Americans fled Lee's invasion, and some were seized by Lee's army and carried away in 1862 and 1863. Peter Vermilyea's research suggests that for Gettysburg, if the fleeing African Americans did not own real estate (only about twenty-seven percent of the African Americans on the tax rolls did), they were not likely to return to the region after the danger from the Confederate army passed. Many area African Americans had portable job skills: agricultural day laborer, barber, hostler, carriage driver, artisan, domestic, laundry woman, and boarding house keeper. They could start again elsewhere if needed. Because of the region's vulnerability, some who fled during the Gettysburg campaign may not have felt safe returning to south central Pennsylvania until after the war ended. By then, they may have set down roots elsewhere.[20]

Some of those seized in the raids also did not return for many years, if at all. In 1863, a local minister reported that several Franklin County African Americans had been seized by Confederate forces, including two young men named James Filkill and Findlay Cuff. Filkill never reappeared in the Franklin County census, although there is a James Filkill listed in Philadelphia in 1870. Findlay Cuff is not in the 1870 Franklin County census either, although he does reappear in the 1880 census. This suggests that either he was missed in 1870, or he was elsewhere: in the South, perhaps, or in Philadelphia.[21] Jack Hopkins, the Pennsylvania College janitor whose flight had forced the school to appoint another person to ring the bell, did return. But he owned a house in town.[22]

Captures and flight, however, were not the only factors weakening the postwar African American community in south central Pennsylvania. Many of its leading young men had joined the Union army—over eighty in the Mercersburg area joined the prestigious Massachusetts 54th and 55th Infantry alone.[23] A number of the recruits were temporary migrants, but many were sons of the area's African American families. Jack Hopkins' son Edward joined the U.S. Colored Troops. Some of these returned if their families had solid roots in the area—Edward did. But others, like their white brethren, may have wished to make a start elsewhere. An 1873 historical novel by Ellwood Griest, an antislavery journalist from Lancaster, suggests that some of southern Pennsylvania's African American troops chose to stay in Florida at war's end, at least temporarily.[24] Whether African American Union soldiers chose to return and stay after their service ended may be important, because in later eras, African American veterans played a key role leading the community to struggle for equal rights. After World War II, they were significant in preparing the soil for the civil rights movement of the 1960s; Civil War veterans may have been able to play a similar role. For example, the noted Underground Railroad conductor Harriet Tubman, who had served in the Union Army in a combat role, spoke out against segregated Northern trains and Philadelphia's segregated streetcars when she lectured. In fact, the organizer of the successful protests against the streetcars, Octavius V. Catto, had served in an African American militia unit. African American soldiers from south central Pennsylvania may have also been able to confront injustices; it is just unclear whether enough of them returned to form a critical mass.[25]

The migration of African Americans created a void at the lower ends of the socioeconomic ladder that was soon filled. Many African Americans relocated to south central Pennsylvania after the war from Maryland and Virginia, especially from the Shenandoah Valley; others came from North or South Carolina.[26] Before the war, fugitive slaves would enter Pennsylvania as the first free state north of the Mason-Dixon Line; now after the war, Pennsylvania would be the first historically free state that freedpeople would encounter as they moved north. South central Pennsylvania would be the first part of the state that many would enter. For ex-slaves from the Shenandoah Valley and North Carolina, the region had a familiar form of agriculture. As new arrivals, however, they did not have the established relationships of their predecessors. It may have been harder for them to push for equal rights and full citizenship in the North after many of them had just come out of slavery. Furthermore, these newcomers were also divided. Some migrants from Virginia resented those from the Carolinas and vice versa. In 1847, Aaron Constant had organized a petition, which claimed to include the names of every African American resident in Gettysburg. In 1867, it might not have been possible to gain such unity, although the need for it was just as great.[27]

Through all of this transformation, the region's border character remained. Ties to the South persisted, and many within the border community desired rapid rapprochement with Southern customers, kin, and friends. In addition to these long-standing connections, the aftermath of the war brought a new one. Gettysburg's emerging status as a tourist destination and pilgrimage site for visitors and mourners from both North and South also helped contribute to a desire for sectional reconciliation that ignored African Americans. Evidence of this conciliatory sentiment appears very early; the "romance of reunion" identified by scholars as an important later expression of reconciliationist sentiment in the North came early here.[28]

For example, the continued anti-black rhetoric of the pages of the Democratic newspaper the *Republican Compiler* showed that this newspaper was not prepared to let emancipated African Americans come between it and readers both North and South of the Mason-Dixon Line. The same invective employed against "wooly head" John C. Fremont in 1856, and then against "nigger regiments," "contrabands," and emancipation during the war, was now turned against African American aspirations to full citizenship. This rhetoric broadly reflected the views of the area's now dominant political party, the Democrats. In one example, the *Compiler* gleefully recorded details of a Democratic celebration in 1868. One display in a parade had come from southwest of Gettysburg. According to the paper,

> Among other things, they had a "Freedman's Bureau," consisting of an old case of drawers, with two persons representing negroes sitting on top and enjoying themselves with a fiddle, whilst a white man was at work sawing wood in the rear part of the wagon.

An accompanying banner stated that while African Americans would not work, "White Men Work! White Men Pay Taxes!" therefore, "White Men at the Ballot Box!" The paper stated it was a "good hit" enjoyed by all.[29]

In short, the social and political atmosphere of the region was transitioning. Residents were weary of war's destruction. The slavery issue was gone, the sectional crisis over. The coalition of former Whigs, Republicans, Free Soilers, antislavery Democrats, and Know Nothings that had put real political power behind at least moderately antislavery positions in the 1850s was finished. While the Republicans remained strong, the party in Pennsylvania was gradually shifting toward supporting business interests and away from the concerns of Northern farmers or African Americans.[30] It also faced a powerful state Democratic Party, which wrote into their 1866 and 1869 Pennsylvania platforms its support for continued, complete disfranchisement of African Americans. They were willing to contest elections on it.[31]

The Republican Party's support of African American voting rights was tepid at best in southern Pennsylvania. African American men were not granted the right to vote in Pennsylvania until the Fifteenth Amendment was ratified in 1870. Pennsylvania's Democrats opposed the amendment, claiming that it infringed on the traditional right of a state to control "the privilege of suffrage within it." When the state finally did ratify it, some Dickinson College students wanted to attend a public gathering with a dual purpose: celebrating the amendment's passage and memorializing recently deceased former professor John McClintock. While he had resigned as professor several years after the fugitive slave riot associated with his name, McClintock had served as a trustee at Dickinson until 1859. His name still had abolitionist associations, however, and the school forbade the students to go. When they did anyway, scores were suspended. That led to a student strike, which became known as the "Rebellion of 1870." Eventually the school, facing ruin, had to restore most of the suspended ringleaders. The students' actions had exceeded local sentiment, however.[32]

Thaddeus Stevens was the great exception to the temporizing in southern Pennsylvania over African American rights. The Republican congressman from Lancaster had lived several decades in south central Pennsylvania and maintained life-long connections and business interests there. Soon, death came to Thaddeus Stevens' door, too, however. He passed away in August 1868, refusing to be interred in a cemetery that did not permit the burial of African Americans, and with his commitment to the "Equality Of Man Before His Creator" inscribed on his tombstone.

Within days of Stevens' death, Jack Hopkins, the College's African American janitor, died as well. The Pennsylvania College trustees, at their August 1868 meeting, remembered both of them. The resolutions passed to commemorate Hopkins lauded his demeanor and his service to the College. Hopkins had been a beloved figure on campus and respected by the administration.[33] The resolutions were to be published in the local papers, and Hopkins was honored by a funeral procession, a rare honor for Gettysburg College.[34]

The resolutions for Stevens, reported by Edward McPherson, acknowledged only his efforts to further education generally. They said nothing about his lifetime of service or about the thousands of dollars he had raised in state appropriations to the College during some of its darkest days. They also did not acknowledge that much of the land for the college had been sold to them by Stevens. While 20,000 turned out for Stevens' funeral in Lancaster, which may have been the largest funeral ever held in Pennsylvania at that time, the College administration wanted to distance itself from Stevens' Reconstruction policies. The administration had made this abundantly clear when it dedicated Stevens Hall on campus the year before.[35]

Stevens had reportedly helped fugitives in person and in the courtroom in his Gettysburg years; later, he represented area abolitionists such as Daniel Kaufman. Hopkins, too, had reputedly worked on the Underground Railroad in Adams County, helping in particular when fugitives needed to be spirited through Gettysburg. His name is affixed to the 1847 Gettysburg petition, asking that the state legislature protect fugitive slaves. Hopkins' and Stevens' deaths, along with those of William Wright, James McAllister, and Cyrus Griest, removed five key individuals with links to the prewar aid to fugitives.

Over time, the character of the region changed—or perhaps it did not progress while so much around it changed. So many links to the South still existed that ex-Confederates found the area congenial. Several of them created resort homes in the 1880s. Colonel Walter Taylor, Gen. Robert E. Lee's trusted aide, purchased a home in Cascade, Maryland just yards from the border with south central Pennsylvania. Many other Confederates came to visit the area during the summer.[36] In Gettysburg, the town tried consciously to attract Southern tourists, both to the battlefield and to the springs that were briefly popular with northern and southern visitors.[37]

Even local literature reflected a growing conservatism. In southern Pennsylvania, early post-war work memorialized the Underground Railroad and acknowledged the agency of local African Americans. Ellwood Griest, a Lancaster journalist who had participated in an anti–Fugitive Slave Law meeting in 1850, penned a novel set in the area. In Griest's *John and Mary: The Fugitive Slaves*, it is a party of local African Americans, not white Quakers, who rescue the fugitives of the title. They also intimidate a local slave catcher into leaving the region, an incident based on a pre-war event in Pennsylvania. A decade later, George Alfred Townsend, a noted Civil War correspondent, settled in Maryland's Catoctin region, below south central Pennsylvania. In *Katy of Catoctin* (1884), he celebrated the Underground Railroad. For literary reasons, Townsend moved many of the events from south central Pennsylvania to north-central Maryland. An important character based on Thaddeus Stevens is present, as well as a fictional daughter of Pennsylvania Governor Joseph Ritner, a sort of "white witch" who helps fugitive slaves. Unlike in Griest's novel, African Americans are ciphers in Townsend's book, but they make their own decisions, as one black character shows when he refuses the entreaties of the protagonist to abandon the Harpers Ferry raid.[38]

As the distance from the events of the war increased however, the area's literary output grows more romanticized, such as in Elsie Singmaster's *A Boy at Gettysburg* (1924). Singmaster's family had moved to Seminary Ridge around the turn of the twentieth century, and she spent much of her life producing novels and short stories about the area. *Swords of Steel* (1934) included a fictional account of the capture of Kitty Payne. In *A Boy at Gettysburg*, the hero, Carl Mottern, works at a mill that is a station on the Underground Railroad, a fictionalized version of McAllister's mill. He hides fugitives from slave catchers and leads them to Quaker settlements deeper in the county. A fictionalized Mag Palm is present, as "Maggie Bluecoat," an African American guide to fugitives. She cooks for a local family, sings ethnic songs, and is definitely not the "Mistress/Harlot" the Gettysburg census taker recorded her as. In the novel, Mag does not fight off her kidnappers, as she did in 1858. Instead, she requires the aid of Carl and another white boy to rescue her.[39] In sum, in Singmaster's well-meaning book, African Americans have become part of the local color—with embarrassing details removed, and folksy songs added—and the real events they were involved in have been subtly altered to emphasize the agency of the white characters.

John W. Appel's *The Light of Parnell* (1916) shows a complete reversal of sentiment from the earlier novels of Griest and Townsend. While the book is ostensibly about the Franklin County's Underground Railroad, it actually condemns the institution as illegal. The hero, Tom, cannot be tempted to join this illicit activity or aid the Harpers Ferry expedition. He lifts a finger to help free slaves only once the Civil War begins. The illegal activities are primarily the territory of weak-willed women easily swayed by abolitionist rhetoric. The African American characters are caricatures; Frederick Douglass is reduced to a nameless "distinguished colored gentleman" who says little in a pivotal conference on the Harpers Ferry raid. The book's leading African American character, light-skinned Moses Preston, tries to pass himself off as white, is wracked with guilt over this deception, and dies a horrible death.[40]

Unlike the other books, *Light of Parnell* has little literary merit, but it is significant because it shows shifting attitudes toward African Americans and the region's legacy regarding the fugitive slave. The Appel family was prominent in antebellum Franklin County, and John Appel's father, Theodore, had written an essay advocating African colonization as a class project in 1840. The family relocated to Lancaster in the 1850s, where Theodore and later John were presidents of Franklin and Marshall College. The attitudes expressed in *Light of Parnell* may have been typical. Appel did not support equality for the region's African Americans. Instead, through the character of Moses Preston, he condemned attempts by African Americans to assimilate into the larger white society. The story also shows how, in the racial environment of the early twentieth century, an emphasis on "law and order" was now being used retrospectively to condemn the Underground Railroad. Helping fugitive slaves was portrayed as a crime against the Constitution, and even noted figures like Frederick Douglass become nameless bit players in a drama of white soldiers upholding the Union and law and order.

This fictional limitation of African Americans reflected what was actually occurring in south central Pennsylvania. As time passed, the lack of opportunity for the region's African Americans caused some to despair. In 1879, Mag Palm, now almost blind, was rescued from a pond where she had nearly drowned while apparently attempting suicide. Was she trying to escape physical suffering, or the diminished role that this significant Underground Railroad figure likely had after the war?[41]

As early as 1869, huge mobs attempted to lynch an African American in Franklin County. By the 1920s, in many ways the area was little different from parts of the Jim Crow South. Cross burnings accompanied that decade's battle to integrate Adams County's schools. In Gettysburg, the Ku Klux Klan held a massive rally, with little condemnation from the area residents—in fact, many are believed to have joined in. The Klan rallied at a campground near the national cemetery—one of the most visible locations near the battlefield. In a bizarre piece of local theater, the Klan members even showed up—in robes and hoods—at a local A.M.E. church meeting to donate $115 to help pay off the church's mortgage. The money may have been welcome, but their action reinforced racial hierarchies. Imagine the shock in such a town when the federal government tried to appoint an African American to a senior government position! In the early 1930s, the appointment of Dr. Louis King as an archaeologist at the National Battlefield Park met with pronounced resistance because, according to the National Park Service, the white people of Gettysburg were not used to socializing with black people. During the 1950s, none of the town's thirty-six boarding houses or hotels accepted black lodgers; only three of fourteen restaurants would serve African Americans food, and then only on a case-by-case basis. Even in the 1970s, only threatened action by the town's African Americans resulted in employment opportunities in the drugstores and stores in the "white" part of town. As recently as the 1980s, long-time African American residents complained that there was still little black presence in the retail areas.[42]

Similar conditions existed in Franklin County. Educational and social opportunities for African Americans were sharply limited through much of the twentieth century. Football teams would not play opponents with African American players. After World War II, African American children from Waynesboro still traveled to Hagerstown for haircuts because the local barbershop was "whites only." Even into the late 1960s real estate agents would steer black and white clientele to their "proper" parts of town.[43]

These policies resulted in significant lost human potential. For generations, Franklin County's African Americans could do little more than run "colored boardinghouses," haul bricks, work in the Frick factory, or be a minister to the local African American congregation. Sometimes the racial tensions spilled out into open violence and murder, as during the fatal 1969 race riots in nearby York, Pennsylvania, which convulsed the whole region. Those riots received national attention, but locally, they were only a flare-up of what one writer described as a "two-year intermittent war."[44] This area, that magic land across the Mason-Dixon Line, had always been dangerous for fugitives and free blacks alike. With the Civil War's conclusion, many white residents who had helped fugitives were gone or leaving, but at least one hundred years of living "on the edge of freedom" remained for the area's African Americans. This time the "edge" was not the border between north and south, but the sharp political divide between a grudgingly extended second-class citizenship and full and equal political and civil rights.

Conclusion

*The Postwar Ramifications of the
Fugitive Slave Issue "On the Edge
of Freedom"*

In runaway slave advertisements and illustrations in abolitionist literature,
the fugitive slave was often depicted as traveling, like Bunyan's pilgrim, with
a bundle on his back or tied to a staff. To some, he was a self-made man,
boldly striking out for a better life, heeding a call to freedom, aspiring to equality.
To others, he was a supplicant, a symbol of need and dependency.[1] Even along
the border, where fugitives frequently escaped in groups, this solitary figure represented the image of the fugitive for Northerners and Southerners alike. As a
symbol, he or she was much less threatening than insurrectionists, the influx
of "contrabands" during the war, or the mass migration of emancipated freedpeople. The constitutional historian Harold Hyman believes that it was fear of the
last that largely inspired Northern interest in Reconstruction. As that fear ebbed,
so did the Northern commitment to the welfare of African Americans.[2]

Because of the assumptions perhaps unconsciously embodied in the image
of the runaway, the fugitive slave issue, in some ways, was an ideal form for expressing antislavery sentiment near the border. Humanitarian feeling could draw
in the involvement of some who would not support any other antislavery activity, and compassionate aid could be given without advocating radical, disruptive
change to the nation's social system. This is one reason why Garrisonian abolitionists feared too much attention to fugitive slaves would divert activists from
the goals of freedom for all and achieving a radical, color-blind America. Some
border antislavery activists were true Garrisonians; many were more moderate.
For many years in this area, colonization or abolition were seen as equally viable solutions to the problems of race and slavery, as illustrated by Thaddeus
Stevens and even a leading Lancaster County Underground Railroad family. The
willingness of many south central Pennsylvanians to assist fugitives who showed
up at their door, and the efforts of the few to offer sustained, regular help, did
not translate into effective pressure on the political system to bring full equality
for African Americans. The 1847 personal liberty law was an exception, and it
brought only protection, not equality.

Despite these limitations, the fugitive slave issue was unmistakably significant in south central Pennsylvania. First of all, fugitives were a frequent reality, unlike many states further north where the fugitive was an uncommon figure. The Pennsylvania Abolition Society, the first national antislavery society, was from its inception engaged in promoting legal means to end slavery and prevent kidnapping. In the 1820s and 1830s, the noted African American clergyman James W. C. Pennington, then an anonymous blacksmith, fled through Adams County on his way north to freedom. Daniel Alexander Payne, another important African American clergyman and future educator, although not a fugitive, spent time in the region studying at the Lutheran Theological Seminary in Gettysburg. He even participated in the contentious efforts to establish an antislavery society in Gettysburg. Payne would later lead Wilberforce University. Payne, Pennington, John Peck (a black Carlisle businessman who would later found Allegheny College), and their helpers in south central Pennsylvania had a significant impact on African American education and religious instruction.

The failure of efforts by Payne, James McAllister, William Reynolds, Jonathan Blanchard, and others to spark a mass movement in the 1830s led to a return to older tactics of petitions and legal action. In 1845, an Adams County kidnapper was tried and convicted. The proceedings illustrated how local politicians were branding, not entirely accurately, Pennsylvania as historic "free soil." In 1846, petitions from the York Springs antislavery activists, likely inspired by this case, preceded a significant and successful petition campaign for a strengthened personal liberty law. One of the petitions sent to the legislature claimed to be from every one of Gettysburg's African Americans. Living on the edge of freedom, they were profoundly concerned about their own security and that of future fugitives.

The 1847 law became a central issue in the McClintock riot case, which followed the prosecution of Daniel Kaufman for harboring fugitive slaves. These cases were followed, in 1851, by the treason trials of the Christiana rioters. This legal counterattack forced much of the south central Pennsylvania Underground Railroad to go even further underground. While that work became even more clandestine, Thaddeus Stevens was interjecting his perspective, influenced by the Pennsylvania border, into the debates of Congress. In the aftermath of the 1850 Compromise, opposition to the Fugitive Slave Law briefly became the leading way in which the sectional conflict was expressed, for that law was the only part of the Compromise that Southerners saw as a concession and many Northerners saw as inhumane and onerous. Still, along the border, both parties eventually embraced the Compromise, even if some Whigs were reluctant. Antislavery activists tried agitating fugitive slave cases and then turned again to the prosecution of kidnappings. The Kansas-Nebraska act of 1854, however, which abrogated the Missouri Compromise, shifted the focus to Kansas and free soil, and the fugitive slave issue waned. It returned with a vengeance after John Brown's Harpers Ferry raid. Now, the fearful South saw a fugitive not as a lone runaway, but as a potential murderer or insurrectionist. Now it was the Democrats, generally opponents of helping fugitives, who agitated the issue more than abolitionists. Southern politicians, who had criticized Pennsylvania's personal liberty laws in the 1820s and stepped up the critique after the 1847 law was passed, charged that Northern failure to carry out the Fugitive Slave Law justified secession. This eventually led to a massive, eleventh-hour petitioning effort to encourage compromise, repeal Pennsylvania's personal liberty laws, and promote colonization. The effort failed to prevent the war, and the war failed to end the controversy over escaping slaves.

During the conflict, numerous African Americans emancipated themselves, and many from Maryland and the Shenandoah Valley ended up in south central Pennsylvania. They then became targets of a large-scale slave hunt during the Gettysburg campaign when Lee's Confederate army rounded up hundreds of fugitive slaves and free blacks to send them south to slavery.

These raids constituted a massive displacement of the African American community—of those who were not taken, many had fled, and many did not return. Their places were eventually taken by newly freed Southern slaves. Combined with the aging of the core abolitionist constituency, large-scale westward migration, and the rising ascendancy of a Democratic party which used virulent racist rhetoric, the prewar interest in the fugitive slave did not translate into postwar political gains for former slaves. With many reform-minded individuals headed elsewhere, the region slipped into rural conservatism, unable to sustain lasting economic and social gains for African Americans after the war. By the 1920s, in some ways south central Pennsylvania was indistinguishable from many parts of the Jim Crow South.

The postwar period illustrated the limitations of the abolitionist's prewar legal and political strategy. Antislavery activists had used the law aggressively, crafting new statutes and prosecuting kidnappers. Although they had made significant changes in Pennsylvania's legal code, their reform spirit did not survive into the postwar years. As much as the law was an instrument for liberation and change in the antebellum years, without the reformer's fire, it became an instrument of oppressive conservatism. By 1916, an area author suggested that the region's Underground Railroad simply had been foolish lawlessness. "Law and order" in his literary construct involved punishing African Americans who aspired to equality by passing as white.

Fugitive slaves and antislavery activists from this rural area had doggedly made significant contributions to the sectional crisis through their legal and political strategy. While the valor of the fugitive created momentum for a law that would stir up sectional tensions on the way to the Civil War, the image of the fugitive hindered African Americans from achieving real equality in the face of determined resistance in the border North. Not accorded full and equal status in the community, south central Pennsylvania's African American residents would find themselves living "on the edge of freedom" for many years to come.

Appendixes

A. Selected Fugitive Slave Advertisements, 1818–28

Date Ad Placed / First Run	Date of Escape	Owner Name / Location	Slave Name / Sex	Age (about)	Build / Demeanor	How Left	Reward
3/17/18 (3/18/18)	Sunday night	Edward Stevenson Near Old Liberty Rd., Baltimore Co., Md.	David (M)	24	Slender	"Had on . . . other clothing which it is deemed unnecessary to mention, as he may change his dress—having a free mother living who has very likely furnished him with the means to do so."	$40. $10 if caught within ten miles, $20 twenty miles, if caught out of state and brought home, or secured in jail, the above $40.

Survey of fugitive slave ads for 1818–19 not completed

Date Ad Placed / First Run	Date of Escape	Owner Name / Location	Slave Name / Sex	Age (about)	Build / Demeanor	How Left	Reward
3/14/20 (3/15/20)	9/26/19	George Shield Near Lanesville, Loudoun Co., Va.	Moses (M)	40			$50 if secured in any jail where owner can reach him.
4/18/20 (4/19/20)	Last Sunday morning	Isaac Peirce Georgetown, D.C.	Sam Dover (M)	25	Genteel	Extensive new clothing described; "He stole a very fine bright sorrel horse in Georgetown . . . and was seen near Frederick, on the evening he went away, with a . . . young black woman, who had went off him, and who has	$50 for securing in jail

10/17/20 (10/18/20)	9/18/20	Philip Graft Straban Township, Adams Co, Pa.	Sam Armstrong (M)	45	Stout	free papers—both on the same horse. It is supposed they will pass for man and wife. SAM has been used to the care of horses, driving wagon and carriage—and will probably seek for such employment."	$20 for confining in jail
12/5/20 (12/6/20)	10/30/20	Peter Shriner Liberty Town, Frederick Co., Md.	Thomas Brown (M)	46			$20 for securing in jail; additional for bringing home
1/2/21 (1/10/21)	9/2/20	Levy Phillips Hyattstown, Montgomery Co., Md.	Sophia F	20		Can read print "No doubt she is somewhere in Adams County, Pennsylvania, as she has been there before."	$40 if delivered to him; $30 if secured in out of state jail; $20 in-state
1/9/21 (1/10/21)	12/23/20	Daniel James Daniel Kiler Near Liberty-Town, Frederick Co., Md.	Bob (Robert Brookes) (M)	Not given	Stout	"It is supposed he has procured a pass from some free negro." "Most likely he will change his dress."	$50 for securing in accessible jail

(Continued)

A. Selected Fugitive Slave Advertisements, 1818–28 (cont'd.)

Date Ad Placed/ First Run	Date of Escape	Owner Name/ Location	Slave Name/ Sex	Age (about)	Build/ Demeanor	How Left	Reward
5/8/21 (5/16/21)	4/15/21	James A. McCreary Gettysburg	John Hubbard (M)	15–16	Light mulatto boy	[Unclear if slave or indentured servant]	$5 for bringing him back
6/5/21 (6/27/21)	3 years ago	Evan Dorsey Linganore, Frederick Co., Md.	Philip (M)	25	Strong built		$100 if lodged in Gettysburg jail; $125 if lodged in Frederick Co., Md.
6/5/21 (6/27/21)	12/23/21	Daniel James Near Liberty, Linganore, Frederick Co., Md.	Bob (Robert Brooks) (M)	24	Ambidextrous	"He is supposed to be some where in the State of Pennsylvania"	$100 for lodging in Gettysburg jail; $150 in Frederick jail
6/14/21 (6/27/21)	Saturday night last	John Clabaugh Middleburg, Md.	Walter (M)	45	Singular walk	"He has no pretension to freedom except while running away."	$40 if brought home; $20 if secured
8/28/21 (9/12/21)	7/21/21	Ephraim Gaither Brookeville, Montgomery Co., Md.	John Trip (M)	19	Light made	Raised on Eastern Shore; may get there via Baltimore or Annapolis; ad also ran in the Harrisburg Chronicle, York Recorder, and Lancaster Journal.	$100 for securing out of state, $60 in state

9/1/21 (9/19/21)	8/25/21	Thomas Kernan Carroll's Manor, Tuscarora, Frederick Co., Md.	Harrison (M)	20		Brought from Eastern Shore; "As he has lately been much with persons from Taney-Town, and is ignorant of the country, it is possible that he may have got direction that way into Pennsylvania." Ran away from Mr. Patterson's farm	$50 for lodging in Frederick jail
1/8/22 (1/9/22)	12/26/21	Lloyd Luckett Near Newtown, Frederick Co., Md.	Frank Hill (M)	27		"I have no doubt he has made for Philadelphia." "It is supposed said Negro is in the neighborhood of Gettysburg."	$100 if taken out of state and secured; $40 in state
1/8/22 (1/9/22)	12/29/21	Peter Wolford Franklin Township, York Co., Pa.	Isaac (Cato) (M)	21	Stout / Plays violin / Speaks German & English	"He has perhaps fifteen or twenty Dollars of money with him—and will probably endeavor to pass for a free man."	$60 for securing him in any jail. Indentured Servant
2/5/22	12/25/21	Stephen G. Wooden Reisterstown Md. (20m from Baltimore)	Caleb Bladen (M)	24	Stout	Took coat and clothing	$200—$100 for each (if secured in jail, $150/$75)
	1/23/22		Kinsey Bladen (M)	22	Not so stout	Took coat and clothing	

(Continued)

A. Selected Fugitive Slave Advertisements, 1818–28 (cont'd.)

Date Ad Placed / First Run	Date of Escape	Owner Name / Location	Slave Name / Sex	Age (about)	Build / Demeanor	How Left	Reward
10/16/22	Before 10/5	Henry Frazier (Administrator of James Fenley) Frederick Co., Md.	Peter (M) Nat (M)	50 21	Not very dark	Peter took a variety of clothing	$150 for both if taken out of state, one-half for either. $40 for both in county, $80 for both in-state
6/25/22 (12/11/22)	4/1/22 6/15/22	Wm I. Johnson Barnesville, Montgomery Co., Md.	Luke Adams (M) Samuel Adams (M)	27 37	"It is supposed SAM has a pass" This ad to run until found	Burnt barn Supposed to have stolen horse. Coins counterfeit money—400 half dollars	$200 for any jail more than 200 mi from Barnesville; $100 ($50 each) within 200 mi.
11/30/22 (12/11/22)	11/30/22	Roger Johnson Bloomsbury Forge (near Sugar Loaf Mtn), Frederick Co., Md.	Alick (M)	30	Stout		$60 for securing so I may get him again.
3/4/23 (4/9/23)	3/1/23	Vachel W. Dorsey Near Liberty, Frederick Co., Md.	Jesse Chub (M)	20		"I think it probable he will change both name and clothing; possibly he may have a counterfeit pass."	$50 for securing out of state; $30 within state; reasonable charges if brought home.

Date	Date (ad)	Owner / Location	Name	Age	Description	Notes	Reward
9/16/23 (10/1/23)	9/6/23	Dennis Plummer Montgomery Co., Md.	Dennis Plummer (M)	35	Stout		$10 in Montgomery Co.; $30 in Baltimore or Md. (ad says $50 reward)
11/9/24 (11/10/24)		James Stephens Frederick Co, Md. (about 10 miles from Frederick)	Stephen (M)	21	Mulatto	Went off in company of Charles, belonging to Jacob Whip	$40 reward for lodging him in jail (believes $50 reward issued for Charles)
4/21/25 (5/4/25)		Peter Gardner Martinsburg Va.	Sam Taylor (M)		Stout	"It is supposed that he may be lurking . . . in the neighborhood of Boonsborough, MD., but will, in all probability, make for Pennsylvania. He may . . . have obtained forged papers and will endeavor to pass for a free man."	$50 for securing him in jail
7/12/25 (7/13/25)		C. Birnie Taneytown, Md. (Frederick Co.)	Charles (M)	21		". . . no doubt he will change his dress."	To be lodged in Baltimore or Frederick Co. Jail. $50 if taken in state, $100 if out of it.
9/13/25 (9/28/25)	9/7/25	John Brien Catoctin Furnace, Frederick Co., Md.	James Johnston (M)	28	Stout		$50 for securing him in jail

(Continued)

A. Selected Fugitive Slave Advertisements, 1818–28 (cont'd.)

Date Ad Placed / First Run	Date of Escape	Slave Name / Sex	Owner Name / Location	Age (about)	Build / Demeanor	How Left	Reward
10/25/25 (11/2/25)	10/1/25	William (M)	Wm A Carter Near Opequon Factory, Frederick Co., Md.	19	Slender		$50 for securing in jail out of state
3/1/26 (3/1/26)	2/19/26	Peter	John Sheets Toms' Creek Hundred, Fred Co, Md.	35–40	Stout		$25 for securing in jail
5/1/27 (5/2/27)	4/16/27	Stephen (M)	Leonard Smith 40 mi W of Cumberland, Allegheny Co., Md.	21	Stout	Lengthy description of clothes. Took with him a small dog. "He has no doubt made for Pennsylvania."	$50 for securing in Cumberland, Frederick, or Hagerstown jail
10/30/28 (11/12/28)	10/18/28 (Sat. night)	Jim Hall (M)	John Harry Hagerstown, Md.	25	Well built	"He went away with three other Negroes, and it is supposed that he and a boy belonging to Mr. John Waggoner, separated from their companions somewhere about Gettysburg, Penn."	$100 for securing, and giving immediate notice by mail. $100 for Mr. Waggoner's boy too.

Frequency of fugitive slave advertisements falls off markedly after 1828.

B. 1828 South Central Pennsylvania Petition Opposing Slavery in the District of Columbia

Of the United States of America, in Congress Assembled:
The Memorial
Of the undersigned, Citizens of the State of Pennsylvania
Respectfully Represents—
THAT they, in common with their fellow-citizens, greatly deplore the rapidly growing evil of African Slavery, which pervades a large portion of our otherwise happy Country. There being at least two millions of a colored population in the United States, most of them held in a state of abject slavery, in such a degraded situation as is more likely to make them enemies, than friends to our government; and nearly doubling in number every 25 years—These are considerations, sufficient to rouse the energies of every true Patriot, to unite in adopting suitable measures to remove the evil, before it becomes too great to admit of a remedy. The slave trade was declared Piracy in the early part of the present century, by the united declaration of the American States; and certainly the crime can be no less, to deprive our natural born citizens of their freedom, than persons born on the coast of Africa. If the Africans had been reduced to slavery as a punishment for crimes, of which they had been fairly and legally convicted, that could not have effected the rights of their offspring, for our Constitution declares that "no attainder," even "of treason shall work corruption of blood, or forfeiture, longer than during the life of the person attain[t]ed." And seeing it is a duty enjoined on us by the highest authority, to love our neighbors as ourselves, and to do unto others as we would that they should do to unto us, which clearly implies that our rights and privileges are equal; it is evidently a continuation of the same Piratical practice, to deprive our American born Citizens of that state of liberty and equality, which they [sic] unanimous declaration of the United States has declared to be their unalienable right. The system of slavery is extremely unjust and impolitic in another point of view: by permitting one of our citizens to hold any number of those degraded creatures in Such a situation as to make them become the natural enemies of our government and institutions, and thereby laying as many of our white citizens, liable every day of their lives, to be called to arms, in order to awe, or compel them to remain in subjection. Many of the latter having no interest in the system which lays them under that liability; & receiving no equivalent for the dangers, and difficulties of their situation. And seeing that this system of oppression is tolerated to a considerable extent in the district of Columbia, which is placed under the exclusive jurisdiction of Congress; in

this spot, which above all others, ought to be dedicated to freedom, and purged from all unwarrantable oppression; in the District, where the Representatives of a free republican people meet in council; where travelers from distant parts, and Ambassadors from Foreign Nations, come to transact business at the Capitol, or Temple of Liberty: that they should find the District, not only abounding with this species of oppression, but made the mart; or emporium of slavery, is highly disagreeable to the American People. For these reasons, and many others that might be given, your memorialists solicit the attention of Congress to the subject; praying for the enactment of a law; that all children born in the District of Columbia after a certain day, shall be free. And as the law prayed for, only applies to unborn posterity, to prevent more persons from being enslaved and debased: to persons unto whom the claim of purchase can by no means extend, and far less any principle of right; it can therefore, of course, be no infringement of right. The undersigned, therefore, earnestly entreat your honorable body, to take this subject under serious consideration, and adopt such measures for removing the evil, as its importance demands.

Signatures on 1828 Petition:

. . . Harmon
[Illegible, pencil signatures — probably 6]
Joel Wierman
Jacob Harris
Henry Beals
Wm C. Wierman
J. E. Pearson
John Harris
Saml Hendricks
Benjamin Ocker
Francis Fickes
Henry Snider
William Wilby [Willey?]
[Illegible, torn]
[Illegible, torn]
Sam . . . [torn] . . . stock[Samuel Fahnestock?]
Levi [M]iller Jr.
Thos. John
John Day
Saml White

Wm R Stewart
Daniel Wickes (Fickes?)
Wm Gardner
Jacob Gardner Jr.
John Wierman
Danl Sheffer
Peter Ferree
Jno. Howard Sheffer

HR 20A-G5.1, Committee on the District of Columbia, Slavery in the District of Columbia, January 9 – January 28, 1828, Folder 1 of 8, National Archives.

C. 1847 Gettysburg African American Petition

House File, 71st Session 1, 1847
RG-7, Ser. 11, Folder 7
[January 15, 1847]
To the Senate and House of Representatives of the State of Pennsylvania
The undersigned, inhabitants of Gettysburg Adams county, in the state of Pennsylvania, earnestly desirous to free this Commonwealth from all connection with Slavery, respectfully ask:

1. That you will repeal all laws which permit the holding of slaves for any length of time within the limits of this State.
2. That you will repeal all laws of this Commonwealth which direct or authorize our judges, magistrates, sheriffs, constables, jailors, or other officers, to aid in the capture and removal from this State of persons claimed as fugitive slaves.
3. That you will propose such measures to Congress as will have the effect either to abolish Slavery in the United States, or release this Commonwealth from the legal obligation to aid in its continuance. [Printed].

David Sibbs	Anthony McClure	Mary Consey
Washington Sibbs	John Disnick	Parasilla Consey
Henry William	William Caucus	John Freeland
Maria Palm	Jeremiah	Maria Freeland
Mary Palm	Ann Armstrong	Kissia Thomas
Jordan Dashett	Rebecca McClure	Judy A. Dorcas

Elizabeth Madock
Elizabeth Williams
Mary Williams
Jane A. Thomas
Mary Thomas
Jesse A. Sibbs
Benjamin Devan
Isaac Hill
Nathaniel Russel
Ephraim Palm
John Hopkins
Samuel Rilly
Patty Johnson
Trecy McCibins
Margart Disnick
Isabella Russel
Samuel Armstrong
Martha Johnson
Emanuel Crage
Judy A. Wagoner
Sarah Johnson
Dicey Johnson
Sarah Armstrong
Joseph Williams
Rebecca A. Sibb
Amy Devan
Benjamin Devan
Henderson Brian
Mary M. Pearman
Stephen Harris
William Harris

Abram Brian
Dinah Butler
Charles Pearman
Aaron Constant
Henry Butler
Upton Johnson
James Carnel
Frank Thomas
William H. Williams
George Consey
Mary C. Cole
Rebecca A. Chiler
Sarah A. Williams
Williams Myers
John Myers
Charles Palm
Alfred Palm
Harriet Drowary
Jane Harris
Harriet Cole
Hetty Brian
Hanamary Jackson
Moses Brian
Violet Drowary
Mary J. Brian
Elisha Devan
John M. Constant
Sarah A. Thomas
William Harris
Ephraim Hopkins
Samuel Cole

Margaret Johnson
Jesse A. Sibb
Solomon F. Sitt
Sarah E. Armstrong
Harriet Palm
Angeline William
Manerva A. Williams
Emily G. Q. Cole
Abram Brian
Charles Johnson
Judy A. Roberson
Elizabeth Brian
Mary J. Skelly
Elisha J. Devan
Ann L. Jones
Dennis M. Washing-
    ton [Williams]
John Stanton
Nathaniel Harris
Greenberry Stanton
Moses Brian
William Hopkins
Edward Hopkins
William Devan
Catharine Miles
Asburry Thomas
Thomas Armstrong
Elizabeth Constant
Joahab Chiler

"These are the names of the colored people of Gettys Burg [Gettysburg] Adams [C]ounty. Aaron Constant."

Endorsement: Aaron Constant & 110 others.

D. 1846 Adams County Petition

House File, 70th Session 1, 1846
RG-7, Ser. 11, Folder 7
To the Senate and House of Representatives of the Commonwealth of Pennsylvania

The petition of the undersigned, inhabitants of Pennsylvania, respectfully asks, that you will be pleased to enact a law making it a penal offense for citizens of Pennsylvania to aid Slaveholders, *or their agents*, in arresting fugitive Slaves. [Printed]

D. 1846 Adams County Petition (cont'd.)

County	Page	Dwelling	Family	NAME	Age in 1850	Profession	Real Estate	Notes
Adams	102	1383	1491	William Wright	62	Farmer	5000	Quaker (Q)
Adams	108	1471	1583	Warner Townsend	29	Farmer	5000	Q
York/ Lancaster				Wm W. Wright (of Columbia)[1]				Q
Adams	48a	624	691	William Wright	72	None	3000	Q
				A. G. Garretson				Q?
Adams	101a	1369	1477	Oliver Garretson	36	Wheel- maker	1200	Q
York		1238	1241	Wm Hunt	41	Farmer		
Adams	078	1050	1121	Nathan Griest	45	Farmer	3000	Q
Adams	092	1248	1257	Amos Griest	64	Carpenter	400	Q
Adams	101	1358	1466	D[avid] Newcommer	41	Merchant	3000	
Adams	101	1367	1475	E. G. Vancise	40	Physician	2000	Q
Adams		134	145	Chas S. Wright	33	Carpenter	600	Q
Adams	59	784	864	Josiah Penrose[2]	60	None	—	Q.
York		1509	1509	Peter Griest	57	Farmer	3000	Q?
Adams	047a	614	680	Cyrus Griest	46	Farmer	2500	Q
				John Townsend				
				Samuel Garretson				Q
				Hiram H. Watts?				
				Wm H Mendenhall[3]				
				A E Mendenhall[3]				
Adams	55b	725	798	Wm D Taylor	36	Laborer	500	
Adams	102	1393	1491	Hannah Wright	30	NL. d.		Q
						Wm&Phebe		

County				Name	Age	Occupation	Value	
Adams	102	1383	1491	Phebe Wright	61	NL. Wife of Wm.		Q.
NF				Rachel Wright	28	d. Wm & Phoebe		Q
York	700?	652	652	Barzillae Garretson	39	Farmer	5000	Q
Adams	056a	735	209	Nathan Wright	64	Farmer	3000	Q
Adams	097	1307	1415	Jesse Cook	54	Farmer	1500	Q
Adams	056a	732	806	Josiah Cook	45	Farmer	2000	Q
Adams	047	618	684	H[iram]S. Wright	35	Tanner	4000	Q
Adams	056a	734	808	J. B. Wright (John B)	68	Farmer	3500	Q
Adams	062b	822	904	Able T. Wright	40	Merchant	1500	Q
Adams	107b	1457	1568	Isaac Tudor[4]	61	Farmer	550	Q
Adams		133	143	Wm H Wright	38	Farmer	4500	Q
York?	56a	734	808	Joel Wright	33	Laborer		Q?
Adams	87B	79	1280	Joseph Russell				Q?
Adams	97	1306	1412	[Thomas] Pearson	25	Teacher		
Adams	088	1191	1294	Samuel Miller	53	Carpenter	500	
Adams	96	1290	1394	Joel Wierman	62	Farmer	3500	Q
Adams				A. H. Myers				
Adams	150	1476	1589	Franklin Miller	30	Trader?	900	
Adams				Wm W Hamvesty				
Adams				Wm Humphrey				
Adams				John Morgan				
Adams	108	1461	1572	Jacob Griest	52	Farmer	4000	Q?
Adams	107b	1139		A[llen] Robinette	67	L[aborer]	—	
York?	162		1237	H. N.? Garretson[5]				Q?
Adams				M.? A. Townsend[6]	28	w. of James		
Adams				W. W. Hottinger				
Adams	601	145	154	Henry A. Picking	[33]	[Farmer & lawyer]	[4500]	
(1860)	(Str)				[43]	lawyer]		

(Continued)

D. 1846 Adams County Petition (cont'd.)

County	Page	Dwelling	Family	NAME	Age in 1850	Profession	Real Estate	Notes
York?				S. Townsend				
				J. G. Myers				
Adams	106	1449	1560	John Welsh	36	Carpenter	NL	
Adams	108	1464	1576	Levi Lippy	33	Wheelwright	2500	
				Hiram Myers				
Adams	105	1435	1545	Jacob P. Lerew?	37	Farmer	6000	
				Nath. Pemberton				
Adams/Hamtbn				Jno. B. McCreary[7]				Q?
Adams				Jane McCreary[7]				Q?
Adams	084	1139	1237	James Townsend[8]	35	Farmer	6000	
Adams	107b	1457	1568	Mary Tudor	64	NL. w. Isaac, 61, Farmer, $550		Q
Adams.	107b	1457	1568	M. or N. A. Tudor[9]	28	NL	NL	Q?
				H[ulder]. [Huldah] S. Penrose				
Adams	107b	1461	1572	S[arah?] M. Robinette[10]	25	Live w/ Allen		Q?
Adams	107b	1461	1572	L[ouisa] L. Robinette	22	Live w/ Allen		Q?

Most of names come from Menallen, Latimore, or Huntingdon Townships

LEGEND:

Q = Quaker (as identified in the Menallen Meeting Minutes)

Q? = Possible Quaker, sharing the same last name as a Quaker family identified in the Menallen Meeting minutes

NL = Not Listed.

w. = wife d. = daughter

[1] There were a number of William Wright's in Adams and York Counties at this time, so it is hard to tell exactly who this signer is. William Wright of Adams County's only son was named William Wierman Wright. He would have been 22 at the time of this petition signing. Because I have seen the signature of William Wright of Columbia, I believe that this signature may represent him instead and have represented it as such.

[2] Josiah Penrose appears retired. His son, Elisha, has $4,000 in real estate and lives with him, so the fact he is listed as having no real property could be misleading as to his wealth.

[3] According to genealogical records, there appears to have been a William Mendenhall married in Adams County in 1844. (He would have been 46 at the time of this petition. His father, Aaron Mendenhall, would have been 77.) It is not clear that these are the two individuals here, however—and they are not in the 1850 Adams County census.

[4] This is the only Isaac Tudor listed in Latimore in the 1850 census, and Huntington Friends Meeting House Cemetery records list him as 64 when he died in 1853. However, in 1870, there is a listing for an Isaac Tudor, age 45, $7,000, who would have been 25 in 1850 census if living in Adams.

[5] Possibly Hanah Garretson, 30 in 1850, daughter of Josia Garretson, a farmer with $3000 in real estate. Considered likely because she lived next door to Peter Griest, another signer. Unclear whether Hanah's middle initial is N. Also, the Star and Sentinel of May 1864 indicates that a different Hannah Garretson died at her nephew Charles S. Wright's house on April 11. She was then 88 years old.

[6] Chosen because Mary Townsend is the wife of James Townsend, another signer. Unclear if Mary Townsend's middle initial is A.

[7] There are several John and Jane McCreary's in the Adams County census. The only Johnathan B. and Jane living together are recorded by the census taker as having the last name of McCleary. Jonathan is age 56 in 1850 and worked as a Lumberman. They also live in Hamiltonban, on the far side of Adams County from York Springs. Jane McCleary was 77 years old in 1846—would she have made the trip and signed the petition? In the absence of a Jane and John McCreary, however, these may be plausible.

[8] The only James Thompson in Adams County in the 1850 census; however, the Star and Sentinel of March 1864 records a James Thompson dying in February, nearly aged 50.

[9] Possibly Martha Tudor, d. of Isaac and Mary, 19, but she would have only been 15–16 at the time of the petition. She lives with Huldah S. Penrose, near Allen and Sarah Robinette. Middle initial not known.

[10] Possibly Susan Robinette, 43, married to George, farmer, 60, $4,500, both also on page 107b. I judged Sarah more likely because Allen Robinette, whom she lived with, did sign, but George did not.

Approximate Ages of Signers in 1846

10–19	1
20–29	11
30–39	10
40–49	5
50–59	8
60–69	6
70–79	0

Average approximate age of signers: 41 years old.
Approximate ages calculated by subtracting four from the 1850 census figure.
Data primarily from 1850 Adams County population census.

E. 1861 Franklin County Pro-Colonization Petition

RG-7, Senate File, Folder 85, Petition 484 (sent in with identical petition from Adams County) [Not dated, but petition is from March 1861]

To the Honorable, the Senate and House of Representatives of the State of Pennsylvania

The undersigned, citizens of Pennsylvania, take the liberty respectfully, but earnestly, of requesting you to make an appropriation toward the passage and settlement in Liberia of such of the colored population of this State as are desirous to remove to that interesting and successful African Republic.

During the years 1859 and 1960, the Pennsylvania Colonization Society colonized in Liberia one hundred and eight of the colored residents of this State. At this time there are ninety of the same class impatiently awaiting to avail themselves of the like boon. The Society has not the means to respond favorably to the applications of these and others constantly reaching it.

This population should be liberally assisted to escape from their depressed condition here, and become citizens and freemen of Liberia. There they attain a position in which they benefit themselves and their race; demonstrate their capacity, advance African civilization, suppress the foreign slave trade, and open to this country an extensive theatre for a legitimate, peaceful and valuable commerce. [Standard pro-PCS form petition]

County	Township/ Borough	NAME	Age in 1860	Profession	Real Estate	Personal Property
Not Found (NF)		John L. Heffelman				
NF		B. Bausinleon?				
Franklin (Frnk)	Chambersburg	George R. Colliflower	31	Printer	300	250
CK		P (J?) E. Norris				
CK		J.? B. Doyle				
Frnk	Chambersburg	Wm H. Toms	21	Clerk	—	—
Frnk	Chambersburg	C. M. Duncan	28	Attorney	30,000	10,000
NF		W. S. Stenger				
Frnk	Chambersburg	Augs Duncan	31	Gentleman	20,000	12,000
Frnk	Chambersburg	Geo. W. Welsh	26	Attorney	—	200
Frnk	Chambersburg	W. W. Paxton	49	Merchant	2000	2500
Frnk	Chambersburg	A. D. Caufman	46	Gentleman	11,000	9000
Frnk	Chambersburg	Joseph Clark	35	Merchant	2000	2500
	Chambersburg	Saml R. Fisher	50	Clergy	300	1000
NF		B. B. Henshey				
Frnk	SW Chambersburg	R. M. Reynolds	20	Physician	—	—
Frnk		Jacob Lortz	44	Sch. Teacher		
NF		J. P. Gray				
NF		J. M. Shillett				
NF		B. C. Ross or Boss				
Frnk	Chambersburg	Jno. Oyler	41	Tanner	3200	4000
Frnk	Chambersburg	Thos J. Wright	58	Book Binder	2000	1000
Frnk	Chambersburg	Wm Heyser	64	Gentleman	55,000	22,500
Frnk	SW Chambersburg	James King	48	Stone Cutter	5000	1500
NF		George W. Snider				
Frnk	SW Chambersburg	Lewis Wampler	46	Silver Plater	1000	900
CK	NF	B. S. Schneck		Professor		

All signers born in Pennsylvania except for Jacob Lortz (Germany), James King (Scotland), and George R. Colliflower (Cauliflower), Maryland

Approximate Ages of Petition Signers

10–19	0
20–29	4
30–39	3
40–49	5
50–59	3
60–69	1
70–79	0

Average approximate age: 40 years old.
Approximate ages calculated by adding one to the figures in the 1860 census.
Census results from: Franklin County, Pennsylvania, 1860 Population Census, Valley of the Shadow: Two Communities in the American Civil War, Virginia Center for Digital History, University of Virginia (http://jefferson.village.virginia.edu/govdoc/pop_census.html)

F. 1861 Adams County Pro-Colonization Petition

RG-7, SENATE FILE, Folder 85, Petition 484(B) (with 484, identical petition from Franklin County

No endorsement, but petition is March 1861

To the Honorable, the Senate and House of Representatives of the State of Pennsylvania

The undersigned, citizens of Pennsylvania, take the liberty respectfully, but earnestly, of requesting you to make an appropriation toward the passage and settlement in Liberia of such of the colored population of this State as are desirous to remove to that interesting and successful African Republic.

During the years 1859 and 1960, the Pennsylvania Colonization Society colonized in Liberia one hundred and eight of the colored residents of this State. At this time there are ninety of the same class impatiently awaiting to avail themselves of the like boon. The Society has not the means to respond favorably to the applications of these and others constantly reaching it.

This population should be liberally assisted to escape from their depressed condition here, and become citizens and freemen of Liberia. There they attain a position in which they benefit themselves and their race; demonstrate their capacity, advance African civilization, suppress the foreign slave trade, and open to this country an extensive theatre for a legitimate, peaceful and valuable commerce. [Standard pro-PCS form petition]

County	Township/ Borough	NAME	Age in 1860	Profession	Real Estate	Personal Property
Adams	Gettysburg	David Wills	27	Attorney	7000	3000
Adams	Gettysburg	Jno. H. McClellan	52	Bank Clerk	5200	4000
Adams	Gettysburg	Jas. F. Fahnestock	39	Merchant	4500	10,000
Adams	Gettysburg	J. L. Schick?	37	Merchant	3000	16,000
Adams	Gettysburg	M. L. Stoever	40	Prof, Pa College	3000	4000
Adams	Gettysburg	F[ranklin]. B. Picking	34	Clothier	—	2000
(Adams)	(Liberty)	(S[amuel] J. Welty)	44	(Farmer)	(2300)	(100)
Adams	Gettysburg	W B McClellan	38	Attorney	2200	800
Adams	Gettysburg	George Geyer	59	Coachmaker	1800	500
Adams	Gettysburg	Eph H. Minnigh	28	Confectioner	—	280
Adams	Gettysburg	J. C.? Neely	22	Attorney	—	500
Adams	Gettysburg	J. M. Walter	30	Clerk	3000	—
Adams	Gettysburg	S. S. McCreary	53	Hatter	3000	700
Adams	Gettysburg	Chas Horner	30	Physician	2500	2000
Adams	Gettysburg	Perry J. Tate	30	Furn. Dlr	1000	750
Adams	Gettysburg	Abm Scott	53	Merchant	9000	4000
Adams	Gettysburg	Moses McLean	56	Attorney	16,540	6000
NF	NF	T. R. Russell[1]				
Adams	Gettysburg	T. D. Carson	27	Coach-maker	—	1500?
Adams	Gettysburg	Edw G. Fahnestock	30	Merchant	3000	10,000
Adams	Gettysburg	Wm McElwee	38	Presbyt. Clergy man	—	500
Franklin?	NF	R F McClellan				
Adams	Gettysburg	J. T. Crawford	63	—	12,000	5500
Adams	Gettysburg	Dunlop Paxton	30	Salesman	—	—
NF	NF	James S. Weitz				
Adams	Gettysburg	J[ames] C. Guinn?	25	Merchant	—	2000
Adams	Freedom	Wm M Bigham	36	Farmer	10,000	1840
Adams	Gettysburg	W[illiam] A Duncan	24	Attorney	15,000	8,000
Adams	Gettysburg	Chas X Martin	36	Printer	—	100
NF	NF	Chas A (D) Boyer				

(*Continued*)

F. 1861 Adams County Pro-Colonization Petition (cont'd.)

County	Township/ Borough	NAME	Age in 1860	Profession	Real Estate	Personal Property
Adams	Gettysburg	John [H.] Culp[2]	34	Coach-maker	1600	400
Adams	Gettysburg	R[obert] Horner	25	Physician	2500	2000
Adams	Gettysburg	John L. Tate	52	Hotel Keeper	5000	2000
Adams	Gettysburg	John Scott[3]	48	Merchant	12500	3000
Adams	Gettysburg	Wm McClean	27	Attorney	1500	1200
Adams	Gettysburg	George Little	53	Merchant	4500	10,000
Adams	Gettysburg	F A Muhlenberg Jr.	41	Prof, Penna Coll	2800	5500

[1] Individual indicated as T. R. Russell may be J. R. Russell. In which case, could be John Russell (107/274/278), 22, Farm Laborer, or James Russell (105/259/261), 61, Surveyor, both in Franklin Township.
[2] Two possible John Culps: one that is listed (168/89/109), and John Culp of Mi., listed in census index as John M. Culp, 43, Merchant, 1500 1850 born in PA.
[3] There are a number of other John Scotts in Adams. This one seemed plausible.

Approximate Ages of Petition Signers

10–19	0
20–29	8
30–39	11
40–49	5
50–59	6
60–69	2

Average approximate age: forty years old.
Approximate ages calculated by adding one year to the figures in the 1860 census.
Data from 1860 Adams County Census, www.genealogy.com.

G. [Second] 1861 Adams County Pro-Colonization Petition

RG-7, SENATE FILE, Folder 85, Petition 486 (Second petition, shorter, includes some of same names as 484B)

McClure

Mar 22/61

Fin [likely "Finance Committee"]

To the Honorable, the Senate and House of Representatives of the State of Pennsylvania

The undersigned, citizens of Pennsylvania, take the liberty respectfully, but earnestly, of requesting you to make an appropriation toward the passage and settlement in Liberia of such of the colored population of this State as are desirous to remove to that interesting and successful African Republic.

During the years 1859 and 1960, the Pennsylvania Colonization Society colonized in Liberia one hundred and eight of the colored residents of this State. At this time there are ninety of the same class impatiently awaiting to avail themselves of the like boon. The Society has not the means to respond favorably to the applications of these and others constantly reaching it.

This population should be liberally assisted to escape from their depressed condition here, and become citizens and freemen of Liberia. There they attain a position in which they benefit themselves and their race; demonstrate their capacity, advance African civilization, suppress the foreign slave trade, and open to this country an extensive theatre for a legitimate, peaceful and valuable commerce. [Standard pro-PCS form petition] [Data from 1860 Adams County population census]

County	Township/ Borough	NAME	Age in 1860	Profession	Real Estate	Personal Property
Adams	Gettysburg	David Wills	27	Attorney	7000	3000
Adams	Gettysburg	Jno. H. McClellan	52	Bank Clerk	5200	4000
Adams	Gettysburg	Jas. F. Fahnestock	39	Merchant	4500	10,000
Adams	Gettysburg	J. L. Schick?	37	Merchant	3000	16,000
Adams	Gettysburg	M. L. Stoever	40	Prof, Pa College	3000	4000
Adams	Gettysburg	David McCreary	56	Saddle Making &c	2500	1500
Adams	Gettysburg	A. J. Cover	28	Attorney	—	250
Adams	Gettysburg	T. D. Carson	27	Coachmaker	—	1500?
Adams	Gettysburg	Edw G. Fahnestock	30	Merchant	3000	10,000
Adams	Gettysburg (191/252/295)	Saml S. Forney[1]	70	Druggist	3000	2000
NF		M. E. Doll				
Adams	Gettysburg	J[acob] Brinkerhoff	40	—	5000	5000

[1] Samuel Forney has a Maryland-born wife, Eliza

Approximate Ages of Petition Signers

10–19	0
20–29	3
30–39	2
40–49	3
50–59	2
60–69	0
70–79	1

Average approximate age: 41.5 years old.
Approximate ages calculated by adding one year to the figures in the 1860 census.
Data from 1860 Adams County Census, www.genealogy.com.

H. 1861 Doylestown, Bucks County Pro-Colonization Petition

RG-7, SENATE FILE, Folder 8-, Petition 385
March 1, 1861
To the Honorable, the Senate and House of Representatives of the State of Pennsylvania

The undersigned, citizens of Pennsylvania, take the liberty respectfully, but earnestly, of requesting you to make an appropriation toward the passage and settlement in Liberia of such of the colored population of this State as are desirous to remove to that interesting and successful African Republic.

During the years 1859 and 1960, the Pennsylvania Colonization Society colonized in Liberia one hundred and eight of the colored residents of this State. At this time there are ninety of the same class impatiently awaiting to avail themselves of the like boon. The Society has not the means to respond favorably to the applications of these and others constantly reaching it.

This population should be liberally assisted to escape from their depressed condition here, and become citizens and freemen of Liberia. There they attain a position in which they benefit themselves and their race; demonstrate their capacity, advance African civilization, suppress the foreign slave trade, and open to this country an extensive theatre for a legitimate, peaceful and valuable commerce. [Standard pro-PCS form petition]

County	Township/Borough (Page/Household/Family)	NAME	Age in 1860	Profession	Real Estate	Personal Property	Birthplace
Bucks	Doylestown B (343/274/274)	Wm. Richard Gries	34	Epis. Clergy	—	1000	Pa.
Bucks	Doylestown B	Hiram Lukens	38	Jnr Printer	—	100	Pa.
Bucks	Doylestown B (338/246/246)	George Lear	42	Lawyer	7000	13000	Pa.
Bucks	Buckingham (208/158/166)	James C. Iden	47	Conveyances	10,000	2000	Pa.
Bucks	Warminster (760)	Henry P. Ross	24	Laborer	—	—	Pa.
Bucks	(209/167/179)	Emmor Walton	27	Drover	—	2000	Pa.
Bucks	(329/174/174)	R[obert] J Armstrong	24	Student at law	—	—	N.J.
Bucks	Doylestown (340/252/252)	R Watson	37	Lawyer	1200	5000	Pa.
Bucks	Doylestown (338/245/245)	C. E. DuBois	60	Lawyer	3000	15,000	Pa.
Bucks	(158/809/843)	Jno. I. Brock / J. L. DuBois	40	Farmer	10,000	1300	Pa.
Bucks	Doylestown (311/27/27)	Jno. Beatty[1]	60	Gentleman	5000	—	Pa.
NF		G. E. Donaldson / Jno. P. Brown					
NF		G R. McCoy[2]					
Bucks	Doylestown (337/238/238)	N. C. James	35	Lawyer	5000	2000	Pa.
Bucks	Doylestown (339/247/247)	Lewis R. Thompson	34	Lawyer	2000	1300	Pa.
Bucks	Doylestown (334/208/208)	William E. Pickering	34	Butcher	—	200	Pa.

(Continued)

H. 1861 Doylestown, Bucks County Pro-Colonization Petition (cont'd.)

County	Township/ Borough(Page/ Household/Family)	NAME	Age in 1860	Profession	Real Estate	Personal Property	Birthplace
Bucks	Doylestown (327/151/151)	Benj. Cadwallader	34	Merchant	—	4500	Pa.
Bucks	Doylestown B (314/48/48)	L[ewis]. P Worthington[3]	27	Clerk in Bank			
Bucks	Doylestown B (339/247/247)	Wm J. Stevenson	21	M. E. Preacher	—	300	Pa.
Bucks	Buckingham (230/317/333)	S[amuel] G. Anderson	34	Farmer	—	1600	Pa.
Buck	Doylestown B (340/252/252)	John B. Pugh	51				Pa.
Bucks	Doylestown (335/223/223)	V. Wetherill	59	Farmer	8500	2000	Pa.
Bucks	Doylestown B (327/156/156)	R[euben] F. Scheetz	42	Clerk	2000	500	Pa.
Bucks		W. W. H. Davis	38	Ed. Of paper	13,000	13,000	Pa.
		Thos Crump?					
Bucks	Doylestown (343/272/272)	Henry T. Darlington	25	Editor	3500	500	Pa.
Phil.		Edward L. Rogers[4]					
Phil.	14th Ward (101/647/740)	Enos Prizer	41	Furniture Cars	5000	—	Pa.

All data from 1860 census. For approximation of ages at the time of the petition, add one year to values above.

[1] Another possible John Beatty, 158/809/843, 50, Farmer, $1000 real property, $100 personal property, born in Pa., lived in Falls Township. Above Beatty was chosen because he lived in Doylestown.

[2] Two possible George McCoys lived in Philadelphia as well.

[3] There is another possible Lewis Worthington, living in Bucks County, a 30-year-old farmer, with no real property, $1500 personal property. As the L. Worthington listed in the table lived in Doylestown, he is the most logical choice here.

[4] Two possible Edward Rogerses: the first, 52, Shoemaker, $3000 real property, born in England, lived in the 22nd Ward of Phil. (23/148/146); the second, 21, Clerk, born in Pa., lived in the 8th Ward of Phil. (442/359/422).

Approximate Ages of Petition Signers

10–19	0
20–29	6
30–39	9
40–49	5
50–59	1
60–69	3

Average approximate age: 39 years old.
Approximate ages calculated by adding one year to the figures in the 1860 census.
Data from 1860 Bucks County population census.

I. 1861 Newtown, Bucks County Pro–Personal Liberty Law Petition

RG-7, Senate File, Folder 8-, Petition 375
To the Senate & House of Representatives of the State of Pennsylvania
The undersigned inhabitants of the State of Pennsylvania respectfully ask that you will repeal no part of the Antikidnaping [sic] Law: and that you will not reenact the old Comity Law—[The Comity Law was a name for the law that allowed Southern slaveholders to hold their slaves in Pennsylvania for up to six months.][Handwritten]

I. 1861 Newtown, Bucks County Pro–Personal Liberty Law Petition (cont'd.)

County	Township/Borough (Page/Household/Family)	NAME	Age in 1860	Profession	Real Estate	Personal Property	Birth place
Bucks	(541/290/325)	Hannah A. White	23	NL			Pa
NF		H or A? B. Linton					
Bucks	Lower Makefield	Thomas Janney[1]	65	Landlord & farmer?	Wealthy	Wealthy	Pa.
Bucks	(591/290/325)	Anna L. White	18	NL			Pa.
NF		Halis (A?) H. Trego					
NF		H A Trego					
Bucks	Newtown (558/236/261)	Elizabeth Y. Linton	52	Wife of farmer, 54, 10,000/3000			Pa.
Bucks	Newtown (535/246/277)	Penquite Linton	51	Farmer	8000	2000	Pa.
Bucks	Newtown	Ellen H. Linton (census: "Hellen")	50	Wife of Penquite?			Pa.
Bucks	Newtown (534/241/266)	Edward Linton	38	Farmer	8500	2000	Pa.
Bucks	Newtown (535/246/272)	Thomas B Linton	18	Lives with Penquite (farmer)			Pa.
Bucks	(534/241/266)	Elizabeth B Linton	36	Wife of Edward			Pa.
Bucks	Lwr Makefield (234/186/195)	Isaac B Brown	45	Farmer	14,000	2800	Pa.
Bucks	(558/420/420)	Emma Linton	15	Domestic	—	—	Pa
Bucks	(444A/110/110)	Joseph Willard	52	Farmer	11,300	3000	Pa.
Bucks	Newtown (530/213/238)	Smith Stradling	40	Farmer	—	1500	Pa.
NF	Several Mariann Vanhorns	N? W? Willard					
NF		Maryann Vanhorn					
Bucks	(532/239/254)	Joseph Wildman r?	29	Farmer	415	12,500	Pa.

County	Census Ref	Name	Age	Occupation	Value 1	Value 2	Birthplace
Bucks	(530/213/238)	Matilda Worthington	25	House work			Pa.
Bucks	Newtown (534/238/264)	John Linton	65	Gentleman	11,000	600	Pa.
?		Emily H. Stradling					
?		Jane Linton					
Bucks	Newtown (541/291/326)	Isaiah Heston	35	Asst. Farmer	—	1000	Pa.
Bucks	Newtown (533/238/263)	Anna M. Linton	30	Wife of farmer	—	2800	
Bucks	(240/290/315)	Abbie A White	21				Pa
Bucks	Newtown (533/238/263)	Emily Leedom	15	House maid?			Pa.
Bucks	(541/290/325)	Lydia White	40	NL			Pa
Bucks	(533/239/265)	Joseph Cunningham	46	Farmer	7800	1500	Pa.
Bucks	(541/290/325)	Ephraim A. White	45	Farmer	3500	2000	Pa.
Bucks	(533/239/265)	Rebecca J. Cunningham	37	[w. farmer]			Pa.
Bucks	(541/290/325)	Oscar White	15				Pa.
Bucks	(534/239/265)	Rach(a)el Cunningham	71	[Prob. mother of farmer]			Pa.
Bucks	(235/197/206)	Richard Janney	64	Farmer	4000	12,500	Pa.
Bucks	Newtown (542/292/326)	Mary C. Cunningham	39	[w. farmer]			
Bucks	Lwr Mkfield (208/11/11)	Jos. H. Yardly	62	Farmer	2,000	4000	Pa.
Bucks	(533/239/265)	Mary J. Cunningham	16	[d. farmer]			
Bucks	Newtown (542/293/327)	Silas Car(e)y	44	Farmer	14,000	3,000	Ireland
(Montgomery?)	Plymouth (741/481/495)	Elijah Lukens	52	Farm Hand	—	—	Pa.
Bucks		Thos Janney[1]	20				Pa.

[1]The two Thomas Janneys were not found in the census, but the data in the table was found in genealogical records.

Approximate Ages of Petition Signers

10–19	6
20–29	4
30–39	6
40–49	7
50–59	5
60–69	4
70–79	1

Average approximate age: 41 years old (average age of male signers 47).
Approximate ages calculated by adding one year to the figures in the 1860 census.
Data from the 1860 Bucks County population census.

Notes

Introduction: The Fugitive Slave Issue on the Edge of Freedom

1. C. Vann Woodward to Robert Penn Warren, September 4, 1960, Vann Woodward—Penn Warren Correspondence, Robert Penn Warren Papers, YCAL MSS 51, Box 82, Yale University Library, cited by John Stauffer, "Remarks at David Herbert Donald's Memorial at Ford's Theater," April 9, 2010. I am indebted to John Stauffer for this reference. Robert Penn Warren, "A Mark Deep on A Nation's Soul," *Life*, May 17, 1961, 82–88. This essay was later published in book form as *The Legacy of the Civil War*.

2. Other locales, such as Boston, New York, and the upper Mississippi River Basin, created a sort of "virtual border" because of the extensive economic ties to the South, but this study concentrates on the North-South border.

3. Frederick Douglass, *My Bondage and My Freedom* (New York, 1856), pp. 323–24, cited by Larry Gara, *The Liberty Line: The Legend of the Underground Railroad* (Lexington: University of Kentucky Press, 1961; reprint, 1996), pp. 147–48. Charles L. Blockson, *The Hippocrene Guide to The Underground Railroad* (New York: Hippocrene Books, 1994), pp. 117–20.

4. Congressional Globe, 50th Congress, 1st session, Appendix, April 20, 1848, pp. 501–4, cited by Stanley Harrold, *Border War: Fighting over Slavery before the Civil War* (Chapel Hill: University of North Carolina Press, 2010). Thomas Hart Benton, *Thirty Years' View*, v. 2 (New York: D. Appleton and Company, 1856), pp. 777–80; Henry Wilson, *History of the Rise and Fall of the Slave Power in America*, 5th ed. (Boston: James R. Osgood and Company, 1878); William Still, *The Underground Railroad* (Philadelphia: Porter & Coates, 1872; reprint, Medford, N.J.: Plexus Publishing, 2005); Levi Coffin, *Reminiscences of Levi Coffin* (Cincinnati: Robert Clark & Co., 1880; reprint, Documenting the American South, http://docsouth.unc.edu/nc/coffin/menu.html); R. C. Smedley, *History of the Underground Railroad in Chester and the Neighboring Counties of Pennsylvania* (Lancaster: John A. Hiestand, 1883).

5. Marion G. McDougall, *Fugitive Slaves* (Boston, 1891); Wilbur H. Siebert, *The Underground Railroad from Slavery to Freedom* (New York: MacMillan Company, 1898); Albert Bushnell Hart, *Salmon Portland Chase* (Boston: Houghton, Mifflin and Company, 1899); Albert Bushnell Hart, "Introduction," in Siebert, *Underground Railroad*. Elsie Singmaster (Lewars), a writer who lived in Gettysburg and who did much to popularize southern Pennsylvania's Underground Railroad in her novels and children's books, was also taught by Hart at Radcliffe. Mrs. E. S. Lewars to W. H. Siebert, June 23, 1943, Wilbur H. Siebert Papers, Ohio Historical Society, Roll 12.

6. Charles and Mary Beard, *The Rise of American Civilization*, v. 2 (New York: MacMillan Company, 1930), pp. 3–121; Arthur C. Cole, *The Irrepressible Conflict, 1850–1865* (New York: MacMillan Company, 1934); Avery Craven, *The Coming of the Civil War* (Chicago: University of Chicago Press, 1942; reprint, Baton Rouge: Louisiana University Press,

1959); Henrietta Buckmaster, *Let My People Go: The Story of the Underground Railroad and the Growth of the Abolition Movement* (New York: Harper Brothers, 1941); Buckmaster, *Flight to Freedom: The Story of the Underground Railroad* (New York: Crowell, 1958).

7. James Ford Rhodes, *History of the United States*, v. 2 (New York: MacMillan Company, 1892; reprint, Port Washington, NY: Kennikat Press, 1967), p. 32; Allan Nevins, *The Emergence of Lincoln: Prologue to the Civil War 1859–1861* (New York: Charles Scribner's Sons, 1950), p. 489; Robin Winks, *The Blacks in Canada* (New Haven: Yale University Press, 1971), pp. 233–44. Winks is correct that not as many fugitives reached Canada as was popularly believed. Don E. Fehrenbacher, *The Slaveholding Republic* (Oxford: Oxford University Press, 2001), is one of the few to recognize the limitations of these census statistics.

8. In addition, Southern sympathizers—and Southerners controlled the census bureau for most of its antebellum history—had already shown their ability to manipulate the census data, most notably in a fraudulent assertion that the 1840 census proved that Northern free blacks went insane at a markedly higher rate than Southern slaves. See William Stanton, *The Leopard's Spots: Scientific Attitudes Toward Race in America, 1815–1859* (Chicago: University of Chicago Press, 1960).

9. Stanley W. Campbell, *The Slave Catchers: Enforcement of the Fugitive Slave Law, 1850–1860* (Chapel Hill: University of North Carolina Press, 1968; reprint, New York: W. W. Norton, 1972), p. 147.

10. Gara, *Liberty Line*. At the same time, historians explored new sources and new questions relating to slavery and the sectional crisis. Southern historians turned to wonderfully detailed manuscript plantation records, and produced studies of Southern slavery that aggregated and analyzed these records, census data, and other evidence. Much of this helped inform an analysis of slavery from a class perspective. Some of the great studies of plantation slavery focused on collective actions, "weapons of the weak" resistance such as work slow-downs, destruction of tools, and negotiation of privileges with the master. There was less emphasis on individual escape. A notable exception is John Ashworth, who, in a more sophisticated version of Hart's analysis, considered the agency of the slave (including their ability to escape) to be the key component to the coming of the Civil War. See Eugene Genovese, *Roll, Jordan Roll: The World the Slaves Made* (New York: Pantheon Books, 1974) and John Ashworth, *Slavery, Capitalism and Politics in the Antebellum Republic* (Cambridge: Cambridge University Press, 1995), pp. 1–15.

11. Eric Foner, *Free Soil, Free Labor, Free Men* (New York: Oxford University Press, 1970; reprint, 1995), pp. 134–37; John Hope Franklin and Loren Schweninger, *Runaway Slaves: Rebels on the Plantation* (New York: Oxford University Press, 1999), p. 116.

12. Charles L. Blockson, "Escape from Slavery: the Underground Railroad," *National Geographic* 166 (1984): pp. 3–39; Charles L. Blockson, *The Underground Railroad* (New York: Prentice-Hall Press, 1987); Stuart Seely Sprague, ed., *His Promised Land: The Autobiography of John P. Parker* (New York: W. W. Norton, 1996); Kathryn Grover, *The Fugitive's Gibraltar: Escaping Slaves and Abolitionism in New Bedford, Massachusetts* (Amherst: University of Massachusetts Press, 2001); David W. Blight, ed., *Passages to Freedom: The Underground Railroad in History and Memory* (Washington: Smithsonian Books, 2004).

13. William S. McFeely, *Frederick Douglass* (New York: W. W. Norton, 1991); L. Diane Barnes and Paul Finkelman, eds., *The World of Frederick Douglass 1817–1895* (Oxford: Ox-

ford University Press, 2006); Catherine Clinton, *Harriet Tubman: The Road to Freedom* (New York: Little, Brown and Company, 2004); Kate Clifford Larson, *Bound for the Promised Land* (New York: Ballantine Books, 2004); Jean Humez, *Harriet Tubman: The Life and Life Stories* (Madison: University of Wisconsin Press, 2004).

14. Albert J. Von Frank, *The Trials of Anthony Burns* (Cambridge: Harvard University Press, 1998); Earl M. Maltz, *Fugitive Slave on Trial: The Anthony Burns Case and Abolitionist Outrage* (Lawrence: University of Kansas Press, 2010); Nat Brandt with Yanna Kroyt Brandt, *In the Shadow of the Civil War: Passmore Williamson and the Rescue of Jane Johnson* (Columbia: University of South Carolina Press, 2007); H. Robert Baker, *The Rescue of Joshua Glover* (Athens: Ohio University Press, 2006); J. Blaine Hudson, *Fugitive Slaves and the Underground Railroad in the Kentucky Borderland* (Jefferson, N.C.: McFarland & Company, 2002); Keith Griffler, *Front Line of Freedom: African Americans and the Forging of the Underground Railroad in the Ohio Valley* (Lexington: University Press of Kentucky, 2004).

15. Stanley Harrold, *Border Wars: Fighting over Slavery before the Civil War* (Chapel Hill: University of North Carolina Press, 2010); Stanley Harrold, *Subversives: Antislavery Community in Washington, D.C., 1828–1865* (Baton Rouge: Louisiana University Press, 2003).

16. Phillip S. Paludan, "The American Civil War Considered as a Crisis of Law and Order," *American Historical Review* 77 (1972): pp. 1,013–34.

17. Ed Ayers and John C. Willis, eds., *The Edge of the South* (Charlottesville: University Press of Virginia, 1991); Ed Ayers, "Worrying about the Civil War," in Karen Halttunen and Lewis Perry, *Moral Problems In American Life* (Ithaca: Cornell University Press, 1991); Ed Ayers, "Momentous Events in Small Places," Frank Klement Lecture Series, Marquette University, 1997; Ed Ayers, Patricia Limerick, et. al., eds., *All over the Map: Rethinking American Regions* (Baltimore: Johns Hopkins University Press, 1996), pp. 145–65; Valley of the Shadow project, http://valley.vcdh.virginia.edu; Ed Ayers, *In the Presence of My Enemies: War in the Heart of America, 1859–1863* (New York: W. W. Norton, 2003). Thanks to Bill Blair, who knew of my admiration for Ayers's work, for suggesting this book's title.

18. David Donald, "Toward a Reconsideration of the Abolitionists," in Donald, *Lincoln Reconsidered* (New York: Knopf, 1956), pp. 19–36. For one example of this piece's many critics, see Robert A. Skotheim, "A Note on Historical Method: David Donald's 'Toward a Reconsideration of the Abolitionists,'" *Journal of Southern History*, 25 (August 1959): pp. 356–65; reprinted (without footnotes) as "The 'Status Revolution' Thesis Criticized," in Richard O. Curry, ed., *The Abolitionists*, 2nd ed. (Hinsdale, Ill.: Dryden Press, 1973), pp. 47–51.

19. Winthrop D. Jordan, *Tumult and Silence at Second Creek: An Inquiry into a Civil War Slave Conspiracy* (Baton Rouge: Louisiana University Press, 1993).

1. South Central Pennsylvania, Fugitive Slaves, and the Underground Railroad

1. Scott Hancock considers the meaning of the Mason-Dixon Line to both white and African American residents of the region in "Crossing Freedom's Fault Line: The Under-

ground Railroad in South Central Pennsylvania," at the Dickinson College Conference on the Underground Railroad in South Central Pennsylvania, February 23–24, 2003. See also Bill Encenberger, *Walkin' the Line: A Journey from Past to Present along the Mason-Dixon* (New York: M. Evans and Company, 2001).

2. Abolitionist networks and the Underground Railroad are not confined to single counties. This study examines three south central Pennsylvania counties. However, because Edward Ayers has studied Franklin County and Richard Tritt is researching fugitive slaves in Cumberland County, this study focuses on Adams County, which has the richest source material, while discussing the other counties as well.

3. James W. Livingood, *The Philadelphia-Baltimore Trade Rivalry 1780–1860* (Harrisburg: Pennsylvania Historical and Museum Commission, 1947; reprint, New York: Arno Press, 1970), pp. 4–6, 13–17, 142–59. Clarence P. Gould, "The Economic Causes of the Rise of Baltimore," in *Essays in Colonial History Presented to Charles McLean Andrews By His Students* (New Haven: Yale University Press, 1931), pp. 225–51. Jo N. Hays, "Overlapping Hinterlands: York, Philadelphia, and Baltimore, 1800–1830," *Pennsylvania Magazine of History and Biography* 116 (1992), pp. 295–322. See also Joseph E. Walker, ed., *Pleasure and Business in Western Pennsylvania: The Journal of Joshua Gilpin, 1809* (Harrisburg: Pennsylvania Historical and Museum Commission, 1975), p. 19. (Bridge) "Governor's Message," *Star and Republican Banner*, January 12, 1855, p. 2 c. 5; Untitled, *Star and Republican Banner*, February 16, 1855, p. 2 c. 5; Paul L. Garber, "The Bridges of Columbia, Pennsylvania," Columbia Historic Preservation Society, http://mysite.verizon.net/vzer4lo3/id15.html. (Railroad) The first section of the Cumberland Valley Railroad did not open until 1837. It was extended to Hagerstown in 1841, and to Baltimore in 1849. "Cumberland Valley Railroad, Chambersburg," http://d_cathell.tripod.com/cham.html. Even the Gettysburg spur was of limited effectiveness until it was integrated into a continuous line in 1884. *History of Cumberland and Adams County*, pp. 55–56, 238. James Powell Weeks, "Gettysburg: Memory, Market, and an American Shrine," (Ph.D. diss., Penn State University, 2001), 78.

4. Keith P. Griffler emphasizes the importance of the Ohio River in both the Underground Railroad and the ties between Kentucky and the Northern states of the Midwest. Griffler, *Front Line of Freedom: African Americans and the Forging of the Underground Railroad in the Ohio Valley* (Lexington, Ky.: University Press of Kentucky, 2004). Philip S. Klein and Ari Hoogenboom, *History of Pennsylvania* (University Park: Pennsylvania State University Press, 1980), pp. 199–201. R. C. Smedley, *History of the Underground Railroad in Chester and the Neighboring Counties of Pennsylvania* (Lancaster, Pa.: John A. Hiestand, 1883; reprint, Mechanicsburg, Pa.: Stackpole Books, 2005), p. 37; Wilbur H. Siebert, *The Underground Railroad from Slavery to Freedom* (New York: The Macmillan Company, 1898), pp. 118–19; Paul A. Wallace, *Pennsylvania: Seed of a Nation* (New York: Harper & Row, 1962), cited by John Albert Shughart, Jr., "The Underground Railroad in Cumberland County 1840 to 1860," (Research paper, Shippensburg State College, 1973), 1. Clifford Dowdey, "In the Valley of Virginia," *Civil War History*, 3 (1957): pp. 401–2; Comte de Paris, *The Battle of Gettysburg from the History of the Civil War in America* (Philadelphia: Porter and Coates, 1886; reprint, Baltimore: Butternut and Blue, 1987), pp. 27, 53–55, 75, 89–92.

5. David Hackett Fischer, *Albion's Seed: Four British Folkways in America* (New York: Oxford University Press, 1989), pp. 605–39; Klein and Hoogenboom, *History of Pennsylvania*, pp. 199–201; John Fraser Hart, *The American Farm* (New York: Barnes and Noble, 1998), pp. 31–36.

6. I. Daniel Rupp, *The History and Topography of Dauphin, Cumberland, Franklin, Adams, and Perry Counties* (Lancaster, Pa.: Gilbert Halls, 1846), p. 527. J. Howard Wert, "Gettysburg: A Brief Sketch of a Rural Town," in G. Craig Caba, ed., *Episodes of Gettysburg and The Underground Railroad* (Gettysburg, Pa.: G. Craig Caba Antiques, 1998), p. 13. Victor S. Clark, *History of Manufactures in the United States*, v. 1 (1607–1860) (Washington: Carnegie Institution of Washington, 1929; reprint, New York: Peter Smith, 1949), pp. 475–76.

7. A provocative, brief account of the Quakers' radical origins is Christopher Hill, *The World Turned Upside Down: Radical Ideas During the English Revolution* (New York: Penguin Books, 1972), pp. 186–207. (Thrift and Business) Frederick B. Tolles, *Meeting House and Counting House: The Quaker Merchants of Colonial Philadelphia, 1682–1763* (Chapel Hill: University of North Carolina Press, 1948; reprint, New York: W. W. Norton, 1963); James Walvin, *The Quakers: Money & Morals* (London: John Murray Publishers, 1997), 123–26. Christopher Hill recounts a 1674 verse mocking the evolving Quakers: "The Quaker who before / Did rant and did roar / Great thrift now will tell ye on." Hill, *World Turned Upside Down*, p. 205. For the Quakers and the Underground Railroad, the best source is Fergus Bordewich, *Bound for Canaan: The Underground Railroad and the War for the Soul of America* (New York: Amistad, 2005).

8. Gary B. Nash and Jean R. Soderlund, *Freedom by Degrees: Emancipation in Pennsylvania and Its Aftermath* (New York: Oxford University Press, 1991), pp. 41–55; Henry J. Cadbury, "An Early Quaker Anti-slavery Statement," *Journal of Negro History* 22 (1937): pp. 488–93, cited by Nash and Soderlund, *Freedom by Degrees*, 45. Edward R. Turner, *The Negro in Pennsylvania, 1639–1861* (Washington: American Historical Association, 1911; reprint, New York: Arno Press, 1969), pp. 3–5; Bordewich, *Bound for Canaan*, pp. 48–55; David Brion Davis, *The Problem of Slavery in the Age of Revolution, 1770–1823* (Ithaca: Cornell University Press, 1975; reprint, New York: Oxford University Press, 1999), pp. 213–54.

9. Thomas D. Morris, *Free Men All: The Personal Liberty Laws of the North, 1780–1861* (Baltimore: Johns Hopkins University Press, 1974), pp. 5–7.

10. *Miller v. Dwilling* (1826), in Thomas Sergeant and William Rawle, *Pennsylvania Reports*, 3rd ed. v. 14 (Philadelphia: Kay and Brother, 1874), pp. 441–45.

11. Nash and Soderlund, *Freedom by Degrees*. Carl D. Oblinger, "New freedoms, old miseries: The emergence and disruption of black communities in southeastern Pennsylvania, 1780–1860," (Ph.D. diss., Lehigh University, 1988).

12. Appendix A, "Percentages of Germans in Pennsylvania Counties," taken from Mark A. Hornberger, "Germans in Pennsylvania, 1800, 1850, and 1880: A Spatial Perspective," *Yearbook of German-American Studies* 24 (1989): p. 99, cited in Christian B. Keller, "Germans in Civil War-Era Pennsylvania: Ethnic Identity and the Problem of Americanization," (Ph.D. diss., Penn State University, 2001), p. 325.

13. Leon Higgenbotham, *In the Matter of Color*, cited by John Alosi, *Shadow of Freedom: Slavery in Post-Revolutionary Cumberland County, 1780–1790* (Shippensburg, Pa.: Ship-

pensburg University Press, 2001), pp. 41–42. The Germantown Petition is discussed, with varying degrees of accuracy, in many treatments of early Pennsylvania or early antislavery. See Katherine Gerbner, "'We are against the traffick of mens-body': The Germantown Quaker Protest of 1688 and the Origins of American Abolitionism," *Pennsylvania History* 74 (2007), the best academic treatment; and "1688 Germantown Quaker Petition Against Slavery," Wikipedia. I am indebted to Christopher Densmore for these references.

14. Larry Bolin, "Slaveholders and Slaves of Adams County," *Adams County History* 9 (2003): pp. 10, 19. Twenty percent is a significant percentage, but less than the proportion of the county's overall population that was of Germanic origin. Bolin's list of Adams County slaveholders from 1770 to 1830 shows many German family names interspersed with English, Scottish, and Irish ones. In one township alone, these include Barnitz, Brosius, Dutterer, Felty, Groft, Hinkle, Hoke, Keller, Kurtz, Maus, Metzger, Pellentz, Reinaker, Shorb, Shriver, and Slagle. Bolin, "Slaveholders," List B: Distribution of Slaveholders, Heidelberg Township, pp. 50–51.

15. Alosi, *Shadow of Freedom*, pp. 66, 75.

16. Oblinger, "New Freedoms, Old Miseries," pp. 45–47; Sara Findlay Rice, "The Findlay Family," in *Old Mercersburg* (Williamsport, Pa.: Women's Club of Mercersburg, 1949), pp. 67–69.

17. Oblinger, "New Freedoms, Old Miseries," pp. 78, 83, 181–82; "1820: York Co. man dies in Africa," *Never to Be Forgotten, 1816–1827, York Daily Record*, http://ydr.com/history/ntbf/2ntbf7.shtml.

18. Turner, *Negro in Pennsylvania*, pp. 93–94; Griffler, *Front Line of Freedom*, p. 13; *Miller v. Dwilling* (1826), pp. 441–45.

19. While tobacco was still cultivated in the tidewater region of both states, that crop had been largely abandoned for cereals in the interior. Robert D. Mitchell, *Commercialism and Frontier: Perspective on the early Shenandoah Valley* (Charlottesville: University Press of Virginia, 1977). All three groups experienced natural increase also.

20. Karen James, personal communication, summer 2003.

21. Griffler, *Front Line of Freedom*, pp. 7, 30–31, Barbara Fields, *Slavery and Freedom on the Middle Ground* (New Haven: Yale University Press, 1985), p. 1. Oblinger, "New Freedoms, Old Miseries," pp. 10, 86, 90, 93.

22. William J. Switala, *Underground Railroad in Pennsylvania* (Mechanicsburg, Pa.: Stackpole Books, 2001), pp. 87–88; "First three African American physicians," http://ohoh.essortment.com/africanamerican_rqdo.htm. Daniel A. Payne, http://www.amecnet.org/payne.htm; Ira V. Brown, "Miller McKim and Pennsylvania Abolitionism," *Pennsylvania History* 30 (1963): p. 57; Oblinger, "New Freedoms, Old Miseries," 92.

23. William Still, *The Underground Railroad* (Philadelphia: Porter & Coates, 1872; reprint, Medford, N.J.: Plexus Publishing, 2005), pp. 494–95; Caba, *Episodes of Gettysburg*, 93; "The Underground Railroad in Adams County," *Gettysburg Times*, undated but c. 1940s, p. 47, Adams County Historical Society, Antislavery File.

24. Recent studies like Richard Newman's *The Transformation of American Abolitionism* do an excellent job describing the PAS's legal and legislative tactics, often (but not entirely accurately) described as "conservative." Overlooked are some of the radical arguments advanced by PAS lawyers, and the fact that the Society had national impact,

encouraging manumissions in the Shenandoah Valley, Tennessee, and the Carolinas. In addition, many of the antislavery societies started in Southern states had ties to the PAS. Edward Turner recognizes "the diligence of the Pennsylvania Abolition Society in helping to found similar societies in other states." He proclaims, "If not the parent, she was at least the foster-mother of most similar societies elsewhere." (Turner, *Negro in Pennsylvania*, p. 214).

25. "Lists of Membership, 1784–1819," Records of the Pennsylvania Abolition Society (microfilm), Reel 25. No members were listed from Cumberland or Franklin County.

26. *Adams Centinel*, November 22, 1820, Adams County Historical Society, Anti-Slavery File. There was a general effort statewide to start protection societies around this time, stemming from a case where a fugitive killed a slave catcher trying to enter his home. For York County, see Mr. Webb to Thomas Shipley, January 19, 1822, Papers of the Pennsylvania Abolition Society, Miscellaneous Correspondence, Reel 13, 9:19.

27. Morris, *Free Men All*, pp. 3–4, 25–27.

28. Nash and Soderlund, *Freedom by Degrees*, p. 80. An insightful study of the kidnapping of African Americans is Julie Winch, "The Other Underground Railroad," *Pennsylvania Magazine of History and Biography*, 111 (1987): pp. 3–26.

29. "To the American Convention for Promoting the Abolition of Slavery, and Improving the Affairs of the African Race," Pennsylvania Abolition Society (1825). In addition, William Rawle of the PAS was president of the Convention in 1825, and was the signer of "To the Abolition and Manumission Societies of the United States of America," which complained, "We fear the practice of kidnapping free people of colour is still continued in our country." In fairness to the critics of the Pennsylvania's abolitionists before Garrison, the Chester County address largely concerned manumissions, not kidnapping. *The American Convention for Promoting the Abolition of Slavery . . .* (New York: Arno Press, 1969), pp. 819–22, 878, 841.

30. Bernard Bailyn, *Ideological Origins of the American Revolution* (Cambridge, Mass.: Harvard University Press, 1967), pp. 94–159.

31. Turner, *Negro in Pennsylvania*, p. 233. Bolin, "Slaveholders and Slaves," pp. 87–90.

32. Adams County Prothonotary's Office, Miscellaneous court records

33. Ulrich B. Phillips, *American Negro Slavery* (New York: D. Appleton and Co., 1918; reprint, Gloucester, Mass.: Peter Smith, 1959), facing p. 370.

34. *State v. negro Jim and Ephraim Valentine*, 1834, Miscellaneous court records, Office of the Prothonotary, Adams County Courthouse. Conversely, magistrate King owned a slave himself as late as 1830, so this may be a misreading of this case.

35. I used Adams County fugitive slave records collated by individuals in the Adams County Office of the Prothonotary for researchers Larry Bolin and Debra McCauslin. Other records may exist, but I and the courthouse staff were unable to find them. See Debra S. McCauslin, *Reconstructing the Past: Puzzle of a Lost Community at Yellow Hill*, Appendix II (Gettysburg, Pa.: For the Cause Productions, 2005), pp. 48–50.

36. Historians have long used runaway slave advertisements as a source of information on Southern slavery and fugitive slaves. See Lathan A. Windley, *Runaway Slave Advertisements: A Documentary History from 1730s to 1790*, 4 vols. (Westport, Conn.: Greenwood Press, 1983); Freddie L. Parker, *Running for Freedom: Slave Runaways in North Carolina*

1775–1840 (New York: Routledge, 1993); Graham R. Hodges and Alan E. Brown, eds. *"Pretends to Be Free": Runaway Slave Advertisements from Colonial and Revolutionary New York and New Jersey* (New York: Routledge, 1994); Daniel Meaders, *Advertisements for Runaway Slaves in Virginia, 1801–1820* (New York: Garland Publishing, 1997); John Hope Franklin and Loren Schweninger, *Runaway Slaves: Rebels on the Plantation* (New York: Oxford University Press, 2000), 209–33, 295–300, 328–32.

37. Franklin and Schweninger, *Runaway Slaves*, 97–123.

38. Ad for Jason Chub, *Adams Centinel*, April 9, 1823.

39. Ads for Philip and Bob (Robert Brooks), *Adams Centinel*, June 27, 1821.

40. Oblinger, "New Freedoms, old miseries," pp. 60–63 and Turner, *Negro in Pennsylvania*, pp. 89–120 describe the apprenticeship and indentured servant systems as they applied to African Americans.

41. "Forty Dollars Reward," *Adams Centinel*, January 10, 1821, p. 1 c. 1.

42. (Christmas) John W. Blassingame, *The Slave Community* (New York: Oxford University Press, 1972), p. 112; (Solstice) Jean Humez, *Harriet Tubman: The Life and Life Stories* (Madison, Wis.: University of Wisconsin Press, 2003), p. 233. Conversely, an early historian of the Underground Railroad and a scholar of Chester County Pennsylvania believe escapes were more likely in the summer and fall. William C. Kashatus, *Just Over the Line: Chester County and the Underground Railroad* (West Chester, Pa.: Chester County Historical Society, 2002), p. 18; see also J. C. Furnas, *Goodbye to Uncle Tom* (New York: William Sloan Associates, 1956), p. 215.

43. Graceanna Lewis, Manuscript Memoir, Lewis-Fussell Family Papers, RG-5/087, Friends Historical Library, Swarthmore University.

44. Franklin and Schweninger, *Runaway Slaves*, p. 117. Albert von Frank has questioned whether only exceptional slaves tried to flee north. Albert J. Von Frank, *The Trials of Anthony Burns* (Cambridge, Mass.: Harvard University Press, 1998), p. 6. William Still's accounts (*The Underground Railroad*) also include many instances of escaping elderly, children, and "non-exceptional" runaways.

45. Ad for Isaac, *Adams Centinel*, January 9, 1822, p. 3 c. 5. The owner claimed Isaac was an indentured servant.

46. Ad for Frank Hill, *Adams Centinel*, January 9, 1822, p. 3 c. 4.

47. In his narrative, Pennington identifies the Wrights simply as "W. W." and "P. W." J. W. C. Pennington, *The Fugitive Blacksmith* (London: Charles Gilpin, 1849; reprint, Westport, Ct.: Negro Universities Press, 1971); Herman E. Thomas, *James W. C. Pennington: African American Churchman and Abolitionist* (New York: Garland Publishing, 1995). John Blassingame, et. al., eds., Frederick Douglass, *The Narrative of the Life of Frederick Douglass, An American Slave, Written By Himself* (1845; reprint, New Haven: Yale University Press, 2001), p. 76.

48. Benjamin Drew, *The Refugee: A North-Side View of Slavery* (1856; reprint, New York: Negro Universities Press, 1969), pp. 73–75.

49. Drew, *Refugee*, 75. This reference to Shippensburg, a town on the border between Franklin and Cumberland counties, makes it likely that Bentley's party was in southern Franklin or Adams County when they encountered this family.

50. Keith Griffler makes the same point about border Ohio in *Front Line of Freedom*.

51. Larry Gara, *The Liberty Line: The Legend of the Underground Railroad* (Lexington: University of Kentucky Press, 1961; reprint, 1996), pp. 97–98, 100.

52. Oblinger, "New Freedoms, Old Miseries," pp. 10, 86, 93, 151, 155. Oblinger studied eight communities including Columbia, where there was a black middle class and even an elite whose social position could be threatened by the misbehavior of new arrivals.

53. Ted Alexander, personal communication, August 2003; S. R. McAllister to J. Howard Wert, December 2, 1904, in G. Craig Caba, ed., *Episodes of Gettysburg*, p. 58; Robert F. Engs, commentary at 2002 Pennsylvania Historical Association Meetings. As Ervin Jordan has noted concerning African Americans who volunteered to help the Confederate army, each individual had to make the best choices for himself and his family, even if such choices may appear illogical from today's perspective. Ervin L. Jordan, *Black Confederates and Afro-Yankees in Civil War Virginia* (Charlottesville: University Press of Virginia, 1995).

54. "Slave's Refuge Society," *Pennsylvania Freeman*, February 2, 1841, Black Abolitionist Papers, Reel 3, frame 866.

55. Barbara Fields, *Slavery and Freedom on the Middle Ground* (New Haven: Yale University Press, 1987).

56. Charles L. Blockson, *The Underground Railroad in Pennsylvania* (Jacksonsville, N.C.: Flame International, 1981), pp. 145–46; Switala, *Underground Railroad in Pennsylvania*, 110.

57. See Appendix C and Chapter 3 for a discussion of this petition. "To The Senate and House of Representatives of the State of Pennsylvania," [Petition of inhabitants of Adams County], January 15, 1847, Petition no. 54, Senate File, Pennsylvania State Archives (this number includes many petitions).

58. See Chapter 4 for a discussion of this case.

59. Gara, *Liberty Line*, pp. 59–61.

60. Lewis, Manuscript Memoir, Lewis-Fussell Family Papers, RG-5/087, Friends Historical Library, Swarthmore University. Tracey Weis, "Mapping the Underground Railroad From Maryland to New York Through Central Pennsylvania." Presentation to The Underground Railroad in South Central Pennsylvania Symposium at Dickinson College, February 24, 2003.

61. (Mountains) R. C. Smedley, *History of the Underground Railroad in Chester and the Neighboring Counties of Pennsylvania* (1883; reprint, Mechanicsburg, Pa.: Stackpole Books, 2005), p. 37; Wilbur H. Siebert, *The Underground Railroad from Slavery to Freedom* (New York: Macmillan Company, 1898), pp. 118–19; Paul A. Wallace, *Pennsylvania: Seed of a Nation* (New York: Harper & Row, 1962), cited by John Albert Shughart, Jr., "The Underground Railroad in Cumberland County 1840 to 1860," (Research paper, Shippensburg State College, 1973), 1. (Woods) Bob Hill, "Forests & Freedom: Forgotten Links to Pennsylvania's Underground Railroad," The Resource v. 3 issue 2–3, Pennsylvania Dept. of Conservation and Natural Resources, February and March, 1999. (Trails) Switala, *Underground Railroad in Pennsylvania*, pp. 104–5.

62. Today Havre de Grace is a stop on Maryland's Underground Railroad tour.

63. J. Blaine Hudson, *Fugitive Slaves and the Underground Railroad in the Kentucky Borderlands* (Jefferson, N.C.: McFarland & Company, 2002), p. 11.

64. Still, *Underground Railroad*, p. 92; Frederick Douglass, who fled by train and then by boat from eastern Maryland, had a set of seaman's travel papers.

65. A Rand McNally road map from 1922 clearly shows the old major roads. See also Elwood L. Bridner, "The Fugitive Slaves of Maryland," *Maryland Historical Magazine* 66 (1971), pp. 42, 46. Still, *Underground Railroad*, p. 92.

66. Stanley Harrold, *Subversives: Antislavery Community in Washington, D.C., 1828–1865* (Baton Rouge: Louisiana State University Press, 2003), pp. 57, 204.

67. Drew, *Refugee: A North-Side View of Slavery* (Account of R.S. Sorrick), 83; (Account of Nelson Moss), 107; (George Williams), pp. 241–42; (James Smith) pp. 247–48; (John Hatfield), p. 256.

68. Franklin and Schweninger, *Runaway Slaves*, pp. 116–20.

69. Mitchell, *Commercialism and Frontier*. Keith Griffler has commented on how Ohio's free black communities also created opportunities for escaping slaves to stop and put down roots, rather than pushing on for Canada. *Front Line of Freedom*, pp. 30–31.

70. Charles L. Blockson, *The Hippocrene Guide to The Underground Railroad* (New York: Hippocrene Books, 1994), pp. 117–20; Switala, *Underground Railroad in Pennsylvania*, pp. 103–7. Hiram Wertz, "A Paper read on 'The Underground Railway' Before the Hamilton Library Association of Carlisle, Penna., February 24, 1911," Cumberland County Historical Society, Carlisle, Pa.

71. Blockson, *Underground Railroad in Pennsylvania*, pp. 142–43. Blockson took this account from Drew, *Refugee: A North-Side View of Slavery*, p. 81.

72. Switala, *Underground Railroad in Pennsylvania*, pp. 107–8; Philip Van Doren Stern, *The Drums of Morning* (Garden City, N.Y.: World Publishing, 1942), pp. 331–32, 346.

73. "Leading Colored Citizen—Was an Active Agent in the Underground Railroad," *Gettysburg Compiler*, June 13, 1906, p. 5, c. 3; *Gettysburg Star and Sentinel*, June 13, 1906, p. 2.

74. Blockson, *Underground Railroad in Pennsylvania*, pp. 145–46; Switala, *Underground Railroad in Pennsylvania*, p. 108; Palm, who was listed in the 1860 census as a "mistress/harlot," purportedly wore the coat to be recognizable to fugitive slaves, a reasonable precaution in an area abounding with kidnappers and informants. She is romanticized in Elsie Singmaster, *A Boy at Gettysburg* (Boston: Houghton Mifflin and Company, 1924).

75. Blockson, *Hippocrene Guide*, p. 114; Switala, *Underground Railroad in Pennsylvania*, pp. 109–10. Peter Vermilyea, "Tour of Gettysburg's Historic African American Sites," Civil War Institute, June 2003. Some claim that the house of Daniel Sell and Mary Long Thompson on the Chambersburg Pike was also an Underground Railroad station, and had been interpreted that way by Gettysburg tour guides in the mid-20th century. Stevens and Mrs. Thompson were sufficiently close that there were rumors of a possible affair.

76. Caba, *Episodes of Gettysburg*, pp. 72–77; G. Craig Caba, "Episodes of Gettysburg and the Underground Railroad," 1st Conference on Gettysburg and the Underground Railroad, Harrisburg Area Community College, Gettysburg, Pa., February 24, 2001. Peter Vermilyea, personal communication, June 2003.

77. G. Craig Caba deserves credit for bringing the "Black Ducks" story to light. Caba, *Episodes of Gettysburg*.

NOTES TO PAGES 35–37

78. Caba, "Episodes of Gettysburg and the Underground Railroad"; Bordewich, *Bound for Canaan*, p. 52; Bolin, "Slaveholders and Slaves," *Adams County History* 9 (2003), inside cover and p. 24; E. S[ingmaster] Lewars to Wilbur H. Siebert, October 25, 1943, Wilbur H. Siebert Underground Railroad Collection, Ohio Historical Society.

79. Smedley, *History of the Underground Railroad*, p. 37; Graceanna Lewis, Manuscript Memoir, Lewis-Fussell Family Papers RG-5/087, Friends Historical Library, Swarthmore University; Still, *Underground Railroad*, pp. 494–97.

80. Still, *Underground Railroad*, pp. 691–93.

81. Letters from J. Bigelow, Esq., to William Still, June 22, 1854 and September 9, 1855, in Still, *Underground Railroad*, pp. 41–42, 178; Mrs. E. S[ingmaster]. Lewars to W. H. Siebert, July 24, 1945, Siebert Collection, Ohio Historical Society, Roll 13. Singmaster's information was based on an article on William Chaplin and Adams County's Underground Railroad by J. Howard Wert. Harrold, *Subversives*, p. 204.

82. "Leading Colored Citizen," *Gettysburg Compiler*, June 13, 1906, p. 5 c. 3; Shughart, "The Underground Railroad in Cumberland County," Copy at Cumberland County Historical Society (CCHS); "Report of the Board of Managers of the York Springs Anti-Slavery Society," *Star*, March 17, 1840, p. 2 c. 1–2.

83. Shughart, "The Underground Railroad in Cumberland County," CCHS. In 1855, Harder became Carlisle's sheriff, a position where he was likely even more helpful to abolitionists.

84. Shughart, "The Underground Railroad in Cumberland County," CCHS. Edward H. Magill, "When Men Were Sold, Reminiscences of the Underground Railroad in Bucks County and Its Managers," *A Collection of Papers Read Before the Bucks County Historical Society*, 2 (1909): 511–15.

85. This would be consistent with the networks of slaves and free blacks in the South, which Tony Kaye has identified as vital to African Americans' sense of place and worldview. Anthony E. Kaye, "Neighborhoods and Solidarity in the Natchez District of Mississippi: Rethinking the Antebellum Slave Community," *Slavery and Abolition* 23 (2002): pp. 1–24.

86. "Leading Colored Citizen," *Gettysburg Compiler*, June 13, 1906; *Gettysburg Star and Sentinel*, June 13, 1906, p. 2. "Basil Biggs," Veterinary Register, 1889–1920, Adams County Prothonotary's Office, Gettysburg, Pa.

· 87. Daniel Wolfe, "History of Union Bridge," in Joseph M. Getty, ed., *The Carroll Record: Histories of Northwestern Carroll County Communities* (Westminster, Md.: Historical Society of Carroll County, 1994), p. 65. Lydia L. Wierman to Halliday Jackson, [undated but apparently 1831], Letter Book 1, Letter 11, p. 2, Halliday Jackson Papers, Friends Historical Library, Swarthmore University.

88. "Memorial of the undersigned, Inhabitants of Fred'k Co.," February 2, 1829, Committee on the District of Columbia, Slavery in the District of Columbia, HR 20A-G5.1, National Archives. Mark Lewis, "Garfield's 'Big Charlie' Misner was a larger-than-life legend," *Middletown Valley Citizen*, April 26, 2001, Slavery-Underground Railroad File, Frederick County Historical Society, Frederick, Md.

89. The literature on rural patterns of shared work, mutual assistance, and mutual dependency is extensive. Some sources in which this phenomenon and its implications are

discussed include: Frank L. Owsley, *Plain Folk of the Old South* (Baton Rouge: Louisiana State University Press, 1949); Michael Merrill, "Cash Is Good to Eat: Self-Sufficiency and Exchange in the Rural Economy of the United States," *Radical History Review* 4 (1977): pp. 42–71; James A. Henretta, "Families and Farms: Mentalité in Pre-Industrial America," *William and Mary Quarterly* 35 (1978): pp. 3–32; John T. Schlotterbeck, "The 'Social Economy of an Upper South Community': Orange and Greene Counties, 1815–1860," in Orville Vernon Burton and Robert C. McMath, Jr., eds., *Class, Conflict, and Consensus: Antebellum Southern Community Studies* (Westport, Conn.: Greenwood Press, 1982); John Mack Faragher, *Sugar Creek: Life on the Illinois Prairie* (New Haven: Yale University Press, 1986).

90. (Deardorff) Caba, "Episodes of Gettysburg;" (Cook) "Albert Cook Myers traces Underground Route from Gettysburg north to Jesse Cook's Mill," A. C. Myers to W. H. Siebert, April 19, 1944, and Mrs. Daniel C. Jacobs, Arendtsville, Pa., to E. S. Lewars, Gettysburg, March 21, 1944, both in Wilbur H. Siebert Collection, Ohio Historical Society, Rolls 13 and 1, respectively. Myers was a noted historian at Swarthmore. (McAllister, Shriver) Switala, *Underground Railroad in Pennsylvania*, 108, 111.

91. Various Wiermans and Werts served on the bank board. John McPherson, a close friend and business associate of Thaddeus Stevens, was a senior bank officer for many years. There is some credible evidence that his farm served as an Underground Railroad station. (West) Henrietta Buckmaster, *Let My People Go* (Boston: Peter Smith, 1941; reprint, Boston: Beacon Press, 1959), p. 78; Bordewich, *Bound for Canaan*, pp. 219–20.

2. Thaddeus Stevens' Dilemma, Colonization, and the Turbulent Years of Early Antislavery in Adams County, 1835–39

1. On the contention that early antislavery organizing was apolitically conceived, and then changed, see Gilbert H. Barnes, *The Anti-Slavery Impulse* (Washington: American Historical Association, 1933; reprint, New York: Harcourt, Brace & World, 1964), pp. 79, 84, 119, 178–79; Dwight Lowell Dumond, *Antislavery Origins of the Civil War in the United States* (Ann Arbor: University of Michigan Press, 1939; reprint, 1960), pp. 35–36; Richard H. Sewell, *Ballots for Freedom* (New York: Oxford University Press, 1976; reprint, New York: W. W. Norton, 1980), pp. 2–23; Aileen S. Kraditor, *Means and Ends in American Abolitionism* (New York: Vintage Books, 1967; reprint, Chicago: Ivan R. Dee, Inc., 1989), pp. 25–26, 28; Ronald G. Walters, "Antislavery," in *American Reformers, 1815–1860* (New York, Hill and Wang, 1978), p. 89.

2. Leonard L. Richards, "The Jacksonians and Slavery," in Lewis Perry and Michael Fellman, eds., *Antislavery Reconsidered* (Baton Rouge: Louisiana State University Press, 1979), pp. 99–118. Jonathan H. Earle, *Jacksonian Democracy & the Politics of Free Soil, 1824–1854* (Chapel Hill: University of North Carolina Press, 2004), touches on this process but focuses on Democrats. To examine where the decline of Antimasonry led to the formation of the Whig Party and the agitation of the temperance issue, see Paul E. Johnson, *A Shopkeeper's Millennium* (New York: Hill and Wang, 1978), pp. 128–35.

3. See, for example, two excellent reviews, Byron C. Andreasen, "Review Essay: Hans L. Trefousse, *Thaddeus Stevens: Nineteenth Century Egalitarian,*" *Journal of the Abraham*

Lincoln Association, 21 (2000), http://www.historycooperative.org/journals/jala/21.2/and reasen.html, and Jean V. Berlin, "Thaddeus Stevens and His Biographers," *Pennsylvania History* 60 (1993): pp. 153–62.

4. Alexander Hood, "Thaddeus Stevens," in Alexander Harris, ed. *The Biographical History of Lancaster County* (Lancaster, Pa.: Elias Barr & Co., 1872); Alexander Harris, *Political Conflict in America . . . Comprising Also a Resume of the Life of Thaddeus Stevens* (New York: T. H. Pollock, MacMillan Company, 1876); George Fort Milton, *The Age of Hate: Andrew Johnson and the Radicals* (New York: Coward-McCann, 1930); James G. Randall, *Civil War and Reconstruction* (New York: D. C. Heath, 1937); Thomas F. Woodley, *Great Leveler, the Life of Thaddeus Stevens* (New York: Stackpole Sons, 1937); Richard N. Current, *Old Thaddeus Stevens: A Story of Political Ambition* (Madison: University of Wisconsin Press, 1942); Henrietta Buckmaster, *Let My People Go: The Story of the Underground Railroad and the Growth of the Abolition Movement* (New York: Harper and Brothers, 1941); see also Henrietta Buckmaster, *Freedom Bound* (New York: MacMillan Company, 1965), p. 6; Elsie Singmaster, *I Speak for Thaddeus Stevens* (Boston: Houghton Mifflin Company, 1947).

5. Ralph Korngold, *Thaddeus Stevens, A Being Darkly Wise and Rudely Great* (New York: Harcourt Brace & Company, 1955); Fawn M. Brodie, *Thaddeus Stevens: Scourge of the South* (New York: W. W. Norton, 1959); Milton Melzer, *Thaddeus Stevens and the Fight for Negro Rights* (New York: Thomas Y. Crowell, 1967); Hans L. Trefousse, *Thaddeus Stevens: Nineteenth Century Egalitarian* (Chapel Hill: University of North Carolina Press, 1997); Bradley R. Hoch, *Thaddeus Stevens in Gettysburg: The Making of an Abolitionist* (Gettysburg: Adams County Historical Society, 2005).

6. "Remarks by Mr. Dickey," *Memorial Addresses on the Life and Character of Thaddeus Stevens* (Washington: Government Printing Office, 1869), pp. 1–3; Brodie, *Thaddeus Stevens*, pp. 22–33; Korngold, *Thaddeus Stevens*, p. 14; Meltzer, *Thaddeus Stevens and the Fight for Negro Rights*, pp. 8–15. *Adams Centinel*, December 18, 1816, Thaddeus Stevens Papers (Scholarly Resources, Inc.), Reel 1, Frame 10. Advertisement dated October 1, 1816.

7. *Butler et. al. v. Delaplaine* (1821), Sergeant and Rawle, *Pennsylvania Reports*, 3rd ed., v. 7 (Philadelphia: Kay and Brother, 1872), pp. 378–79. Brodie believes that Charity Butler carefully tallied up her days in Pennsylvania, but owing to her young age, this seems unlikely. Brodie, *Thaddeus Stevens*, p. 33.

8. *Butler v. Delaplaine*, pp. 382–85; Harris, *Review of the Political Contest in America*, 19. Recently, fiction author Dolen Perkins-Valdez has highlighted another reason for the six-month transit law: Southern slaveowners wanted to be able to take their slave mistresses to Northern resorts. Dolen Perkins-Valdez, *Wench: A Novel* (New York: HarperCollins Publishers, 2010).

9. Brodie, *Thaddeus Stevens*, p. 33; *Gettysburg Sentinel*, July 9, 1823.

10. Trefousse, *Thaddeus Stevens*, p. 14, citing "Remarks by Mr. Orth," *Memorial Addresses*, p. 53.

11. Trefousse, *Thaddeus Stevens*, pp. 14–15, citing *Memorial Addresses*, pp. 53–54; Current, *Old Thad Stevens*, pp. 34–35. Current complained that no proof of Stevens' involvement in fugitive slave cases has emerged from Adams County court records, but if Stevens

was successful and no warrant of removal was issued, it is not clear that there would have been any record made.

12. *Cobean v. Thompson* (1829), in W. Rawle, C. B. Penrose, and F. Watts, eds. *Pennsylvania Reports*, 3rd ed. v. 1 (Philadelphia, 1880), p. 93. Bradley Hoch explicitly states that after the Butler case, Stevens "never again represented a slave owner against [a] slave." In light of the *Cobean* case, this appears incorrect. Hoch, *Stevens in Gettysburg*, p. 20.

13. The most cogently presented counterargument to this interpretation is by Bradley Hoch. Hoch cites a freedom suit in which Stevens was involved at the same time as the Butler case, which went through five trials and sixty Adams County jurors. Hoch believes that Stevens' determination shows that he had had a change of heart regarding slavery, but it could also be evidence that he was a good lawyer who represented his clients well and liked to win. Bradley R. Hoch, *Stevens in Gettysburg*, pp. 20–21.

14. Brodie, *Thaddeus Stevens*, pp. 38–39, 45; Current, *Old Thad Stevens*, p. 10; Melzer, *Thaddeus Stevens*, p. 17; Trefousse, *Thaddeus Stevens*, pp. 17, 21, 24–27.

15. Brodie, *Thaddeus Stevens*, pp. 38–39; Trefousse, *Thaddeus Stevens*, pp. 17, 27. A good account of the movement is Michael Holt, "The Antimasonic and Know Nothing Parties," in Michael Holt, *Political Parties and American Political Development* (Baton Rouge: Louisiana University Press, 1992), pp. 88–112.

16. Current, *Old Thad Stevens*, 17; Trefousse, *Thaddeus Stevens*, pp. 13, 28–33; Brodie, *Thaddeus Stevens*, p. 57.

17. Membership Lists, 1816–19, "Lists of Membership, 1786–1819," Records of the Pennsylvania Abolition Society (microfilm), Reel 25.

18. Charles Osborn, *Journal of that Faithful Servant of Christ, Charles Osborn* (Cincinnati: Achilles Pugh, 1854), pp. 163, 169. Merton Dillon believes that Osborn, who stopped in Ohio near Lundy in 1815, was the "immediate inspiration" for Benjamin Lundy's antislavery organizing. Merton Dillon, *Benjamin Lundy and the Struggle for Negro Freedom* (Urbana: University of Illinois Press, 1966), pp. 17–18. See also Richard F. O'Dell, "The Early Antislavery Movement in Ohio," (Ph.D. diss., University of Michigan, 1948), pp. 206–10.

19. Dillon, *Benjamin Lundy*, p. 251; William Still, *The Underground Railroad* (Philadelphia: Porter & Coates, 1872; reprint, Medford, N.J.: Plexus Publishing, 2005), p. 494.

20. Garry Wills, *Negro President: Jefferson and the Slave Power* (Boston: Houghton Mifflin, 2003); Leonard Richards, *Gentlemen of Property and Standing* (Oxford: Oxford University Press, 1970), pp. 10–19; "900 Souls in Hell," Cleveland Family Papers, Penn State University; "George Duffield III (1794–1868)," http://chronicles.dickinson.edu/encyclo/d/ed_duffield Gthree.htm; Susan Fritschler, "Art from the President's House: A Portrait of John McClintock," *Cumberland County History* 9 (1992), p. 12.

21. Current, *Old Thad Stevens*, p. 19; Trefousse, *Thaddeus Stevens*, pp. 34–41.

22. Trefousse, *Thaddeus Stevens*, pp. 41–42; "Symbols," Pennsylvania: Past and Present, http://www.phmc.state.pa.us /bah/pahist/symbols.asp?secid=31 (*Aurora* 1803); Sanford W. Higginbotham, *The Keystone in the Democratic Arch: Pennsylvania Politics, 1800–1816* (Harrisburg: Pennsylvania Historical and Museum Commission, 1952).

23. Trefousse, *Thaddeus Stevens*, pp. 42–43.

24. Trefousse, *Thaddeus Stevens*, pp. 45–46. On the vice presidential nomination, see also "Thaddeus Stevens Esq.," *Gettysburg Star and Republican Banner*, October 19, 1835, p. 3 c. 2.

25. Brodie, *Thaddeus Stevens*, p. 57.

26. Higginbotham, *Keystone in the Democratic Arch*, passim.

27. In his study of Vermont, Hal Barron has a useful discussion of Antimasonry as a rural movement against the local elites who were Jeffersonian Republican-Democrats. He describes the movement as "an attack on local privilege and a home-grown aristocracy centered in the village instead of the countryside." Hal S. Barron, *Those Who Stayed Behind: Rural Society in Nineteenth Century New England* (Cambridge, U.K.: Cambridge University Press, 1984), pp. 23–25, 134.

28. Brodie, *Thaddeus Stevens*, pp. 35–44; *Harrisburg Chronicle*, March 14, 1836, cited by Trefousse, *Thaddeus Stevens*, p. 46. See also Trefousse, *Thaddeus Stevens*, 253 fn. 35.

29. Trefousse, *Thaddeus Stevens*, p. 20; Brodie, *Thaddeus Stevens*, pp. 98–99.

30. The standard works on colonizationism include Early L. Fox, *The American Colonization Society, 1817–1840* (Baltimore: Johns Hopkins University Press, 1919) and P. J. Staudenraus, *The African Colonization Movement, 1816–1865* (New York: Columbia University Press, 1961), but in the 1960s they were challenged by works such as Leon Litwack's *North of Slavery* (Chicago: University of Chicago Press, 1961) and Leonard Richards' *Gentlemen of Property and Standing*. Now, after decades of neglect, newer scholarship is emerging, such as Eric Burin, *Slavery and the Peculiar Solution* (Gainesville: University Press of Florida, 2005), Beverly Tomek's *Colonization and Its Discontents: Emancipation, Emigration, and Antislavery in Antebellum Pennsylvania* (New York: New York University Press, 2011), and Karen Fisher Younger's *America's Forgotten Women: Northern Women and the Colonization of Liberia* (in progress).

31. Negro Entry Book, 1820–1849, Folder 4b, MG-240, The Slave Records of Lancaster County, 1780–1849, Lancaster County Historical Society; Leroy T. Hopkins, Jr., "The Negro Entry Book: A Document of Lancaster County's Antebellum African American Community," *Journal of the Lancaster County Historical Society*, 88 (1984): pp. 142–80; Carl D. Oblinger, "New Freedoms, Old Miseries: The emergence and disruption of black communities in southeastern Pennsylvania, 1780–1860," (Ph.D. diss., Lehigh University, 1988), pp. 62–64; Peter C. Vermilyea, "Jack Hopkins' Civil War," *Adams County History* 11 (2005), p. 5.

32. Carl D. Oblinger, "New Freedoms, Old Miseries," pp. 114–20; Oblinger says one advertisement for a "moral lecture" promised attendees they would see "real live negroes" stuck with pins, presumably to show African American insensitivity to pain. William R. Stanton, *The Leopard's Spots: Scientific Attitudes Toward Race in America, 1815–1859* (Chicago: University of Chicago Press, 1960); Stephen Jay Gould, *The Mismeasure of Man* (New York: W. W. Norton, 1981). Gould argued that Morton's methodologies were fatally flawed and his investigation suffered from a pervasive, if possibly unconscious, bias. Recently Gould's conclusions have also come under attack. "Scientists Measure the Accuracy of a Racism Claim," *New York Times*, June 13, 2011.

33. Letter from W. M. Paxton, Greencastle Franklin Co., Pa., April 16, 1850, Papers of the American Colonization Society, Letterbook, Reel 62; "Capture of Slaves," *Keystone* (Harrisburg), July 4, 1837, p. 3 c. 5.

34. Paul A. Baglyos, "Samuel Schmucker's American Seminary," in Frederick K. Wentz, ed., *Witness at the Crossroads: Gettysburg Lutheran Seminary Servants in the Public Life*

(Gettysburg: The Lutheran Theological Seminary of Gettysburg, 2001), pp. 1–9; Dale A. Johnson, "Lutheran Dissension and Schism at Gettysburg Seminary, 1864," *Pennsylvania History* 33 (1966): pp. 13–29. P[aul] Anstadt, *The Life and Times of Dr. S. S. Schmucker* (York, Pa.: P. Anstadt & Sons, 1896), pp. 293–94.

35. "Colonization Meeting," *Star and Republican Banner*, July 27, 1835, p. 2 c. 6; the same piece was also printed in *The People's Press* (Gettysburg), August 31, 1835, p. 3. c. 3. Daniel Alexander Payne, *Recollections of Seventy Years* (Nashville: A.M.E. Sunday School Union, 1888), pp. 57–58, available at Documenting the American South, http://docsouth.unc.edu/church/payne70/menu.html.

36. "Letter from Prof. Reynolds," *Liberator*, December 24, 1836, p. 2 c. 4; *African Repository* subscription lists, ACS Papers, Series V, v. 44, Reel 298. Minutes of the Pennsylvania Colonization Society (PCS), January 2, 1838 to December 11, 1849; Minutes of the PCS, 1856–64, and Minutes of the PCS, 1864–77, Papers of the Pennsylvania Colonization Society, Special Collections, Lincoln University. Schmucker's name does not appear on the list of "Names and Residences of Members" for 1857–58, 1858–59, 1860–61, 1861–62.

37. Theodore Appel, "Our Country in Years to Come" (also titled "Our Country in the Future—A Prophecy—1841"), Notebook, v. 2, 1840–94, Theodore Appel papers, Franklin and Marshall College.

38. Oblinger, "New Freedoms, Old Miseries," pp. 123–32; William Frederic Worner, "The Columbia Race Riots," *Papers Read Before the Lancaster County Historical Society* 26 (1922), pp. 175–87; Deborah Wright to Nephew, 1835, Parrish Papers, Friends Historical Library, Swarthmore University.

39. Keith Griffler, *Front Line of Freedom: African Americans and the Forging of the Underground Railroad in the Ohio Valley* (Lexington: University Press of Kentucky, 2004), p. 21.

40. "Colonization Meeting," *Star and Republican Banner*, July 27, 1835, p. 2 c. 6; the same piece was also printed in *The People's Press* (Gettysburg), August 31, 1835, p. 3 c. 3. Current, *Old Thad Stevens*, p. 33.

41. The paper itself was sensitive about Stevens' role. Stevens' handpicked editor Robert W. Middleton had to defend it from charges that he was only the printer for Stevens' views. Trefousse, *Thaddeus Stevens*, pp. 27–28; Brodie, *Thaddeus Stevens*, p. 39.

42. "African Colonization," *Gettysburg Star and Republican Banner*, July 17, 1832, p. 4 c. 3; Untitled, *Gettysburg Star and Republican Banner*, August 14, 1832, p. 2 c. 5; "Liberia in Africa," *Gettysburg Star and Republican Banner*, November 6, 1832, p. 2 c. 2; "Colonization Society," *Gettysburg Star and Republican Banner*, December 4, 1832, p. 3 c. 2.

43. "State Legislature—December 6," *Gettysburg Star and Republican Banner*, December 11, 1832, p. 3 c. 5. Anti-immigration petitions from southern Pennsylvania were frequent. Edward Raymond Turner, *The Negro in Pennsylvania History* (Washington: American Historical Association, 1911; reprint, New York: Negro Universities Press, 1969), pp. 153–54; Oblinger, "New freedoms, old miseries," pp. 121–22.

44. "Emigrants to Liberia," *Gettysburg Star and Republican Banner*, January 1, 1833, p. 4 c. 1. In 1832, when Stevens was locked in a bitter battle with Jacob Lefevre, the *Compiler's* editor, the *Star* made its first efforts to link Masonry and slavery; Middleton republished comments that said that Masons, bound by oaths, were also slaves—except that slaves

were freer than Masons, because their bondage was only physical, not volitional. "Democracy," *The A.M. Star and Republican Banner*, April 25, 1832, p. 2, c. 4 (reprinted from the *Pennsylvania Whig*); "Freemen to the Polls," October 2, 1832, p. 2 c. 4.

45. "To the honorable the Senate and House of Representatives . . ." [For aid to persons of color, to go to Liberia], H. R. January 18, 1828, House File 1827–28, Folder 2, RG-7, Pennsylvania State Archives.

46. Henry Mayer, *All on Fire: William Lloyd Garrison and the Abolition of Slavery* (New York: St. Martin's Press, 1998), pp. 80–81.

47. Richards, *Gentlemen of Property and Standing*, pp. 20–30.

48. Richards, *Gentlemen of Property and Standing*, pp. 131–55.

49. Oblinger, "New Freedoms, Old Miseries," pp. 123–32; Worner, "The Columbia Race Riots," pp. 175–87; John Runcie, "'Hunting the Nigs' in Philadelphia: The Race Riot of August 1834," *Pennsylvania History* 39 (1972): pp. 187–218. For Northern opposition to abolitionism generally, see Lorman Ratner, *Powder Keg: Northern Opposition to the Antislavery Movement, 1831–1840* (New York: Basic Books, 1968).

50. Richards, *Gentlemen of Property and Standing*, pp. 25–26; "Colonization Meeting," *Star and Republican Banner*, July 27, 1835, p. 2 c. 6, and *The People's Press* (Gettysburg), August 31, 1835, p. 3. c. 3. In the future, such as the "Friends for the Integrity of the Union" meeting in Harrisburg in 1837, Stevens would deliberately go to a meeting whose sentiments he did not agree with to try to derail its agenda. In the absence of further evidence, however, the participation of Stevens, Schmucker, and Baugher (and their consent to serve on various committees and fundraising drives) needs to be taken at face value. Later Schmucker would describe himself as "a very warm friend to colonization" even as he adopted an antislavery position.

51. Eli Seifman, "The United Colonization Societies of New-York and Pennsylvania and the Establishment of the African Colony of Bassa Cove," *Pennsylvania History* 35 (January 1968), pp. 23–44. I am indebted to Beverly Tomek for pointing out this reference and this period as the high point of the PCS.

52. Current, *Old Thad Stevens*, p. 33; "Public Meeting (For the *Star and Banner*)," *Star and Republican Banner*, October 19, 1835, p. 2 c. 3–4. Stevens was sometimes crafty about meetings he attended and why, but he was also careful to correct the public record if he felt constituents were getting the wrong impression about his participation. He let this stand without comment; indeed, it appears that this was a special report that only appeared in a newspaper to which he was closely connected.

53. "Anniversary Celebration," *Star and Republican Banner*, February 29, 1836, p. 2 c. 3.

54. "Anti-Slavery," *Star and Republican Banner*, January 2, 1837, p. 2 c. 2; *American Advertiser* (Philadelphia), January 29, 1838, cited by Current, p. 51. Eventually, colonizationists got to use the hall while abolitionists were prohibited, a matter of some controversy. "Just Remarks," *Star and Republican Banner*, February 20, 1837, p. 3 c. 2; "Disingenuous," *Star and Republican Banner*, March 3, 1837, p. 1 c. 6.

55. Current, *Old Thad Stevens*, p. 33; Trefousse, *Thaddeus Stevens*, pp. 46–47.

56. During the months preceding this report, the *Star* had defended Pennsylvania's "states' rights" several times; these items were related to the perception that Southern

states were trying to dictate policy to the Commonwealth. "The Slave Question," *Star and Republican Banner*, June 6, 1836, p. 2 c. 1; "Great Celebration—Huzza for Pennsylvania," *Star and Republican Banner*, March 14, 1836, p. 2 c. 2; "Pennsylvania," *Star and Republican Banner*, March 21, 1836, p. 3 c. 3.

57. Trefousse, *Thaddeus Stevens*, p. 47. "The Slave Question," *Star and Republican Banner*, June 6, 1836, p. 2 c. 1.

58. Ira V. Brown, "Miller McKim and Pennsylvania Abolitionism," *Pennsylvania History* 30 (1963): pp. 56–57.

59. "Freedom vs. Slavery," *Star and Republican Banner*, July 11, 1836, p. 2 c. 5–6. Emphasis in the original. The importance of the trope "of one blood" to abolitionists is explored in Paul Goodman, *Of One Blood: Abolitionism and the Origins of Racial Equality* (Los Angeles: University of California Press, 1998).

60. "Anti-Slavery," "Mobism," and "Anti-Slavery Meeting at McAllister's," *Star and Republican Banner*, July 11, 1836. Middleton's unfamiliarity with abolitionist rhetoric was reflected by his misspelling the epithet for pliable Northern politicians as "doe faces" rather than "dough faces."

61. The fact that September 17, Constitution Day, was a second symbolic date after July 4 was first noted by Library of Congress scholars working with G. Craig Caba. G. Craig Caba, "Episodes of Gettysburg and the Underground Railroad," First Annual Conference, Harrisburg Area Community College, February 24, 2001.

62. *Niles Register*, XLV, p. 147 (Nov. 2, 1833), cited by Leonard D. White, *The Jacksonians: A Study in Administrative History, 1829–1861* (New York: Macmillan, 1954), p. 10. Richard Sewell maintains that the technique was based on British abolitionists' success with the topic. Sewell, *Ballots for Freedom*, pp. 10–13.

63. "Anti-Slavery Meeting," *Star and Republican Banner*, September 26, 1836, p. 1 c. 5; Sewell, *Ballots for Freedom*, pp. 12–13 indicates that the interrogation tactic started in 1837, and Gilbert Hobbs Barnes, *The Anti-Slavery Impulse*, p. 147, includes it in his chapter discussing 1838 (when it was used in New York's gubernatorial campaign to ask candidates if they would support jury trials for fugitive slaves). Barnes also describes the practice of printing the correspondence in the papers. Adams County's 1836 use of the tactic predates any of the examples mentioned in these two works. "To this Complexion it Must Come," *National Enquirer*, December 24, 1836, p. 62 c. 4–5.

64. "Correspondence . . . ," *Star and Republican Banner*, October 3, 1836, p. 2 c. 3. Sheffer was not a recent convert, although he did not mention in his correspondence that he had also signed the same 1828 antislavery petition as Joel and William Wierman. See Appendix B.

65. G. Craig Caba, ed. *Episodes of Gettysburg and the Underground Railroad* (Gettysburg, Pa.: G. Craig Caba Antiques, 1998), p. 96.

66. "To This Complexion It Must Come," *National Enquirer*, December 24, 1836, p. 62 c. 4–5. Sewell, *Ballots for Freedom*, pp. 10–13.

67. "Anti-Slavery," *Star and Republican Banner*, November 14, 1836, p. 3 c. 2. Emphasis in original.

68. "Anti-Slavery," *Star and Republican Banner*, November 21, 1836, p. 2 c.4.

69. "Anti-Slavery," *Star and Republican Banner*, November 28, 1836, p. 2 c. 3.

70. I. Daniel Rupp, *The History and Topography of Dauphin, Cumberland, Franklin, Adams, and Perry Counties* (Lancaster, 1846), p. 527; J. Howard Wert, "Gettysburg: A Brief Sketch of a Rural Town," in Caba, *Episodes of Gettysburg*, p. 13.

71. "For the Compiler" by "A Spectator," *Republican Compiler*, December 20, 1836, p. 3 c. 2; Payne, *Recollections of Seventy Years*, 58n.

72. Stanley Harrold, *Subversives*, pp. 40–41. Payne, *Recollections of Seventy Years*, pp. 74–75.

73. "Extracts of a letter . . . " *National Enquirer*, December 17, 1836, pp. 58–59. "Public Meeting" and "Anti-Slavery Meeting," *Republican Compiler*, December 13, 1836, p. 3 c. 2–3; Richards, *Gentlemen of Property and Standing*, pp. 30–33; "For the Compiler" by "A Spectator," *Republican Compiler*, December 20, 1836, p. 3 c. 2; "Anti-Slavery Meeting," *Star and Republican Banner*, December 12, 1836, p. 1 c. 4.

74. "Extracts," *National Enquirer*, December 17, 1836, pp. 58–59. Emphasis in original.

75. Ira Brown, "An Antislavery Agent: Charles C. Burleigh in Pennsylvania, 1836–1837," *Pennsylvania Magazine of History and Biography* 55 (1981), pp. 78, 81–82; "Charles C. Burleigh," *National Enquirer*, January 21, 1837, [p. 3].

76. *Republican Compiler*, December 20, 1836, p. 1 c. 4. Brodie, *Thaddeus Stevens*, 64; Trefousse, *Thaddeus Stevens*, p. 49; "Governor Ritner's Message" and "The Governor's Message," *Star and Republican Banner*, December 19, 1836, p. 2 c. 1 and p. 3 c. 1.

77. Blanchard in *The Christian Cynosure*, September 22, 1868, December 29, 1868, and April 5, 1883, cited by Current, *Old Thad Stevens*, p. 34, and Brodie, *Thaddeus Stevens*, pp. 64–65. Trefousse, *Thaddeus Stevens*, p. 47. Various accounts differ as to whether the date of their first meeting was in December 1836 or January 1837. Like Stevens, Blanchard was from Vermont, and his parents were associates of Stevens. For background on Blanchard see Payne, *Recollections of Seventy Years*, 58n; Richard S. Taylor, "Beyond Immediate Emancipation: Jonathan Blanchard, Abolitionism, and the Emergence of American Fundamentalism," *Civil War History* 27 (1981), pp. 260–74. Blanchard became a prominent abolitionist in Cincinnati; his activities in the 1840s to 1850s are discussed in Victor B. Howard, *Conscience and Slavery: The Evangelistic Calvinist Domestic Missions, 1837–1861* (Kent, Oh.: Kent State University Press, 1990). See also Stanley Harrold, *Border War* (Chapel Hill: University of North Carolina Press, 2010), p. 122.

78. One historian believes that Weld insightfully perceived that the great cities were dependent on rural areas for their trade; others simply hold that Weld, like many antebellum ministers and rural Americans, merely believed that the city was a giant sump of sin. Gilbert Hobbs Barnes, *The Antislavery Impulse* (New York: Appleton-Century, 1933), p. 107; Fergus M. Bordewich, *Bound for Canaan* (New York: Amistad, 2005), p. 156.

79. Richard S. Newman, *The Transformation of American Abolitionism* (Chapel Hill: University of North Carolina Press, 2002), pp. 152–75.

80. Brodie, *Thaddeus Stevens*, pp. 64–65; Robert Fortenbaugh's Notes on Thaddeus Stevens, Anti-Slavery File, Adams County Historical Society.

81. "Abolition Meeting," *Star and Republican Banner*, March 20, 1837, p. 3 c. 2; "Integrity of the Union," March 20, 1837, p. 3 c. 4; "The Pro-Slavery Meeting," *Star and Republican Banner*, April 10, 1837, p. 3 c. 2.

82. "Remarks of Mr. Blanchard on the Question, 'Will the agitation of the Abolition Question cause a dissolution of the Union,'" *Star and Republican Banner*, April 17, 1837, p. 1 c. 1.

83. "Remarks of Mr. Blanchard on the Question, 'Will the agitation of the Abolition Question cause a dissolution of the Union,'" *Star and Republican Banner*, April 17, 1837, p. 1 c. 1. The "genius of emancipation" was a phrase of Irish reformer John Philpot Curran that Lundy appropriated. Dillon, *Benjamin Lundy*, p. 46.

84. "Mr. Cooper's Remarks," *Star and Republican Banner*, May 29, 1837, p. 1 c. 1. The *Star* republished Cooper's remarks in their entirety on June 2. This may have been to goad the *Compiler* into publishing Blanchard's remarks (which was unsuccessful), but it also may have been a subtle step back for the *Star* and an attempt to show readers that the paper also accepted a moderate position on antislavery.

85. "Mr. Cooper's Remarks," *Star and Republican Banner*, May 29, 1837, p. 1 c. 1.

86. "Mr. Cooper's Remarks," *Star and Republican Banner*, May 29, 1837, p. 1 c. 1.

87. "Abolition Discussion," *Star and Republican Banner*, March 20, 1837, p. 3 c. 2. Miller would go on to notoriety (for abolitionists) as a judge in the Booth Wisconsin fugitive slave case.

88. "Abolition Discussion," *Star and Republican Banner*, March 20, 1837, p. 3 c. 2.

89. Brodie, *Thaddeus Stevens*, p. 65. "Abolition Discussion," *Star and Republican Banner*, March 20, 1837, p. 3 c. 2–3.

90. Minutes of the Agency Committee, American Anti-Slavery Society, March 15, 1837, in Gilbert Hobbs Barnes, *Anti-Slavery Impulse*, pp. 262–63 n. 17.

91. "Abolition Discussion," *Star and Republican Banner*, March 20, 1837, p. 3 c. 3.

92. "Mr. Blanchard," *Adams Sentinel*, May 8, 1837, p. 3 c. 2–3; Brodie, *Thaddeus Stevens*, p. 65; Meltzer, *Thaddeus Stevens*, p. 51.

93. *Star*, April 10, 1837, p. 2 c. 1; April 24, 1837, p. 2 c. 1; and May 1, 1837, p. 3 c. 2. Blanchard also apparently returned to Gettysburg to speak at a "Friends of the Integrity of the Union" meeting.

94. Citing intense "interest," Harper had published Cooper's remarks in the *Adams Sentinel*—"Mr. Cooper's Reply," May 22, 1837, *Adams Sentinel*, p. 2 c. 2 and p. 3 c. 2; "Mr. Cooper's Remarks," May 29, 1837, *Star and Republican Banner*, p. 1 c. 1 and p. 3 c. 2; "Mr. Cooper's Speech on Abolition," *Star and Republican Banner*, June 9, 1837, p. 2 c. 1. (Heathen and Hell comments) "Mr. Blanchard," *Adams Sentinel*, May 8, 1837, p. 3 c. 2–3. "Integrity of the Union," *Adams Sentinel*, May 22, 1837, p. 2 c. 2–3.

95. Joel Wierman to Adam Wert, August 6, 1837, J. Howard Wert Collection, G. Craig Caba, curator.

96. Current, *Old Thad Stevens*, pp. 39–41.

97. Current, *Old Thad Stevens*, p. 51.

98. Ira V. Brown, "Miller McKim and Pennsylvania Abolitionism," pp. 56–72; Still, *Underground Railroad*, pp. 470–71; "Letter of J. M. McKim [From the *Emancipator*], August 28, 1839, *The [Pennsylvania] Freeman*, September 12, 1839, p. [2].

99. Frederick J. Blue, *Salmon P. Chase: A Life in Politics* (Kent, Oh.: Kent State University Press, 1987); Albert Bushnell Hart, *Salmon P. Chase* (Boston: Houghton, Mifflin and Company, 1899; reprint, New York: Chelsea House, 1980), pp. 28–90; L. Belle Ham-

lin, "Selections from the Follett Papers," *Quarterly Publications of the Ohio Historical and Philosophical Society*, XI (1916), pp. 11–15, cited by Eric Foner, *Free Soil, Free Labor, Free Men* (Oxford: Oxford University Press, 1970; reprint, 1999), p. 73.

100. "Political Abolition," *Compiler*, March 21, 1837, p. 3 c. 4; see also, "Abolition," *Compiler*, May 9, 1837, p. 3 c. 1; *Pennsylvania Reporter* (Harrisburg), December 30, 1836, cited by Current, *Old Thad Stevens*, p. 31.

3. Antislavery Petitioning in South Central Pennsylvania

1. Charles W. Griest to Friend David, February 1884, pp. 1–2; copy courtesy Debra Mc-Causlin. "Report of the Board of Managers of the York Springs Anti-Slavery Society," *Star*, March 17, 1840, p. 2 c. 1–2. Petitioning, like pamphleting and lending libraries, was aided by new technological developments, which allowed for low cost printing. For information about the brief, late 1830s popularity of lending libraries and pamphlets, see Gilbert H. Barnes, *The Anti-Slavery Impulse, 1830–1844* (Washington: American Historical Society, 1933; reprint, New York: Harcourt Brace & World, 1964), pp. 139–40.

2. [Letter from Charles C. Burleigh], *The Pennsylvania Freeman*, April 2, 1840, p. 3 c. 3–5.

3. Theophane Geary, *A History of Third Parties in Pennsylvania, 1840–1860* (Washington: Catholic University of America, 1938), pp. 45–46.

4. "Letter from B. S. Jones," *Pennsylvania Freeman*, May 8, 1845, p. 1 c. 2; Benjamin S. Jones to Adam Wert, Gettysburg, April 7, 1845, J. Howard Wert Gettysburg Collection, G. Craig Caba, curator.

5. "Letter from C. M. Burleigh," *Pennsylvania Freeman*, October 1, 1846, p. 1 c. 2–4. The case of Thomas Finnegan is discussed in Chapter 4.

6. Richard S. Newman, *The Transformation of American Abolitionism* (Chapel Hill: University of North Carolina Press, 2002), pp. 39–59.

7. Angelina E. Grimke, *Appeal to the Christian Women of the South* (New York: American Anti-Slavery Society, 1836), pp. 25–26, quoted by Carolyn L. Williams, "Religion, race and gender in antebellum American radicalism: The Pennsylvania Female Anti-Slavery Society, 1833–1870," (Ph.D. diss., UCLA, 1991), p. 229; James Brewer Stewart, *Holy Warriors: The Abolitionists and American Slavery* (New York: Hill and Wang, 1976), p. 88. Interestingly, when Grimke appeared before the Massachusetts legislature, she argued the act had political as well as moral implications; perhaps because her *Appeal* was written to Southerners, she downplayed the political implications. Gerda Lerner, *The Grimke Sisters from South Carolina* (Chapel Hill: University of North Carolina Press, 1967; reprint, New York: Schocken, 1971), p. 7.

8. The Gag Rule controversy has been extensively covered in the historiography of the antislavery movement. Perhaps the best account remains that of Gilbert Hobbs Barnes in *The Antislavery Impulse*, pp. 109–45. The sheer volume of this campaign, and the fact that the petitions are uncatalogued, make using the antislavery petitions from 1835–44 extremely difficult. Although abolitionist claims of tall stacks of petitions lining the hallways of the House of Representatives may be exaggerated, in the U.S. House of Representative's archives there are twelve linear feet of the paper-thin petitions for 1835 alone.

9. Minutes of the Adams Co. A[nti] Slavery Society, December 1, 1837, p. 23, J. Howard Wert Gettysburg Collection, G. Craig Caba, curator.

10. George Chambers to Adam Wert, Washington, January 30, 1837; Joel Wierman to Adam Wert, August 6, 1837; Daniel Sheffer to Adam Wert, Washington, May 14, 1838; all three in the J. Howard Wert Gettysburg Collection, G. Craig Caba, curator.

11. "1783 Quaker Anti-Slavery Petition," http://www.rootsweb.com/~quakers/petition .htm.

12. David Brion Davis, *The Problem of Slavery in the Age of Revolution 1770–1823* (Ithaca: Cornell University Press, 1975; reprint, New York: Oxford University Press, 1999), pp. 39–83; Newman, *Transformation of American Abolitionism*, pp. 58–59. In 1799, the Quaker petitions were joined by one from fifty African Americans from Philadelphia, led by Absalom Jones.

13. "Records that Pertain to Slavery and the International Slave Trade," http://www .archives.gov/research_room/alic/reference_desk/slavery_records.html; Walter B. Hill, "Living with the Hydra: Documenting of Slavery and the Slave Trade in Federal Records," *Prologue*, 32 (2000), available at: http://www.archives.gov/publications/prologue/ winter_2000_hydra_slave_trade_documentation_1.html; "Slave Trade," *American State Papers* (1789–1809) 37 (Miscellaneous volume 1), Document 44, p. 76. Newman, *The Transformation of American Abolitionism*, pp. 55, 58–59. As an example of Congress refusing to act on antislavery petitions because they judged jurisdiction over slavery to lie with the states, see "Abolition of Slavery," *American State Papers* (1789–1809) 37 (Miscellaneous volume 1), Document 13, p. 12.

14. Merton L. Dillon, *Benjamin Lundy and the Struggle for Negro Freedom* (Urbana: University of Illinois Press, 1966). For PAS petitioning campaigns and strategies, see Newman, *Transformation of American Abolitionism*, pp. 39–59. Lundy's journal title probably reinforced free soil concepts and possibly resistance to fugitive slave law in the mind of his readers. It was taken from a quotation by Irish reformer John Philpot Curran, who, speaking of Irish emancipation, stated: "[T]he spirit of British law . . . makes liberty commensurate with, and inseparable from, British soil; [and] proclaims, even to the stranger and sojourner, the moment he sets his foot on British earth, that the ground on which he stands is holy, and consecrated by the genius of Universal Emancipation."

15. Don E. Fehrenbacher, *The Slaveholding Republic* (Oxford: Oxford University Press, 2001), p. 68. Newman, *Transformation of American Abolitionism*, p. 51. Miner was a member of the PAS when he was not in office.

16. Merton L. Dillon, *Benjamin Lundy and the Struggle for Negro Freedom* (Urbana: University of Illinois Press, 1966), pp. 121–26. Fehrenbacher, *Slaveholding Republic*, pp. 68–69.

17. "Memorial of the undersigned, Citizens of Pennsylvania," February 5, 1827, Committee on the District of Columbia, Slavery in the District of Columbia, HR 19A-G4.2, National Archives.

18. "Memorial of the undersigned . . . ," February 5, 1827. In an even closer corollary to Pennsylvania's law, a later version of the petition recommended that children be freed only after reaching as certain age.

19. Why south central Pennsylvania was involved on the leading edge of this petition campaign is not completely clear. It likely was because of Lundy and the Wierman family. Lundy had several children living in Adams County into the 1830s; one daughter married a Wierman. William Wierman also moved to Baltimore in this period.

20. HR 20A-G5.1, Committee on the District of Columbia, Slavery in the District of Columbia, January 9 – January 28, 1828, Folder 1 of 8, National Archives. Dillon. *Lundy*, pp. 121–26.

21. Dillon, *Lundy*, 126, pp. 133–37; Newman, *Transformation of American Abolitionism*, p. 152; Lydia Lundy to W. Hicks, 12 Month [December] 7, 1828, Halliday Jackson Papers, Letterbook 3, No. 25, Friends Historical Library, Swarthmore University.

22. HR 20A-G5.1, Committee on the District of Columbia, Slavery in the District of Columbia, 1829, Folders 3–8, National Archives. The Vermont petitions are in folder 6.

23. HR 20A-G5.1, Committee on the District of Columbia, Slavery in the District of Columbia, January 19–26, 1829, Folder 4 of 8, National Archives. William J. Switala, *Underground Railroad in Pennsylvania* (Mechanicsburg, PA: Stackpole Books, 2001), pp. 70–71, 76–78. Barnes, *Anti-Slavery Impulse*, p. 33.

24. Fehrenbacher, Slaveholding Republic, pp. 72–73; Newman, *Transformation of American Abolitionism*, p. 51.

25. Citing Acting Committee Minutes, c. 1822 and c. 1828, PAS Papers, Reel 2, Newman maintains that the PAS refused to join this petition campaign. Newman, *Transformation of American Abolitionism*, pp. 55, 203 n. 63. Yet many members of the PAS had relationships with Benjamin Lundy, and the American Convention would have been unlikely to support the campaign without the acquiescence of the PAS.

26. Newman, *Transformation of American Abolitionism*, pp. 58–59. Dillon, Lundy, pp. 125–26.

27. Barnes, *The Anti-Slavery Impulse*, p. 109; Fehrenbacher, *Slaveholding Republic*, pp. 72, 75.

28. Barnes, *The Anti-Slavery Impulse*, pp. 109–45. (Immediatism) Barnes, *The Anti-Slavery Impulse*, p. 111. (Politicization) James Brewer Stewart, *Holy Warriors: The Abolitionists and American Slavery* (New York: Hill and Wang, 1976), pp. 82–85. See also Dwight L. Dumond, *Antislavery Origins of the Civil War in the United States* (Ann Arbor: University of Michigan Press, 1939), p. 51; Aileen S. Kraditor, *Means and Ends in American Abolitionism* (New York: Pantheon, 1967, reprint, 1969), pp. 6–7; Stephen John Hartnett, *Democratic Dissent and the Cultural Fictions of Antebellum America* (Urbana: University of Illinois Press, 2002), pp. 15, 176–77.

29. "Petitioning," *National Enquirer*, December 24, 1836, p. 62 c. 4–5. For instruction to succeed, legislation on the issue would have to be pending before Congress. Instruction was a highly controversial tactic, seen by some as anti-democratic, and was used very rarely by the Pennsylvania legislature. Technically, most antebellum politicians believed that U.S. Senators could be instructed by the state legislature on how to vote, since the legislature had chosen them, but U.S. Representatives could only be urged to vote in certain ways. There were some noted but controversial uses of "instructions" on slavery in the Midwestern states.

30. Jonathan Stayer, archivist, Pennsylvania State Archives, personal communication, spring 2003. Newspapers and antislavery societies, and even the House and Senate journals, sometimes claim the submission of more petitions than can be found in the files in the twenty-first century. In some years, it appears as if only petitions from a specific area have been retained.

31. A number of works have attempted to characterize, in various areas, the demographic makeup of antislavery supporters through analyzing antislavery petitions, subscription lists to antislavery newspapers, or membership records of antislavery societies. Perhaps the best monograph using petitions to analyze the demographic makeup of an antislavery community remains Edward Magdol, *The Antislavery Rank and File: Profile of the Abolitionists' Constituency* (New York: Greenwood Press, 1986).

32. Carl D. Oblinger, "New freedoms, old miseries: the emergence and disruption of black communities in southeastern Pennsylvania, 1780–1860," (Ph.D. diss., Lehigh University, 1988), pp. 121–22; Edward Turner, *The Negro in Pennsylvania* (Washington, 1911: American Historical Association; reprint, New York: Negro Universities Press, 1969), p. 153.

33. Photocopy of February 18, 1845 petition, "Taken from Carl Swisher Papers," Box 21, National Archives Record Group 233, from the "Negroes-Slavery" file, Adams County Historical Society, Gettysburg, Pa. It was sent by some of Gettysburg's professionals, and did not include town abolitionists such as William Reynolds or Samuel Schmucker, or, apparently, any members of the Adams County Anti-Slavery Society.

34. The unsorted petitions to the Congress during the Gag Rule controversy are too daunting for this kind of work; in 1835 alone, there were 12 linear feet of paper-thin petitions from all over the North.

35. There was a third flurry of petitions in 1837–38, but almost all of these went to the state constitutional convention, not the legislature.

36. William Still, *The Underground Railroad* (Philadelphia: Porter & Coates, 1872; reprint, Medford, N.J.: Plexus Publishing, 2005), pp. 470–72; Ira V. Brown, "Miller McKim and Pennsylvania Abolitionism," *Pennsylvania History* 30 (1963): pp. 56–72; "James Miller McKim (1810–1874)," http://chronicles.dickinson.edu/encyclo/m/ed_McKimJM.htm. (Duffield) Richard J. Carwardine, *Evangelicals and Politics in Antebellum America* (Knoxville: University of Tennessee Press, 1997), pp. 140–41. (Seventy) John L. Myers, "Organization of the 'Seventy': To Arouse the North Against Slavery," in John R. McKivigan, ed., *Abolitionism and American Reform* (New York: Garland Publishing, 1999), p. 39.

37. Poster sent by Mariette Rutter to Dr. Hiram Corson, Corson Papers, Historical Society of Montgomery County, quoted in Charles L. Blockson, *The Underground Railroad in Pennsylvania* (Jacksonville, N.C.: Flame International, 1981), p. 49. Still, *Underground Railroad*, pp. 471–72.

38. Williams, "Religion, race and gender," p. 181; Records of the General Assembly, RG-7, Senate File 1847, Box 19, Folder 26, Petition No. 74 (this number includes many petitions), Pennsylvania State Archives.

39. Laws of the General Assembly of the Commonwealth of Pennsylvania Passed at the Session of 1847 (Harrisburg, Pa.: The Commonwealth, 1847), pp. 206–8; Thomas D. Morris, *Free Men All: The Personal Liberty Laws of the North, 1780–1861* (Baltimore: Johns

Hopkins University Press, 1974), p. 118; Thomas Hart Benton, *Thirty Years View*, v. 2 (New York: D. Appleton and Company, 1856), pp. 777–78. The clause on riot and disorder was directly suggested by Story's opinion in Prigg.

40. "To The Senate and House of Representatives of the State of Pennsylvania," [Petition of inhabitants of Adams County], January 15, 1847, Petition No. 54, Senate File, Pennsylvania State Archives [this number includes many petitions]. See Appendix C.

41. "Extract From the Quarterly Conference of the A.M.E. L. Church, Gettysburg, commenced June 20th, and closed July 11th, 1857," *Adams Sentinel*, July 10, 1857, p. 3 c. 3; "Letter of S. R. McAllister Furnishing Data on the Underground Railroad," (S. R. McAllister to J. Howard Wert, December 2, 1904), in G. Craig Caba, ed., *Episodes of Gettysburg and the Underground Railroad* (Gettysburg: G. Craig Caba Antiques, 1998), p. 59. Several other members of the Devan family were included as signers, however.

42. "A Petition of the Inhabitants of Adams County . . . , Jan 15 '47," Petition File, Petition No. 54, Senate File, Pennsylvania Archives, RG-7. Different Northern states had varying policies on how long slaves could be brought into the state by Southern visitors; it was in large part an effort to retain business by Southern tourists. In the late antebellum period, several other states, such as Pennsylvania, adopted legislation that slaves would be freed immediately if brought to the state; New Hampshire even passed a law that said that fugitive slaves would be freed immediately by setting foot on that state's soil.

43. Stanley Harrold, *Border War: Fighting over Slavery before the Civil War* (Chapel Hill: University of North Carolina Press, 2010), p. 70 and *passim*.

44. Barnes, *The Anti-Slavery Impulse*, p. 84.

45. William Wierman Wright was William Wright's 22-year old son. He would move from Adams County in the next year, become a trusted aide of General Sherman's during the Civil War, and eventually rise to the rank of general in the engineers. He assisted the International Technical Commission in investigating potential canal routes across Panama, before dying in a Philadelphia prison in 1882 from complications of alcoholism. "Description," William W. Wright Collection, Georgetown Library Special Collections, http://www.library.georgetown.edu/dept/speccoll/cl178.htm.

46. David Donald, *Lincoln Reconsidered* (New York: Alfred A. Knopf, 1956; reprint, New York: Vintage Books, 1961), pp. 21–36; Robert A. Skotheim, "A Note on Historical Method: David Donald's 'Toward a Reconsideration of Abolitionists,'" *Journal of Southern History* 25 (1959): pp. 356–65; reprinted in Richard O. Curry, *Abolitionists: Reformers or Fanatics* (New York: Holt, Rinehart and Winston, 1965), pp. 49–52.

47. Margaret B. Walmer, *Menallen Minutes, Marriages, and Miscellany* (Bowie, Md.: Heritage Books, 1992). Some of the signers were identifiable in the meeting minutes only and not the census records. Some of the signers would have belonged to the Huntington Meeting or to meetings in York County. Thanks to Debra McCauslin for pointing this out.

48. Aging of the antislavery community is a likely reason why no antislavery petitions were sent from this area to the state legislature in 1861. The fact that south central Pennsylvania could lie (and, events proved, did lie) on a major invasion route from the South was probably another. See Chapter 7.

49. Magdol, *Antislavery Rank and File*, p. 88. In Table 6-5, Magdol cites an occupational average of 6.3% as farmers among the fifteen hundred petitioners he analyzed from seven Massachusetts and New York cities. This figure, however, does not appear to be consistent with Table 6-3, "1830s Petitioners' Occupation Groups by Age Group," or Table 6-14, "Occupational Structure of Lynn, Massachusetts Abolitionist Petitioners and Anti-Abolitionists." Magdol, *Antislavery Rank and File*, pp. 68, 65, 87. Regardless, in terms of numbers of petition signers, there are fewer farmers than workers.

50. "Communicated," *Star*, July 16, 1847, p. 3 c. 3. A manuscript letter indicates that the last meeting of the antislavery society was in 1847. Charles W. Griest to Friend David, February 1884. Copy courtesy of Debra S. McCauslin.

4. The Fugitive Slave Issue on Trial: The 1840s in South Central Pennsylvania

1. The U.S. court system would serve a similar role one hundred years later for civil rights advocates, as in *Brown v. Board of Education* (1954).

2. Despite the best efforts of Pennsylvania's activists, there were no jury trials in fugitive slave cases.

3. William Wright played an important role in Pennsylvania's small Liberty Party, but I found little documentation for that aspect of south central Pennsylvania's antislavery efforts.

4. Stanley Harrold has uncovered evidence that free soil ideas were present among those who helped fugitive slaves from early on; they were reluctantly willing for a slave to be recaptured in the South, but felt that he should be free the moment he reached Northern soil. Others believed that only the Fugitive Slave Law kept runaways from being free, but all slaves brought north by their masters instantly became free. Stanley Harrold, *Border War: Fighting Over Slavery Before the Civil War* (Chapel Hill: University of North Carolina Press, 2010), pp. 55, 67. Thomas Morris has argued that resistance to the rendition of fugitive slaves and resistance to slavery extension into the territories were two sides of the same coin. One opposed the expansion of slavery into western territories, the other into the North. Regardless of whether this provocative point is completely supported, Northerners who were concerned about the aggrandizement of the Slave Power regarding the western territories were also concerned about its ability to effect law and practice in the North. Through these "free soil" arguments in Adams County's courts, these two issues could be linked in the minds of the judge, jury, and an attentive local populace. Thomas D. Morris, *Free Men All! The Personal Liberty Laws of the North* (Baltimore: Johns Hopkins University, 1974).

5. Richard S. Newman, *Transformation of American Abolition: Fighting Slavery in the Early Republic* (Chapel Hill: University of North Carolina Press, 2002), pp. 39–59.

6. "Letter from Mr. R[awle] to ---- ------- Esq., June 27, 1834," published in John Agg, et al., *Proceedings and Debates of the Convention of . . . Pennsylvania*, v. 11 (Harrisburg, Pa.: Packer, Barrett & Parke, 1838), pp. 287–88.

7. "[J.G. Blount] To The Sheriff or Jailer of the County of Beaufort [S.C.]," June 17, 1822, in "Documents Concerning cases in which slaves were awarded freedom, 1773–1833," Papers of the Pennsylvania Abolition Society, Reel 24; also in Appendix A, pt. 3, Papers of the PAS.

8. "The Committee to Whom was referred the letter from Richard D. Baily . . . ," May 10, 1821, Papers of the Pennsylvania Abolition Society, Reel 13. Edward Turner stated, "If not the parent, she [the PAS] was at least the foster mother of similar societies elsewhere," including in the South. Edward Turner, *The Negro in Pennsylvania* (Washington, 1911: American Historical Association; reprint, New York: Negro Universities Press, 1969), pp. 214–15.

9. Fergus M. Bordewich, *Bound for Canaan* (New York: Amistad, 2005), p. 57.

10. Bordewich, *Bound for Canaan*, pp. 56–57; William Still, *The Underground Railroad* (Philadelphia: Porter & Coates, 1872; republished Medford, N.J.: Plexus Publishing, 2005), p. 494.

11. Larry C. Bolin, "Pennsylvania Legislation Regarding Slavery," in Bolin, "Slaves and Slaveholders of Adams County," *Adams County History* 9 (2003): pp. 81–82, 85.

12. See three south central Pennsylvania cases, *Respublica v. William Findlay* (1801), *Cook v. Neaff* (1801), and *Commonwealth v. Blaine* (1811). *Commonwealth v. Blaine*, in Horace Binney, ed., Reports of Cases Adjudged in the Supreme Court of Pennsylvania [Pennsylvania Reports], v. 4 [1811–1812]. J. Levering Jones and Thos. I Wharton, eds. (Philadelphia: Kay and Brother, 1891), pp. 185–88; *Cook v. Neaff* and *Respublica v. Findlay*, in Albert B. Weimer, ed., Reports of Cases Adjudged in the Supreme Court [Pennsylvania Reports] with some select cases at *nisi prius* and in the Circuit Court, by the Honorable Jasper Yeats, 3rd edition, with notes, v. III (Philadelphia: T. & J. W. Johnson & Co., 1889), 259–61.

13. Newman, *Transformation of American Abolition*, pp. 81–82; *Wilson v. Belinda*, in Thomas Sergeant and William Rawle, Jr., *Reports of Cases Adjudged in the Supreme Court of Pennsylvania [Pennsylvania Reports]* v. 3 [1817–1818], 3rd ed. (Philadelphia: Kay & Brother, 1872), pp. 396–401.

14. Thomas Morris, *Free Men All! The Personal Liberty Laws of the North, 1780–1860* (Baltimore: Johns Hopkins University Press, 1974), p. 6.

15. Stanley W. Campbell, *The Slave Catchers: Enforcement of the Fugitive Slave Law, 1850–1860* (Chapel Hill: University of North Carolina Press, 1970; reprint, New York: W. W. Norton, 1972), pp. 7–8.

16. An insightful study of kidnapping in Philadelphia is Julie Winch, "The Other Underground Railroad," *Pennsylvania Magazine of History and Biography* 111 (1987): pp. 3–26.

17. See, for example, "Address of the Chester Co. Society for Preventing Kidnapping, &c. (1823)," and "To the American Convention for Promoting the Abolition of Slavery, and Improving the Affairs of the African Race," Pennsylvania Abolition Society (1825). In addition, William Rawle of the PAS was president of the Convention in 1825, and was the signer of "To the Abolition and Manumission Societies of the United States of America," which complained, "We fear the practice of kidnapping free people of colour, is still continued in our country." *The American Convention for Promoting the Abolition of Slavery and Improving the Conditions of the African Race* (New York: Bergman Publishers, 1969), pp. 819–22, 878, 841.

18. J. P. M., "Three Fugitive Slaves," in William Burkhart, et al., eds. *Shippensburg in the Civil War* (Shippensburg: Shippensburg Historical Society, 1964), pp. 8–11; "Slavery," Jeremiah Zeamer papers, Container 40, Folder 7, Cumberland County Historical Society.

O. P. M. letter to Jeremiah Zeamer, Sep. 25, 1901, typescript, "Underground Railroad" file, Zeamer Papers [original indicated as in Zeamer Papers, Container 40, folder 9]. O. P. M. chose not to sign his letter to Zeamer; I believe he and J. P. M. may be the same person.

19. R. Kent Newmyer, *Supreme Court Justice Joseph Story* (Chapel Hill: University of North Carolina Press, 1985), p. 370; "Governmental Powers: Edward Prigg v. Pennsylvania (1842)," in Louis M. Waddell, *To Secure The Blessings of Liberty: Pennsylvania and the Changing U.S. Constitution* (Harrisburg, Pa.: Pennsylvania Historical and Museum Society, 1986), pp. 3–4. In 1832, after Nat Turner's failed rebellion in Virginia, the Maryland legislature urged the state's free blacks to emigrate to Liberia, and passed a restrictive black code, tightening documentation requirements for proving free status. This may explain why Margaret and Jerry Morgan left, particularly if their freedom was not well documented.

20. Newmyer, *Supreme Court Justice Joseph Story*, p. 370; Waddell, "Governmental Powers," pp. 3–4. For a discussion of the transition from tobacco to grain farming, see Robert Mitchell, *Commercialism and Frontier: Perspectives on the Early Shenandoah Valley* (Charlottesville, 1977).

21. Waddell, "Governmental Powers," p. 3.

22. Carl D. Oblinger, "New freedoms, old miseries: The emergence and disruption of black communities in southeastern Pennsylvania, 1780–1860," (Ph.D. diss., Lehigh University, 1988), pp. 85–87, 93.

23. Waddell, "Governmental Powers," pp. 5–6.

24. Waddell, "Governmental Powers," p. 6.

25. The relevant part of Article 4, Section 2, reads: "A person charged in any State with Treason, Felony, or other Crime, who shall flee from Justice, and be found in another State, shall on Demand of the executive Authority of the State from which he fled, be delivered up, to be removed to the State having Jurisdiction of the Crime. No Person held to Service or Labour in one State, under the Laws thereof, escaping into another, shall, in Consequence of any Law or Regulation therein, be discharged from such Service or Labour, but shall be delivered up on Claim of the Party to whom such Service or Labour may be due."

26. Waddell, "Governmental Powers," p. 6; *Prigg v. Com. of Pennsylvania* (1842) 41 US 539, January Term 1842, at http://caselaw.lp.findlaw.com/scripts/.

27. Waddell, "Governmental Powers," p. 6.

28. Waddell, "Governmental Powers," p. 6; Newmyer, *Supreme Court Justice Joseph Story*, p. 377.

29. Waddell, "Governmental Powers," p. 6; *Prigg v. Com. of Pennsylvania* (1842) 41 US 539, January Term 1842, at http://caselaw.lp.findlaw.com/scripts/.

30. Newmyer, *Supreme Court Justice Joseph Story*, pp. 372, 376–77.

31. Story based his logic on Chief Justice John Marshall's opinion in *Sturgis v. Crowninshield* (1819) that certain grants of power to Congress were intended to exclude any state interference whatsoever.

32. As early as 1789, Benjamin Franklin, then president of the Pennsylvania Abolition Society, proposed a national police force to, in part, police emancipated African Ameri-

cans. Stephen J. Hartnett, *Democratic Dissent & the Cultural Fictions of Antebellum America* (Urbana: University of Illinois Press, 2002), pp. 41–42.

33. Newmyer, *Supreme Court Justice Joseph Story*, p. 372; Edward Turner, *The Negro in Pennsylvania* (Washington: American Historical Association, 1911; reprint, New York: Negro Universities Press, 1969), p. 49; John Hope Franklin and Loren Schweninger, *Runaway Slaves: Rebels on the Plantation* (New York: Oxford University Press, 1999), pp. 175, 178–81.

34. "Address to the People of Maryland, Virginia, North Carolina, South Carolina, Florida, Alabama, Tennessee, Kentucky, Louisiana, Texas, Missouri, Mississippi, and Arkansas," "The Nashville Convention," *Daily National Intelligencer*, July 13, 1850, p. 2 c. 4. Thomas Hart Benton, *Thirty Years' View*, v. 2 (New York: D. Appleton and Co., 1856), pp. 777–78.

35. Philip S. Klein and Ari Hoogenboom, *A History of Pennsylvania*, 2nd ed. (University Park, Pa.: Penn State Press, 1980), p. 34.

36. In Adams County, some biographers of Thaddeus Stevens claim he aggressively defended fugitives during this period, but no proof has yet emerged from the Adams County court records. Hans Trefousse, *Thaddeus Stevens: Nineteenth-Century Egalitarian* (Chapel Hill: University of North Carolina Press, 1997), pp. 14–15, citing "Remarks by Mr. Orth," *Memorial Addresses*, p. 53–54. Milton Meltzer titled an entire chapter in his 1967 biography of Stevens, "The Runaways' Lawyer." Meltzer, *Thaddeus Stevens and the Fight for Negro Rights* (New York: Thomas Y. Crowell, 1967), pp. 41–58; Richard Current, *Old Thad Stevens: A Story of Ambition* (Madison: University of Wisconsin Press, 1942), pp. 34–35.

37. "The Case of Johnson v. Tompkins, and others," Wilbur H. Siebert Papers, Ohio Historical Society, Columbus, Ohio, Roll 12. "The State vs. Negro Jim and Ephraim Valentine," Miscellaneous Court Records, Adams County Office of the Prothonotary (records pulled for Larry Bolin and Debra McCauslin).

38. "Gross Outrage," *Adams Sentinel*, August 11, 1845, p. 3 c. 2. See also the "Great Outrage—Man Stealing," (Reprint from *Gettysburg Star*), *Chambersburg Times*: August 11, 1845, p. 2 c. 2, Kittochtinny Historical Society and "Kidnapping," (Reprint from *Gettysburg Star*), *Compiler*, August 18, 1845.

39. "Finnegan Arrested," *Adams Sentinel*, May 25, 1849, p. 2 c. 1. Mary (Goins) Gandy, *Guide My Feet, Hold My Hand* (Privately published, 1987), p. 21 (copy in the Adams County Historical Society). Gandy, in her highly valuable and generally accurate family history on the case, maintains that Finnegan was a slave catcher from Virginia. Most other local historians hold that he lived in Hagerstown; reading newspaper accounts of the court case, I had believed he was from Franklin County, Pennsylvania.

40. "Letter to the Editor," *Republican Compiler*, April 15, 1846, p. 2 c. 4; Brodie, *Thaddeus Stevens*, pp. 41–45.

41. "Court of Quarter Sessions—August Term," *Star and Republican Banner*, August 28, 1846, p. 2 c. 1. Debra McCauslin maintains that Samuel Maddox Jr. was heavily indebted and had already used the slaves—which he did not yet own—as collateral on loans. Debra S. McCauslin, "Yellow Hill and the Quaker Valley," Adams County Historical Society Meeting, March 7, 2006.

42. "Court of Quarter Sessions—August Term," *Star and Republican Banner*, August 28, 1846, p. 2 c. 1; "Gross Outrage," *Adams Sentinel*, August 11, 1845, p. 3 c. 2. Gandy, *Guide My Feet*, pp. 18–19.

43. "Court of Quarter Sessions—August Term," *Star and Republican Banner*, August 28, 1846, p. 2 c. 1.

44. "Court of Quarter Sessions—August Term," *Star and Republican Banner*, August 28, 1846, p. 2 c. 1.

45. "Court of Quarter Sessions—August Term," *Star and Republican Banner*, August 28, 1846, p. 2.

46. "Court of Quarter Sessions—August Term," *Star and Republican Banner*, August 28, 1846, p. 2. McKaig did state that most Southerners saw Northern abolitionism as a force that worked against voluntary slave manumissions and any easing of the slave's lot.

47. In 1837, Cooper opposed Jonathan Blanchard in Gettysburg, but he had helped Stevens at Harrisburg's "Friends of the Integrity of the Union" meeting, diverting it from pro-Southern pronouncements.

48. This sort of "slippery slope" reasoning, used here to justify Pennsylvania's laws protecting free blacks and punishing kidnapping, had been a staple of American political rhetoric since the colonial period. The premise was that the smallest infringement of the liberty of one held the risk of ultimate enslavement for all. See Bernard Bailyn, *The Intellectual Origins of the American Revolution* (Cambridge, Mass.: Harvard University Press, 1967), pp. 94–160.

49. "Court of Quarter Sessions—August Term," *Star and Republican Banner*, August 28, 1846, p. 2 c. 1. As a judge in Virginia had just declared the 1788 Pennsylvania emancipation statute unconstitutional, Cooper's encomium to that law both supported his legal case but also appealed to the jury's pride and emotion.

50. Kitty Payne and her children returned to Adams County in November of 1846. She died an early death, probably from tuberculosis. Before her death, she was married to Abraham Brien, a local African American who lived on what would come to be called Cemetery Ridge. Gandy, *Guide My Feet*, pp. 38–39.

51. "Court of Quarter Sessions—August Term," *Star and Republican Banner*, August 28, 1846, p. 2 c. 1.

52. Eric Foner, *Free Soil, Free Labor, Free Men: The Ideology of the Republican Party before the Civil War* (New York: Oxford University Press, 1970; reprint, 1995); see also Richard H. Sewell, *Ballots for Freedom: Antislavery Politics in the United States, 1837–1860* (New York: W. W. Norton, 1976), pp. 152–232; Reeve Huston, "Land and Freedom: The New York Rent Wars and the Construction of Free Labor in the Antebellum North," in Eric Arnesen, Julie Greene, and Bruce Laurie, eds., *Labor Histories: Class, Politics and the Working-Class Experience* (Urbana: University of Illinois Press, 1998), pp. 19–44. Jonathan Earle, Jacksonian Democracy & the Politics of Free Soil (Chapel Hill: University of North Carolina Press, 2004), also examines the complicated antecedents of Free Soil doctrine.

53. Beverly Wilson Palmer and Holly Byers Ochoa, eds., *Selected Papers of Thaddeus Stevens*, v. 1 (1814–1865) (Pittsburgh, Pa.: University of Pittsburgh Press, 1997), pp. 110–30.

54. "Court of Quarter Sessions—August Term," *Star and Republican Banner*, August 28, 1846, p. 2 c. 1.

55. "William Neill Irvine," http://www.irvineclan.com/wni1782.htm; "William Irvine," http://www.famousamericans.net/williamirvine/.

56. "Court of Quarter Sessions—August Term," *Star and Republican Banner*, August 28, 1846, p. 2 c. 1–6. "Finnegan Sentenced," *Star and Republican Banner*, November 20, 1846, p. 3 c. 1.

57. Gandy, *Guide My Feet*, pp. v, 33–36. Megan Bishop and Debra McCauslin are currently researching what will likely be the comprehensive account of the Payne case.

58. (Franklin County) "Kidnapping," *Chambersburg Repository and Whig*, August 26, 1847, p. 3 c. 2; "The Kidnappers," *Repository and Whig*, September 2, 1847, p. 2 c. 2, Kittochtinny Historical Society, Chambersburg, Pa.; "Court of Quarter Sessions: Trial for Kidnapping," *Herald and Expositor* (Carlisle), April 10, 1850, Slavery File, Cumberland County Historical Society. Special thanks to Richard L. Tritt and his assistants for finding this case and placing it in the Historical Society's files.

59. "Extraordinary Attempt to Kidnap," *Star*, July 13, 1855, p. 3 c. 2.

60. The leader of the resistance at Christiana, William Parker, made a similar point about Lancaster County: "The whites of that region were generally such negro-haters, that it was a matter of no moment to them where fugitives were carried." William Parker, "The Freedman's Story," *The Atlantic Monthly*, 17 (1866): p. 162, cited in Jonathan Katz, *Resistance at Christiana* (New York: Thomas Y. Crowell, 1974), p. 25.

61. The Senate committee that developed the original 1793 Fugitive Slave Law had added a legislative proviso calling for African Americans who had lived in the area from which they were taken for a term of years to be tried under the laws of that state instead of being seized under the federal law. It is not clear that the term of years was ever spelled out (the draft reads "term of ----- years immediately previous to such arrest"), and the proviso was dropped by amendment before the bill was passed. Morris, *Free Men All!*, pp. 20–21.

62. Garrett Hardin, "The Tragedy of the Commons," *Science* 162 (1968): pp. 1243–48. In 2009, Elinor Ostrom received the Nobel Prize in Economics for her work proving that under certain circumstances the tragedy of the commons could be avoided, but she did not destroy the essential validity of the concept.

63. Ralph L. Ketcham, "Uncle James Madison and Dickinson College," in *Early Dickinsonia: The Boyd Lee Spahr Lectures in America 1957–1961* (Carlisle, Pa.: Dickinson College, 1961), p. 175.

64. Dickinson College Alumni biographies (1826–50) http://chronicles.dickinson.edu/encyclo/a/alumni/alumni3.html. James Henry Morgan, *Dickinson College* (Harrisburg, Pa.: Mount Pleasant Press, 1933), pp. 147–48.

65. "The Fight for the Border Conferences," in Emory Stevens Bucke, et. al., *The History of American Methodism*, v. 2 (New York: Abingdon Press, 1964), pp. 159–67; "Border Troubles," *Christian Advocate and Journal* (New York) [hereinafter referred to as *Christian Advocate*], March 17, 1847, p. 3 c. 4–5, is one of a number of similar examples appearing in the *Advocate* in this period. See also "Letter of Bishop Capers," *Christian Advocate*, April 21, 1847, p. 3 c. 2–4.

66. J. P. Durbin, "Plan for the Removal of Slavery," *Christian Advocate*, February 10, 1847, p. 1 c. 2–3; J. P. Durbin, "Border War," *Christian Advocate*, March 3, 1847, p. 2 c. 5–6; "Reply to Dr. Durbin," *Christian Advocate*, March 10, 1847, p. 1 c. 4–5; "'Dr. Durbin's Plan

to Extinguish Slavery' Considered," *Christian Advocate*, March 17, 1847, p. 1 c. 2–3; "Plan for the Removal of Slavery," *Christian Advocate*, March 24, 1847, p. 1 c. 6.

67. Richard J. Carwardine, *Evangelicals and Politics in Antebellum America* (Knoxville: University of Tennessee Press, 1997), pp. 142–43; Charles Sellers, *Dickinson College: A History* (Middletown, Ct.: Wesleyan University Press, 1973), ch. 9, available at: chronicles .dickinson.edu/histories/sellers/chapter_nine.htm, p. 27 of 30 of web version. Susan Fritschler, "Art from the President's House: A Portrait of John McClintock," *Cumberland County History* 9 (1992): p. 17. John McClintock, "Slavery—No. I," *Christian Advocate*, March 24, 1847, p. 1 c. 5–6; John McClintock, "Slavery—No. II," *Christian Advocate*, March 31, 1847, p. 1 c. 6–7; John McClintock, "Slavery—No. III," *Christian Advocate*, April 21, 1847, p. 1 c. 5–6; John McClintock, "Slavery—No. IV," *Christian Advocate*, May 28, 1847, p. 1 c. 7–p. 2 c. 1.

68. J. P. M., "Three Fugitive Slaves," pp. 8–11; McClintock appears to have been charged as "ringleader" for the same reason Castner Hanway would be for the Christiana Riot in 1851: a paternalistic assumption that African Americans could not organize for effective intervention without white assistance. See Thomas P. Slaughter, *Bloody Dawn: The Christiana Riot and Racial Violence in the Antebellum North* (New York: Oxford University Press, 1991), pp. 66, 92.

69. McClintock's personal letters contain numerous references to his ailments and conditions, and less charitable biographers have labeled him as a hypochondriac. John T. Cunningham and Regina Diverio, *Drew University* (Charleston, S.C.: Arcadia Publishing, 2000), p. 18. (Genius, best preacher) Sellers, *Dickinson College* (web version), ch. 9, p. 11.

70. Sellers, *Dickinson College* (web version), ch. 9, p. 27; Charles D. Cashdollar, "Unexpected Friendship: John McClintock and Auguste Comte," *Pennsylvania Magazine of History and Biography* 105 (1991): pp. 85–98; Fritschler, "Art from the President's House," 17. Moncure Conway, a student at Dickinson at the time, wrote in his autobiography that a witness at McClintock's trial admitted that several individuals had resolved to drive McClintock from the town. Morgan, *Dickinson College*, pp. 278–79.

71. Thomas Slaughter, in his book on Christiana, points out that riots by their very nature are "wild, confusing, and frightening" and it can be impossible, over a hundred years later, to sort out exactly what happened. Slaughter, *Bloody Dawn*, p. 59.

72. Sellers, *Dickinson College* (web version), ch. 9, pp. 27–28; Fritschler, "Art from the President's House," p. 15 (quoting McClintock's diary); "Remarks of Charles W. Carrigan, at the Centennial Anniversary of Dickinson College," June 27, 1873, pp. 1–4.

73. Sellers, *Dickinson College* (web version), ch. 9, p. 28; Morgan, *Dickinson College*, p. 277.

74. Thaddeus Stevens to John McClintock, August 2, 1847, Thaddeus Stevens Papers (microfilm), Reel 1 (General Correspondence), item TS0361. Palmer and Ochoa, eds. *Selected Papers of Thaddeus Stevens*, v. 1, pp. 88–89 In a subsequent letter to the anxious McClintock, Stevens accurately predicted, "I doubt not of *your* acquittal, but I fear for the colored Defts [defendants]—their skin testifies against them. . . . " Stevens to McClintock, August 9, 1847, item TS0362.

75. Sellers, *Dickinson College* (web version), ch. 9, pp. 29–30; Morgan, *Dickinson College*, p. 280–81.

76. McClintock trial transcript, Jeremiah Zeamer papers, Cumberland County Historical Society, Carlisle, Pa.

77. John McClintock to [Stephen Olin], Carlisle, June 26, 1847, p. [2], McClintock Papers, Drew University; Fristchler, "Art from the President's House," p. 17. Morgan, *Dickinson College*, p. 279. James Henry Morgan believes that the African American defendants received harsh sentences because of Hepburn's anger at the McClintock verdict, but it may have been more a result of their being black and being charged with a serious crime with sectional ramifications.

78. John McClintock to Stephen Olin, May 21, 1848, McClintock Papers, Emory University, cited by Sellers, *History of Dickinson College*, ch. 9, p. 29 (web).

79. "Riot at Carlisle," *New York Commercial Advertiser*, June 5, 1847, p. 2 c. 5; "The Fugitive Slave Case," *New York Commercial Advertiser*, August 28, 1847, p. 1 c. 7. "The Carlisle Riot," *New York Daily Tribune*, June 12, 1847, p. 3 c. 1. "Application of the Gag," *New York Daily Tribune*, May 26, 1847.

80. "Alarming Riot—Maryland Runaway Slaves," *News and Courier* (Charleston), June 8, 1847, p. 2 c. 6; "The Slave Riot at Carlisle," *Baltimore Sun*, p. 1 c. 6; "The Riot at Carlisle," *Baltimore Sun*, June 9, 1847, p. 2 c. 1; "Death of Mr. Kennedy," June 29, 1847, p. 2 c. 1; "Acquittal of Professor McClintock," and "The Carlisle Slave Case," *Baltimore Sun*, September 4, 1847, p. 2 c. 1. (Trial Transcript) "The Slave and Riot Case," *Baltimore Sun*, August 30, 1847 – September 1, 1847, p. 1.

81. "The Carlisle Riot," *Richmond Whig and Public Advertiser*, July 16, 1847, p. 2 c. 3.

82. "Death of Mr. Kennedy, of Hagerstown," *Richmond Whig & Public Advertiser*, July 2, 1847, p. 2 c. 2. "A Subscriber," *Richmond Whig and Public Advertiser*, July 6, 1847, p. 1 c. 3. (Personal Liberty Law) "To the Editors of the Whig," *Richmond Whig and Public Advertiser*, July 6, 1847, p. 4 c. 2. This letter was originally published in the *Daily Whig* on July 1. *Daily Richmond Enquirer*, August 23, 1847, quoting Winchester *Virginian*, cited by Larry Gara, *The Liberty Line* (Lexington, Ky.: University of Kentucky Press, 1961; reprint, 1996), p. 159.

83. Charles T. Furlow journal, late June 1863, Charles T. Furlow papers, Fredericksburg and Spotsylvania National Battlefield Park (originals at Yale University), cited in Joseph T. Glatthaar, *General Lee's Army* (New York: Free Press, 2008), p. 271.

84. "Kaufman, David Spangler (1813–1851)," Index to Politicians: Kaufman, The Political Graveyard, http://politicalgraveyard.com/bio/kaufman.html#R9MoJ2IR6.

85. [Testimony of Robert Cole], Court records of *Mary Oliver, et. al., v. Daniel Kaufman*, November Court of 1847, Papers No. 32, File box November 1847 – January 1848, pp. 4–5, Office of the Prothonotary, Cumberland County Courthouse, Carlisle, Pennsylvania. Hereafter referred to as "Cole testimony." Some local historians believe African American workers sometimes hid fugitives in limestone caves near the furnace.

86. Richard L. Tritt, "The Underground Railroad at Boiling Springs," in Richard L. Tritt and Randy Watts, eds., *At a Place Called the Boiling Springs* (Carlisle, Pa.: Sesquicentennial Publications Committee, 1995), p. 113; [Cross-examination of Robert Cole], *Oliver v. Kaufman*, Papers No. 32, loose, unnumbered sheet of paper.

87. "Cole testimony"; Tritt, *Boiling Springs*, pp. 113–14.

88. Tritt, *Boiling Springs*, p. 114.

89. Tritt, *Boiling Springs*, pp. 114–15.

90. "Cole Testimony"; "To the Jury," *Oliver v. Kaufman*, court records.

91. An individual named Cole was implicated in an attempted fugitive slave rescue in Lancaster in 1851. Whether the individual was Robert Cole, a relative, or unrelated I could not determine.

92. As a result, the final legal documents at the federal level read *Oliver v. Weakly*, not *Oliver v. Kaufman*.

93. "A Statement of Facts," Handbill, Cumberland County Historical Society, 1848, [Folder] P-4-6.

94. "A Statement of Facts." Receipt, "Received of Samuel May . . . ," March 31, 1854, and "Received of Samuel May . . . ," May 10, 1854, Ms B.1.6.v.5 no. 19 and no. 25, Miller-McKim papers, Weston Sisters Collection, Rare Book Department, Boston Public Library. The odd figure in the last amount indicates that it was probably an accumulation of small contributions from a number of individuals.

95. [Notes on Michael Buck], Jeremiah Zeamer Papers, Container 40, Folder 7, "Slavery," Cumberland County Historical Society (CCHS), Carlisle, Pennsylvania. Mary C. Bobb, "An Underground Railroad," *Lamberton and Hamilton Library Prize Essays*, v. 1 (1923), 2, CCHS.

96. G. Craig Caba, "Episodes of Gettysburg and the Underground Railroad," First Annual Underground Railroad and Abolition Conference, Harrisburg Area Community College, February 24, 2001.

5. Controversy and Christiana: The Fugitive Slave Issue in South Central Pennsylvania, 1850–51

1. G. Craig Caba, "Episodes of Gettysburg and the Underground Railroad," First Annual Underground Railroad and Abolition Seminar, Harrisburg Area Community College, February 24, 2001. Charles W. Griest to Friend David, February 1884. Courtesy of Debra McCauslin.

2. John F. Coleman, *The Disruption of the Pennsylvania Democracy 1848–1860* (Harrisburg, Pa.: Pennsylvania Historical & Museum Commission, 1975), p. 11. Mark E. Neely, Jr., *The Divided Union* (Cambridge, Mass.: Harvard University Press, 2002), pp. 62–64.

3. In early 1850, the *Compiler* reprinted a piece from the *Harrisburg Keystone*, which admitted that there was no doubt "the people of Pennsylvania are opposed to the extension of slavery into the territories." "Slavery and Instructions," *Compiler*, January 28, 1850, p. 2 c. 3.

4. Untitled [New volume of the *Star*], *Star*, March 19, 1852, p. 2 c. 3.

5. Jonathan H. Earle, *Jacksonian Democracy and the Politics of Free Soil* (Chapel Hill: University of North Carolina Press, 2005).

6. Arthur C. Cole, *The Irrepressible Conflict 1850–1865* (New York: The Macmillan Company, 1934), pp. 228–29; Avery Craven, *The Coming of the Civil War* (Chicago: University of Chicago Press, 1942; 2nd ed. 1957), pp. 340–44, 365, 371. As the 1850s progressed, however, the tone in south central Pennsylvania became more biting and partisan on issues such Kansas and the status of African Americans.

7. *Congressional Globe*, 31st Congress, 1st session, 21:99, 103; appendix, p. 79 cited by Stanley W. Campbell, *The Slave Catchers* (Chapel Hill: University of North Carolina Press, 1968; reprint, New York: W. W. Norton, 1972), pp. 15–16. "Clay on Slavery Question," *Star*, February 8, 1850, p. 2, c. 2–3.

8. "Sick of the discussion of the Slave Question," *Compiler*, February 4, 1850, p. 2 c. 3; "Union Meetings," *Compiler*, March 4, 1850, p. 2 c. 1; "Democratic Union Meeting in New York," *Compiler*, March 11, 1850, p. 2 c. 2; "Democratic Union Meeting in Philadelphia on the 22d," *Compiler*, March 4, 1850, p. 2 c. 4.

9. "Dissolution of the Union," *Compiler*, January 21, 1850, p. 3 c. 2; "Disunion," *Sentinel*, May 6, 1850, p. 2 c. 5; "Slavery and Disunion," *Star*, February 8, 1850, p. 2 c. 3. "Congressional," *Star*, February 1, 1850, p. 2 c. 5.

10. "Congress: The Slavery Question in the House," *Compiler*, February 25, 1850, p. 2 c. 2; "Mr. McLanahan's Speech," *Compiler*, March 4, 1850, p. 2 c. 1.

11. "Speech of Mr. Cooper of Pennsylvania on the Compromise Bill," *Daily National Intelligencer*, July 4, 1850. Cooper's speech was so long that none of the Adams County newspapers carried it in full. Later, Cooper would oppose the fugitive slave provisions while supporting the rest of the Compromise. He would claim to be personally opposed to slavery, but warned, "However our sympathies are towards the fugitive, we cannot take him from his master's service." "Compliment to the Hon. James Cooper," *Star*, October 25, 1850, p. 2 c. 1; "Tender of a Public Dinner—Letter from the Hon. James Cooper," *Star*, November 22, 1850, p. 2 c. 4–5.

12. Michael F. Holt, *Rise and Fall of the American Whig Party* (New York: Oxford University Press, 1999), p. 507.

13. J., "Senator Cooper," Chester County, Pa., May 11, 1850, *National Era*, August 8, 1850.

14. "Congressional," *Star*, February 15, 1850, p. 2 c. 5–6; "Speech of the Hon. James Cooper," *Star*, March 1, 1850, p. 2 c. 3; "Disunion Petition," *Compiler*, February 18, 1850, p. 2 c. 2. The petitions advocated peaceable separation rather than continued entanglement between the free North and the slaveholding South, a position then held by some Quakers and some Garrisonian abolitionists.

15. Isaac Fisher to Samuel Calvin, July 22, 1850, Calvin Manuscripts, cited by Holt, *Rise and Fall*, p. 507; J. Howard Wert, "Old Time Notes of Adams County," *Star & Sentinel*, October 4, 1905.

16. "Congress," *Star*, April 26, 1850, p. 2 c. 5. Cooper had been one of the few Northern Whigs to support the committee. Holt, *Rise and Fall of the Whig Party*, pp. 495, 504, 506–9, 512–13. Holman Hamilton, *Prologue to Conflict: The Crisis and Compromise of 1850* (Lexington, Ky.: University of Kentucky Press, 1964).

17. Stevens' June 10th speech opposing the Compromise has been generally slighted by his biographers, undeservedly so. Richard N. Current, *Old Thad Stevens: A Study of Ambition* (Madison: University of Wisconsin Press, 1942), p. 88; Fawn Brodie, *Thaddeus Stevens: Scourge of the South* (New York: W. W. Norton, 1959), p. 113. However, Beverly Wilson Palmer and Holly Byers Ochoa are to be commended for including the entire speech in the *Selected Papers of Thaddeus Stevens* (Pittsburgh: University of Pittsburgh Press, 1997), pp. 110–30.

18. "Congressional," *Star*, June 14, 1850, p. 2 c. 6–7; "Speech of Thaddeus Stevens of Pennsylvania on the California Question," *Star*, June 28, 1850, p. 2 c. 2ff; Palmer and Ochoa, eds., *Selected Papers of Thaddeus Stevens*, pp. 110–30.

19. "Last Speech of Thaddeus Stevens," *Compiler*, July 8, 1850, p. 2 c. 6. "Mr. Stevens' Speech," *Star*, June 28, 1850, p. 3 c. 2.

20. "Governor's Message: Special Message of the Governor," *Sentinel*, April 1, 1850, p. 1 c. 5–6.

21. Untitled, *Star*, March 19, 1850, p. 2 c. 3; "Governor's message," *Star*, April 5, 1850, p. 2 c. 4.

22. "The Fugitive Slave Bill [State PLL]," *Star*, April 26, 1850, p. 2 c. 7; "The Dough Faces in Council," *Star*, May 3, 1850, p. 2 c. 6; Joel H. Sibley, "James Buchanan," in Paul S. Boyer, et. al., eds., *The Oxford Companion to United States History* (New York: Oxford University Press, 2001), pp. 89–90.

23. Thomas Morris confirms that Buchanan's "partisans were at the back of the movement to repeal the state law." Thomas Morris, *Free Men All! The Personal Liberty Laws of the North 1780–1860* (Baltimore: Johns Hopkins University, 1974), p. 154.

24. "The Fugitive Slave Bill [PLL repeal]," *Star*, April 5, 1850, p. 2 c. 4; "The Fugitive Slave Bill [State PLL]," *Star*, April 26, 1850, p. 2 c. 7.

25. "A Chase," *Star*, June 14, 1850, p. 2 c. 6. Gettysburg had an African American–led Slave Rescue Society since 1841, but it was not clear if this individual was affiliated with it.

26. "Slave Hunting" and "More Negro Catching," *Star*, August 23, 1850, p. 2 c. 6; Untitled, *Compiler*, August 19, 1850, p. 2 c. 6. See Stanley Harrold, *Border War: Fighting over Slavery Before the Civil War* (Chapel Hill: University of North Carolina Press, 2010), p. 136.

27. "Our Country—Its Perils—Moral/Religious Decline," *Star*, April 5, 1850, p. 2 c. 6–7.

28. "Address of the Whig State Central Committee to the Freemen of Pennsylvania," *Star*, September 12, 1850; "Address of the Lancaster County Whig Committee, To their Brother Whigs of Lancaster and Other Counties of Pennsylvania," *Star*, October 4, 1850, p. 1 c. 3; "Address of the Democratic State Committee," *Compiler*, September 2, 1850, p. 2 c. 1.

29. "Slave Excitement at Harrisburg," *Compiler*, September 2, 1850, p. 2 c. 5; "Slave Excitement at Harrisburg," *Star*, August 30, 1850, p. 2 c. 2; Untitled, *Compiler*, December 2, 1850, p. 3 c. 1.

30. Slave catchers used similar tactics to evade Massachusetts' personal liberty laws.

31. Untitled, *Star*, November 15, 1850, p. 2 c. 6.

32. Gerald Eggert, "The Fugitive Slave Law in Harrisburg: A Case Study," *Pennsylvania Magazine of History and Biography* 109 (1985): pp. 537–70. "Affairs in Kansas," *Star*, March 21, 1857, p. 2 c. 2.

33. Jonathan Katz, *Resistance at Christiana* (New York: Thomas Y. Crowell Company, 1974), pp. 54, 42–43; Thomas P. Slaughter, *Bloody Dawn: The Christiana Riot and Racial Violence in the Antebellum North* (New York: Oxford University Press, 1991), pp. 46–51.

34. Irene E. Williams, "The Operation of the Fugitive Slave Law in Western Pennsylvania from 1850 to 1860," *Western Pennsylvania Historical Magazine* 4 (1921): p. 152; "Fugitive

Slaves," *Compiler*, October 21, 1850, p. 2 c. 6; Harrold, *Border War*, p. 149; Untitled, *Star*, October 25, 1850, p. 2 c. 2.

35. Hiram E. Wertz, "The Underground Railroad Along South Mountain [1912]," in Caba, ed., *Episodes of Gettysburg and the Underground Railroad* (Gettysburg, Pa.: G. Craig Caba Antiques, 1998), p. 99; "The Fugitive Slave Law," *Star*, October 25, 1850, p. 2 c. 6–7. "Gamaliel Bailey," Answers.com.

36. "Detestable Doctrine," *Compiler*, October 28, 1850, p. 2 c. 6; Untitled, *Star*, October 25, 1850, p. 2 c. 7; Untitled [Weakly case] *Sentinel*, October 28, 1850, p. 2 c. 2; "The Fugitive Slave Law," *Sentinel*, November 4, 1850, p. 2 c. 3–4.

37. "The Fugitive Slave Law—Opinion of Mr. Crittenden," *Compiler*, October 28, 1850, p. 2. c.1.

38. "President Fillmore and the Fugitive Slave Law," *Compiler*, November 4, 1850, p. 2 c. 2; "President Fillmore and the Fugitive Slave Law," *Sentinel*, November 4, 1850, p. 2 c. 3; "Semi-Official Declaration," *Star*, November 8, 1850, p. 2 c. 4; "Letter from President Fillmore Relative to the Fugitive Slave Law," *Compiler*, November 25, 1850, p. 3 c. 1; "Letter from President Fillmore Relative to the Fugitive Slave Law," *Star*, November 22, 1850, p. 2 c. 3; Michael Holt, *The Fate of Their Country* (New York: Oxford University Press, 2003), p. 82.

39. "Vermont and the Fugitive Slave Law," *Star*, December 13, 1850, p. 2 c. 5; "Address to the People of Maryland, Virginia, North Carolina, South Carolina, Florida, Alabama, Tennessee, Kentucky, Louisiana, Texas, Missouri, Mississippi, and Arkansas," "The Nashville Convention," *Daily National Intelligencer*, July 13, 1850, p. 2 c. 4; "Georgia Convention," *Star*, December 20, 1850, p. 2 c. 6; Untitled [Vermont nullification], *Sentinel*, December 23, 1850, p. 2 c. 2. In Gettysburg, the *Compiler* labeled this "treason in Vermont," an indicator that Democrats were willing to label resistance to the fugitive slave as treason nine months before Christiana. "Treason in Vermont," *Compiler*, December 23, 1850, p. 2 c. 6; "The Vermont Nullification Law," *Compiler*, December 30, 1850, p. 3 c. 2.

40. Untitled, *Star*, November 22, 1850, p. 2 c. 7.

41. "Whig County Ticket," *Compiler*, August 5, 1850, p. 2 c. 4.

42. Coleman, *Disruption of Pennsylvania Democracy*, pp. 26–28, 34–35. In 1848, Pennsylvania had not created the office of lieutenant governor, so the Speaker of the Senate was next in line.

43. Coleman, *Disruption of Pennsylvania Democracy*, p. 35; [Untitled—Alleged Planned Duel], *Compiler*, February 2, 1852, p. 2 c. 3.

44. "Silver Grays and Wooly Heads," and "Very Good," *Compiler*, December 23, 1850, p. 2 c. 5 and p. 3 c. 1; Coleman, *Disruption of the Pennsylvania Democracy*, pp. 33–34. The terms had originated in New York to indicate the split between the followers of William H. Seward and Martin Van Buren, but they were widely applied in Pennsylvania as well.

45. "William F. Johnston's Message, Jan. 7, 1851," *Compiler*, January 13, 1851, p. 2 c. 5–6; "Governor's Message," *Sentinel*, January 13, 1851, p. 2 c. 1.

46. "Speech of Hon. Joshua R. Giddings," *Star*, February 28, 1851, p. 1 c. 2; Untitled [Comment on Giddings' Speech], *Star*, February 28, 1851, p. 3 c. 1; Michael F. Holt, *Fate of Their Country*, p. 82; "Important Pledge by Members of Congress," *Compiler*, January 27,

1851, p. 2 c. 5; "Congressional," *Star*, January 17, 1851, p. 2 c. 7; "Congress," *Compiler*, January 20, 1851, p. 2 c. 5.

47. "Congressional," *Star*, February 21, 1851, p. 3 c. 3–5; William C. Davis, *Rhett* (Columbia, S.C.: University of South Carolina Press, 2001), pp. 293–94.

48. "Union Meeting at York," *Compiler*, January 20, 1851, p. 2 c. 2; "Another Union Meeting," *Star*, March 7, 1851, p. 2 c. 4.

49. "African Colonization and the Recognition of Liberia," *Star*, January 31, 1851, p. 3 c. 2; "American Colonization Society," *Star*, January 31, 1851, p. 1 c. 6–7; "The Colonization Cause," *Star*, February 7, 1851, p. 2 c. 2; "Emigration to Liberia," *Star*, May 16, 1851, p. 2 c. 5; "Penn'a Colonization Society," *Star*, May 23, 1851. This was the first time the paper had noted the colonization society's Address to the Clergy of All Denominations in many years, even though it was issued annually.

50. "Another Fugitive Slave Case—Rescue by a Boston Mob," *Compiler*, February 24, 1851, p. 2 c. 2; "Another Arrest of a Fugitive Slave" and "The Affair at Boston," *Star*, February 15, 1851, p. 2 c.3; "Government Officer Arrested in Boston," *Compiler*, March 3, 1851, p. 2 c. 1.

51. "The Boston Slave Case—Proclamation of the President" and "Important Document," *Compiler*, February 24, 185, p. 2 c. 4.; "Boston Mob—Proclamation of the President" and "A Proclamation," *Star*, February 21, 1851, p. 3 c. 2. "The Boston Slave Case—Proclamation of the President" and "Important Document," *Compiler*, February 24, 185, p. 2 c. 4.

52. "A Fugitive Slave Case," *Star*, January 3, 1851, p. 2 c. 6–7; "Fugitive Slave Case," *Compiler*, January 6, 1851, p. 2 c. 3.; "Conflict with Fugitive Slaves," *Star*, January 10, 1851, p. 3 c. 2.

53. "Fugitive Slave Case in Pottsville," *Star*, March 7, 1851, p. 3 c. 3.

54. "Riot at Columbia, Pa.," *Star*, February 21, 1851, p. 3 c. 2.

55. "The Mitchel[l] Case," *Star*, March 21, 1851, p. 2 c. 2; "Kidnapping," *Star*, March 21, 1851, p. 2 c. 5; "More Kidnapping," *Star*, March 28, 1851, p. 2 c. 3.

56. "The Penalty for Kidnapping," *Star*, March 28, 1851, p. 2 c. 1; W. U. Hensel, "The Christiana Riot, Chapter II," *Journal of the Lancaster County Historical Society* 15 (1911): p. 8.

57. "Boston Fugitive Slave Case," *Star*, April 11, 1851, p. 3 c. 4; "The Boston Fugitive Slave Case," *Star*, April 18, 1851, p. 2 c. 1; "The Fugitive Slave Simms," *Star*, May 2, 1851, p. 2 c. 5; "More Trouble in Boston," *Compiler*, April 7, 1851, p. 2 c. 2; Untitled, *Compiler*, April 7, 1851, p. 3 c. 2; "Great Excitement in Boston," *Compiler*, April 14, 1851, p. 2 c. 6; "Interesting from Boston," *Compiler*, April 21, 1851, p. 2 c. 2.

58. G. Craig Caba, "Episodes of Gettysburg and the Underground Railroad," February 24, 2001; "Leading Colored Citizen . . . Active Agent in the Underground Railroad," *Gettysburg Compiler*, June 13, 1906, p. 5 c. 3; "Arrest of a Fugitive Slave—Threatened Riot," *Harrisburg Daily American (DA)*, April 7, 1851, p. 3 c. 2; "The Boston Slave Case," *DA*, April 8, 1851, p. 2 c. 1; "Further Particulars of the Boston Slave Case," *DA*, April 9, 1851, p. 2 c. 5 and April 10, 1851, p. 2 c. 4; "Fugitive Slave Case—Mr. Webster," *DA*, April 11, 1851, p. 2 c. 5; "The Boston Slave Case—The Fugitive Remanded," *DA*, April 14, 1851, p. 3 c. 1–3.

59. "Lebanon Kidnapping Case," *Star*, April 25, 1851, p. 2 c. 2.

60. "Wooly Heads and Silver Grays," *Compiler*, March 17, 1851, p. 2 c. 3; "Kidnapping Law," *Compiler*, March 31, 1851, p. 2 c. 2.

61. "The Anti-Kidnapping Law," *Star*, April 4, 1851, p. 3 c. 1; "From Harrisburg," *Star*, April 4, 1851, p. 3 c. 2; "From Harrisburg," *Star*, April 18, 1851, p. 3 c. 2. "The Next Presidency—Pennsylvania," *Compiler*, May 5, 1851. The *Star* claimed that all Whigs had voted for the one section that passed. This was not technically correct—all of the Whigs had voted to eviscerate the House bill and limit it to one section. Then seven Whig Senators refused to vote for even that.

62. In Pennsylvania, the governor could keep a bill passed late in the session "in his pocket" and refuse to sign it until three days after the next legislative session convened in December.

63. Untitled [Harrisburg case], *Star*, May 2, 1851, p. 3 c. 1.

64. "Fugitive Slave Law in the South," *Star*, May 23, 1851, p. 3 c. 1; "The Fugitive Slave Law in Massachusetts," *Star*, May 23, 1851, p. 3 c. 3.

65. "Nigger Catching," *Star*, May 30, 1851, p. 3 c. 3.

66. "Orful [Awful]," *Star*, June 13, 1851, p. 3 c. 2.

67. Mr. Webb to Thomas Shipley, January 1822, Papers of the Pennsylvania Abolition Society, Miscellaneous Correspondence, reel 13, 9:19; *Albany Patriot*, February 7, 1844, cited by Harrold, *Subversives*, p. 91; (Shippensburg constable J. Thompson Rippey) O.P.M. to Jeremiah Zeamer, September 25, 1901, p. 2, Jeremiah Zeamer Papers, Folder 40:9, Cumberland County Historical Society; "The Chambersburg Telegrams," *New York Herald*, June 19, 1863, p. 2 c. 2. Arnold C. Hackenbruch Collection, University of Notre Dame. The *New York Times* called Rippey "Sheriff Ripley." "The Rebels in Pennsylvania," *New York Times*, June 25, 1863, p. 1 c. 1.

68. "The Fugitive Slave Law," *Star*, June 20, 1851, p. 1 c. 6; "Sound Democratic Principles [Reading Platform], *Compiler*, June 23, 1851, p. 2 c. 5; "Bigler's Inconsistency Clearly Proved," *Star*, June 20, 1851, p. 3 c. 3; "The Thousand-legged Party," *Star*, June 6, 1851, p. 2 c. 1. The *Compiler* tried to excuse these two politicians' support by portraying the bill as passing in a fever of excitement.

69. "Whig State Convention," *Star*, June 27, 1851, p. 3 c. 2; "Gov. Johnston's Speech," *Star*, July 4, 1851, p. 2 c. 1; "Gov. Johnston Renominated," *Compiler*, June 30, 1851, p. 2 c. 3.

70. "Gov. Johnston's Speech," *Star*, July 4, 1851, p. 2 c. 1.

71. "Governor Johnston will be with us in September," *Star*, July 25, 1851, p. 2 c. 5; "The Fourth at Easton," *Star*, July 25, 1851, p. 1 c. 6–7. Varying accounts of the visit can be found in "The Welcome to Governor Johnston," *Star*, September 5, 1851, p. 2 c. 5. "Governor Johnston's Visit to Gettysburg," *Star*, September 12, 1851, p. 2 c. 4; "Governor Johnston's Visit to Gettysburg—A Humiliating Spectacle," *Compiler*, September 8, 1851, p. 2 c. 2–3.

72. Katz, *Resistance at Christiana*, p. 67. Myles and Florence Jackson, producers, "Two Man War at Christiana, 1851," (recording), Viewpoints on American Abolition (Random House, 1971), cited by Katz, *Resistance at Christiana*, pp. 69–70. Living near the border of the free states often locked slaves and their masters into a dance of resistance, special privileges, promised freedom, and uncertainty. Brenda E. Stevenson, *Life in Black and White* (New York: Oxford University Press, 1996).

73. Katz, *Resistance at Christiana*, pp. 28, 35–43; Slaughter, *Bloody Dawn*, p. 51.

74. Gorsuch had first tried to get the slaves extradited as criminals, but Johnston had turned down the request. Katz, *Resistance at Christiana*, pp. 72–73; Slaughter, *Bloody Dawn*, pp. 44–45, 52.

75. Katz, *Resistance at Christiana*, pp. 81–82; Slaughter, *Bloody Dawn*, pp. 57–58.

76. Katz, *Resistance at Christiana*, pp. 83–86; Slaughter, *Bloody Dawn*, pp. 59–62.

77. Katz, *Resistance at Christiana*, pp. 87–91; Slaughter, *Bloody Dawn*, p. 62. Katz based his supposition on a number of contemporary accounts and a 1911 account of Christiana published by the Lancaster County Historical Society. Katz, *Resistance at Christiana*, pp. 91, 328–29, and n. 20.

78. Katz, *Resistance at Christiana*, pp. 92–109; Slaughter, *Bloody Dawn*, pp. 63–75.

79. Katz, *Resistance at Christiana*, pp. 137–38, 161–62. *Baltimore American*, September 20, 1851, handwritten copy in the Thaddeus Stevens papers (microfilm), Reel 1 (General Correspondence), TSP 9920.

80. "Attempted Arrest of Fugitive Slaves," *Compiler*, September 15, 1851, p. 2 c. 6; "The Christiana Tragedy," *Compiler*, September 22, 1851, p. 2 c. 2; "Governor Johnston, the Christiana Tragedy, His Tardy Proclamation," *Compiler*, September 22, 1851, p. 2 c. 4–5; "The Christiana Outrage: Letter from Rev. Mr. Gorsuch to Gov. Johnston," *Compiler*, September 29, 1851, p. 1 c. 5–6; Katz, *Resistance at Christiana*, pp. 156–61.

81. "Noble Letter from Gov. Johnston" and "The Christiana Riot and Locofoco Demagoguism," *Star*, September 19, 181, p. 2 c. 1–4; "The Rev. J. S. Gorsuch" and "The Slander Repelled" and "The Insolence of Slavery," *Star*, September 26, 1851, pp. 2–3; "Attorney General Franklin in Reply to Rev. Gorsuch," *Star*, October 3, 1851, p. 3 c. 1.

82. Jonathan Katz, *Resistance at Christiana*, pp. 156–61; Slaughter, *Bloody Dawn*, pp. 94–104.

83. "The Christiana Murder," *Star*, October 3, 1851 p. 1 c. 3; "The Union in Danger—False Alarm!" *Star*, October 3, 1851, p. 1 c. 6; "The Proof of the Atrocious Conspiracy," *Star*, October 10, 1851, p. 1 c. 4.

84. Reah Frazer Papers, Folder 13 (Runaway Slave Case), MG-53, Pennsylvania State Archives.

85. "Meeting at Hanover on Friday Last," *Star*, October 3, 1851, p. 2 c. 1–3; "Good Riddance," [at Frazer leaving Democratic party], *Compiler*, November 6, 1854, p. 3 c. 2; "Libel," *Adams Sentinel*, January 20, 1845, p. 3 c. 2. Frazer's speech was not the only sign that the 1851 election in south central Pennsylvania was becoming racially charged. In Gettysburg, the *Star* complained that Daniel Durkee, the defeated Whig candidate for local presiding judge, had been unfairly labeled an abolitionist and a "friend of the Niggers." (The paper admitted, however, that it was the charge that Durkee favored temperance that had likely damaged him the most). "President Judge—Official," *Star*, October 24, 1851, p. 2 c. 4. Bradley R. Hoch, *Thaddeus Stevens in Gettysburg* (Gettysburg, Pa.: Adams County Historical Society, 2005), p. 59.

86. "Fred. Douglass and the 'Silver Grays'" *Star*, November 14, 1851, p. 2 c. 7; "Emigration to Liberia," *Star*, October 17, 1851, p. 3 c.2. See also "For Liberia," *Star*, November 7, 1851, p. 3 c. 1–2.

87. With three selected jurors, Adams County matched Lancaster County for the most residents on the jury.

88. "The Christiana Rioters," *Star*, November 21, 1851, p. 2 c. 5; "The Treason Trials," *Star*, November 28, 1851, p. 2 c. 6; "Trial of the Christiana Rioters," *Compiler*, December 1, 1851, p. 2 c. 2; "The Christiana Trials," *Star*, November 14, 1851, p. 2 c. 3; "Indictments in the Christiana Outrage, &c." *Compiler*, November 3, 1851, p. 2 c. 1; "The Christiana Trials," *Compiler*, November 17, 1851, p. 2 c. 6.

89. "The Treason Trials," *Star*, December 4, 1851, p. 2 c. 4; "The Treason Trials," *Star*, December 12, 1851, p. 2 c. 4; "The Christiana Trials," *Compiler*, December 4, 1851, p. 3 c. 3.

90. "The Treason Trials," *Star*, December 12, 1851, p. 2 c. 4; "End of the 'Treason' Trials," *Star*, December 19, 1851, p. 2 c. 4–5; Katz, *Resistance at Christiana*, pp. 228–34.

91. "End of the 'Treason' Trials," *Star*, December 19, 1851, p. 2 c. 4–5.

6. Interlude: Kidnapping, Kansas, and the Rise of Race-Based Partisanship: The Decline of the Fugitive Slave Issue in South Central Pennsylvania, 1852–57

1. Stanley Harrold, *Border War: Fighting over Slavery before the Civil War* (Chapel Hill: University of North Carolina Press, 2010), p. 66. Harrold is discussing the right of transit, but a similar principle applies.

2. "Another Kidnapping Case," *Star*, January 9, 1852, p. 2 c. 6; "The Kidnapping Case," *Star*, January 16, 1852, p. 2 c. 4; "The Kidnapping Case at Baltimore," *Compiler*, January 19, 1852, p. 3 c. 1. The best treatment of this tangled and important case is George F. Nagle, "Kidnapping and Murder: How the Rachel Parker Case Galvanized Pennsylvania Popular Opinion Against the Fugitive Slave Law," First Annual Underground Railroad Conference, Temple University, February 13, 2004, http://www.afrolumens.org/ugrr/parker.html.

3. "A Most Righteous Act [Alberti Pardon]," *Compiler*, February 9, 1852, p. 2 c. 5; "Pardon of Alberti, the Kidnapper," *Star*, February 6, 1852, p. 2 c. 3. Stanley Harrold gives several examples from Kentucky, Ohio, Michigan, and Indiana of similar sorts of border *quid pro quo* pragmatism. Harrold, *Border War: Fighting over Slavery before the Civil War* (Chapel Hill: University of North Carolina Press, 2010), pp. 111, 180–2.

4. "Fugitive Slave Case—Fugitive Shot," *Compiler*, May 3, 1852, p. 3 c. 1; "Particulars of the Fugitive Slave Case," *Compiler*, May 3, 1852, p. 3 c. 1; "Murder of an Alleged Fugitive Slave in Columbia," *Star*, May 7, 1852, p. 2 c. 1; "The Columbia Homicide," *Star*, May 21, 1852, p. 2 c. 5. "Return of a Free Colored Boy from Baltimore to Harrisburg," *Compiler*, June 14, 1852, p. 3 c. 1. Gerald G. Eggert, "The Impact of the Fugitive Slave Law on Harrisburg: A Case Study," *Pennsylvania Magazine of History and Biography* 109 (1985), pp. 551–52.

5. Untitled, *Star*, June 18, 1852, p. 2 c. 3.

6. Untitled [Reprint from the York *Republican*], *Star*, June 25, 1852, p. 3 c. 1.

7. Eggert, "The Impact of the Fugitive Slave Law on Harrisburg," *Pennsylvania Magazine of History & Biography*, pp. 537–70; William E. Gienapp, "Nebraska, Nativism, and Rum: The Failure of Fusion in Pennsylvania, 1854," *Pennsylvania Magazine of History & Biography* 109 (1985): pp. 425–72; Nat Brandt and Yanna Brandt, *In the Shadow of the Civil War; The Passmore Williamson Case and the Coming of the Civil War* (Columbia, S.C.: University of South Carolina Press, 2007); John F. Coleman, *The Disruption of the Penn-*

sylvania Democracy, 1848–1860 (Harrisburg, Pa.: Pennsylvania Historical and Museum Commission, 1975), pp. 78, 84. This was largely a symbolic vote as Republicans fought against Know Nothings and others who sought to co-opt the new party at the state convention. Eventually, Williamson stood aside for another candidate.

8. (Wierman farm seizure) Untitled, *Star*, July 6, 1855, p. 2 c. 2; "The Negro-hunt at York Springs," *Star*, July 13, 1855, p. 3 c. 1; "Slave Hunt in Petersburg [York Springs]," July 13, 1855, p. 2 c. 3; Untitled, *Star*, July 20, 1855, p. 2 c. 2. (Fugitive slave case during election campaign) "Suspended Operations!" "That Habeas Corpus!" "Con-Fusion Train Off the Tracks," *Compiler*, November 10, 1856, p. 2 c. 1 and p. 2 c. 3. Curiously, no account of this case can be found in the *Star*, but additional details are in the *Sentinel*, Untitled, September 29, 1856, p. 2 c. 3.

9. "Freemen Look Here," *Star*, August 22, 1856, p. 2 c. 1; "Congress," *Star*, August 29, 1856, p. 3 c. 1; "A Challenge," *Star*, September 5, 1856, p. 2 c. 4; "Slave Hunt in America," *Star*, August 10, 1855, p. 2 c. 3.

10. Jean H. Baker brilliantly traced the importance of opposition to African Americans in Democratic political thought without fully exploring why this happened. This trend did not appear in Adams County until the 1856 presidential campaign, suggesting that in south central Pennsylvania, at least, it was tied to determined, if not desperate, efforts by Democrats to prevent Fremont from becoming the first Republican president. Baker, *Affairs of Party* (Ithaca: Cornell University Press, 1983; reprint, New York: Fordham University Press, 1998), pp. 177–258; Coleman, *Disruption of the Pennsylvania Democracy*, p. 92.

11. "Slavery Code of Kansas," *Adams Sentinel*, January 5, 1857, p. 2 c. 7; Untitled, *Adams Sentinel*, January 12, 1857, p. 5 c. 1.

12. "Who Are the Democratic Leaders," "Reasons for the Existence of an American Party," and "Amending the Naturalization Laws," *Star*, January 30, 1857, p. 2 c. 2–4.

13. "Affairs in Kansas," *Star*, March 21, 1857, p. 2 c. 2; "For Kansas," *Star*, May 8, 1857, p. 3 c. 1. Even a black resident of Gettysburg, probably Daniel Alexander Payne, had commented on the westward migration as early as the 1840s. "To the Church and Congregation at T.," *The Colored American* (New York), October 20, 1838.

14. "Union Convention," *Star*, March 27, 1857, p. 2 c. 3; "Meeting of the Republican and American State Convention," *Sentinel*, March 30, 1857, p. 3 c. 3.

15. "Call for a Union State Convention," *Star*, March 6, 1857, p. 2 c. 2; "Another Coalition," *Compiler*, March 2, 1857, p. 2 c. 2.

16. "The Black Republicans and Know Nothing State Convention," *Compiler*, April 6, 1857, p. 2 c. 3; "Abolitionism and Know Nothingism Below Par," *Compiler*, April 27, 1857, p. 2 c. 2.

17. "The Nomination," "State Convention," "State Convention—The State Ticket," *Star*, April 3, 1857, p. 2 c. 1–4; "The Platform," *Star*, April 3, 1857, p. 2 c. 5–6; "The Platform," *Sentinel*, April 6, 1857, p. 2 c. 6. Five of the platform's eight position planks dealt with slavery, slavery extension, Kansas, and *Dred Scott*. One plank rehearsed the position of the national Republican Party, that it was the "duty of Congress to prohibit in the Territories, those twin relics of barbarism, Polygamy and Slavery."

18. "Read! Read!" *Compiler*, September 21, 1857, p. 2 c. 5.

19. This important election approached with the *Star* under new leadership. In May, D. A. Buehler turned over the editorship to John T. McIlhenny. Both men assured readers that the paper would continue to urge both American (Know Nothing) and Republican principles, although Know Nothing issues such as immigration and "Jesuitism" were mentioned first. Still, McIlhenny promised that "nor will that 'sum of all villainies'—the curse of human slavery—receive aid or comfort at our hands." "To The Patrons of the *Star*," and "To Our Friends," *Star*, May 8, 1857, p. 2 c. 3. McIlhenny may have been a recent convert to slavery agitation, however, because he only dated the "unchristian" policy of the South as extending from the Kansas-Nebraska act. According to the new editor, slavery must not be interfered with in the South, but its blighting institution must not be permitted to spread. With the transition of the *Star* to McIlhenny, an evidence problem arises, as a continuous run of the newspaper during his stewardship does not exist, and this valuable source is mostly unavailable until 1868. For the rest of 1857, we must rely on the *Compiler* and the *Sentinel*, whose coverage was dominated by the statewide election.

20. "Panic in New York," *Compiler*, August 31, 1857, p. 2 c. 3; "Suspension of the Bank," *Compiler*, October 5, 1857, p. 3 c. 1.

21. Coleman, *Disruption of the Pennsylvania Democracy*, pp. 108–9; "A Chilling Affair," *Compiler*, October 5, 1857, p. 2 c. 5–7.

22. "The Last of the 'Proviso,'" and "Exit Mr. Wilmot," *Compiler*, October 26, 1857, p. 2 c. 2.

23. Coleman, *Disruption of the Pennsylvania Democracy*, 110.

7. Revival of the Fugitive Slave Issue, 1858–61

1. Eric Foner, *Free Soil, Free Labor, Free Men* (New York: Oxford University Press, 1970), pp. 134–35. I am indebted to William Blair for sharpening my thinking about border Democrats.

2. The experience of border Pennsylvania was this time different from Ohio, where Republicans had agitated the fugitive slave issue after the Oberlin fugitive slave rescues. In the process, the party nearly split. Foner, *Free Soil, Free Labor, Free Men*, pp. 136–37.

3. "Democratic Meeting in Philadelphia," *Compiler*, January 4, 1858, p. 2 c. 2; "Kansas," *Compiler*, January 11, 1858, p. 3 c. 2; "Important Message from the President," *Compiler*, February 9, 1851, p. 2 c. 1 and p. 3 c.1; "Pennsylvania with the President," February 22, 1858, p. 2 c. 2; "Senate Bill to Admit Kansas," *Compiler*, April 5, 1858, p. 2 c. 2–4; "Speech of Hon. Geo. Brewer," March 29, 1858, p. 1 c. 4–7; "Speech of Hon. Wilson Reilly of Pennsylvania In Favor of the Admission of Kansas, Under the Lecompton Constitution," *Compiler*, April 12, 1858, p. 1 c. 3–7; "Decline of the Anti-Slavery Sentiment," *Compiler*, April 26, 1858, p. 2 c. 6; "Mr. Reilly's Speech," *Compiler*, April 26, 1858, p. 2 c. 5.

4. "Attempt to Kidnap," *Sentinel*, February 8, 1858, p. 2 c. 3; [Untitled], *Sentinel*, February 15, 1858, p. 2 c. 4; "An Alleged Attempt to Kidnap," *Compiler*, February 15, 1858, p. 2 c. 6.

5. Elsie Singmaster, *A Boy at Gettysburg* (Boston: Houghton Mifflin and Company, 1924), pp. 59–61.

6. "Union of 'Sam' and 'Sambo,'" *Compiler*, July 19, 1858, p. 1 c. 7.

7. "The Mulatto State Convention," *Compiler*, July 26, 1858, p. 2 c. 4. This was a reprint from the *Pennsylvanian*.

8. "Republican Scheme," *Compiler*, August 16, 1858 p. 2 c. 3; "The Re-Construction of Parties," *Compiler*, August 30, 1858, p. 1 c. 7; Bruce Collins, "The Democrats' Loss of Pennsylvania in 1858," *Pennsylvania Magazine of History and Biography* 109 (1985): pp. 499–536.

9. "The People's County Ticket," *Sentinel*, August 9, 1858, p. 2 c. 3; "County Convention," *Sentinel*, August 9, 1858, p. 2 c. 1; "Our Candidate for Congress," *Sentinel*, August 16, 1858, p. 2 c. 3; "Congressional Conference," *Sentinel*, August 16, 1858, p. 2 c. 5; "Opposition Convention," *Compiler*, August 9, 1858, p. 2 c. 1–4.

10. "Opposition Convention," *Compiler*, August 9, 1858, p. 2 c. 1–4; "The 'Kane Letter' and the Opposition State Convention," *Compiler*, September 20, 1858, p. 2 c. 4; "Free Trade McPherson—Keep it Before the People," *Compiler*, October 4, 1858, p. 1 c. 5.

11. "The XVIIth Congressional District," *Sentinel*, October 18, 1858, p. 2 c. 4. The district also included some parts of Cumberland County, which went for the Democratic candidate.

12. Eric Foner identifies a radical Republican-led campaign to nullify the fugitive slave law in "almost every northern state." He discusses well-known examples in Massachusetts, Wisconsin, and Ohio, but I have not found anything similar in Pennsylvania. Foner, *Free Soil, Free Labor, Free Men*, pp. 133–43.

13. "By Their Fruits Shall Ye Judge Them," *Compiler*, January 3, 1859, p. 2 c. 4; "Blacks in Office," January 3, 1859, p. 2 c. 2; "The Directors of the Republican Party and Their Object," *Compiler*, January 31, 1859, p. 2 c. 3.

14. "News, etc." and "One of the Fruits of the People's Party," *Compiler*, May 23, 1859, p. 2 c. 1 and p. 2 c. 3. "What is Black Republicanism?" *Compiler*, June 20, 1859, p. 2 c. 2; Untitled, *Compiler*, July 4, 1859, p. 2 c. 4; "The Two Year Amendment," *Compiler*, August 15, 1859, p. 1 c. 7.

15. "Republicanism," *Compiler*, April 4, 1859, p. 2 c. 2. The paper stated that the abolitionists "could not prevail on the people to swallow their hash of white and black meat, in the style introduced by cooks Garrison and Giddings, and cookess Abby Kelley," so "Republican negroism" had emerged as "a snake in the grass."

16. "Important Decision of the U.S. Supreme Court," *Compiler*, March 1, 1859, p. 3 c. 1. For the particulars of the case, see Jenni Parrish, "The *Booth* Cases: Final Step to the Civil War," in John R. McKivigan, *Abolitionism and American Law* (New York: Garland Publishing, 1999), pp. 237–78 and H. Robert Baker, *The Rescue of Joshua Glover: A Fugitive Slave, the Constitution, and the Coming of the Civil War* (Athens: Ohio University Press, 2006).

17. "Fugitive Slave Arrested," *Compiler*, April 11, 1859, p 3 c. 1. The evening gathering was probably an after-hours meeting with speeches and resolutions.

18. The tangled ambiguities of Maryland manumissions are explored in Max Grivno, *Gleanings of Freedom: Free and Slave Labor along the Mason-Dixon Line, 1790–1860* (Urbana: University of Illinois Press, 2011).

19. Samuel P. Bates, et al., *History of Cumberland and Adams Counties, Pennsylvania* (Chicago: Warner Beers, 1886), p. 222; "Negro Excitement," *Compiler*, June 20, 1859, p. 2 c. 5; "Negro Abduction Case," *Compiler*, June 27, 1859.

20. A Hard Dose for Old Whigs," *Compiler*, September 26, 1859, p. 1 c. 7; "The Republican Creed," *Republican Compiler*, October, 1859, p. 1 c. 6–7; Don Fehrenbacher, *The Slaveholding Republic* (New York: Oxford University Press, 2001), pp. 238–39; Untitled and "The [Opposition] Platform," *Compiler*, July 4, 1859, p. 2 c. 4 and p. 3 c. 1.

21. A. K. McClure, *Old Time Notes of Pennsylvania* (Philadelphia: J. C. Winston Company, 1905), pp. 360–61; William McFeely, *Frederick Douglass* (New York: W. W. Norton, 1991), pp. 195–97; W. E. B. Du Bois, *John Brown* (Philadelphia: George W. Jacobs & Company, 1909; reprint, New York: Modern Library, 2001), pp. 177–78; Edward L. Ayers, *In the Presence of Mine Enemies* (New York: W. W. Norton, 2003), pp. 13–14.

22. Ayers, *In the Presence*, pp. 7–9; Benjamin Quarles, *Allies for Freedom: Blacks and John Brown* (Oxford: Oxford University Press, 1974 and Urbana: University of Illinois Press, 1972; New York: combined Da Capo Press edition, 2001), pp. 76–77; see also McFeely, *Frederick Douglass*, pp. 95–97.

23. McFeely, *Frederick Douglass*, pp. 196–97; Ayers, *In the Presence*, p. 16.

24. A. K. McClure, *Old Time Notes*, pp. 364–69; Ayers, *In the Presence*, pp. 38–40.

25. See the Annual Report of the American Anti-Slavery Society by the Executive Committee for the Year Ending May 1, 1860 (The Anti-Slavery History of the John Brown Year) (New York: Anti-Slavery Society, 1861; reprint, New York: Arno Press, 1969), pp. 138–39.

26. I have been unable to determine whether Adams County's Robert Goodloe Harper was related to Robert Goodloe Harper, the procolonization Congressman from South Carolina and later Maryland.

27. Untitled, *Sentinel*, May 14, 1860, p. 2 c. 2; "The Chicago Platform," *Sentinel*, May 28, 1860, p. 2 c. 1–3; "Mr. Lincoln a Conservative Man," *Sentinel*, June 4, 1860, p. 2 c. 7.

28. McClure, *Old Time Notes*, p. 352; Collins, "Democrats' Loss," pp. 535–36.

29. "National Democratic Platform," *Compiler*, July 23, 1860, p. 1 c. 6–7; "Mr. Douglas' Letter of Acceptance" and "Acceptance of Hon. John C. Breckenridge of the Nomination to the Presidency," *Compiler*, July 16, 1860, p. 1 c. 4–6.

30. David M. Potter, *The Impending Crisis, 1848–1861* (New York: Harper Torchbooks, 1976), p. 516; William C. Wright, *The Secession Movement in the Middle Atlantic States* (Rutherford, N.J.: Rutgers University Press, 1973); Untitled [*Chambersburg Valley Spirit's* early endorsement of Breckenridge], *Compiler*, May 30, 1859, p. 2 c. 2; "Secession," *Compiler*, August 13, 1860, p. 2 c. 5.

31. "The Two Candidates for Governor—The Contrast," *Compiler*, June 11, 1860, p. 2 c. 2.

32. Singmaster, *Boy at Gettysburg*, pp. 43–44; "'Wide Awakes,'" *Compiler*, June 20, 1860, p. 3 c. 1; "Flag Raising," *Compiler*, June 10, 1861, p. 1 c. 6; "History of a Wide Awake," *Compiler*, February 25, 1861, p. 1 c. 7.

33. "Plan of Union Adopted by the Democratic State Committee," *Compiler*, July 23, 1860, p. 2 c. 1; "Union on the National Electoral Ticket," *Compiler*, August 27, 1860, p. 2 c. 3; John Coleman, *Disruption of the Pennsylvania Democracy, 1848–1860* (Harrisburg, Pa.: Pennsylvania Historical and Museum Commission, 1975), p. 141; "Official Vote of Pennsylvania—1860 [Gov.]," *Compiler*, November 12, 1860, p. 3 c. 1; "Freemen, Read—The Regard of the Republicans for the Constitution of the United States," *Compiler*, October 22, 1860, p. 1 c. 7; "Mechanics and Workingmen," *Compiler*, October 29, 1860, p. 1 c. 6.

34. "The Fugitive Slave Case in Chicago," *Compiler*, November 19, 1860, p. 2 c. 7 – p. 3 c. 1; "The Nail Hit on the Head," *Compiler*, November 26, 1860, p. 2 c. 2.

35. "Political Meanness," *Compiler*, November 26, 1860, p. 2 c. 2.

36. Vernon Burton, "Lincoln and Secession," Speech to the Capitol Hill Society, Washington, May 5, 2010, available at http://www.c-spanvideo.org/program/Secess; Chandra Manning, *What This Cruel War Was Over* (New York: Alfred A. Knopf, 2007), pp. 18–51.

37. "The Secession Movement in the South," *Compiler*, November 26, 1860, p. 2 c. 4; Untitled, *Compiler*, December 3, 1860, p. 2 c. 1; "Rumors from Washington," *Compiler*, December 10, 1861, p. 1 c. 7.

38. House Executive Documents, no. 7, 36th Congress, 2nd session, pp. 450–51, cited by Philip S. Foner, *Business & Slavery: The New York Merchants and the Irrepressible Conflict* (Chapel Hill: University of North Carolina Press, 1941), p. 162; Christian B. Keller, "Keystone Confederates?" in William A. Blair and William Pencak, *Making and Remaking Pennsylvania's Civil War* (University Park: Penn State University Press, 2001), pp. 6–7. Tyler was still in Richmond in the spring of 1863, predicting success for Lee's army when it invaded Pennsylvania.

39. Untitled, *Compiler*, December 17, 1860, p. 2 c. 1; "Speech of Judge Woodward," *Compiler*, December 31, 1860, p. 1 c. 5–7.

40. Cong. Globe, 36th Cong., 2d sess., Dec. 3, 1860, Appendix, p. 1 ff, in Philip S. Klein, *President James Buchanan: A Biography* (University Park: Pennsylvania State University Press, 1962), cited by Thomas D. Morris, *Free Men All! The Personal Liberty Laws of the North 1780–1860* (Baltimore: Johns Hopkins University Press, 1974), p. 202. See also Harold Hyman, "The Narrow Escape from a 'Compromise of 1860': Secession and the Constitution," in H. Hyman and L. Levy, eds., *Freedom and Reform* (New York: Harper & Row, 1967), p. 153.

41. [Joshua Francis Fisher?], "Concession and Compromise," [Philadelphia? 1860?], Microprint edition, Louisville, Ky., 1962. Authorship of this pamphlet is attributed to Fisher; this appears to be confirmed by a December 1860 diary entry in his brother Sidney George Fisher's diary. Jonathan White, ed., *A Philadelphia Perspective: The Civil War Diary of Sidney George Fisher* (Philadelphia: Historical Society of Pennsylvania, 1967; reprint, New York: Fordham University Press, 2007). A bill to hold counties liable for slave rescues was introduced into the Pennsylvania legislature, and Henry Clay had tried to add to the 1850 Fugitive Slave Law a provision for a jury trial in the Southern county from which the slave had fled.

42. [Fisher?], "Concession and Compromise."

43. "Mr. Crittenden's Resolutions," *Compiler*, December 24, 1860, p. 2 c. 3; Allan Nevins, *The Emergence of Lincoln* (New York: Charles Scribner's Sons, 1950), p. 391; Jean Humez, *Harriet Tubman: The Life and Life Stories* (Madison: University of Wisconsin Press, 2003), pp. 27, 45–46.

44. See in particular Foner, *Free Soil, Free Labor, Free Men*.

45. Vernon Burton, "Lincoln and Secession"; Stanley Harrold, *Border War: Fighting Over Slavery Before the Civil War* (Chapel Hill: University of North Carolina Press, 2010), pp. 194–213.

46. This conflict, especially in the border context, is admirably captured by Harrold's *Border War.*

47. William A. Link, *Roots of Secession: Slavery and Politics in Antebellum Virginia* (Chapel Hill: University of North Carolina Press, 2003), pp. 110–18.

48. "Declaration of the Immediate Causes which Induce and Justify the Secession of South Carolina from the Federal Union," The Avalon Project at Yale Law School, www.yale.edu/ lawweb/avalon/csa/scarsec.htm; "Confederate States of America—Georgia Secession," Avalon Project, Yale University, http://avalon.law.yale.edu/19th_century/csa _geosec.asp.

49. Foner, *Free Soil, Free Labor, Free Men,* pp. 133–140. Both privately before his inauguration and in his address itself, Lincoln indicated a willingness to enforce the Fugitive Slave Law; it was the territorial issue that was the sticking point. Nevins, *Emergence of Lincoln,* pp. 447, 459.

50. Carl Oblinger, "New Freedoms, Old Miseries: The emergence and disruption of black communities in southeastern Pennsylvania, 1780–1860," (Ph.D. diss., Lehigh University, 1988), pp. 121–22. I have not been able to locate these petitions in the Pennsylvania Archives. See also Edward R. Turner, *The Negro in Pennsylvania, 1639–1861* (Washington: American Historical Association, 1911; New York: Arno Press, 1969), pp. 150–54.

51. Edward Magdol, *The Antislavery Rank and File* (New York: Greenwood Press, 1986).

52. "To the Honorable Senate and House . . . ," [March 1861], RG-7, Senate File, Folder 85, Petitions 484 and 484[B]; Jane Dice Stone, ed., "Diary of William Heyser," *Papers Read Before the Kittochtinny Historical Society* 16 (Mercersburg, Pa.: Kittochtinny Historical Society, 1978), pp. 54–58, available electronically at the Valley of the Shadow, www.iath .Virginia.edu/vshadow2/personal/wmheyser.html; (Heyser—RR) "To The President and Managers of the Cumberland Valley Railroad," *Star,* December 8, 1848, p. 1 c. 6.

53. I. Daniel Rupp, *The History and Topography of Dauphin, Cumberland, Franklin, Bedford, Adams and Perry Counties* (Lancaster, Pa.: Gilbert Hills, 1846), p. 527; J. Howard Wert, "Gettysburg: A Brief Sketch of a Rural Town," in Caba, *Episodes of Gettysburg and the Underground Railroad* (Gettysburg: G. Craig Caba Antiques, 1998), p. 13. (Adams County) "To the Honorable Senate and House . . . ," RG-7, Senate File, Folder 85, Petition 486, Pennsylvania State Archives.

54. Doylestown, Bucks County 1861 Pro-colonization petition, March 1, 1861, Pennsylvania State Archives, RG-7, Senate File, Petition 358.

55. No published account of the society exists after its 1847 celebration of the passage of the personal liberty law; in 1884, Charles W. Griest wrote to an inquirer that the Anti-Slavery society had met in a school house for nine years and described its last meeting, indicating it had probably ceased meetings around 1847. Charles W. Griest to Friend David, February 1884. Copy provided by Deb McCauslin.

56. One newspaper claims that a petition supporting the Republican position was sent to Edward McPherson in Congress.

57. "To the Senate & House . . . ," Pennsylvania State Archives RG-7, Senate File, Petition 375. Repeal of the personal liberty law and restoration of this "Comity Law" were goals of many others who were petitioning the legislature in a bid to reconcile the seceding South.

Even before 1860, Missouri Senator Thomas Hart Benton believed that restoring such comity laws was critical to rekindling kind feelings between the North and South. *Thirty Years' View*, v. 2 (New York: D. Appleton and Company, 1856), pp. 778, 780.

58. Carolyn L. Williams, "Religion, race and gender in antebellum American radicalism: The Pennsylvania Female Anti-Slavery Society, 1833–1870," (Ph.D. diss., UCLA, 1991).

59. David Donald, *Lincoln Reconsidered* (New York: Alfred A. Knopf, 1956; reprint, New York: Vintage, 1961), pp. 19–36; Robert A. Skotheim, "The 'Status Revolution' Thesis Criticized," in Richard O. Curry, ed., *The Abolitionists* (Hinsdale, Ill.: Dryden Press, 1973), pp. 47–51.

60. Hal S. Barron, *Those Who Stayed Behind: Rural Society in Nineteenth Century New England* (Cambridge: Cambridge University Press, 1984), pp. 23–25, 134.

61. "Message of Wm. F. Packer, Governor of Penn.," *Compiler*, January 3, 1861, p. 2 c. 1. As the 1826 act had been declared unconstitutional in *Prigg*, there were significant questions as to whether it could be reapplied.

62. "Very Important Intelligence! Message of Gov. Letcher, of Va.," *Compiler*, January 14, 1861, p. 2 c. 1. In late 1860, Letcher had been in correspondence with Philadelphia conservative Lewis D. Vail over Pennsylvania's personal liberty law. Morris, *Free Men All*, p. 216.

63. "The Difference," *Compiler*, January 14, 1861, p. 2 c. 5. The states in the border state committee were Maryland, Virginia, Missouri, North Carolina, Kentucky, Delaware, Arkansas, Texas, Ohio, Indiana, Illinois, Pennsylvania, Iowa, and New Jersey.

64. Untitled, *Compiler*, January 21, 1861, p. 2 c. 2; "The People Speaking," *Compiler*, January 21, 1861, p. 2 c. 3.

65. "Highly Important Proposition by Gov. Bigler," *Compiler*, January 21, 1861, p. 1 c. 3–4; Untitled, *Compiler*, January 21, 1861, p. 2 c. 2. This concept was similar to the one advocated in "Concession and Compromise," and which became Article 4, Section 3 of the new Confederate Constitution, one of the few changes in that document from its U.S. predecessor.

66. Untitled, January 21, 1861, p. 2 c. 2; Untitled, *Compiler*, January 28, 1861, p. 2 c. 2; "PETITIONS TO CONGRESS," *Compiler*, January 28, 1861, p. 2 c. 6; Nevins, *Emergence of Lincoln*, p. 393; "Let the People Speak," *Compiler*, February 4, 1861, p. 2 c. 2; "Thaddeus Stevens" [Lancaster], February 11, 1861, p. 2 c. 2; "What the People Say [Massachusetts]," *Compiler*, February 18, 1861, p. 2 c. 2.

67. "Union Meeting at Philadelphia," *Compiler*, January 21, 1861, p. 3 c. 2. Even for those Southerners who did not wish to visit Pennsylvania, Philadelphia was a frequent steamboat stop on the way North.

68. "Union Meeting at Philadelphia." For a discussion of the secession movement in Pennsylvania, see William C. Wright, *The Secession Movement in the Middle Atlantic States* (Rutherford, N.J.: Rutgers University Press, 1973), pp. 125–63.

69. "Effects of Civil War Upon the North," *Compiler*, February 4, 1861, p. 2 c. 3; "Senator Bigler," *Compiler*, February 11, 1861, p. 1 c. 3. Bigler's biblical tones echoed those of Henry Clay in 1850.

70. "Union Meeting at Mount Rock [in Mountpleasant]," *Compiler*, February 4, 1861, p. 2 c. 5.

71. "Southern Rights and Concessions," *Compiler* [reprint], February 11, 1861, p. 2 c. 4; "Democratic State Convention," *Compiler*, February 25, 1861, p. 2 c. 2–3.

72. "The Great Difficulty," *Compiler*, February 25, 1861, p. 3 c. 1; "The Peace Congress— Adjournment after Adopting the Guthrie Modified Plan," *Compiler*, February 25, 1861, p. 3 c. 2; "Guthrie, James," *Biographical Directory of the United States Congress*, bioguide. congress.gov.

73. Untitled, *Compiler*, February 25, 1861, p. 2 c. 5.

74. "No Compromise!" *Compiler*, March 4, 1861, p. 2 c. 4. The *Compiler* countered that a pro-compromise campaign near Littlestown had garnered many more signatures than those opposing compromise.

75. "Coming to Their Senses," March 25, 1861, p. 2 c. 3; "The Constitution As it Is," April 1, 1861, p. 1 c. 6.

8. Contrabands, "White Victories," and the Ultimate Slave Hunt: Recasting the Fugitive Slave Issue in Civil War South Central Pennsylvania

1. General Benjamin Butler coined the phrase "contrabands" to justify his refusal to return escaped slaves to Southerners who sought them. Because the South considered slaves as property, and that "property" could dig trenches, build roads and engage in other activities in support of the military, he classified them as "contraband of war," or militarily useful property. The phrase stuck, and was soon used to refer generally to all African American slaves who had fled, regardless of whether they had traveled to a specific U.S. military encampment.

2. A historical debate over how emancipation was accomplished—whether Lincoln was the initiator or whether fleeing slaves forced his hand—can be found in what is called the "Who Freed the Slaves?" Debate. Key readings include Ira Berlin, Barbara Fields, et al., "The Destruction of Slavery, 1861–65" in *Slaves No More: Three Essays on Emancipation and the Civil War* (Cambridge: Cambridge University Press, 1992), pp. 1–76; Ira Berlin, "Who Freed the Slaves? Emancipation and Its Meaning in American Life," *Quaderno* 5 (1993): pp. 27–34, http://www.library.vanderbilt.edu/Quaderno/Quaderno5/Q5.C3.Berlin. pdf. James McPherson, "Who Freed the Slaves," *Proceedings of the American Philosophical Society*, 139 (1995), pp. 1–10. This author believes that the actions of the slaves to free themselves had a profound impact on the border North. By emphasizing the importance of the contrabands issue, and its continuity with the prewar debate over fugitive slaves, my work tends to support those who emphasize the roles that the slaves themselves played by their flights to freedom, but McPherson is certainly correct that Lincoln stood against even those in his own party who were willing to reunify the country on the backs of the slaves.

3. James M. McPherson, *Battle Cry of Freedom: The Civil War Era* (Oxford: Oxford University Press, 1988), p. 506.

4. Untitled, *Compiler*, May 13, 1861, p. 2 c. 5.

5. *Semi-Weekly Dispatch* [Franklin County], April 19, 1861, p. 2, column 1, quoted in Edward L. Ayers, *In the Presence of Mine Enemies: War in the Heart of America, 1859–1863* (New York: W. W. Norton, 2003), p. 144.

6. In Gettysburg, a similar meeting was attended by members of both political parties. While it condemned the seizure of the fort as rebellion and treason, it did not cast aspersions on any party. "Union Meeting," *Compiler*, April 22, 1861, p. 3 c. 1.

7. "Horrible Occurrence," *Compiler*, June 10, 1861, p. 2 c. 3; "Horrible Occurrence," *Sentinel*, June 12, 1861, p. 3 c. 3; "Murder Trials in Franklin County," *Compiler*, April 25, 1864, p. 2 c. 5.

8. "Head Quarters Dept. of Penna., Chambersburg, June 3, 1861," *Compiler*, June 10, 1861, p. 2 c. 6. Major General Robert Patterson, "To the United States' Troops of this Department," June 1861, U.S. War Department, *War of the Rebellion: The Official Records of the Union and Confederate Armies*, 128 vols. (Washington, 1890–1901), ser. 1, v. 2, p. 662 (hereinafter cited as *OR*), cited by Edward H. Phillips, *The Lower Shenandoah Valley in the Civil War* (Lynchburg: H. E. Howard, 1993), p. 110. Patterson's proclamation had been preceded by an almost identical order that General McClellan made to his troops in western Virginia. [McClellan] Proclamation, "To the Union Men of Western Virginia," 26 May 1861, in Negro Military Service, Roll 1, frame 0401, cited by Ervin Jordan, *Black Confederates and Afro-Yankees in Civil War Virginia* (Charlottesville: University Press of Virginia, 1995), p. 177.

9. The best introduction to the extensive literature on Northern perceptions of Southern leadership is Leonard Richards, *The Slave Power: The Free North and Southern Domination, 1780–1860* (Baton Rouge, 2000). On early Northern belief in Southern unionism, see Mark Grimsley, *The Hard Hand of War: Union Military Policy toward Southern Civilians, 1861–1865* (Cambridge, UK: Cambridge University Press, 1995).

10. Dudley Taylor Cornish, *The Sable Arm: Black Troops in the Union Army, 1861–1865* (Lawrence: University Press of Kansas, 1956; reprint, 1987), pp. 10–11; "Army Movements—The Arrival of Gen. [Cadwalder] at Greencastle," *Compiler*, June 17, 1861, p. 2 c. 3.

11. "The War & Its Relation to Slavery," *Compiler*, June 17, 1861, p. 1 c. 7.

12. Untitled [Contrabands], *Sentinel*, November 4, 1862, p. 2 c. 4 and November 25, 1862, p. 2 c. 5; "Abolition of Slavery in the District of Columbia," September 30, 1862, p. 2 c. 6.

13. J. Howard Wert, "Old Time Notes of Adams County . . . John T. McIlhenny and the 'Copperheads,'" *Star & Sentinel*, January 2, 1907, p. 1. c. 2–3.

14. For more on the impact of "contrabands," see Leslie A. Schwalm, "'Overrun with Free Negroes': Emancipation and Wartime Migration in the Upper Midwest," *Civil War History* 50 (June 2004): pp. 145–74.

15. "Who Are The Union Breakers?" *Compiler*, July 1, 1861, p. 1 c. 6; McPherson, *Battle Cry of Freedom*, p. 506.

16. James Francis Crocker, "Prison Reminiscences," February 2, 1904, cited by William Frassanito, *Early Photography at Gettysburg* (Gettysburg: Thomas Publications, 1995), pp. 377–78; R. C. Smedley, *History of the Underground Railroad in Chester and the Neighboring Counties of Pennsylvania* (Lancaster, Pa.: John A. Hiestand, 1883; reprint, Mechanicsburg: Stackpole Books, 2003), p. 36; H. L. Baugher, "Subjection to Law, the Constitution of Man's Nature" (Gettysburg, 1852), esp. p. 16; Baugher, "The Men for the Times" (Gettysburg, 1854). esp. p. 5; Baugher, "Let No Man Despise Thee," (Gettysburg, 1855), esp. p. 16; Baugher Family Papers, Special Collections, Musselman Library, Gettysburg College.

17. H. L. Baugher, *The Christian Patriot: A Discourse Addressed to the Graduating Class of Pennsylvania College, September 15, 1861* (Gettysburg: A.D. Buehler / H.C. Neinstedt, 1861), pp. 15-16, Baugher Family Papers, Special Collections, Musselman Library, Gettysburg College. Anarchy undoubtedly was particularly troubling to a descendant of Germans familiar with the carnage created as a result of the Thirty Years' War in Europe, when disputes over sovereignty led to carnage and mass starvation in central Europe. The role of America as a beacon of hope to the world in the mid-nineteenth century is explored in Mark E. Neely, Jr., *Last Best Hope of Earth: Abraham Lincoln and the Promise of America* (Cambridge, Mass.: Harvard University Press, 1993).

18. Baugher, "Christian Patriot," pp. 5-6, 20-21, 23-24.

19. Baugher, "Christian Patriot," pp. 12, 16-17.

20. Frassanito, *Early Photography*, pp. 379-80.

21. For the importance of this concept to Civil War Americans, see Phillip S. Paludan, "The American Civil War Considered as a Crisis of Law and Order," *American Historical Review* 77 (1972): pp. 1013-34. The power of appeals to law and order and the sacredness of the Constitution should not be minimized; they may have helped contribute to the heavy military turnout in this border state. For concepts of treason during and after the Civil War, see William A. Blair, "Why Didn't the North Hang Some Rebels?" in James Marten and A. Kirsten Foster, eds., *More Than a Contest Between Armies: Essays on the Civil War Era* (Kent, Ohio: Kent State University Press, 2008), pp. 189-218, and his forthcoming book on the subject of treason from the University of North Carolina Press.

22. "Beware," *Compiler*, August 5, 1861, p. 1 c, 5; "Aid and Comfort to the Enemy," *Compiler*, September 6, 1861, p. 1 c. 4; "The President and the Abolitionists," *Compiler*, September 30, 1861, p. 1 c. 7; "The Ohio Resolutions," *Compiler*, August 19, 1861, p. 1 c. 4.

23. Ohio became a leading center for opposition to the war as the Republican administration was fighting it. For more about Vallandigham and Copperheadism in general, see McPherson, *Battle Cry of Freedom*, pp. 591-99; Frank L. Klement, *The Limits of Dissent: Clement L. Vallandigham and the Civil War* (New York: Fordham University Press, 1998); Frank L. Klement, *The Copperheads in the Middle West* (Chicago: University of Chicago Press, 1960); and Jennifer L. Weber, *Copperheads: The Rise and Fall of Lincoln's Opponents in the North* (New York: Oxford University Press, 2006). The *Compiler*'s publication of Vallandigham's speeches and letters may belie Alan Nevins' contention that the Ohioan "never gained a substantial following outside of his own state." Alan Nevins, *The War for Union: War Becomes Revolution* (New York: Charles Scribner's Sons, 1960), p. 396.

24. "The Ohio Resolutions," *Compiler*, August 19, 1861, p. 1 c. 4.

25. "The Result in the County," *Compiler*, October 14, 1861, p. 2 c. 1; "The Election," *Compiler*, October 14, 1861, p. 2 c. 2; "The Lessons of the Hour," *Compiler*, December 2, 1861, p. 1 c. 6.

26. "Emancipation as a Means of Subduing Rebellion," *Compiler*, November 4, 1861, p. 2 c. 3; "How to Turn the World Topsy-Turvy," *Compiler*, November 25, 1861, p. 2 c. 2; "Consequences of Universal Emancipation," *Compiler*, November 25, 1861, p. 2 c. 2; "Slaves at Hilton Head," *Compiler*, December 9, 1861, p. 1 c. 7. Cornish, *The Sable Arm*, pp. 33-34.

27. "Fugitive Slaves in Camp," *Compiler*, December 16, 1861, p. 2 c. 4-5; Untitled, *Compiler*, January 6, 1862, p. 1 c. 7; "General Dix's Proclamation," *Compiler*, December 30, 1861,

p. 2 c. 1; Cornish, *Sable Arm*, pp. 25. Halleck issued a similar proclamation in St. Louis on February 23, 1862, for which the Democratic paper renewed its applause, saying "it is the only proper rule." "Important Order of Gen. Halleck Regarding Slaves and Other Property of the Rebels," *Compiler*, March 3, 1862, p. 2 c. 7; Untitled, *Compiler*, March 10, 1862, p. 2 c. 1.

28. Herman Hattaway and Archer Jones, *How the North Won the Civil War* (Urbana: University of Illinois Press, 1991); "White Victory," *Compiler*, March 31, 1862, p. 1 c. 4. This piece was a reprint from another paper, but the sentiments were shared by the *Compiler*.

29. "Progress of Abolition," *Compiler*, May 4, 1862, p. 1 c. 4; "The Necessity of a White Man's Party," *Compiler*, May 4, 1862, p. 1 c. 5.

30. "The Emancipation Bill," *Compiler*, March 17, 1862, p. 2 c. 3–4; "Sick of the Negro," *Compiler*, February 17, 1862, p. 2 c. 2; "The Negro to Be Excluded from Illinois," *Compiler*, March 17, 1862, p 1 c. 7; "Necessity of a White Man's Party," *Compiler*, May 4, 1862, p. 1 c. 5; "Calmly Think of It," *Compiler*, May 5, 1862, p. 2 c. 6; "The Evil Beginning to Be Felt," *Compiler*, July 21, 1862, p. 1 c. 6. Movements to ban African Americans also occurred in Illinois and Ohio. The *Compiler* was actually critical of the movement in Ohio because the paper felt that given that state's long history of harboring fugitive slaves, it should accept its proportional share of refugees now.

31. Untitled, *Compiler*, October 28, 1861, p. 2 c. 3.

32. Untitled, *Compiler*, April 28, 1862, p. 3 c. 1 (reprint from the *Bedford Gazette*).

33. O. P. M. to Jeremiah Zeamer, January 1901, Zeamer Papers, File 40–9, Cumberland County Historical Society, p. [5]. Conversely, shortly before the war, in January 1861, several fugitive slaves were captured in Adams County without any resistance from the local citizenry—which was cited as proof that "the Southern people have no just cause of complaint against Pennsylvania, in this respect." "Runaways," *Sentinel*, January 30, 1861 (reprint from the *Hanover Spectator*). Thanks to Timothy Smith, Adams County Historical Society, for bringing this to my attention.

34. "Little McPherson's Great Speech," *Compiler*, July 14, 1862, p. 1 c. 7. McPherson was also criticized for opportunism. Like many politicians, he had volunteered for military service when the expectations had been for a short war. As Congress returned to session, he had to resign from the leadership of troops and serve as a volunteer aide-de-camp to various generals. "Capt. McPherson vs. Buncombe," *Compiler*, October 10, 1862, p. 2 c. 6.

35. Henry Wilson, *History of the Antislavery Measures of the Thirty-Seventh and Thirty-Eighth United-States Congresses, 1861–1864* (Boston: Walker, Wise and Company, 1864; reprint, New York: Arno Press, 1969), pp. 15–16, 86.

36. Wilson, *Antislavery Measures*, pp. 14, 65–66, 73, 76–77.

37. "Military Colonies," *Compiler*, July 14, 1862, p. 2 c. 5.

38. Untitled, *Compiler*, August 11, 1862, p. 2 c. 3.

39. "The Issue," *Compiler*, October 10, 1862, p. 2 c. 1.

40. McPherson, *Battle Cry of Freedom*, pp. 560–62; Allan Nevins, *The War for the Union: War Becomes Revolution, 1862–1863* (New York: Charles Scribner's Sons, 1963), pp. 318–22.

41. Frank B. Evans, *Pennsylvania Politics, 1872–1877* (Harrisburg, Pa.: Pennsylvania Historical and Museum Commission, 1966), facing p. 1.

42. Untitled, *Compiler*, January [5], 1863, p. 2 c. 6.

43. "The Negro Proclamation," *Compiler*, January [5], 1863, p. 2 c. 1; "A Negro Salute!" *Compiler*, January 12, 1863, p. 2 c. 2; "Relief of the Contrabands," January 5, 1863, p. 1 c. 6; "What It Costs to Superintend Contrabands," *Compiler*, January 12, 1863, p. 1 c. 5.

44. "The Contrabands," *Compiler*, January 26, 1863, p. 1 c. 2; McPherson, *Battle Cry of Freedom*, p. 491.

45. "State Legislature," *Compiler*, January 26, 1863, p. 2 c. 1.

46. Untitled, *Compiler*, January 26, 1863, p. 2 c. 1; "The Legislature," *Compiler*, March 2, 1863, p. 3 c. 1; "Negro Emancipation in Pennsylvania," *Compiler*, March 9, 1863, p. 2 c. 6–7; Untitled, *Compiler*, March 23, 1862, p. 2 c. 1.

47. "Let 'Er Rip—The Spring Elections—Democracy Triumphs," *Compiler*, March 30, 1863, p. 2 c. 2; Untitled, *Compiler*, May 4, 1863, p. 2 c. 3; Untitled, *Compiler*, May 11, 1863, p. 2 c. 4.

48. "The Negro Tax," *Compiler*, February 2, 1863, p. 1 c. 5; "Paying Dear for the Negro," *Compiler*, February 2, 1863, p. 2 c. 5; "What the Soldiers Think of the War," *Compiler*, February 2, 1863, p. 1 c. 6; "Letter from the 165th," *Compiler*, January 26, 1863, p. 1 c. 3; "Case of C. L. Vallandigham," *Compiler*, May 18, 1863, p. 2 c. 3; "Address of C. L. Vallandigham to the Democracy of Ohio," *Compiler*, May 18, 1863, p. 2 c. 4.

49. "The Negro Brigade," *Compiler*, February 2, 1863, p. 2 c. 4; Untitled, *Compiler*, February 9, 1863, p. 2 c. 1; "Is it Not Time . . . ," *Compiler*, February 9, 1863, p. 2. c. 3; "Stevens' Negro Bill," *Compiler*, February 16, 1863, p. 2 c. 4; "Mr. Wright speaks again," *Compiler*, February 16, 1863, p. 3 c. 1; "Negroes as Soldiers," *Compiler*, March 9, 1863, p. 2 c.4.

50. Noel Ignatiev, *How the Irish Became White* (New York: Routledge, 1995); George Frederickson, *The Black Image in the White Mind* (New York: Harper & Row, 1972); "Africans vs. Dutchmen," *Compiler*, May 4, 1863, p. 2 c. 4; "Will Be Repealed," *Compiler*, February 9, 1863, p. 4 c. 1.

51. The "herrenvolk [master race] democracy" concept was developed by George Frederickson building on the ideas of a South African researcher, Pierre L. van den Berghe. Frederickson, *The Black Image in the White Mind*, esp. pp. 61–64, 94.

52. At least 88 African Americans from the Mercersburg area enlisted in the war ("African American Historic Sites of Mercersburg," www.mercersburg.com/blackhistory/black01.htm). A separate list shows 46 African Americans from Mercersburg who enlisted in the 54th or 55th Massachusetts, as well as 20 from Carlisle, 12 from Chambersburg, and 11 from Shippensburg. Thomas L. Doughton, "Pennsylvania Men in Massachusetts Colored Infantry Units," (www.geocities.com/afroyankees/Military/penn1.html). See also Woman's Club of Mercersburg, *Old Mercersburg* (New York: Frank Allaben Genealogical Company, 1912; reprint, Williamsport, Pa.: Grit Publishing Co., 1949), p. 196. This wave of recruitment for Massachusetts units seemed to concentrate on African American communities located near rail lines.

53. "Recruiting Negroes," *Compiler*, March 9, 1863, p. 4 c. 1;

54. "First Negro Regiment," *Compiler*, April 6, 1863, p. 2 c. 7; Untitled, *Compiler*, June 22, 1863, p. 2 c. 6. The Massachusetts 54th was featured in the movie *Glory* (1989).

55. David Wills to Andrew Curtin, 15 June 1863, Military Dispatch Books, Book 18, RG 19.181, Pennsylvania State Archives, cited in Margaret S. Creighton, *Colors of Courage*

(New York: Basic Books, 2005), pp. 66–67 (Timothy Smith unearthed this information). See also William Frassanito, *Early Photography at Gettysburg*, p. 110.

56. "Outrages against Newspapers," *Compiler*, March 23, 1863, p. 2 c. 2; "Gen. Cooper Rebukes the Mob Spirit," *Compiler*, March 23, 1863, p. 2 c. 2; "Death of General James Cooper," *Compiler*, April 1, 1863, p. 2 c. 1.

57. "Case of C. L. Vallandigham," *Compiler*, May 18, 1863, p. 2 c. 3; "Address of C. L. Vallandigham to the Democracy of Ohio," *Compiler*, May 18, 1863, p. 2 c. 4; "Arrest of Adams County Citizens by the Provost Martial [sic]," May 18, 1863, p. 2 c. 1; Untitled, *Compiler*, June 1, 1863, p. 2 c. 6. For more information on the Knights of the Golden Circle, a shadowy organization whose impact and possibly very existence may have been exaggerated, see Frank L. Klement, *Dark Lanterns: Secret Political Societies, Conspiracies, and Treason Trials in the Civil War* (Baton Rouge: Louisiana State University Press, 1984); Robert M. Sandow, *Deserter Country: Civil War Opposition in the Appalachian North* (New York: Fordham University Press, 2009). Jennifer Weber and Robert Churchill have suggested that Northern anti-war secret societies may have posed a greater threat than Klement maintained. Weber, *Copperheads*, and Robert H. Churchill, "Liberty, Conscription, and Delusions of Grandeur: The Sons of Liberty Conspiracy of 1863–1864," *Prologue* 30 (Winter 1998): pp. 295–303.

58. "Another Victim," *Compiler*, July 13, 1863, p. 2 c. 2; "Mr. Stahle's Arrest and Imprisonment," *Compiler*, July 20, 1863, p. 2 c. 1; "Imprisonment of an Editor," *Compiler*, August 3, 1863, p. 2 c. 1; "Return of the Editor," *Compiler*, August 10, 1863, p. 2 c. 1; "Four Weeks Under Arrest," *Compiler*, August 17, 1863, p. 2 c. 1.

59. Margaret S. Creighton, "Living on the Fault Line: African American Civilians and the Gettysburg Campaign," in Joan E. Cashin, ed., *The War Was You and Me* (Princeton: Princeton University Press, 2002), pp. 225–27.

60. George M. Neese, *Three Years in the Confederate Horse Artillery* (New York: Neale Publishing Company, 1911), p. 61; Edward H. Phillips, *The Lower Shenandoah Valley in the Civil War* (Lynchburg: H. E. Howard, 1993), pp. 114, 118; Alonzo H. Quint, *The Potomac and the Rapidan* (Boston: Crosby and Nichols, 1864), p. 235; Jedediah Hotchkiss to Sara Hotchkiss, 17 September 1862, Letters of Jedediah Hotchkiss, 1860–65, Valley of the Shadow project website; David G. Smith, "Race and Reconciliation: The Capture of African Americans during the Gettysburg Campaign," in *Virginia's Civil War*, ed. P. Wallenstein and B. Wyatt-Brown (Charlottesville: University of Virginia Press, 2005), pp. 137–51.

61. Smith, "Race and Retaliation"; Wilbur S. Nye, *Here Come the Rebels!* (Baton Rouge: Louisiana State University Press, 1965), pp. 144–45; Edwin B. Coddington, *The Gettysburg Campaign: A Study in Command* (New York: Charles Scribner's Sons, 1968), p. 161; John W. Schildt, *Roads to Gettysburg* (Parsons, W. Va.: McClain Printing Company, 1978), p. 106; W. P. Conrad and Ted Alexander, *When War Passed This Way* (Shippensburg, Pa.: Beidel Publishing House, 1982), p. 137; McPherson, *Battle Cry of Freedom*, p. 649; Alan Nolan, *Lee Considered* (Chapel Hill: University of North Carolina Press, 1991), pp. 16–18; Ted Alexander, "A Regular Slave Hunt," *North & South* 4 (2001): pp. 82–89; Peter C. Vermilyea, "The Effect of the Confederate Invasion on Gettysburg's African American Community," *Gettysburg Magazine* 24 (2001): pp. 112–28; James F. Epperson, "Lee's Slave Makers," *Civil War Times* 41 (August 2002): pp. 44–51; Margaret S. Creighton, "Living on the Fault Line:

African American Civilians and the Gettysburg Campaign," in Cashin, ed., *The War Was You and Me*, pp. 209–36; Creighton, *Colors of Courage*, pp. 75–76.

62. Taliaferro N. Simpson to Caroline V. T. Miller, June 28, 1863, in Guy R. Everson and Edward H. Simpson, Jr., eds., *"Far, Far from Home:" The Wartime Letters of Dick and Tally Simpson Third South Carolina Volunteers* (New York: Oxford University Press, 1994), pp. 251–52; Salome Myers Stewart, "Recollections of the Battle of Gettysburg," Diary entry for June 21, 1863, Adams County Historical Society, cited by J. Matthew Gallman with Susan Baker, "Gettysburg's Gettysburg: What the Battle Did to the Borough," in Gabor S. Borrit, ed., *The Gettysburg Nobody Knows* (New York: Oxford, 1997), p. 161.

63. James Elton Johnson, "A History of Camp William Penn and its Black Troops in the Civil War, 1863–1865," (Ph.D. diss., University of Pennsylvania, 1999), pp. 36–38; Mark E. Neely, Jr., "Pennsylvania Politics [1863]," Penn State 16th Annual Mont Alto Civil War Conference, June 5, 2002.

64. Diary entry for Rachel Cormany, June 16, 1863, in James Mohr and Richard Winslow III, eds., *The Cormany Diaries: a Northern Family During the Civil War* (Pittsburgh: University of Pittsburgh Press, 1982), pp. 328–30 (also available at the Valley of the Shadow Project); Creighton, "Living on the Fault Line," 215; Capt. W. S. How to Mr. Wills, 31 August 1865, in "Letters from Captain W. S. How in relation to colored people at White Post," Freedmen's Bureau Records, RG 105, National Archives, Virginia: Winchester 1865–1867, Box 64. It is not clear whether the captain's threat referred to all local African Americans or just to the remaining "family slaves" he believed were in the area.

65. Schildt, *Roads to Gettysburg*, p. 106; Creighton, "Living on the Fault Line," pp. 228–29. This account of the fate of "Old Liz" is based on the account of Albertus McCreary, who was a young boy during the battle. His description of Gettysburg during wartime includes inconsistencies, exaggerations, and some outright incorrect statements, but other portions appear as if they may be true. I am indebted to Timothy Smith, Adams County Historical Society, for pointing out some of the inconsistencies in McCreary's account. Albertus McCreary, "Gettysburg: A Boy's Experience of the Battle," *McClure's Magazine* 33 (July 1909), p. 250.

66. Diary Entry for William Heyser, June 18, 1863, in Jane Dice Stone, ed., "Diary of William Heyser," *Papers Read Before the Kittochtinny Historical Society* 16 (Mercersburg, Pa.: Kittochtinny Historical Society, 1978): pp. 54–58, available electronically at the Valley of the Shadow, www.iath.Virginia.edu/vshadow2/personal/wmheyser.html. George W. Davis to Family, 7 July 1863, Rebecca Pitchford Davis Papers, Southern Historical Collection (SHC), University of North Carolina. Department of Henrico Papers, Section 13, Virginia Historical Society, reproduced in Joseph T. Glatthaar, Confederate Military Manuscripts, Series A, Microfilm Reel C591, frame 830, undated list of African Americans received at the prison from Spring 1863 until July 31, 1863. At least one of the eleven African Americans received in July, William Sprigge, claimed to be a free black from Pennsylvania. Frames 793–794 contain "Lis[t] No. 1 from 1st to August 1863," which includes the names of twenty-seven African Americans. Six of these were identified as claiming to be free and captured in Pennsylvania.

67. G. M. Sorrel to George Pickett, July 1, 1863, *OR*, Series I, v. 51, pt. 2, pp. 732–33. This significant order was first noted by Coddington, *Gettysburg Campaign*, p. 161. Alfred Nofi has stated that Longstreet and several other Confederate commanders directly ordered

their soldiers to recapture fugitive slaves during the campaign, but offers no documentation; presumably he had the above order in mind. Alfred A. Nofi, *The Gettysburg Campaign* (New York: Combined Books, 1986), p. 37.

68. Kent Masterson Brown, *Retreat from Gettysburg* (Chapel Hill: University of North Carolina Press, 2005), pp. 12–33; David G. Smith, "Clear the Valley: The Shenandoah Valley and the Genesis of the Gettysburg Campaign," *Journal of Military History*, 74 (2010), pp. 1069–96. James A. Seddon, Secretary of War, to General R. E. Lee, January 12, 1863, in *OR*, ser. 3, v. 3, p. 13. An examination of just two (reels 102 and 110) of the potentially two dozen relevant reels of microfilm in the Letters Received by the Confederate Secretary of War, National Archives Microfilm 437, revealed eight letters from residents in or near the Valley urging action to clear the Valley of Union soldiers and bemoaning the loss of slaves. Wm Simmons, Madison County, January 1, 1863, S15 W[ar] D[ept.], Reel 110, frame 59; W. Skeen, Provost Marshal to Quarter Master General, March 13, 1863, S188 WD, Reel 110, frame 733; W. Skeen, April 2, 1863, S258 WD, 110: frames 1045–47; Charles Moore, Mt. Jackson, February 11, 1863, M111 WD, Reel 102, frame 82; J. G. Meen, Lynchburg, February 24, 1863, Reel 102; Thomas B. Massi, Rappahanock County, March 10, 1863, M239 WD, Reel 102, frame 541.

69. A. A. Anderson to C. Anderson, 8 July 1863, in Patrick H. Cain Letters, Duke University Special Collections.

70. Heyser diary entries, 26–27 June, 30 June 1863; Diary entry of Rev. Philip Schaff, 27 June 1863, in, "The Gettysburg Week," *Old Mercersburg*, p. 169. Smith, "Race and Retaliation," pp. 140–41, 144–46. Southern fears, at least as concerns soldier motivations, are ably discussed in Chandra Manning, *What This Cruel War Was Over* (New York: Alfred A. Knopf, 2007), pp. 28–34.

71. "The Treatment of Conquered Cities," *Richmond Daily Whig*, September 12, 1862, p. 2 c. 1; "Our Army in Maryland," *Richmond Dispatch*, September 17, 1862, p. 1 c. 1. The *Richmond Dispatch's* comments were noted in Gettysburg. Untitled, *Adams Sentinel*, September 30, 1862, p. 2 c. 5.

72. W. H. Taylor to General[s], 21 March 1863, Orders and Circulars Issued by the Army of the Potomac and the Army and Department of Northern Virginia, C.S.A., 1861–65, National Archives Microfilm M921, Reel 1, frame 1391. The order directed the army to comply with an early March directive by the Confederate Adjutant General, General Orders No. 25, 6 March 1863. See the *OR*, ser. 2, vol. 5, pp. 844–45.

73. See, for example, Newman Feamster's note that his brother Thomas and his men had "captured several Negroes and are sending them back," or Lt. John Gay, 4th Georgia, writing from Chambersburg, "We . . . captured . . . over a hundred negroes. All are sent back . . . " This implies there was a policy to send captured African Americans, like other captured supplies, back to the quartermasters. S. W. N. Feamster to mother, June 23, 1863, Feamster Family Papers, Library of Congress. Lt. John T. Gay to [Newspaper?], June 28, 1863, University of Georgia Archives and Special Collections. Thanks to Robert Wynstra for this reference. For use of this "sent back" phraseology with supplies, see Robert E. Lee to General John D. Imboden, June 10, 1863, in Clifford Dowdey and Louis H. Manarin, eds., *The Wartime Papers of Robert E. Lee* (Boston: Little, Brown, 1961; reprinted New York: Da Capo Press, 1987), p. 510.

74. Diary entry of Lucy Rebecca Buck, July 3, 1863, in Elizabeth R. Baer, ed., *Shadows on My Heart: The Civil War Diary of Lucy Rebecca Buck of Virginia* (Athens, Ga.: University

of Georgia Press, 1997), p. 228. The need for military slave labor in Virginia was great; see Jordan, *Black Confederates and Afro-Yankees*, and James H. Brewer, *The Confederate Negro* (Durham, N.C.: Duke University Press, 1969).

75. T. V. Moore to James Seddon, December 3, 1863 C (WD) 1025, Letters Received by the Confederate Secretary of War, National Archives microfilm M437, reel 88; William D. McKinstry et. al. to Amos Barnes, November 5, 1863; and Thomas Creigh to T. V. Moore, November 10, 1863, Department of Henrico Papers, Section 11, Virginia Historical Society, reproduced in Glatthaar, Confederate Military Manuscripts, Series A, Microfilm C591, frames 61–63. (Lafayette College) *Adams Sentinel*, October 14, 1850.

76. Moore to Seddon, December 3, 1863; J. A. Campbell to John Winder, December 14, 1863, *OR*, Series 2, volume 6, p. 705; "Just from 'Dixie,'" *Mercersburg Weekly Journal*, December 25, 1863, p. 2 c. 1.

77. Based on the Barnes evidence, Mark Neely believes that all the captured African Americans were ultimately freed. I have been unable to find the kind of documentation for their releases, however, that accompanied the Barnes case. James Epperson believes the Confederates held on to their African American hostages from Pennsylvania, and may have offered to trade them for runaway slaves. Mark E. Neely, Jr., *Southern Rights: Political Prisoners and the Myth of Confederate Constitutionalism* (Charlottesville, Va.: University Press of Virginia, 1999), pp. 139–40; Epperson, "Lee's Slave Makers," p. 51. According to a Mercersburg newspaper, Rev. Moore offered to undertake similar intercessions for other prisoners, but it is not clear if Creigh or other south central Pennsylvanians pursued this. "Rev. Dr. Moore—Richmond—Our Colored Prisoners," *Mercersburg Journal*, January 1, 1864, p. 2 c. 1.

78. The *Compiler* would call for both Robert Ould and Solomon Meredith, the Southern and Northern exchange commissioners, to be replaced. "Exchange of Prisoners," *Compiler*, December 7, 1863. Civil War prisoner of war policy is covered in a number of texts; Lonnie R. Speer, *War of Vengeance* (Mechanicsville, Pa.: Stackpole Books, 2002) is good, if especially critical of Northern policy.

79. Isaac H. Carrington to Capt. W. S. Winder, August 26, 1863, in Letters Received by the Confederate Secretary of War, C (WD) 604, National Archives microfilm M437, reel 86, frames 919–921. I am indebted to Mark Neely for both this reference and the December 3 reference to Amos Barnes. Jacob Hoke, *Historical Reminiscences of the War, In and About Chambersburg, During the War of Rebellion* (Chambersburg: M. A. Foltz, 1884; reprint, Evansville, Ind.: Whipporwill Publications), p. 144.

80. Department of Henrico Papers, Section 13, Virginia Historical Society, Microfilm C591, Frame 830, undated list of African Americans received at the prison from Spring 1863 until July 31, 1863. At least one of the eleven African Americans received in July, William Sprigge, claimed to be a free black from Pennsylvania. Frames 793–794 contain "Lis[t] No. 1 from 1st to August 1863," which includes the names of twenty-seven African Americans. Six of these were identified as claiming to be free and captured in Pennsylvania, but a comparison of names to the Franklin County census indicates that at least eight others may have been from Pennsylvania as well.

81. The activities of African American prisoners at Castle Thunder are not documented, but for Libby Prison, the morning reports contain frequent references to placing African American prisoners out for work. The October 10, 1862 report mentions, "Rec'd 12 negroes

returned from President of Y[orktown] RRd, October 9, 1862," and on November 19, 1862 the report reads, "Off 19 Negroes who are at work outside at various places." Morning Reports of the C.S. Eastern Military District Prison [Libby], March 22, 1862 – December 16, 1863, Ryder Collection of Confederate Archives, Tufts University.

82. (Sent from Richmond to Salisbury) Special Orders No. 36, July 29, 1864, "Special Orders Relative to Federals Held as Prisoners, 1864," RG 109, Chapter IX, v. 250, p. 54. From August 1864 on in this valuable volume is severely damaged, making it impossible to ascertain if additional African Americans were sent later. ("negroes confined at Salisbury") Lt. Col. H. L. Clay, with endorsement by Robert Ould, November 19, 1864, *OR*, Series 2, v. 7, 1145, cited by Alexander, "Regular Slave Hunt," p. 89. Captain Louis R. Fortescue, "Salisbury," in "Pennsylvania at Salisbury, North Carolina" (Harrisburg, Pa.: C. E. Aughinbaugh, 1910), p. 59, Special Collections, Penn State University. Louis A. Brown, *The Salisbury Prison* (Statesville, N.C.: Published by the author, 1992), pp. 85–86, 283.

83. Conrad and Alexander, *When War Passed This Way*, 219. Gregory Coco, *A Vast Sea of Misery* (Gettysburg: Thomas Publications, 1988).

84. Johnson, "History of Camp William Penn," pp. 41–46; James M. Paradis, *African Americans and the Gettysburg Campaign* (Lanham, Md.: Scarecrow Press, 2005), pp. 65–66. It appears that the 1862 recruiters for the Massachusetts regiments only visited communities easily accessible by rail line because that would be the primary method for transporting recruits to New England. Gettysburg was on a spur, which would impose significant delays on recruiters traveling to it.

85. Neely, "Pennsylvania Politics." The Democratic leadership insisted he stay on the Supreme Court, making it impossible for him to campaign on his own behalf.

86. Neely, "Pennsylvania Politics"; "The Decision of the Supreme Court," *Compiler*, June 2, 1862, p. 1 c. 6; "The Soldiers' Vote Unconstitutional," *Compiler*, June 2, 1862, p. 2 c. 4. As the *Compiler* pointed out, had the soldiers' vote been prohibited in 1861, Henry Myers would have been elected to the state legislature from the district including Adams County, instead of Henry Busbey triumphing by two votes in a disputed election.

87. Neely, "Pennsylvania Politics"; "Abolition Falsehoods," *Compiler*, October 12, 1863, p. 2 c. 2; "The Pennsylvania Election," *Compiler*, October 19, 1863, p. 2 c. 2; "Gen. McClellan's Woodward Letter," *Compiler*, October 19, 1863, p. 4 c. 1. This letter was released too late to appear in Pennsylvania newspapers before the election. It did nothing but hurt McClellan in 1864.

88. "Farmers of Adams County, Read! General Stuart's Raid," *Compiler*, October 12, 1863, p. 2 c. 3; "White Men, Remember," *Compiler*, October 5, 1863, p. 1 c. 5.

89. "Pennsylvania Elections—Returns, (1863)—Official," *Compiler*, November 2, 1863, p. 2 c. 4.

90. "Slavery Must Die," *Compiler*, February 22, 1864, p. 1 c. 6; "Speech of Hon. A. H. Coffroth of Pennsylvania," *Compiler*, July 4, 1864, p. 1 c. 6.

91. "America for White Men," *Compiler*, May 23, 1864, p. 2 c. 2.

92. "Nigger Driving in Congress," *Compiler*, January 18, 1864, p. 2 c. 4; "Equality of Whites and Blacks," and Untitled, *Compiler*, February 22, 1864, p. 2 c. 1 and 3; "The Miscegenation Agitators," *Compiler*, May 30, 1864, p 4 c. 1. On the stigma of permitting Afri-

can Americans equal access to streetcars, see also Untitled, *Compiler*, February 13, 1865, p. 2 c. 1.

93. "The Battle of Monocacy," *Compiler*, July 25, 1864, p. 2 c. 6–7; "Wisdom and Patriotism Demand an Armistice—An Immediate Peace," *Compiler*, July 18, 1864, p. 1 c. 4–5.

94. U. S. Grant to Hon. E. B. Washburne, August 16, 1864, quoted in W. J. Tenney, *The Military and Naval History of the Rebellion in the United States* (New York: D. Appleton and Company, 1866; reprint Mechanicsburg, PA: Stackpole Books, 2003), p. 591.

95. Liva Baker, "The Burning of Chambersburg," in Stephen W. Sears, ed., *The Civil War: The Best of American Heritage* (Boston, 1991), pp. 165–73; Everard H. Smith, "Chambersburg: Anatomy of a Confederate Reprisal," *American Historical Review* 96 (1991): pp 432–55; "Gen. M'Causland in Chambersburg! . . . The Town Sacked and Burned," *Franklin Repository*, August 24, 1864, p. 1 c. 6–7.

96. "Retaliation," *Compiler*, August 29, 1864, p. 1 c. 6; "The Burning of Chambersburg— The Object of that Act as Stated by Gen. Early," *Compiler*, August 29, 1864, p. 1 c. 4.

97. "Abolition County Ticket," *Compiler*, August 15, 1864, p. 2 c. 2; "The Peace Negotiations," *Compiler*, August 8, 1864, p. 1 c. 3; "Why Not Negotiate," *Compiler*, August 15, 1864, p. 4 c. 1; "Peace, Union and the Laws: General A. H. Coffroth Address," September 12, 1864, p. 2 c. 3; "Democratic County Convention," *Compiler*, September 5, 1864, p. 2 c. 6.

98. "Peace with Union," *Compiler*, August 29, 1864, p. 4 c. 1; Untitled, *Compiler*, September 19, 1864, p. 1 c. 7.

99. "The County," *Compiler*, November 14, 1864, p. 2 c. 1; "524!," *Compiler*, November 21, 1864, p. 2 c. 1; "The Election," *Compiler*, November 14, 1864, p. 2 c. 2. Gloomily, the *Compiler* predicted a return to the draft: "The Draft Wheel Again in Motion," *Compiler*, November 21, 1864, p. 2 c. 6.

100. Untitled, *Compiler*, February 6, 1865, p. 2 c. 1.

101. "The Assassin: Important Letter from John Wilkes Booth," *Compiler*, May 1, 1865, p. 1 c. 6–7.

102. Untitled, *Compiler*, May 1, 1865, p. 2 c. 2; Untitled, *Compiler*, May 29, 1865, p. 2 c. 1.

9. After the Shooting: South Central Pennsylvania after the Civil War

1. Confederate irregulars and spies failed to burn down St. Alban's, Vermont, or Manhattan, giving south central Pennsylvania and Missouri undisputed claims to the most devastated areas of the North. For the disruption that accompanied mobilization, see Reid Mitchell, *The Vacant Chair: The Northern Soldier Leaves Home* (New York: Oxford University Press, 1993); and William Marvel, "A Poor Man's Fight: Civil War Enlistment Patterns in Conway, New Hampshire," *Historical New Hampshire* 43 (1988): pp. 21–40.

2. Eric Foner, *Reconstruction: America's Unfinished Revolution, 1863–1877* (New York: Harper & Row, 1988), p. xxvi.

3. *Mercersburg Journal*, July 17, 1863, p. 3 c. 2 (page 1 dated June 26, 1863). *Gettysburg Star and Banner*, June 25, 1863, cited by Margaret Creighton, "Living on the Fault Line: African American Civilians and the Gettysburg Campaign," in Joan Cashin, ed., *The War Was You and Me* (Princeton: Princeton University Press, 2003), p. 230.

4. "The K K K," *Mercersburg Journal*, August 14, 1868, p. 2 c. 4; "Rev. Thomas Agnew," *Mercersburg Journal*, August 21, 1868, p. 2 c. 4.

5. Personal communication, G. Craig Caba, curator of the J. Howard Wert Gettysburg Collection, 2004.

6. W. P. Conrad and Ted Alexander, *When War Passed This Way* (Shippensburg, Pa.: Beidel Publishing House, 1982), p. 219.

7. Clarke Garrett, "The Great Migration to Kansas in the '70s," *Cumberland County History*, 15 (1998): pp. 83–95; Clarke Garrett, "Leaving the Cumberland Valley: Patterns of Migration from 1750 until 1890," *Cumberland County History* 17 (2000): pp. 93–102; "To the Church and Congregation at T.," *The Colored American* (New York), October 20, 1838. "What is to be Done?," *Star*, March 20, 1857, p. 2 c. 1; "Kansas to be a Slave State," *Star*, March 27, 1857, p. 2 c. 1; "Westward Ho!" *Star*, p. 2 c. 3; Untitled, *Compiler*, March 23, 1857, p. 2 c. 1; Untitled, *Adams Sentinel*, April 13, 1857, p. 2 c. 3.

8. Helen Hinchliff, "Going West to Ohio: The Andrew Mumper Family of York county," *Pennsylvania Genealogical Magazine*, 42 (2002): pp. 197–211.

9. Robert M. Preston, "The Great Emmitsburg Fire," Emmitsburg Area Historical Society, http://emmitsburg.net/archive_list/articles/history/stories/emmitsburg_fire.htm; Garrett, "Cumberland Valley Patterns of Migration," and "The Great Migration to Kansas."

10. (Wiermans) "Fire", *Adams Sentinel*, March 1, 1860, p. 2 c. 4; (Wright) "Albert Cook Myers traces Underground Route from Gettysburg north to Jesse Cook's Mill," A. C. Myers to W. H. Siebert, April 19, 1944, Wilbur H. Siebert Collection, Ohio Historical Society, Rolls 13 and 1; "Creigh, Dorothy Wyer," and "Creigh, Thomas, Jr." *Adams County [Nebraska]: The People, 1872–1972* (Hastings, Neb.: Adams County—Hastings Centennial Commission, 1971), pp. 48–49.

11. Sally McMurry, *From Sugar Camps to Star Barns: Rural Life and Landscape in a Western Pennsylvania Community* (University Park: Penn State University Press, 2001), p. 39.

12. Bruce Laurie, *Beyond Garrison: Antislavery and Social Reform* (New York: Cambridge University Press, 2005), p. 289.

13. Samuel L. Daihl, "1865: Our Johnnies Came Marching Home," *Papers Read before the Kittochtinny Historical Society*, XV, March 24, 1966, available at the Valley of the Shadow website.

14. Marvel, "A Poor Man's Fight." Marvel shows that farm families, short on labor, often left the poorest fields lie fallow during the war. Sometimes these fields were to be the land of one of the sons, and on returning after the war, he might head west rather than undertake the arduous task of clearing this marginal land. For migration south by soldiers, financiers, and capitalists, see Lawrence N. Powell, *New Masters: Northern Planters During the Civil War and Reconstruction* (New York: Fordham University Press, 1999). See also Dixon Wecter, *When Johnny Comes Marching Home* (Boston: Houghton-Mifflin Co., 1944), pp. 201–7.

15. Henry Mayer, *All on Fire: William Lloyd Garrison and the Abolition of Slavery* (New York: Saint Martin's Griffin, 1998), p. 620. Letter from Henry Blackwell, early 1843, Weld-Grimké Papers, William L. Clements Library, University of Michigan, cited in Gerda

Lerner, *The Grimké Sisters* from South Carolina (Boston: Houghton Mifflin, 1967; reprint, New York: Schocken Books, 1971), p. 314.

16. Stanley Elkins and Eric McKitrick, "The Founding Fathers: Young Men of the Revolution," *Political Science Quarterly* 76 (1961): p. 181–216; James N. Shubert, "Age and the Active-Passive Leadership Style," *American Political Science Review* 82 (1988), pp. 763–72; Lynn Botelho and Pat Thane, eds., *Women and Aging in British Society* (Essex, UK: Longman, 2001).

17. "Yellow Hill and Quakers in the Vicinity," Debra S. McCauslin lecture, March 7, 2006, Adams County Historical Society; "Died" [Isaac Wright], *National Era*, October 24, 1850, v. IV, no. 199, p. 171; G. Craig Caba, "Episodes of Gettysburg and the Underground Railroad," Lecture, Abolition and Underground Railroad Seminar, February 24, 2001.

18. Minutes, Menallen Monthly Meeting of Women Friends, November 20, 1861, and Minutes, Menallen Monthly Meeting, April 15, 1863, September 24, 1863, January 21, 1864, February 18, 1864, Microfilm, Friends Historical Library, Swarthmore University. See also Margaret B. Walmer, *Menallen Minutes, Marriages, and Miscellany, Quaker Records, 1780–1890* (Bowie, Md.: Heritage Books, 1992), p. 135.

19. John G. Brinkerhoff to Charles W. Griest, April 4, 1891, Adams County Historical Society, Folder 190 (Anti-Slavery Movement 1828–1865), 190.05, Members, Anti-Slavery Movement.

20. Peter C. Vermilyea, "The Effect of the Confederate Invasion of Pennsylvania on Gettysburg's African American Community," *Gettysburg Magazine* 24 (2001): pp. 112–25. Gerald Eggert discusses similar issues with Harrisburg. Eggert, *Harrisburg Industrializes* (University Park: Penn State University Press, 1993), pp. 251–53.

21. Diary entry for June 26, 1863, in J. D. Edmiston Turner, "Civil War Days in Mercersburg as related in the Diary of Rev. Thomas Creigh," Papers Read before the Kittochtinny Historical Society, February 29, 1940, available at the Valley of the Shadow project. 1880 Census, Montgomery Township, Franklin County, Pennsylvania, p. 403B, lists Findlay Cuff as 42 years old. "Cuff(e)," 1880 United States Census, www.geocities.com/cuff1880/pennsyl.htm.

22. Peter C. Vermilyea, "Jack Hopkins' Civil War," *Adams County History* 11 (2005): p. 11.

23. At least 88 African Americans from the Mercersburg area enlisted in the war ("African American Historic Sites of Mercersburg," www.mercersburg.com/blackhistory/black01.htm). A separate list shows 46 African Americans from Mercersburg who enlisted in the 54th or 55th Massachusetts, as well as 20 from Carlisle, 12 from Chambersburg, and 11 from Shippensburg. Thomas L. Doughton, "Pennsylvania Men In Massachusetts Colored Infantry Units," (www.geocities.com/afroyankees/Military/penn1.html). See also Woman's Club of Mercersburg, *Old Mercersburg* (New York: Frank Allaben Genealogical Company, 1912; reprint, Williamsport, PA: Grit Publishing, 1949), p. 196.

24. Ellwood Griest, *John and Mary: The Fugitive Slaves* (Lancaster, Pa.: Enquirer Printing and Publishing Company, 1873), pp. 153–63. Available at Documenting the American South, http://docsouth.unc.edu/neh/griest/griest.html.

25. John Ditmer, *Local People: The Struggle for Civil Rights in Mississippi* (Urbana: University of Illinois Press, 1995), pp. 1–18. Jean Humez, *Harriet Tubman: The Life and Life*

Stories (Madison: University of Wisconsin Press, 2003), pp. 69–71. Harry C. Silcox, "Nineteenth Century Black Militant: Octavius V. Catto (1821–1871)," in Joe William Trotter and E. L. Smith, *African Americans in Pennsylvania* (University Park, Pa.: Penn State University Press, 1997), pp. 198–219. Thanks to Christopher Densmore for encouraging me to be more precise about Catto's militia service.

26. Peter Vermilyea has found that 90 percent of the African Americans who moved to Gettysburg from 1863 to 1870 were natives of Maryland or Virginia. Vermilyea, "Jack Hopkins' Civil War," p. 14. See also Eggert, *Harrisburg Industrializes*, p. 252.

27. Earl "Cookie" Johnson and Philip Lowman, Waynesboro, interview by author, tape recording, Waynesboro, Pa., November 18, 2002. Stella M. Fries, et. al., *Some Chambersburg Roots: A Black Perspective* (Chambersburg, Pa.: Privately published, 1980), p. 241.

28. Nina Silber, *Romance of Reunion: Northerners and the South, 1865–1900* (Chapel Hill: University of North Carolina Press, 1993).

29. "The Mass Meeting," *Compiler*, October 16, 1868, p. 2 c. 4.

30. David Montgomery, "Pennsylvania: An Eclipse of Ideology," in James C. Mohr, ed., *Radical Republicans in the North: State Politics During Reconstruction* (Baltimore: Johns Hopkins University Press, 1976), pp. 50–65; Grace Palladino, *Another Civil War: Labor, Capital and the State in the Anthracite Region of Pennsylvania, 1840–1868* (Urbana: University of Illinois Press, 1990).

31. The 1838 Pennsylvania constitution limited the franchise to whites only. Edward McPherson, *Political Manual for 1866* (Washington: Philip & Solomons, 1866), p. 123; Edward McPherson, *A Hand-Book of Politics for 1870* (Washington: Philip & Solomons, 1870), p. 484. Both books are available at the "Making of America" website.

32. "The Fifteenth Amendment," *Mercersburg Journal*, February 5, 1869, p. 2 c. 1. A. Lee Fritschler, "Abolitionist professor's story fascinating," Letter to the Editor, *Harrisburg Patriot-News*, March 23, 1999, p. A10. James Henry Morgan, *Dickinson College* (Carlisle, Pa.: Dickinson College, 1933), pp. 330–33 covers the events in some detail but omits any mention of McClintock. "John McClintock (1814–1870)," *Encyclopedia Dickinsonia*, http://chronicles.dickinson.edu/encyclo/m/ed_mcClintockJ.htm.

33. James Q. Waters, "Jack the Janitor," *Odds and Ends: Or Things Wise and Otherwise, Pennsylvania College* (Hagerstown, Md.: Daniel Dechert, 1860), pp. 17–99, cited in Vermilyea, "Jack Hopkins' Civil War," pp. 5–6, 9, 18.

34. Charles H. Glatfelter, *A Salutary Influence: Gettysburg College, 1832–1985* (Gettysburg, Pa.: Gettysburg College, 1987), pp. 150–51; Peter Vermilyea, "Jack Hopkins' Civil War." (Raise) Minutes, May 22, 1867, Board of Trustees, Gettysburg College, v. 2, 1854–1879, p. 96, Special Collections, Musselman Library, Gettysburg College. (Resolutions) Minutes, August 13, 1868, Board of Trustees, Gettysburg College, v. 2, 1854–1879, pp. 113–14, Special Collections, Musselman Library, Gettysburg College.

35. Minutes, August 13, 1868, Board of Trustees, Gettysburg College, v. 2, 1854–1879, pp. 113–14, Special Collections, Musselman Library, Gettysburg College; "Funeral of Thaddeus Stevens," *Mercersburg Journal*, August 28, 1868, p. 2 c. 2; "Addresses Delivered at the Laying of the Corner Stone of Stevens Hall," August 8, 1867 (Gettysburg, 1867), pp. 16–22, 23–26, 30; Glatfelter, *Salutary Influence*, 115.

36. "Summer Home of Lee's Trusted Staff Officer for Sale," *Battlefield Journal*, July 2001.

37. James Powell Weeks, *Gettysburg: Memory, Market, and an American Shrine* (Princeton: Princeton University Press, 2003).

38. George Alfred Townsend, *Katy of Catoctin* (New York: D. Appleton and Company, 1886).

39. Elsie Singmaster, *Gettysburg: Stories of Memory, Grief and Greatness*, Introduction by Lesley J. Gordon, (Tuscaloosa: University of Alabama Press, 2003), xiv; "Interesting Facts about the Lutheran Seminary," *Gettysburg Experience* (March 2003), p. 17; Elsie Singmaster, *A Boy at Gettysburg* (Boston: Houghton Mifflin Company, 1924).

40. John W. Appel, *The Light of Parnell* (Philadelphia: The Heidelberg Press, 1916; reprint, Mercersburg, Pa.: Mercersburg Printing, 1986).

41. "Attempted Suicide," Newspaper Clipping, Folder 140, Blacks in Adams County, Adams County Historical Society. A reference to the upcoming school year for Pennsylvania College dates this to 1879.

42. Joseph Santora, "Race and Violence in the Valley: The 1869 Attempted Lynching of Cain Norris," in Stephen B. Burg, ed., *Black History of Shippensburg, Pennsylvania, 1860–1936* (Shippensburg, Pa.: Shippensburg University Press, 2005), pp. 45–74; Margaret S. Creighton, *The Colors of Courage* (New York: Basic Books, 2005), pp. 223–24, 231. "Colored Church Gets Klan Gift Sunday Evening," *Star and Sentinel*, [1921], Adams County Historical Society, Black History File. Clark Foreman to Harold Ickes, 8 September 1933, 7 November 1933, 9 November 1933, New Deal Agencies and Black Americans, papers, microfilm, reel 14, cited by Patricia Sullivan, *Days of Hope: Race and Democracy in the New Deal Era* (Chapel Hill: University of North Carolina Press, 1996), p. 54. Shelley Jones and Harry Stokes, "Black History in Our Community," Pamphlet, January 15, 1987, Adams County Historical Society. One researcher completed an extensive, 150-page study of *de facto* segregation in Gettysburg: Donald H. Becker, "Trends in Negro Segregation in Gettysburg from 1900 to 1953," (Master's thesis, University of Maryland, 1953), Adams County Historical Society, Black History File.

43. Lowman and Johnson interview.

44. Lowman and Johnson interview; Jim Kalish, *The Story of Civil Rights in York, Pennsylvania* (Mechanicsburg, Pa.: Stackpole Books, 2000), pp. 72–85.

Conclusion: The Postwar Ramifications of the Fugitive Slave Issue "On the Edge of Freedom"

1. Allan Nevins made similar comments relating to fugitive slaves and need and perceived dependency in *Ordeal of the Union: Fruits of Manifest Destiny 1847–1852* (New York: Charles Scribner's Sons, 1947), p. 380.

2. Regarding Northern commitment to reconstruction, I follow an interpretive line briefly suggested by Harold Hyman in *A More Perfect Union: The Impact of the Civil War and Reconstruction on the Constitution* (New York: Alfred A. Knopf, 1973).

Archives Consulted

Adams County Courthouse, Office of the Prothonotary, Gettysburg, Pa., Miscellaneous court records (Fugitive Slave Cases); Veterinary Register, 1889–1920

Boston Public Library, Rare Books Department, Boston, Mass., Weston Sisters Correspondence; McKim-Chapman Papers

Cumberland County Courthouse, Carlisle, Pa., Court Records of *Mary Oliver, et al. v. Daniel Kaufman*, November Court of 1847, Papers No. 32 in November 1847 – January 1848

Drew University, Methodism Collection, Madison, N.J., John McClintock Collection, 1830–68

Duke University, Special Collections, Perkins Library, Durham, N.C., George Besore Papers; various letters and diaries from Confederate soldiers in the Gettysburg campaign; Patrick H. Cain Letters

Franklin and Marshall University, Special Collections, Lancaster, Pa., Theodore Appel Family Papers (MS 4)

Freedman's Bureau Papers, University of Maryland, College Park, Md., Records Relating to Freedpeople in Pennsylvania

Friends Historical Library, Swarthmore College, Swarthmore, Pa.
Menallen Minutes
Graceanna Lewis, Manuscript Memoir Describing Underground Railroad Activities (RG-5/087), Lewis-Fussell Family Papers, Series 1, Box 1
Letters of Lydia Lundy (Wierman) in the Halliday Jackson Papers
Letters of William and Deborah Wright, Parrish Papers

Gettysburg College, Musselman Library, Special Collections, Gettysburg, Pa.
Samuel Simon Schmucker Papers, MS-023
Baugher Family Papers, MS-034
Newspaper Files
Minutes, Board of Trustees, v. 1, 1832–53; v. 2, 1854–79
Faculty Minutes, 1832–70

Gettysburg National Battlefield Park Library, Gettysburg, Pa.

Peter Vermilyea, "We did not know where our colored friends had gone," Undergraduate Thesis, Gettysburg College

"Gettysburg African Americans" file

Historical Society of Pennsylvania, Philadelphia, Pa., Papers of the Pennsylvania Abolition Society, Microfilm

Library of Congress, Manuscript Division, Washington, D.C., Feamster Family papers, 1794–1967

Lincoln University, Langston Hughes Memorial Library, Oxford, Pa., Pennsylvania Colonization Society Records

Millersville University, Special Collections, Lancaster, Pa.

National Archives, Washington, D.C.

Records of the United States House of Representatives

Petitions, Committee on the District of Columbia, Slavery in the District of Columbia (HR 19A-G4.2; HR20A-G5.1), RG 233.10

War Department Collection of Confederate Records

Manuscripts

Order book, Battle's and Rodes's Brigade

Registers, rolls, lists, and other records of Confederate, federal, political, and civil prisoners received, transferred, escaped, paroled, died, buried, discharged, and released, 1861–65; and Descriptive Lists of Prisoners, 1862–65. Records Relating to Prisoners, Oaths and Paroles, RG 109.14.2

General and Special Orders, 1861–65, Records of the Adjutant and Inspector General's Department, RG 109.7.1

Letters of Telegrams Sent, Letters Received, and other records of the Department of Henrico, 1862–1863, RG 109.9.2

Registers, day books, daily lists of arrivals, and other records relating to federal prisoners confined in Libby Prison, Castle Thunder, and other prisons at Richmond, Va., 1861–65, Records relating to individual federal prisoners of war, RG 249.3.2

"Special Orders Relative to Federals Held as Prisoners, 1864," RG 109, Chapter X, v. 250.

Microfilm

"Letters Received by the Confederate Secretary of War, 1861–65," RG 109, M437

"Orders and Circulars Issued by the Army of the Potomac and the Army and Department of Northern Virginia, C.S.A.," 1861–65, M921

National Archives, Mid-Atlantic Region, Philadelphia, Pa.

Pennsylvania, Eastern District Court Records, RG-21

   Oliver v. Weakly case records

Ohio State Historical Society, Columbus, Ohio, Wilbur H. Siebert Underground Railroad Collection

Pennsylvania State Archives, Harrisburg, Pa.

   Harrisburg Daily American, 1851

   Maclay Family Papers, MG-352, Charles Templeton Maclay Diary, 1863

   Records of the General Assembly, RG-7

   House File, 1790–1903 (House petitions)

   Senate file, 1832–1973 (Senate petitions)

   Senate Petition Books, 1832–1943

Runaway Slave Case, Reah Frazer Papers, MG-53

Pennsylvania State University, Pattee Library Special Collections, University Park, Pa., Cleveland Family Papers 2000–0325H and Cleveland Family Scrapbook, 1827–1869

Swarthmore University, Friends Historical Library, Swarthmore, Pa.

Graceanna Lewis, Manuscript Memoir, Lewis-Fussell Family Papers, 1698–1978, Series 1, Box 1, RG-5/087

Lydia Lundy (Wierman) Correspondence, Halliday Jackson Papers

Menallen (Adams County) Monthly Meeting Minutes, 1733–1993

Parrish Family Papers [Deborah Parrish Wright], 1780–1966, RG-5/229

Tufts University, Digital Collections and Archives, Medford, Mass.

William H. Ryder Collection of Confederate Archives, 1861–65

Morning Reports of the C.S. Eastern Military District Prison

Virginia Historical Society, Richmond, Va., Confederate States of America. Department of Henrico records, 1861–64, Mss3C7604a, Microfilm reels C589–C591

University of North Carolina, Wilson Library, Manuscripts Department, Chapel Hill, N.C.

Southern Historical Collection

Letters and diaries from Confederate soldiers in the Gettysburg campaign

Rebecca Pitchford Davis Letters #3328

University of Notre Dame, Hesburgh Library, Special Collections, South Bend, Ind., Arnold C. Hackenbruch Newspaper Collection

Washington and Lee University, Leyburn Library, Special Collections, Lexington, Va., Jefferson Davis Papers, Collection 011–011a

Local Historical Societies and Private Collections

Adams County Historical Society, Gettysburg, Pa.
  Anti-Slavery Collection
  Newspaper files
  Black History file
  Underground Railroad files
  Mary (Goins) Gandy, *Guide My Feet, Hold My Hand*

Baltimore County Historical Society, Cockeysville, Md., Slavery files

Carroll County Maryland Historical Society, Westminster, Md., Antislavery files, Union Bridge Quaker Meeting

Chester County Historical Society, West Chester, Pa., Underground Railroad and Anti-slavery files

Cumberland County Historical Society, Hamilton Library, Carlisle, Pa., Jeremiah Zeamer Papers

Frederick County Historical Society, Frederick, Md., Slavery—Underground Railroad file

Handley Regional Library, Archive Room, Winchester, Va., Civil War Shenandoah Valley letters and papers

J. Howard Wert Gettysburg Collection, G. Craig Caba, Curator, Enola, Pa.
  Minutes of the Adams Co. A[nti] Slavery Society
  Correspondence to Adam Wert
  Miscellaneous handbills, receipts, diaries, and so on

Kittochtinny Historical Society, Franklin County, Pa., Antislavery and Underground Railroad materials; Franklin County newspapers
Lancaster County Historical Society, Lancaster Pa.
Negro Entry Book, Folder 4b, MG-240, The Slave Records of Lancaster County, 1780–1849
Underground Railroad and antislavery materials
York County Historical Society, York, Pa., Underground Railroad files

Index

THE NORTH'S CIVIL WAR
Paul A. Cimbala, series editor

Paul A. Cimbala and Randall M. Miller, eds., *Union Soldiers and the Northern Home Front: Wartime Experiences, Postwar Adjustments.*

Mark A. Snell, *From First to Last: The Life of Major General William B. Franklin.*

Paul A. Cimbala and Randall M. Miller, eds., *An Uncommon Time: The Civil War and the Northern Home Front.*

John Y. Simon and Harold Holzer, eds., *The Lincoln Forum: Rediscovering Abraham Lincoln.*

Thomas F. Curran, *Soldiers of Peace: Civil War Pacifism and the Postwar Radical Peace Movement.*

Kyle S. Sinisi, *Sacred Debts: State Civil War Claims and American Federalism, 1861–1880.*

Russell L. Johnson, *Warriors into Workers: The Civil War and the Formation of Urban-Industrial Society in a Northern City.*

Peter J. Parish, *The North and the Nation in the Era of the Civil War.* Edited by Adam L. P. Smith and Susan-Mary Grant.

Patricia Richard, *Busy Hands: Images of the Family in the Northern Civil War Effort.*

Michael S. Green, *Freedom, Union, and Power: The Mind of the Republican Party During the Civil War.*

Christian G. Samito, ed., *Fear Was Not In Him: The Civil War Letters of Major General Francis S. Barlow, U.S.A.*

John S. Collier and Bonnie B. Collier, eds., *Yours for the Union: The Civil War Letters of John W. Chase, First Massachusetts Light Artillery.*

Grace Palladino, *Another Civil War: Labor, Capital, and the State in the Anthracite Regions of Pennsylvania, 1840–1868.*

Christian B. Keller, *Chancellorsville and the Germans: Nativism, Ethnicity, and Civil War Memory.*

Robert M. Sandow, *Deserter Country: Civil War Opposition in the Pennsylvania Appalachians.*

Craig L. Symonds, ed., *Union Combined Operations in the Civil War.*

Harold Holzer, Craig L. Symonds, and Frank L. Williams, eds., *The Lincoln Assassination: Crime and Punishment, Myth and Memory.* A Lincoln Forum Book.

Earl F. Mulderink III, *New Bedford's Civil War.*

George Washington Williams, *A History of the Negro Troops in the War of the Rebellion, 1861–1865.* Introduction by John David Smith.

Randall M. Miller, ed., *Lincoln and Leadership: Military, Political, and Religious Decision Making.*

David G. Smith, *On the Edge of Freedom: The Fugitive Slave Issue in South Central Pennsylvania, 1820–1870.*